NO END TO
WAR

NO END TO
WAR

TERRORISM IN THE
TWENTY-FIRST CENTURY

WALTER LAQUEUR

continuum
NEW YORK • LONDON

2004

The Continuum International Publishing Group Inc.
15 East 26th Street, New York, NY 10010

The Continuum International Publishing Group Ltd
The Tower Building, 11 York Road, London SE1 7NX

Printed in the United States of America

Library of Congress Cataloging-in-Publication Data

Laqueur, Walter, 1921-
    No end to war : terrorism in the 21st century / Walter Laqueur.
      p. cm.
    Includes bibliographical references and index.
    0-8264-1435-4 (hardcover : alk paper)   0-8264-1656-X (paperback : alk paper)
    1. Terrorism. 2. World politics – 21st century. I. Title
    HV6431.L366 2002
    303.6′25 – dc21

                        2002151954

Contents

Introduction

TERRORISM HAS BEEN on the international agenda for a long time, but until fairly recently it was relegated to a lowly place. From time to time, following some spectacular attack, terrorism would figure prominently in the media for a few days. There would be deliberations on the highest level of government, committees would be appointed and resolutions passed. But when calm returned the issue would be forgotten, for there seemed to be no particular urgency to deal with it. There were always some very important domestic and foreign issues that would take precedence, and in any case terrorism never threatened all countries in an equal measure. This has now changed, and terrorism is bound to remain high on the list of our priorities. True, acute apprehension is bound to decline if no major attacks take place for a considerable time. The lack of vigilance during the period before September 11, 2001, can be explained, in part, with reference to the fact that during the preceding two years terrorist activities had been rare.

It was only to be expected that there should be voices arguing that the events of September 2001 had been unique and unlikely to recur, as time had passed without many major terrorist attacks. Memories are short and wishful thinking is deeply rooted. Terrorism will be given less attention if a full scale war breaks out. But no war lasts forever. It is too expensive in every respect in our day and age, whereas terrorism is relatively cheap and will be with us for as long as anyone can envision, ever if not always at the same frequency and intensity.

Terrorism has become the subject of a great deal of study, comment, debate, and controversy. There has been an enormous amount of comment on the roots of terrorism as well as the best ways to deal with it. Unfortunately, these debates have been distinguished very often more by passion and emotion (and, of course, preconceived notions) than by knowledge and insight. The history of terrorism remains an essential key to understanding the phenomenon; most of the new terms that have appeared in the literature in recent years refer to concepts that have been known since time immemorial. Guerrilla warfare and terrorism were always "asymmetric warfare," and the discovery that terrorists need "failed countries" (or regions of failed countries) would have been considered less than sensational in biblical times, let alone by Mao Tse-tung (from the caves of Adulam to the caves of Yenan).

But past experience is no longer the only key for understanding terrorism. The crucial new elements are, as I tried to show in a book several years ago, easier access to weapons of mass destruction and the greater importance of religious-political fanaticism as a motive. At the present time, radical Islamism is the single most important force in international terrorism, and it will probably remain so for a considerable time to come. But there is always the danger of being blinded by current events; radical Islamism was not always the main threat and it may not always be in the future.

There is no authoritative systematic guide to terrorism — no Clausewitz, not even a Jomini — and perhaps there never will be one, simply because there is not one terrorism but a variety of terrorisms and what is true for one does not necessarily apply to others. There are major obstacles on the road toward understanding terrorism; perhaps no other topic in our time has provoked such violent emotions.

Those who have been commenting with the greatest assurance on terrorism are usually concerned with one group, ethnic or political. They are not preoccupied with the general phenomenon of terrorism, but the fate and the interests of the specific group with which they identify or which they oppose. Those preoccupied with terrorism in the Israeli-Palestinian context (except for a small group of professional experts) are usually unwilling to give even passing thought to events in Algeria or Sri Lanka; the fact that, to give another example, suicide terrorism occurs in various parts of the world and not just in one will merely be regarded as confusing by those engaging in sweeping generalizations on the subject. People preoccupied with the Kashmir conflict have little interest in events in Colombia or the Balkans — faraway countries about which little is known and that seem irrelevant to the problems at hand. Those finding justifications for the violence of the extreme left (which leads them to far-reaching generalizations about the progressive character *tout court* of global terrorism) tend to forget that there is also a terrorism of the far right of which they do not approve at all. The student of terrorism has to consider the general picture; any fixation on one specific aspect of terrorism is bound to lead to wrong conclusions.

The use of terms like "left" and "right" has become more and more problematical with the passing of time; it has become more often than not misleading in an age of growing populism that can with equal ease adopt views and politics that used to be considered "left" and "right." Terrorist groups of the extreme "left" have often become aggressively nationalistic, whereas those of the far right are second to none with their ardent anticapitalism and anti-Americanism. Trotskyites have given critical support to Ayatollah Khomeini and the Taliban with their radical "anti-imperialism," and neo-Nazis are suggesting a "third position," an anti-Westernism that should unite extremists from the left and the right. Anti-Semitism, once the preserve of the extreme right, has spread to the far left. Is Osama bin Laden a man of the left or the right? The question is, of course, absurd: The religious-nationalist terrorists have nothing in common with the ideas of the traditional, secular left;

they may have in common certain features with fascism. But such comparisons are of limited relevance only; traditional Western political categories do not apply to them. They are premodern and postmodern at the same time.

Another major obstacle to understanding terrorism is the psychological resistance against accepting uncomfortable facts. Such resistance to accept new facts running counter to deeply ingrained beliefs is not, of course, new. It has occurred whenever a new movement appeared on the scene; fascism and communism, to give but two examples, were interpreted in the light of the past, and what was essentially new in these movements was overlooked. This form of resistance has been frequent even in the history of science, and it should have come as no surprise that in the study of terrorism in which scientific proof and prediction do not exist, resistance should be even stronger. As a result, the debate on terrorism has resembled quite often a parade of old hobby horses. People who have ready-made explanations of why terrorism occurs will not easily give up their beliefs, however much proof to the contrary is produced.

My interest in terrorism and guerrilla warfare goes back some three decades. I dealt with the history of these subjects in two volumes in the 1970s. My assumption at the time was that while terrorism was a topic of great fascination, its political importance was limited. But I did not exclude that a time might come when, for a variety of reasons, terrorism might assume a far more important role. I mentioned in my earlier writing growing fanaticism, religious and nationalist, on the one hand and the access to weapons of mass destruction on the other.

Fanaticism per se is of course not new, but it has had a major rebirth — much to the surprise of those in Europe and America who had believed that it was a thing of the past. The use of the weapons of mass destruction by fanatics is yet to come. Awareness of this danger has not yet percolated in the public consciousness: the possibility, indeed the probability, that even very small groups of people will be able to inflict enormous damage on societies and that the number of victims could be infinitely greater than in the past.

There is yet another crucial difference between the old terrorism and the new: until recently, terrorism was, by and large, discriminate, selecting its victims carefully — kings and queens, government ministers, generals, and other leading political figures and officials. It was, more often than not, "propaganda by deed." Contemporary terrorism has increasingly become indiscriminate in the choice of its victims. Its aim is no longer to conduct propaganda but to effect maximum destruction. Another important difference between the old terrorism and the new is the crucial importance of paranoiac elements in the terrorism of the far right and the extreme left, perhaps most of all in terrorists inspired by religious fanaticism. National oppression (to give but one example) is not a delusional disorder, but it is precisely in individuals and groups of religious-nationalist extremists that aggression and hostility toward others become unmanageable, and that the all-consuming concern with nonexistent hidden motives leads to a loss of the sense of reality. The outlook is poor; there are no known cures for fanaticism and paranoia.

Present debates about the causes of terrorism deal with topics such as ethnic and religious tensions, globalism and antiglobalism, poverty and exploitation. But these issues could be less important with regard to the terrorism of the future; the smaller the terrorist group, the more outlandish its doctrine is likely to be and the greater the relevance of psychological factors. There is bound to be great resistance to accepting this. But there is no accounting for the perceived complaints and injuries of a handful of people by means of invoking broad social, economic, and political trends. Eventually the old science-fiction scenario of the mad scientist taking vengeance on society could become reality.

I had no wish in the present study to go over the same ground as in earlier books originally published in the 1970s. *Terrorism* and *History of Guerrilla Warfare* provide a historical introduction for those interested in the subject. There have been in recent years excellent books surveying the terrorism of the 1980s and 1990s and on specialized topics such as the arms of mass destructions that terrorists could use in the future. There have been first-rate accounts of events in New York and Washington in September 2001, about the Taliban and the war in Afghanistan. I list some of these books in my bibliography. Nor was my concern with the Iraq crisis, proliferation and counterterrorism.

My intention in the present work is to deal with the new elements in contemporary terrorism. This includes, among other issues, a critical review of the debate on the causes of terrorism, the specific roots of Islamic terrorism, and the phenomenon of suicide terrorism. I also deal with the reactions toward the emergence of the new terrorism on the part of governments, as well as the media, academic experts, and the general public from the extreme left to the far right of the political spectrum. The book considers the reasons terrorism came so unexpectedly and why it should be so often and so thoroughly misinterpreted. I am concerned with the future of terrorism and its geopolitics — the battlefields of the future. While terrorism is unpredictable and may become even more so (as terrorist groups tend to be smaller) terrorism caused by religious-nationalist tensions will continue for a long time, and this is obviously more likely to occur in some countries than in others. Surprises might always be ahead. Apart from all other considerations, terrorism might trigger off a full-scale war, as it has done in the past.

AMONG THOSE I OWE A DEBT OF GRATITUDE for having helped me in various ways are, above all, Marek Michalewski, Jeffrey Bale, Kevin Coogan, Jeff Thomas, Daniel Rankin, Melissa Goldate, Aidan Higgins, Andrew Noznesky, Marc Svetov, and my friend Irena Lasota. A stay at the American Academy in Berlin helped to conclude this study more quickly than would have been possible in other circumstances.

ONE

Roots of Terrorism?

T O UNDERSTAND TERRORISM one ought to investigate its roots rather than deal with its outward manifestations. This statement, endlessly repeated in recent years, happens to be perfectly correct and is, of course, quite true with regard to any phenomenon in the world. Unfortunately, the statement has very often become a misleading slogan, justifying a parade of hobby horses. Instead of studying the available evidence, preconceived notions have frequently been proclaimed as the received truth.

The causes of terrorism have been a source of bewilderment and misconceptions for a long time. It was widely believed that terrorism was a response to injustice and that terrorists were people driven to desperate actions by intolerable conditions, be it poverty, hopelessness, or political or social oppression. Following this reasoning, the only way to remove or at least to reduce terrorism is to tackle its sources, to deal with the grievances and frustrations of the terrorists rather than simply trying to suppress terrorism by brute force. As an American linguist put it, "Drain the swamp, and the mosquitoes will disappear."

Such views had much justification in past situations. To give but two examples — the Russian revolutionaries and the Irish patriots. Tsarist Russia was at the time the most repressive country in Europe. Its rulers had almost unrestricted power. There was no political freedom, no redress against injustice. The masses lived in grinding poverty; the distance between an extremely rich aristocracy and the peasants was enormous, and the bureaucracy was often corrupt. In these circumstances, some members of a highly idealistic young generation decided to engage in acts of violence against leading figures of the hated regime. Two waves of terrorist activities occurred, in the late 1870s and again in the early years of the twentieth century. As for the motives and character of those participating in the terrorist movement, these were selfless young people without personal ambitions; they wanted to sacrifice themselves so that the people of Russia would enjoy a better life free of oppression. Originally these young people had tried to bring about change by "going to the people," meaning a propaganda campaign. They had opted for terrorism only after having realized that legal action was either impossible or ineffectual. They were sad that they had to kill, and they went out of their way not to hurt innocent people. Their first terrorist actions had been in self-defense and were directed against officials who had been particularly cruel in the treatment of political prisoners. Given the selfless character of the terrorist movement, that it had wide sympathies in Russian society and frequently received help was not surprising.

The Irish terrorists of the nineteenth and early twentieth centuries were fighting for national independence and freedom from foreign occupation. England had ruled Ireland for centuries and faced growing opposition as an Irish national consciousness (fueled by religious antagonism) became stronger. The dismal economic situation — which included periodical starvation leading to mass emigration to America — also played a role in this context. The terrorist attacks carried out by the Fenians (and later the IRB, the IRA, and other organizations) both in Ireland and on mainland Britain were aimed to achieve the old dream: Irish freedom from the British government. As in the case of the Russian revolutionaries, the motivation of the Irish patriots was selfless and idealistic. They enjoyed the moral support of wide sections of society, including even Irish Protestants. The Irish were merely the best known and most prominent of a whole series of small nationalist terrorist groups — some in Europe, others in colonial or semicolonial countries such as Egypt and India.

However, the nineteenth-century terrorists — with all their sterling qualities, heroism, and idealism — encountered for a variety of reasons a great deal of criticism not only on the part of their political opponents but also among those who shared their political aspirations. The majority of Russian socialists (including the young Lenin) decided not to join the terrorists because they thought their policy harmful. The killing of Tsar Alexander II who had come to power in 1881 (and was by Russian standards a relatively liberal ruler with a program of modest reforms) led to a backlash, a more severe policy on the part of the regime. The defeat of Russia in the war against Japan and the upsurge of the democratic forces that ensued forced the Tsarist government to introduce a constitution and make a variety of other concessions, but the terrorist attacks that reached their climax in 1906 made it easier for the reactionary forces to withdraw the concessions.

The struggle of the Irish for national independence evoked much sympathy among the European left at the time, but the left was still doubtful about the means used. England, after all, was a democracy, albeit an elitist one. The Irish had the right to vote and the Irish party (Parnell) had considerable influence; they enjoyed a reasonable prospect of attaining their political aims following the growth of democracy and a persistent political struggle. Karl Marx and Frederic Engels sympathized with the Irish national cause, but at the same time sharply condemned terrorist attacks. Engels called the perpetrators of the Clerkenwell attack in London cannibals, cowards, and stupid fanatics, and Marx wrote in a letter that one could not really expect the London proletarians to be blown up in honor of the Fenians.

The general attitude of the European left was negative toward the anarchists, the third terrorist group at the time and the one which generated the most fear. Individual anarchists engaged in assassinations of heads of state and government ministers, and very infrequently these actions were undertaken by groups. Anarchism had a hallowed ideological tradition; the terrorists among them were a small minority, but they received all the limelight. Opposition to these acts was both a matter of principle as well as rooted in tactics. How could murder be justified in political regimes in which alternative ways existed to register protest? It was one thing to attack dictators and another, very different one to shoot politicians who had been democratically elected. Anarchism also harmed the cause it wanted to promote, for governments and the public at large tended to blame not just the small groups or the individuals who engaged in terrorist acts but socialism and the radical democratic movement as a whole. Lastly the motives of some anarchists were suspect. The majority was deeply idealistic, and their main impulse was the desire to liberate mankind from its shackles. But there were also highly strung, unbalanced figures among them, as well as herostratic personalities, even criminal elements. One of them, after having thrown a bomb, said that victims little mattered as long as the gesture was beautiful, and another just before his execution commented, "Now at last I am a famous man."

Thus even in the nineteenth century, in the heroic period of terrorism, it was clear that the decision to engage in terrorist acts was as much a matter of personality as of ideological conviction.

The Fenians and the Russian revolutionaries had no monopoly as far as their ardent wish to see their country liberated. In fact, we do not even know whether those who were throwing the bombs were the ones most deeply committed to their cause. All we do know is that their thirst for action (or their aggression) was greater than that of their comrades.

After World War I, and even more after World War II, the character of terrorism began to change. Terrorist operations were frequently carried out by groups of far-right and fascist inspiration, such as the Free Corps in Germany, the Romanian Iron Guard, or Japanese terrorists who drew their inspiration from the Samurai. There is no reason to doubt the idealistic inspiration of these terrorists and their willingness if need be to sacrifice their lives. But it became abundantly clear that terrorism was by no means a left-wing or progressive phenomenon. Those, for instance, who in 1922 killed the German Foreign Minister Walther Rathenau (who was of Jewish origin) were the precursors of the Nazi movement. Terrorism still occurred frequently on the basis of national conflicts, but it was no longer primarily directed against political and military leaders of the other side; it became progressively more and more indiscriminate. Furthermore, other forms of terrorism occurred, such as terrorism that was largely religiously motivated and terrorism which consisted of a mixture of ideological and criminal elements, such as the drug trade. All this was quite different from nineteenth-century terrorism, and generalizations trying to cover all these manifestations became difficult if not impossible.

The targets of nineteenth-century terrorism were kings, ministers, and generals. This was true even for terrorism in Europe and elsewhere up to the 1970s, though increasingly middle-level targets were included — such as judges, bankers, or other figures who were not very much in the public eye. True, there had been the occasional pronouncement on the part of terrorists that "there are no innocents," but by and large the killing of bystanders had been accidental, not part of a strategy. More recently, especially in ethnically motivated terrorism, acts of violence have been indiscriminate. Hence the many attacks against "soft" targets such as tourism (Djerba, Bali, Mombasa).Relatively few political leaders or other prominent public figures were killed, and the strategy became to assassinate as many members of the enemy group as possible. The reason might have been, in part, that it is usually more difficult to assassinate a leading political figure who is often well guarded. But mainly the change in strategy was caused by the growing fanaticism, the beliefs (1) that not just a few figures but the whole enemy society was a legitimate target, (2) that the aim was not to propagate an idea but to destroy, and (3) that the murder of children, women, elderly people, and other noncombatants would spread even more fear and panic than attacks against soldiers and security forces.

The geography and the etiology of terrorism — the analysis of where terrorism occurred and where it did not occur in the twentieth century — is of some help in understanding its roots. If terrorism is the result of intolerable oppression, one should have expected terrorism in the most oppressive regimes: Nazi Germany, Fascist Italy, and the Soviet Union. There were a few attempts to kill Hitler and Mussolini (none to assassinate Stalin), but these were the actions of individuals and not systematic terrorism. In the Soviet Union (as in Spain under Franco), terrorism occurred only after the totalitarian regime had been dismantled. In Latin America in the 1970s, terrorism first occurred in Uruguay, the most democratic of the South American countries, not in the harshest dictatorships.

The reasons were obvious: In an effective dictatorship, the political police could prevent attempts to prepare terrorist campaigns. Even in a military dictatorship that was not particularly efficient — such as Franco's Spain — there was no terrorism. The operation of the Basque ETA began only after the dictator had died. Terrorism in Greece started after the Colonels had been ousted, not under their rule. On the other hand, terrorism of the extreme left did occur in democratic regimes such as Germany and Italy in the 1970s as well as regimes that were at least democratic to some extent. These terrorist campaigns led to the overthrow of democratic governments in some Latin American countries that were incapable of stemming the terrorist tide. But the military dictatorships that succeeded them suppressed terrorism without much difficulty. In brief, terrorism did not stand much of a chance against political regimes able to use unrestricted

force against them, unhampered by laws, considerations of human rights, and public protests. Terrorism could flourish only in a surrounding that was at least partly
democratic in character or, alternatively, in a wholly inefficient dictatorship.

It has been widely argued that a direct correlation exists between terrorism
and poverty — that poverty, especially in what used to be called the third world,
is the most important factor responsible for terrorism. However, the historical
evidence does not bear out such categorical statements. It stands to reason that
if all mankind were to live in small countries, preferably in small cities, and if all
human beings were well off, there would be less violence, be it crime or terrorism.
But there is no reason to assume that violence would disappear altogether.

Some European terrorist groups and some Islamists have claimed to act on
behalf and in the interest of the poorest of the poor.[1] But in the forty-nine countries currently designated by the United Nations as the least developed hardly
any terrorist activity occurs. (Among the criteria underlying this list are not only
low per-capita income but also weak human resources and a low level of economic diversification.) In the list of these countries, in particular those located
in Africa (the majority), many have experienced major unrest such as civil war
(e.g., Burundi, Somalia, and Sierra Leone) and others have fought against each
other (Ethiopia and Eritrea), but only one in which terrorism played a certain role,
namely, the Sudan. But in the Sudan too, it was not the native Sudanese element
that played the main role but foreign terrorists who were hiding in the country
and using it as a training ground. They had bought themselves into Sudan, which
was relatively easy in view of the poverty of the country and the radical Islamic
orientation of some of its leaders. The same situation prevailed in Eritrea. But
these countries were not safe havens for terrorists; when the French made an
offer, the Sudanese government turned over Carlos, who was hiding in Sudan,
and Eritrea released Ethiopian terrorists to Addis Ababa.

The Sudanese rulers realized that the presence of foreign terrorists only caused
trouble. The country was put on the list of "rogue states," and economic sanctions
were taken. Furthermore, the Sudanese government was involved in a semiper-
manent war with the non-Muslim tribes in the south of the country and did not
need further complications. Bin Laden, who was residing there and had heavily
invested in the country, had to leave.

What of other, somewhat more developed countries? From what classes of
society were terrorists recruited? Was it not true that the grave economic problems
facing countries such as Algeria or Pakistan, to name but two — a high birth rate
and economic stagnation resulting in high unemployment, mainly among the
young — created a fertile ground for terrorist movements? Again, the evidence
in favor of the poverty argument is not conclusive. While the Irish Republican
Army (IRA) has traditionally recruited its followers from the lower middle class
and the working class, the Basque Euskadi Ta Azkatasuna (ETA) seems to have
been composed mainly of young people of middle-class origin. Whereas Northern

Ireland, the mainstay of the IRA, belonged to the less prosperous regions of the United Kingdom, the Basque provinces are among the most developed of Spain. In the Middle East, Palestinian groups such as Hamas, Islamic Jihad, and particularly the Lebanese Hizbullah are constituted to some extent of relatively poor people, but then the great majority of people in these societies are not wealthy. In any case, the leadership and the early Palestinian terrorists, such as the various popular fronts for the Liberation of Palestine, were strictly middle class, including one of their early heroines, Leila Khaled.

The Algerian Islamist terrorists came mainly from poor families, but the most militant such as the Egyptian and Saudi suicide bombers came from middle- or upper-middle-class families. Their parents were professional people, successful merchants, or belonged to the higher echelons of the bureaucracy. This applies in particular to the Bin Laden network, many of whose members were graduates of universities or technical high schools or military academies. The Egyptian terrorists concentrated their efforts for many years in the cities of Upper Egypt such as Assyut and Minya, which belonged to the more neglected regions of the country, but within that area they looked for their recruits among families who were better off and in particular university students. Ahmed Sheikh, London-born and sentenced to death in Pakistan for the murder of journalist Daniel Pearl, came from a well-to-do family and was educated at private schools, but was thrown out from two of them, which tends to point to more than average psychological trouble.

This phenomenon, the appeal of terrorism to students with a middle-class background, has been observed for a long time in other parts of the world. Ernst Halperin noted with regard to Latin American terrorism in the 1970s that if one were to apply a Marxist class analysis it would appear that terrorism was a movement of middle-class students against entrenched oligarchies, looking for an improvement in their status and their prospects as well as for political power.[2]

The European terrorist groups of the extreme left in Europe were predominantly middle class (more in Germany than in Italy), whereas those of the extreme right — neo-Nazis and skinheads — belonged to a lower social stratum. Shining Path in Peru was definitely a movement of the poor, but the Tamil Tigers in Sri Lanka was not. In brief, one would look in vain for a clear socioeconomic pattern in the composition of terrorist movements. Terrorism rarely occurs in the poorest and richest countries, especially if these happen to be small societies in which there is little anonymity; between these extremes, terrorism can occur almost anywhere.

It has been argued that the leadership of revolutionary movements has always been constituted by the elite. Marx after all did not come from a poor family. Engels owned a factory, and the prophet Muhammad, having married a wealthy widow, was well-off too. But radical Islamic terrorism is not a movement aiming at social revolution. While support for al Qa'ida was strong among the poor in Pakistan, there are obvious reasons that the militants should come from the middle class, even the upper middle class. A contemporary terrorist operating outside his own country has to be educated, have some technical competence, and be able to move without attracting attention in alien societies. In brief, such a person will have to have an education that cannot be found among the poor in Pakistani or Egyptian villages or Palestinian refugee camps, only among relatively well-off town folk.

One other factor has contributed to the terrorist potential in the Arab world: uncontrolled demographic growth and the incapacity of the Arab governments to find jobs for young people leaving the schools and graduating from the universities. Among the regions with the highest total fertility rate (TFR) are Gaza with 7.9 percent and Saudi Arabia with 7 percent. Saudi Arabia is a rich country (even though its income substantially declined over the last decade) whereas Gaza is poor. Both countries have been leading recruiting grounds of terrorists. But relatively few terrorists have come from Jordan and Syria, which also have a TFR of 7 percent. In countries like Egypt and Algeria, hundreds of thousands of young people graduate from the universities each year. Of these young people only about half will find a job, and the percentage of those finding a satisfactory job is even smaller. These young people will be found in the coffee houses drinking coffee, smoking water pipes, and not surprisingly discussing radical politics, and among them the terrorists will find sympathizers. A high percentage of youth unemployment can be found in all Arab and most Muslim countries, rich and poor; governments have failed to make any real effort to find jobs for the younger generation. They left supervision of education in the hands of the Islamists, and secular entertainment for young people hardly exists at all. These seem to be the main causes of radicalization among the young generation, not poverty per se.

The present distribution of wealth between nations and within many nations is not conducive to social and political peace. Many reasons can be adduced in favor of greatly increased efforts on the part of developed nations to help their less fortunate brothers and sisters. But this process will take a long time and cannot possibly be one-sided. Greater prosperity depends not just on the transfer of capital and investment but to a large extent on education and, generally speaking, the creation of a suitable climate for economic development. In recent decades, the Far East has developed relatively quickly, quicker than Europe, whereas in most African countries there has been negative development. The Middle East, by and large, has stagnated.

In the third world, and in particular in the Arab and Muslim countries, another trend has contributed to radicalization: the growing frustration about the social and economic stagnation of the Muslim world and particularly the Arab countries, the oil-rich societies among them. Furthermore, terrorism has, of course, added to the pauperization of the region. This effect was palpably felt through the Muslim world after the events of September 2001 — international companies ceased to invest in the Middle East, the tourism industry (very important in countries like Egypt) collapsed, exports from the Arab countries sharply declined, and unemployment increased.

How to explain the persistent belief that poverty and starvation are the main, if not the only, causes of terrorism in the contemporary world? It has to do in part with certain political assumptions: that the misery of the third world is the fault of imperialism and the third world's exploitation by the developed countries, a version of the Leninist theory of imperialism which lingers on. Westerners have been told not only that the global division of wealth is unjust, but that it is their fault. Of course the colonial powers have exploited their colonies, but the powers also contributed to the colonies' economic development. The colonies rebelled against foreign rule not primarily because of economic exploitation; had they remained colonies, the economic situation of many would be better today. Underlying the belief that terrorism is generated by poverty is the assumption that in this case it might be relatively easy to remedy this state of affairs by offering much greater support to the poor countries, to have a redivision of wealth, by providing employment and thus restoring hope.

The misery of hundreds of millions in North Africa, the Middle East, and South Asia, not to mention Africa, has a variety of reasons; it should figure high on the international agenda. But even those most sympathetic to the cause of the third world have realized for a long time that to account for violence in these parts, more sophisticated explanations are called for. As Kofi Annan, secretary general of the United Nations, put it: The poor of this world suffer enough; one should not in addition brand them as potential terrorists.

Similar misconceptions have prevailed for a long time in a related field: hate crimes. In a famous study more than sixty years ago, two psychologists established a correlation between lynching and cotton prices in the United States. When prices were low, lynchings went up. This finding was accepted for a long time as an established truth. But new studies many years later covering longer periods found no such correlation. Had there been a correlation, one would have expected more lynchings in America during the Great Depression, but this was not the case. Studies concerning the level of unemployment and attacks on foreigners in Germany in the 1990s likewise found no correlation, and that the causes of violence must have been different.

Terrorism, like revolutions, occurs not when the situation is disastrously bad but when various political, economic, and social trends coincide. In the 1970s, social scientists pointed to the concept of relative deprivation and frustration leading to aggression. These concepts were also not very successful trying to account for terrorism, and they led away from the realm of economics to the field of human psychology.

While poverty is sometimes a contributing factory to the emergence and spread of terrorism, national-ethnic tensions are of considerably greater relevance, and much of the present study is devoted to this topic. Such conflicts were at the bottom of the confrontation in Kashmir, in Israel/Palestine, in Chechnya, and in Sri Lanka. They were not a decisive factor in some of the bloodiest terrorist campaigns, such as in Algeria, Colombia, or Central Asia. In other words, resolving national conflicts would be no more of an universal panacea to end terrorism than eradicating poverty. Solving national conflicts and reducing tensions between various ethnic groups remain vital aims but would not provide a magic wand. People who practice terrorism are extremists, not moderates, and the demands of extremists can hardly ever be satisfied without impairing the rights of other ethnic groups, especially if two groups happen to claim the same region or country.

Another reason frequently adduced for the spread of terrorism is the clash of civilizations and the inability of the West to prevent it. There is some truth in these assertions, but mainly in the case of Islam and hardly with regard to the Far East or India, where there is less of an inferiority feeling vis-à-vis the West. Radical Islamists have been trying hard to add fuel to such a potential conflict.[3]

A review of wars, civil wars, and other contemporary conflicts shows indeed a greater incidence of violence and aggression in Muslim societies than in most others. If we ignore tribal warfare in sub-Saharan Africa (notably in Nigeria and Somalia as well as the Sudan), the Islamic factor has been prominently involved; almost 90 percent of these conflicts appear to affect Muslim countries and societies. Of the twenty-two member states of the Arab League and the fifty-seven member states of the OIC (the Organization of the Islamic Conference), hardly any have been free of major political violence during the last twenty years. The United Arab Emirates and perhaps also Morocco and Kazakhstan may provide exceptions, but it is difficult to think of others. Muslims have a hard time living as minorities in non-Muslim countries, be it in India, the Philippines, or in Western Europe. Muslims find it equally difficult to give a fair deal to minorities — Muslim or non-Muslim — in their own midst, be it the Berbers in Algeria; the Copts in Egypt; or the Kurds, the Baha'i, or the Christians in the Sudan, Pakistan, and East Timor.

However, the bloodiest war since 1945 has been between two Muslim countries, namely, Iran and Iraq, and the bloodiest terrorist campaign with about 100,000–150,000 victims took place in Algeria with the Islamist FIS (Front Islamique de Salut) and GIS (Groupe Islamique Armée) attacking Algerian government forces and society. There have been armed conflicts between Morocco and the Polisario, and between the Sudan and its neighbors, not to mention Afghanistan and the two Yemens. Iraq has attacked Kuwait, and Syria has invaded Jordan. There has been trouble between Muslims in the Caucasus as well as in Central Asia.

In some cases Muslims have been the aggrieved party. One needs to think only of the Chechen, Bosnia, Kashmir, the West Bank, or the Uighurs in China. But the moment the Albanians had the opportunity, they turned against their Serbian and Macedonian neighbors; the Chechen invaded Dagestan; the Muslim Kashmiris made it known that they wanted not only a state of their own but to expel those who were not Muslims. The radical Palestinian groups have made no secret that they do not merely want to liberate the territories occupied by Israel in 1967 but to destroy the state of Israel, for which they argue there is no room in an Islamic Middle East.

Given all these conflicts and tensions, it seems unlikely that, despite the hostility against the West (which, after all, is not a monolith either), the Muslim countries have a common cause against what the radicals among them consider the Big Satan. Never in its history has the Organization of the Islamic Conference (OIC) managed to solve a conflict between its members.

In brief, the elements of disunity among these countries are stronger than those making for common action. The radical Islamists have opposed Arab nationalism, which they consider a Western importation because it is a divisive factor. But at the same time they have added fuel to Arab dissension by attacking (following the guidance given by their gurus such as Sayed Qutb) the present Arab governments, all of whom they think unbelievers and corrupt traitors. They are capable of engaging in common action on the diplomatic front, such as voting as a bloc in the United Nations. But it is difficult to imagine the rise of a new Muhammad uniting the various tribes and leading them to war. There is not that much cohesion because Islam has spread much too far: Islam in Africa is more African than Islamic and Moroccan Islamists have not much in common with Albanian, the Uzbek, or the Indonesian. The Islamists violently oppose modernism, but large sections of the Islamic world have been irrevocably affected by Western ideas. It seems hopeless to turn back the wheel of history.

One of the reasons adduced not just for the unpopularity of the United States but for the global spread of terrorism is U.S. military aggression in the postwar world. Ms. Roy, the prominent Indian writer, in a widely publicized essay after the terrorist attacks in September 2001, listed some eighteen or twenty wars in which the United States was involved. The list is correct even if it includes some wars in which the United States intervened on behalf of the United Nations to protect a Muslim minority (Kuwait, Bosnia, and Kosovo). If Ms. Roy had applied the same standard to her own country, she would have found that India fought Pakistan five or six times, and there were military conflicts with China, intervention in Sri Lanka, the conquest of Goa, fighting over many years in Kashmir and the Punjab, in Nagaland and Bodoland, and in Assam, Tripura, and with the Naxalites. In brief, the number of armed conflicts in which India was involved was slightly larger than the number of wars waged by the United States. Islamist terrorism against the United States was rampant in particular during the Carter administration, which tried harder than any other to establish friendly relations with the Muslim world, arming the Afghan rebels, for instance.

The next major upsurge of Muslim terrorism directed against the United States came under the Clinton administration when the Oslo peace process was under way and when Washington intervened to protect the Muslims in former Yugoslavia.

A frequently mentioned cause of terrorism is the state of Israel. As a leading Orientalist put it facetiously many years ago — if it were not for Israel, businessmen would get fat contracts, the supply of cheap oil would be guaranteed, generals and admirals would get bases, and missionaries would face an onslaught of people desiring to be converted to Christianity. To this list one should now add that terrorism would disappear, and democratic and prosperous societies would emerge in the Arab world.

Israel has many critics and enemies, and as a result of its policies on the West Bank and Gaza it has often become difficult for its friends to justify its actions. Israeli domination of the holy places and its unwillingness to share control with the Muslims has been a cause of deep resentment in the Muslim world. It has also been a source of danger of a further spread of the conflict, for there is always the possibility that a religious madman or fanatic, not necessarily Jewish, will try to burn or bomb one of the Muslim holy places. Such an action might have incalculable consequences, given the indoctrination of Muslim masses over many years by religious leaders. Such attempts have occurred in the past and may take place in the future, and they could well lead to a religious war.

Furthermore, Israel should have given up most of the territories occupied in 1967 long ago, for its own sake, not to pacify the outside world. No democratic country can rule in the long run so many hostile subjects and retain its democratic character. Occupation is bound to lead to oppression and armed resistance. The longer the inevitable decision to surrender most of the territories is postponed, the more difficult it will be. Under Barak, Israel offered the return of almost all the territories, but Yasir Arafat refused the offer. Nevertheless, Israel should have gone ahead unilaterally, if need be, despite all uncertainties.

However, the idea that the surrender of the territories and the emergence of a Palestinian state would have a decisive effect on the incidence of global terrorism is far-fetched. For some of Israel's neighbors and, of course, for the Palestinians, Israel is a crucial problem and it is unlikely that the radicals among them will accept its existence even within the borders of 1948. For the Muslim world at large, Israel is a symbol and a catalyst of their rage rather than the cause. An Israeli retreat from the occupied territories will not decisively strengthen the position of the present governments of countries such as Egypt or Saudi Arabia. It will make no great difference (or perhaps no difference at all) with regard to the great majority of present armed conflicts in the Muslim world, be it in North Africa or Nigeria, in Central Asia, Pakistan, the Caucasus or the Philippines, not even in the Persian Gulf, and it is quite unlikely that Israel's retreat would reduce the hostility to the West of the radical Muslims in Western Europe. The radical Islamists have bigger fish to fry; they aim at the punishment and if possible destruction of America and Western civilization. Israel is a small Satan compared with the various big Satans on their political horizon. Far-reaching concessions are in Israel's best interest, but they will hardly induce countries such as Egypt or Syria or Saudi Arabia to move closer to the West.

The attempts to explain contemporary terrorism are quite different in character from the explanations offered a century earlier when anarchism fascinated and frightened public opinion in Europe. Cesare Lombroso, the founder of modern criminology, claimed that he had found one of the main keys for this new startling phenomenon; the anarchists, he claimed, suffered from avitaminosis. For all one knows, some of those who threw the bombs at Lombroso's time may indeed have had an insufficient intake of vitamins, but the same was probably true for many of their less aggressive contemporaries. Lombroso's ideas seem ridiculous one hundred years later, but are present-day explanations closer to reality?

Terrorism has causes; *ex nihilo nihil fit* — nothing comes out of nothing. There is a connection between terrorism and the economic and social situation. There is a connection with the political state of affairs, and at the present time, there is a connection with Islam. If all mankind would be as wealthy as the very richest countries are right now, there would, in all probability, still be violence, but there would be less of it.

Such conclusions do not, however, take us very far. Many terrorisms exist, and their character has changed over time and from country to country. The endeavor to find a "general theory" of terrorism, one overall explanation of its roots, is a futile and misguided enterprise. The motives of the Russian revolutionaries of 1881 have as much to do with al Qa'ida and the various jihads as does the terrorism of Oklahoma City with Peru's Shining Path or the Colombian revolutionaries and drug dealers.

The motives of the Russian terrorists of 1881 and of 1904 can be explained without difficulty against the background of the political situation in Tsarist Russia. But even this relatively obvious and easy explanation cannot account for the fact that some revolutionaries opted for terrorism whereas others preferred political action. These young men and women were by no means more radical in their rejection of the regime than their comrades who rejected terrorism. Of those who survived, more than a few in later life became liberals, conservatives, even die-hard reactionaries. If so, what motivated them: impatience, lack of belief that political action would lead to any results? Was it a matter of personality rather than ideology and objective circumstances? The search for the roots of terrorism has been too frequently lopsided in its endeavor to discover "objective conditions" which, it was believed, always generate terrorism. Such conditions, needless to say, do exist, but they are not the only factors involved. If it were different — if terrorists are, indeed, as some claim, "people like you and me" — there would be billions of terrorists, but there are only relatively few.

Hence it is important to consider psychological factors such as aggression and fanaticism, which are frequently neglected or even ignored in the terrorist context. They are neglected because they are much more difficult to define. While it is always possible to point to ways and means to deal with "objective factors," the psychological motives involved are far more elusive, far more difficult to confront. Such investigations are also neglected because they are repugnant to many as they tend to reduce the importance of the ideological factor in terrorism and lump together terrorists with other individuals showing high degrees of violence and aggression — such as serial murderers. Furthermore, if a strong biological-genetic base were proved, this might lead to a climate of hopelessness, for while there are ways and means to reduce unemployment and defuse national conflicts, there is no known cure at the present time for fanaticism.[4]

The realization that "objective factors" and ideology are usually insufficient to explain the decision of individuals or groups to opt for terrorism has led to a preoccupation with psychological and biological factors: Is there such a thing as a "terrorist personality"?

Psychologists of various schools (behaviorists as well as psychoanalysts) have stressed the importance of childhood experiences. Geneticists have shown a corre-lation between violence, aggression, and biological-genetic factors, while research has focused on the presence of an extra chromosome (Klinefelter's syndrome), on serotonin and testosterone levels, and on the presence of toxic heavy metals and certain brain defects. But however interesting these studies, causation has no more been established than in the case of the objective factors; a great many people may have elevated serotonin and low cholesterol levels and yet do not become terrorists — and vice versa.

The Irish patriots of the nineteenth and twentieth centuries fought for national independence, but their activities cannot explain why other minorities in Europe (even inside the United Kingdom, such as the Scots) did not choose terrorism as their strategy. Why did the radical Basque opt for terrorism whereas the Catalans, also a minority in Spain albeit a more numerous one, did not? Why did the Chechen engage in violent actions, but not the Tatars or other Muslim minorities in Russia? Why did the Tamil Tigers in Sri Lanka opt for terrorism and engage in one of the most protracted and bloody campaigns whereas the Muslims in Sri Lanka have not? And why have the Tamils in Southern India, far more numerous than those in Sri Lanka, been satisfied with their status and not carried out a war for total independence? Many hundred national and religious minorities in the world are persecuted and discriminated against; in fact there are few countries in which minorities do not believe that they are unfairly treated.

To find an explanation to the questions of why and in what circumstances ter-rorism occurs, one ought to consider at least in passing the questions of why and where terrorism does *not* occur even though all the "objective" reasons such as oppression and persecution do exist. To give but a few examples — the untouchables in South and East Asia (scheduled castes or Dalits in India, Burakami in Japan, and similar groups in Sri Lanka, Bangladesh, Myamar, Pakistan, etc.). They number about 240 million and their treatment has been often abominable, yet there has been no terrorism. Could it be that they are so degraded and fearful that they do not dare to protest and oppose their persecutors?

It could be argued that most national and religious minorities have accepted that, given the mixture of national groups in the modern world, it would not be possible to have total independence short of ethnic cleansing such as the world has never witnessed. There is of course also the fact that some ethnic groups demand the same territories as their rivals. But such sober calculation is probably not the main reason for the absence of terrorism in many parts of the globe and its presence in others. In every case, the specifics of the situation have to be considered. There are similarities, but in the end each case is different.

This takes us back to the changes that have taken place in the character of terrorism over the past 150 years. Terrorism in the nineteenth century aimed at social revolution or national liberation. Their quarrel was not with society at large, only with a small layer of oppressors. There were cases of indiscriminate killing, but these were the exception rather than the rule. This situation began to change in the 1970s, a little earlier in the case of nationalist-separatist terrorism. It refers to the brutalization and dehumanization in the choice of targets. That attacks should become indiscriminate was only logical, for the enemy was no longer a thin layer but the whole opposing group. If an anarchist declared in the late nineteenth century that there were no innocents, this declaration came from a fellow traveler, not a terrorist speaking on behalf of his group. It was considered by most of his fellow militants a willfully paradoxical and wicked statement. A hundred years later indiscrimination had become common practice. Terrorist spokesmen would still occasionally claim that they were fighting only wicked governments, not other people, but in practice they aimed to kill as many people as possible. On occasion they would declare that civilian victims were after all taxpayers and young girls would one day be mothers and give birth to babies who would become enemy soldiers. Rape and mutilation were unheard of in nineteenth-century terrorism, but toward the end of the twentieth century they became the rule rather than the exception in some parts of the world.

Old-style terrorists, with the exception of a few marginal cases, would not have considered using weapons of mass destruction or even of leaving their bombs in places such as supermarkets where innocent bystanders would be the victims. This dehumanization is in large part the result of religious fanaticism especially in the case of Islamism, but it is also true in the case of radical nationalist terrorism. It has occurred in particular in the fantasies and the actions of the extreme right in the United States; the case of the Turner Diaries is an obvious example. These groups felt themselves so isolated and so powerless vis-à-vis an omnipotent enemy that every weapon seemed permissible to have a chance in an unequal combat. The greater the fanaticism and the madness, the greater the urge to destroy as many enemies as possible. Whereas nineteenth-century terrorism especially in its anarchist variant had considered terrorism "propaganda by deed," the extreme groups of a later period had no wish to persuade anyone; their aim was to destroy as many of the enemy forces as possible, with "enemy forces" referring to all infidels, including small babies.

Just as the Holocaust would have been unlikely in nineteenth-century Europe, the new terrorism became possible only as the moral values and the whole Zeitgeist changed. Terrorists of an earlier period with all their hatred of the enemy had still felt bound by certain conventions. They would not have engaged in actions considered inhuman, and they would not have declared that they intended to "drink the blood of their enemies" and to "dance on their graves." Some present-day terrorists expect their enemies to drink their own blood and to infect them with AIDS and commit similar cruelties, or at least they claim to believe this. There were, of course, cases of indiscriminate killing by terrorists well before the 1970s, but only thereafter, with bombs placed into jumbo jets or the attack against Olympic athletes, did such practices become the prevailing strategy.

There were not a few unstable personalities among nineteenth-century terrorists, especially the Anarchists and the Russians, but there were few paranoiacs among them. On the other hand, persecution mania plays an important part in the new terrorism. Terrorism adapted itself and was motivated by a fanaticism that manifested itself in, among other things, indiscriminate mass killings and suicide bombings.

The term "fanaticism" comes from the Latin *fanum* (a holy place) but acquired early on the meaning of being possessed. It has frequently been described by theologians and historians of religion, whereas psychologists and psychiatrists have often shied away from investigating the phenomenon. A workable definition has been provided by Adolf Hitler in *Mein Kampf;* more than any other modern leader Hitler invoked fanaticism as an essential element of the Nazi movement.

Hitler noted that the mobilization of the masses could never be achieved by "half-hearted statements and actions" but only by total lack of any (humane) consideration and the fanatical, relentless pursuit of the goal. The enemy had to be smashed and destroyed; he was not just wrong, he was always totally wrong. The greatness of each great movement, Hitler declared, is rooted in a religious fanaticism totally convinced of its own rightness, intolerant against everything else. Seen in this light, the greatness of Christianity was not in attempting to compromise with similar philosophical schools but in fanatically and without compromise pressing its own message.

Hitler's insistence on the religious sources of fanaticism should not blind us to the fact that Hitler and his comrades were by no means motivated by traditional religion, except perhaps in a new, self-made variety. Nor was he reliable as a student of religion. Christianity was, after all, during the first three centuries of its history the religion of persecuted minorities, in contrast to Islam whose founder was — or to be precise, became — a military leader and whose followers in the course of the next three centuries engaged in military expansion in Asia and North Africa.

Religious sources of fanaticism cannot wholly account for contemporary manifestations. The first suicide bombers in the Middle East in the early 1980s were not Muslims but secular Christians. The Tamil Tigers, who produced more suicide bombers in the 1990s than any other terrorist movement, were not motivated by religion either. Nationalism, in other words, could produce a fanatical appeal similar to religion. The kamikaze pilots in World War II are an obvious example, as are soldiers in other armies in all recent wars who went on actions from which the chances of returning were minimal (SS units in so-called *Himmelfahrtskommandos*, the crew of German submarines in 1944, etc.). Nationalism quite apart, esprit de corps — the feeling of loyalty to a group — played an important role.

But with all this, the religious (or quasi-religious) sources of fanaticism are beyond doubt. They appear perhaps most clearly in certain episodes in the history of Christianity, such as the story of the Crusades. The speeches of Pope Urban and other princes of the church called the pious to go to the Holy Land to save the holy places from the Saracenes who had desecrated and destroyed them. The chronicles describe how the scum of France (*faex residua Francorum*) responded with great enthusiasm shouting "Deus lo volt" — God wants it — but how later on the nobles joined the Crusade (as well as many thousands of children and women wholly ill prepared who never made it), how Jerusalem was conquered, and how a bloodbath took place thereafter. Many Jewish communities have been destroyed on the road of the crusaders, but they did not spare Eastern Church congregations either. Many of their contemporaries thought these enthusiasts possessed and crazy, but the movement affected tens of thousands.

It was not, of course, only the Pope who had played a role in this incitement, but demagogic priests also like Peter of Amiens, a type of fanatic who recurs during the Middle Ages up to Savonarola, the Inquisition, and the burning of witches. Fanaticism suffered a decline even before the Enlightenment, but it had a revival in some churches such as the Russian Orthodox church in the late nineteenth century; there was a reaction elsewhere too against a century of tolerance and humanity.

The Russian religious philosopher Nikolai Berdyaev has provided a psychological profile of the fanatic, which may fit the fanatics of all religions. According to Berdyaev, the fanatic sees everywhere treason, betrayal, and the breaking of fidelity. He discovers everywhere conspiracies against his beloved idea, against the object of his faith. He is obsessed with a maniacal pursuit after the snares of the devil. Being in the grip of a persecution mania, it is very difficult to bring him back to reality. He sees enemies all around him, and he always becomes the persecutor. He reacts with force, for the devil seems always very strong and omnipotent, and in many ways the fanatic believes more strongly in Satan than in God. The fanatic in Berdyaev's profile acts with the greatest of malice, coercion, and cruelty. His whole life is devoted to persecuting heresy, and he cannot exist without an enemy.

Berdyaev, who wrote in 1937, noted the tendency of fanaticism to divide the world into two hostile camps. This observation applies to the same degree to radical Islamism at the present time.

It is more difficult to follow Berdyaev's generalizations when he claims that fanaticism is always rooted in fear and a perception of danger. He left out of his purview the element of hatred and aggression. Nor is it true, as Berdyaev argues, that there is a basic difference between the fanaticism of the Middle Ages and modern times, inasmuch as in the Middle Ages there was deep religious faith such as no longer exists in the modern age. Also the Middle Ages carried a great intolerance of culture and intellectual creativity. Torquemada and the other inquisitors believed that they tortured people in order to save their souls from perdition, which cannot be said about the modern inquisition.

For Christianity and the other major religions, the Crusades, the Inquisition, and the burning of witches are a thing of the past. But in Islam, once the most tolerant of religions, fanaticism in various manifestations (Wahabism, Salafism, etc.) had a revival in modern times. In some branches of Islam, such as Shiism, fanaticism has always been stronger than in others (e.g., self-flagellation). But in the decades before Khomeini's rise to power, this tradition seemed to be on the wane.

With the resurgence of fundamentalism came a recurrence of fanaticism. The idea of saving the souls of their victims is certainly alien to the present-day terrorists; on the contrary, victims should be annihilated so that there should be no remembrance of them. Nor is terrorist cruelty limited to unbelievers. One need to think only of the Algerian terrorists who excelled in unspeakable acts of cruelty toward their own coreligionists as well as children. True, some of the Islamic fanaticism could well be pre-Islamic in motivation. The Koran and Hadith, for instance, command a decent burial even to enemies (especially Muslim enemies), whereas the traditional way to deal with the corpses of political enemies in Iraq in the 1950s and 1960s but also elsewhere in Muslim lands has been mutilation. This practice has certainly not been in conformance with the prescriptions of religion; the Taliban has acted in a similar barbaric way.

Fanaticism is an essential part of terrorism, for how can one expect militants to kill and to expect to be killed but on the basis of a very strong, single-minded belief? Hence the upsurge of barbarism in terrorism, religious and secular alike. There was a basic difference between Russian revolutionary terrorists of a hundred years ago, among whom there was the belief that by killing (which was politically necessary) they committed a sin for which they were to be punished. These terrorists of a bygone age had been motivated by a feeling of idealism and duty toward their class or their country. The last words of those about to be executed, such as Fischer, one of the accused in the Haymarket trial in Chicago ("This is the happiest day in my life"), reveal that they were deeply convinced that upon them, like upon Christ, was the burden of deliverance. The fanatical devotion of some of the early Nazis — such as Schlageter, who was executed by the French in 1923 after some acts of sabotage — was paid homage by a leading Soviet communist, Karl Radek. He wrote at the time that the fact that Schlageter risked death showed that he was determined to serve his country. Radek drew the conclusion that the Communists shall do everything in their power to ensure that men like Leo Schlageter, willing to go to their death for an ideal, should not have died in vain but be harbingers of a better world.

To state the obvious again, terrorism has changed over time and so have the terrorists, their motives, and the causes of terrorism. A century ago terrorism was either socialist revolutionary or anarchist, or in some cases, nationalist separatist such as in Ireland and the Balkans. A world map of terrorism around 1970 still showed, broadly speaking, the same trends — left-wing terrorism in some European countries and in Latin America, nationalist terrorism in the Middle East, but also terrorism carried out by groups of the extreme right — in Germany and Romania in the 1920s and 1930s and in later decades also in Italy, Turkey, and other countries. This terrorism was predominantly internal, directed against the ruling government or other parties and social groups. Only in a few cases was terrorism based in one country directed against another, such as in the Middle East and on the Indian subcontinent.

During the 1980s and early 1990s there was a worldwide decline in terrorist action. The left-wing groups with a very few exceptions had disappeared, the right wing had declined in influence, and while the nationalist-separatist trend continued to operate, there were also signs that it was abating. The Irish and the Basque terrorists were negotiating on and off with the governments of their countries, and the peace process in the Middle East also caused a decline in the number of acts of terrorism. Some of the sponsors of state terrorism, including Libya and Sudan, became noticeably less active than they had been before, and the Iranians tried harder to obliterate their traces. As the annual report of the State Department for the year 2000 stated, only nineteen U.S. citizens had been killed that year in acts of international terrorism. (Seventeen of them perished in a single attack — on the USS *Cole* in the port of Aden.)

However, during the 1990s, a new factor arose that became within a few years the most important by far on the map of international terrorism: Islamic terrorism. There had been, of course, such groups before, such as in Algeria, but sometimes they were overlooked; on other occasions they were thought to be mainly local and nationalist rather than religious in character, such as in the case of Kashmir and Palestine. (Kashmir and Palestine had been originally national conflicts, but they have become more and more religious-political — Islamist in other words — in recent years.) In other places the military operations by Islamic groups took the character of guerrilla warfare rather than terrorism in the Caucasus and Central Asia.

But with the attempts of al Qa'ida under Osama bin Laden to establish something like an international coordination bureau of Muslim terrorist groups and an International Brigade, the role of Islamic terrorism became predominant and most other terrorist groups became marginal — except, of course, for the local authorities involved.

All this history has to be recalled for the simple reason that an analysis of the roots of terrorism at the beginning of the twenty-first century cannot be based exclusively on the experience of earlier phases. But to reiterate once again, it would be even more misleading to proceed with such an analysis from the assumption that terrorism has no prehistory. Both the features the new terrorism has in common with the old and the essential differences have to be taken into account. Religious and nationalist fanaticism is the predominant feature of terrorism at the present time, which does not preclude that in future decades terrorism might appear also in other guises.

TWO

The Origins of Islamic Terrorism

D URING THE NINETEENTH and most of the twentieth centuries terrorism in the Muslim and Arab world did not play a significant role. To be more precise, Muslim and Arabic terrorism was a localized phenomenon. It did exist but it was not predominant, nor did it differ essentially in its motivation and outlook from other forms of terrorism. Toward the end of the twentieth century, Muslim and Arabic terrorism became the most prominent component of world terrorism. How did this happen?

Its origins were in the emergence of the revivalist movements promoting a return to fundamentalist Islam, and those of its protagonists who wanted to impose their aims by force. Such movements appeared in several countries: In the Arabian Peninsula it took the form of Wahhabism, the teaching spread by an eighteenth-century sect that was little noticed at the time. On the Indian subcontinent, terrorism was connected with the desire to strengthen the identity of the Muslim minority vis-à-vis the Hindu majority; the founders of Pakistan had been secular politicians, but on the fringes of their movement, religious extremists were active. As time went by, they became more prominent. But the heartland of Islamic fundamentalism was Egypt, even though Salafism (as it was locally known) never gained a politically leading position. The term "Salafi" simply means early Islamic, referring to those who lived in the first centuries after Muhammad. In religious terms it means opposition to reform and the purification of Islam from alien elements. But Salafism was also a reform movement, a reinterpretation of the origins of a religion which as much as other religions (and perhaps even more so) were shrouded in darkness and uncertainty. With what justification could these modern advocates of a pure Islam claim that they were more knowledgeable and more faithful interpreters than those of a bygone time? Salafism opened widely the door to subjectivism. It meant in practice that everyone was, or at any rate could be, his own interpreter of the holy writ — except, of course, that the Salafis thought that they had a monopoly as far as truth was concerned.

Islamic fundamentalism in one form or another had always been present, just as in Christianity and Judaism there had been fundamentalist trends all along. If so, what was specific about the new Islamic fundamentalism? It preached that one should adhere very closely to the Koran; that Allah was the only true Lord, the only God worthy of obedience and true worship; and that one should believe in the uniqueness the of prophet Muhammad. But these basic tenets were common to every Muslim. What was really new was the conviction of the Salafis that *they* were Islam, not just one of several factions; that state and society should be based on the principles of the religious law, the Sharia, and not on secular law; and that this aim could be achieved most likely only by violence.

New also was the strong emphasis on jihad (holy war), even though its exact meaning was not always made clear. Many fundamentalists also believed in the necessity to reestablish the Khilafah (the unity of political and religious rule) which had vanished with the break-up of the Ottoman Empire after World War I. However, on this point there were differences of opinion, and the Muslim Brotherhood in Egypt, for instance, which had first been in favor later dropped this demand. These basic beliefs were bound to collide with the existing order in the Muslim world and also with nationalism and the national states that had developed over time.[1]

What were the roots of the rise of fundamentalism? They varied from religion to religion and from country to country. In Egypt and other Middle Eastern countries it was the general dissatisfaction with the prevailing state of affairs, the imperfections of politics and society, and fear of and resistance against Western ideological and material influences. The Muslim Brotherhood, the main agent of fundamentalism, which spread over the years to many countries, was never a monolithic political party. It changed its tactics and even some of its doctrine in the course of time. It engaged in many activities — educational, political, social as well as "military" (that is to say, terrorist). In this respect, the Muslim Brotherhood was not different from movements in other parts of the world: IRA had been part of Sinn Fein, a political party; ETA was in close contact with its political wing, Hari Batasuna; the Zionist Revisionist party had Irgun as its terrorist branch; and more recently Hizbullah in Lebanon has not only engaged in suicide bombing but also managed hospitals and schools. Hamas did the same.

This book primarily addresses the terrorist activities of the Muslim Brotherhood and its offshoots. The terrorist acts have to be considered in a wider political context; the IRA and Irgun did not always follow the political leadership but slipped out of their control, and sometimes even turned against it. So did the armed wing of the Brotherhood.

The Muslim Brotherhood in Egypt was founded in 1928 in the city of Ismailya. The original impulse for its creation came from a number of observant Muslims who were appalled at the actions of Mustafa Kemal, the ruler of Turkey who was transforming his country into a secular state. The Brotherhood's founder, Hassan al Banna, saw its main assignment as dissemination of religious propaganda. He created his organization to engage in missionary activities, acting not only through religious education and the building of mosques but also all kinds of social activities (including sports and youth clubs — among them ninety-nine football and

sixteen boxing teams) and even economic enterprises such as building firms and
small banks — all in the spirit of Islam.

The history of the Muslim Brotherhood has been the subject of many Arab
and a few English language studies.[2] By the late 1930s the Brotherhood had
established many local branches in Egypt and also initiated foreign contacts. It
had also become more politicized and radical. As al Banna announced: Islam was
both a religion and a state. The Koran and the sword were inseparable.

At about this time the "special unit" (also called the "secret apparatus") was
established. This armed wing of the Brotherhood would buy (or steal) weapons,
recruit new members from among the army and police, assassinate enemies of
the Brotherhood, and eventually carry out a coup.[3] The secret apparatus had
in the early days a Mufti of its own to decide on the religious legitimacy of an
assassination. On the eve of such an action there would be a ritual trial in the
absence of the accused.[4]

During World War II the British tried to persuade or bribe the Brotherhood
to help them with the war effort, but without much success. The sympathies of
the Brotherhood were with the Axis forces. They tried to establish contact with
Rommel's advancing forces but nothing much became of these feelers. The secret
organization engaged in attacks against Jewish citizens living in Egypt, trying
without success to burn down the Jewish quarter of Cairo. The first great activist
period in the history of the Brotherhood took place in the years between the end
of the world war up to the revolution resulting in the deposition of King Faruq.
The Brotherhood was in the forefront of the struggle against the British; it sent
thousands of volunteers to join the war against the Jews in Palestine; above all the
Brotherhood engaged in a campaign of terror against its domestic foes. Among
the victims were two prime ministers of the day (1948) — Ahmed Maher and
Mahmoud Fahmi en Noqrashi — but among those attacked were also foreign and
domestic journalists. In retaliation, Hassan al Banna was killed by the police in
a Cairo street in February 1949. Al Banna's antagonism vis-à-vis the West was
profound and unshakeable. In an open letter to the heads of Muslim states in
1946, he called the West not only unjust and tyrannical but also very weak and
decadent; one strong push by the army of the faithful, according to al Banna, and
the whole world would find calm and peace under the banner of Islam.[5]

There is reason to believe that al Banna was unhappy during the last years of
his life about the activities of the special apparatus, which had become largely
independent under Abdel Rahman al Sanadi. Al Banna did not want to burn
his bridges with the leading political parties, such as the Wafd, or with the government. His successor, the judge Hassan Hodaibi, was even more moderate. As
a result, a period of ideological and tactical confusion set in, with various factions pulling in different directions. The Brotherhood supported the Free Officers
who had taken over power, but they also dissociated themselves from the new
leadership; they bitterly opposed the godless Communists but also found at times

common cause with them. Eventually one of the Brothers tried to kill Nasser as he made a speech in the city of Minya (the so-called "Minya incident"), whereupon four thousand members of the organization were arrested; thousands fled from Egypt, and a few were executed. The Brotherhood was effectively smashed and for the next fifteen years amounted to very little inside Egypt.

In 1964, Nasser granted a general amnesty to all members of the Muslim Brotherhood. However, while accepting the amnesty, the Brotherhood had no wish to collaborate with Nasser and immediately continued their own operations aiming to overthrow the government. The ideology was provided by Sayed Qutb, whose writings in prison became the doctrine of the militant wing of the Brotherhood in the years that followed.

About Qutb the theologian a great deal has been written; our interest in his teaching and influence is limited to Qutb as the philosopher and instigator of terrorism.[6] Qutb was born in 1906 in a middle-class family near Assyut in Upper Egypt, the heartland of the radical Islamist groups. He was a literary critic, teacher, and school inspector in later years, and relatively late in life, following a visit to the United States in 1948–50, he became a convert to fundamentalism and joined the Muslim Brotherhood, which had been in existence at that time for about two decades. Within a very short time he emerged as one of its leaders, the most radical and the most influential but also a very divisive figure. He taught that Islam was the only true religion; that all other religions and civilizations were barbarian, evil, and animal-like, and that any contact with them was to be shunned. The West was the enemy par excellence of the Muslims, afraid of Islam and aware of its spiritual superiority. As Qutb saw it, there could never be peace with the West. The struggle was not about territory but about truth and which truth should prevail in the world. All that is known about his life points to a fanatic, a man totally dedicated to the cause he thought right, a person beset with deep psychological difficulties. He did not have any formal theological education, and in the early years his books were banned as those of a deviationist if not apostate by Al Azhar, the leading religious study center in the Islamic world. He did have the urge to die a martyr to his cause, which in the end he did.

Together with other Muslim Brotherhood militants, he spent many years in prisons and concentration camps under the rule of Gamal Abdel Nasser, and according to his sympathizers he was tortured. But conditions cannot have been too harsh, because while detained he wrote some twenty books. The most important of them, on top of a thirty-volume interpretation of the Koran (half of them written in prison), was a book entitled *Milestones*.

Milestones amounted, no more and no less, to the ex-communication (*taqfir*) of all Muslims who did not agree with his brand of Islam. The book claimed that all existing Islamic states and their rulers were not true Muslims but pagans against whom relentless war should be waged up to their destruction. This claim was tantamount to a declaration of war, not just on the present rulers but on society in general. This kind of radicalism repelled most of the older members of the Muslim Brotherhood, including those in prison, but it strongly appealed to the younger radicals. In 1964, trying to appease the Brotherhood and to induce them to join his Arab Socialist Union (the only existing political party), Nasser had most of the Brotherhood's leaders released from detention. But the Brotherhood had no desire to collaborate with Nasser, whom they considered an enemy. Following several more attempts on Nasser's life, the leadership of the Brotherhood was again arrested. Several ringleaders, including Qutb, were hanged. Thus he died a martyr and became a hero of the extremists who were attracted precisely by his appeals to violence.[7]

After his death, hundreds of thousands, perhaps millions, of copies his works were printed throughout the Islamic world. While some spiritual leaders continued to reject his views, others accepted them, wholly or in part. In the canon of the Muslim Brotherhood, Qutb figures today as the leader and thinker second in importance only to the founder, Hassan al Banna. But since al Banna wrote much less than Qutb, it is safe to say that the latter has been the most influential thinker of the Brotherhood. He has certainly been the greatest influence as far as the Muslim terrorists in the Arab world and North Africa are concerned. As some observers have pointed out, many terrorists, including some of their leaders, never read Qutb, but his message of holy war, shorn of theological refinements, filtered down even to those who had never even heard his name. Not one of the reformist Muslim religious thinkers, nor all of them taken together, had even remotely as much influence as Qutb did.

Nasser's defeat in the war against Israel and his death a few years later gave the Brotherhood new freedom of maneuver, and Anwar el Sadat, who succeeded the "Rais" (as Nasser had been known), had another general amnesty declared. Sadat believed that he needed their help to purge the country from Nasserists and Communists. Thus the Muslim radicals received for a while a free hand to remove their enemies, who happened also to be the rivals of the new regime, from positions of influence in the field of education, the universities, and cultural and public life. But this fatal miscalculation on Sadat's part eventually led to his murder. The Muslim radicals considered the purge of the secular only the first stage of their fight for power which, as they envisaged it, should result in a coup d'état. For them Sadat, even though he was a practicing Muslim, was no better than Nasser.

Qutb's teachings inspired a variety of underground organizations. One of them was headed by Shukri Mustafa; it was the first to establish a guerrilla band called Taqfir va'l hejra (also called Jama'at al Muslimin, society of Muslims) in the neighborhood of Assyut.[8] Shukri's group, active between 1971 and 1977, was a typical sect which, for all intents and purposes, established a religion of its own so ultra-orthodox that it turned anti-Islamic and rejected the teaching of all the *ulema* (religious leaders) past and present because they had been corrupted by the governments of the day and could not be trusted. Like Pol Pot, Shukri reached the conclusion that society in general was so corrupt that there was no way to reform it; it had to be destroyed. But since in contrast to Pol Pot the guerrilla group was too weak to do so, it decided in its early stages to withdraw from the sinful cities and their temptations to caves in remote hilly districts. However, they found life in these primitive conditions too difficult, so they returned to the cities where they attracted some new members.

Next, internal splits occurred in their ranks. Other, competing Islamic extremist groups tried to wean members over to their organizations, but since leaving the group was tantamount to treason (like apostasy from Islam), Shukri reacted violently.[9] He also decided to put the finances of his organization on a more solid basis by kidnapping a prominent personality and asking for ransom. The best-known victim was Muhammad al Dhahbi, a former government minister of *waqf* (religious properties), and when the authorities refused to pay the two hundred thousand Egyptian pounds that the kidnappers had demanded, the sheikh was killed by his abductors. This led within a few days to the arrest of most active members of this group, who had been under police observation for some time. Astonishing facts emerged in the trial such as, for instance, that Shukri could not quote a single verse from the Koran, and that in all probability, he would not have been able to understand it in any case. Shukri and some of his fellow conspirators were sentenced to death and executed in 1977.

The religious establishment regarded Shukri and his gang as marginal figures outside the camp of faithful Muslims. But at the same time they put the responsibility for the Taqfir va'l hejra phenomenon on the government which, it argued, was secular, not rooted in Islamic religious tradition.

This was not quite the end of Taqfir, which reemerged in 1985 under the name al Wawaquf wal tabayun, a terrorist group which tried to assassinate two ministers of the interior and also the editor-in-chief of *Al Mussawar*, Egypt's leading illustrated weekly. Members of the group were duly arrested; one of the defendants in the trial claimed that they firmly believed that they would be the only ones to be saved from hell. Lastly, a local terrorist gang in Fayoum in 1990 also maintained that it was a successor of Taqfir. They were headed by a local militant named Shawqi el Sheikh; it is difficult to establish to what extent this group was motivated by religion or whether it was mainly criminal in character. It certainly raised funds by running protection rackets that intimidated local farmers. The farmers complained, the police intervened, and in the shootout that followed nineteen people were killed. At one time Shawqi almost succeeded in establishing in a village named Khak a "liberated zone" on the Maoist model. The social composition of his gang was interesting; its leaders without exception were local notables and men of substance, while their followers were farmers, seasonal workers, and fishermen. The group had local backing because of widespread antigovernment resentment, but it always remained restricted to the district where it originated.[10]

Several other terrorist groups emerged in the 1970s, some more or less spontaneous and short-lived, such as the gang headed by a Palestinian Arab named Salah Sariya. He had arrived from Jordan only a few years earlier and on the fringes of the Muslim Brotherhood recruited a group of students at the military academy at Heliopolis. In April 1974, they engaged in a highly amateurish coup, trying to gain hold of the academy and to kill Sadat. But they were overpowered by the guards; two were executed, more given lengthy prison terms.

Far more serious and long-lived were two groups that entered the history of Egyptian terrorism under the name of Jihad and Gama'a Islamiya.[11] They too derived their doctrine from Sayed Qutb and developed among students on the university campuses and the youth organizations of the Muslim Brotherhood.

Qutb was dead and they needed a living guru. They found him in a blind sheikh named Umar Abdel Rahman who had been a professor in a religious institute affiliated with Al Azhar in Assyut. Abdel Rahman had the reputation of an extreme fundamentalist, very critical of the government and in favor of the use of violence. According to some sources, Umar became the mufti of terrorist groups in 1980 (according to others in 1981), but he certainly did play for years a central role in Egyptian terrorism.[12] There was a long theological discussion among his followers about whether he could ever be the official head or commander because of his infirmity, but he certainly was the power in the background. He issued the fatwas they needed, be it for robbing and killing local goldsmiths (usually Christian) or for launching war against America, which, according to him, was the source of all evil and the main enemy of Islam, responsible for the unhappy condition of the Muslim world. Every conspiracy against Islam, every bit of scheming emanated from America and the task of the terrorists was to strike terror against America, and not to be afraid of the "terrorism" label. This approach was what Jihad was all about: jihad with the sword, with the cannon, with grenades, and with the missile, jihad against God's enemies.[13]

When most members of his group were arrested, the blind sheikh fled, or was permitted to escape, to the United States in late 1990. The circumstances are not clear why Washington would give exile to one so prominently involved in terrorist activities. Perhaps he was considered harmless. The Egyptian government later claimed to have asked for his extradition, but the U.S. government certainly did not respond and seems not to have paid attention until 1993, when the sheikh was arrested in connection with the attempt to bomb the World Trade Center as well as with other terrorist activities. Perhaps they thought him a lesser danger value at liberty, since his freedom made it easier to observe Muslim radical activities in the United States. If so, their judgment was not, as it later appeared, very sound.

The blind sheikh's connection was mainly with el Jihad, but he was by no means the terrorists' only inspiration. Another was an electrician named Abd al Salam Faraj, author of a book entitled *The Hidden Imperative*, which became the bible of the group that killed Anwar Sadat. Faraj's hidden imperative was jihad, armed attacks against the domestic tyrants (the "Pharaoh"); everything else — the building of mosques, religious education, and other religious obligations — was unimportant. Even the war against the Jews and Israel was subordinated to the supreme duty of "establishing the rule of God in our own country first."[14]

Faraj's book became a cult book among radical Muslims and has been republished countless times. It is a bitter attack against all those who for one reason or another want to interpret jihad in a different, more liberal way or even postpone it. Faraj was particularly caustic about those refusing to fight because among those opposing them were Muslims too. Had not Muhammad said: Verily the killer and the killed will be in Hell Fire? Whence the scruples to kill fellow Muslims? The intellectual level of this tract is very low. To compare it with the writings of medieval Islamic jurists and philosophers of Baghdad or Andalusia is to invite ridicule. It consists of a string of quotations from the Koran and what certain interpreters (carefully selected by the author) said about them. However, the *Hidden Imperative* was not written for intellectuals, but for semiliterate young militants thirsting for violent action.

Sadat's peace initiative with Israel was anything but popular in the ranks of the Muslim Brotherhood and allied groups, but it certainly was not the only reason for his murder; after all, they had try to kill Nasser too, even though he had not wanted to make peace with the Jews. In any case, the first attempts to kill Sadat date back several years before a peace treaty with Israel was signed.

The circumstances of the murder of Sadat in September 1981 during a military parade emerged in detail at the trial of the assassins. It seems to have been a more or less impetuous decision by an army lieutenant named Khaled al Istambuli, a native of Minya district, following the detention of his brother in one of the periodic mass arrests of the local radicals. The plan was submitted to the Cairo leadership of the Gama'a, envisaging not just the murder of the president but a general revolution. It seems to have been a combined action carried out by Gama'a and Jihad of which the young Al Zawahiri, bin Laden's deputy in later years, was one of the leaders. While the first part of the plan was relatively easy — three of a tank crew would jump from their vehicle and open fire on Sadat — the second part, the general uprising, was in the realm of fantasy. Some of the more experienced and mature conspirators had their misgivings about it from the very beginning.

Istambuli and four other conspirators were executed after the first of several trials. Sadat was replaced by his deputy Hosni Mubarak, and the only tangible political result of the assassination was a split in the ranks of the radical Islamists. The Muslim Brotherhood distanced itself from the murder. Some of the leading members of Gama'a who had escaped arrest left the group, and it took several years until the practitioners of violence in Egypt would be able to reorganize.[15]

Thus the murder of Anwar Sadat, far from bringing about the hoped-for revolution, merely ended a chapter in the history of Muslim terrorism in Egypt.

SEVERAL QUESTIONS REMAIN to be addressed, including the geopolitics of terrorism in Egypt. The heavy concentration of terrorist acts from the early days to
the present time in the provinces of Minya and Assyut in southern Egypt can be
explained without great difficulty. These districts are quite populous. The cities
of Minya have almost four hundred thousand inhabitants and those of Assyut
close to half a million, but they suffer from neglect by the central authorities.
They are far from Cairo, and government control has been traditionally difficult
to impose. There are sizeable universities in both cities and, above all, there are
major concentrations of Copts. The approximate number of Coptic Christians in
Egypt is six million or more;[16] the accurate number has not been published for a
long time and is thought to be a state secret.

The Copts have been considered second-class citizens not only by the Islamic
radicals but also the Muslim Brotherhood; even the present chief guide of the
Brotherhood has demanded that they should pay a special tax to the Muslims for
protection against an outside attack.[17]

If there had been substantial colonies of Europeans and Jews in Egypt, the
Muslim Brotherhood would undoubtedly have chosen them as their main, immediate target, but since Europeans and Jews had been thrown out under Nasser,
another enemy had to be found: the Copts of southern Egypt. Individual Copts
were killed, their churches and institutions attacked and sometimes burned, their
shops pillaged. The religious enmity quite apart, there were tensions between
neighboring villagers and resentment of the better-off Copts. According to the
Islamists, the Copts behaved as if they were equal in status to the Muslims. The
Islamists also demanded that no Copt should be promoted to a leading position
in the state apparatus or the security forces. The Copts were accused of buying
weapons, which was quite correct, but they did so mainly in self-defense. In any
case, beating up Copts, while not the only pastime of the Brotherhood and especially the radical terrorist groups in Southern Egypt, became one of their main
preoccupations, much to the embarrassment of the government and also, for different reasons, to the dismay of the radical Islamic leadership in Cairo. They were
as hostile as their brethren in the south to the "crusaders," but they regarded the
attacks against native Egyptians a diversion from the main targets and a waste of
energy. The main aim was to attack the Islamic infidels at home and, of course,
the Americans. Minya and Assyut remain two of the main strong points of the
Gama'a to the present day.

From time to time, the authorities would launch a new campaign to bring
the situation in the south under control — for instance, after the massacre of
foreign tourists in Luxor in November 1997 — but sporadic attacks against Copts
and police patrols did continue. Thousands were arrested, and in an average
year between one hundred and two hundred people were killed in these two
districts alone.[18] The government never quite succeeded in stamping out terrorism
altogether.

After the assassination of Sadat and the failed revolution of 1981, individual radicals continued their efforts to penetrate the army to gain new recruits
among the junior officers and through them to obtain weapons. The authorities,
though, were now doubly watchful, and some of these attempts at insurrection
failed because of the presence of informers, others because of the inexperience of
the plotters.[19] One of their more successful ventures was the escape of Esam el
Qamari, a former army officer, and a couple of his comrades from Tura prison, but
he was apprehended soon after and killed in a shootout with the police. Next,
the terrorists provoked clashes with the security forces in the al Shams quarter
of Cairo, one of their strongholds. But this action again led to mass arrests and
four executions. The terrorists retaliated by trying to kill the minister of interior and the information minister Sawfat al Sharif. A little girl was killed, but
the minister escaped the ambush. The terrorists were more successful when they
ambushed and shot Rauf Khairat, a general in the state security service.[20] At one
stage Gama'a declared several quarters of Cairo "liberated zones." But the next
ambush, the most ambitious, again ended in failure. The plan had been to kill
President Mubarak in Addis Ababa, where he was participating in a conference.

Other operations included an attack against the U.S. embassy in Islamabad
and a group of Israeli tourists in Egypt. By 1991 the movement was again wholly
underground, and it had declared open war on the government; more than a
thousand people were killed as a result of its attacks in the 1990s. But inside the
Gama'a there was a feeling of lack of achievement. More than twenty thousand
of its members and sympathizers had been arrested, various small groups still
at liberty were acting without close coordination, and the leadership in prison
seemed to have lost control over the militants outside. While the leaders in prison
gradually came to consider a truce with the authorities, a small group of terrorists
carried out the massacre of more than fifty Western tourists in Luxor in 1997,
which had a very negative reaction both inside Egypt and even more outside.

By that time the leading members of el Jihad had moved to Afghanistan. Al
Zawahiri, who served there with bin Laden, writes that the chance to transfer
their activities to Afghanistan was a golden opportunity because in Egypt they
had always been closely watched by state security. He quotes a friend, el Banshiri,
a former military commander of el Jihad, who said that he felt as if a hundred
years had been added to his life when he came to Afghanistan.[21]

Afghanistan gave them security to plan their operations, the presence of volunteers eager to undertake missions, unlimited quantities of weapons, and money
supplied by bin Laden and others. But the leaders of Jihad were not the only ones
to go to Afghanistan; Kamal el Sananiri, the head of the Muslim Brotherhood
"special organization" that had been revived, also went there. He later visited
Croatia, and then was extradited to Egypt where he died (or was killed) in prison.

In brief, the terrorist scene had become more than somewhat chaotic in view
of the spreading of various groups acting without coordination. Bin Laden tried

on several occasions to act as an honest broker and, without much success, to restore unity between the various groups. Incidentally, this situation also made it more difficult for the Egyptian authorities to watch the terrorists.

Al Zawahiri and those of his comrades who had gone to Afghanistan eventually came to be part of al Qa'ida (about which more below) and thus lost contact with the militants inside Egypt. They strongly disapproved of the leaders in prison who had opted for a truce. The moving spirits behind this initiative were Khalid Ibrahim, a leader from Aswan, and Muntasar el Zayat, who had acted as the lawyer of the various Islamic groups and was an active sympathizer if not a member. Zayat, who later wrote a book about his efforts to reunite the Islamic groups, also contacted Sheikh Umar, who was now in an American prison but still enjoyed authority among the terrorists in Egypt.[22] He too was in favor of a truce as far as terrorist operations in Egypt were concerned. But some of the brothers in exile, especially those in Afghanistan, proved to be intransigent. El Zayat noted that while violence was sometimes justified, it had no justification if it was no longer rooted in sound judgment and turned into an indiscriminate strategy directed against innocent people, as in the case of the foreign tourists in Luxor.

Al Zawahiri gave his reply in a book in which he bitterly attacked the Muslim Brotherhood leadership in Egypt which, as he claimed, had become tame and reformist, unwilling even to avenge their comrades who had been executed or killed in prison.[23] This did not do Zawahiri's reputation in Egypt any good; who was he, living in relative safety abroad, to teach those in Egyptian prisons?

If the leadership of the Muslim Brotherhood had changed its strategy in the meantime, it had good reasons to do so. While the authorities did not permit it to participate in the elections under their name, it could join the Labor Party, which was headed by a former Communist turned fundamentalist. Above all, the Brotherhood correctly recognized the political vacuum in the country that could be filled by them and which would give them a position of crucial importance. This refers to the labor unions and the associations of the free professions such as the engineers, the physicians, dentists, pharmacists, and so on.

In the late 1980s and 1990s, the Brotherhood took over the leadership of all these groups. The last bastion to fall was the association of lawyers that had earlier been a stronghold of the secular society and liberals. The Brotherhood also strengthened its influence in the private mosques as well as in Al Azhar. Whereas the terrorists had planned to impose Islamization from above, the leadership of the Brotherhood was exceedingly successful with their policy of Islamization from below.[24]

A new type of leadership had taken over, Westernized in many respects, disposing of considerable sums of money (mainly from Saudi Arabia and the Gulf states). They were modern orthodox (to use a term from Israeli society) rather than radical fundamentalists of the old style. Yet they also stood for making Sharia the state law.

All this belongs only indirectly to the history of Egyptian terrorism but it explains why the terrorist trend in Egypt was weakened, at least temporarily. It is quite possible, and indeed likely, that the new leadership of the Brotherhood envisaged a double strategy: They wanted to exhaust the legal possibilities fully and at the same time keep the military (terrorist) option open, so that if the authorities would change their relatively liberal attitude the Brotherhood would be in a position to continue their struggle by other means. The Mubarak government was quite aware of this, hence the new wave of arrests (mainly among professional people) and trials in 2001–2.

Terrorist activities in Egypt throughout the 1990s were as uncoordinated as before: Gama'a, like the Muslim Brotherhood in former years, had been engaged in all kinds of activities, educational and semilegal as well as terrorist. It was stronger than Jihad but its strength was in southern Egypt rather than in Cairo, where their influence was limited to some popular quarters such as Imbaba and Ain Shams in Cairo, where many of the recent arrivals from Upper Egypt had settled. When they tried to extend their activities in the capital, the security forces warned them, and when they did not heed the warnings, some seventeen of them were shot in Cairo streets whereupon the other militants fled to Afghanistan, Britain, and other countries. Gama'a would organize social services such as a soup kitchen for the poor, summer camps for the young, and some cultural institutions, but at the same time they engaged in terrorist activities such as the murder of Rifaat Mahgoub, the speaker of the parliament; the attempted murder of some other ministers; the assassinations of policemen and intellectuals, including the killing of Farag Foda, one of their chief intellectual adversaries; and the attempted murder of Neguib Mahfouz, the writer and Nobel prize laureate. A new, third group of terrorists based in Assyut also planned attacks against foreign tourists and embassies, but their leaders were arrested early on and sentenced to death. Jihad continued to be active, to be sure, but mainly within the framework of bin Laden's new umbrella organization and their terrorist operations now taking place outside Egypt.

Two questions remain to be addressed. One concerns the sources of attraction which the terrorist organizations had inside Egypt. Gama'a invested many of its efforts in gaining support among the urban poor in Cairo, whereas Jihad was an elitist organization that never aimed at mass support and attempted to win over students, young professionals, and, above all, army and police officers. But the leaders and militants of Gama'a too came predominantly from the educated middle class and upper middle class. According to a breakdown concerning social origin and status, about two-thirds of Sayed Qutb's original group were young people with a university education. In the case of the Taqfir it was 85 percent. In the trials of the Jihad organization (1981) of 326 members, at least half had a university education and the majority had a modern education. They were students not of Islamic theology but more often than not science and engineering.[25] Some of the leaders came from very prominent families; al Zawahiri was an example but there were quite a few others.

What attracted them was certainly not class interest or commiseration with the poor peasants and workers. It was the restlessness of the young who were dissatisfied with the government and the quality of politics in their country, who wanted quick change and who fifty years earlier would have joined fascist or Communist organizations. But the fascists and the Communists were no longer around, so there was an ideological void that the military rulers certainly did not know how to fill. This is where radical Islamism entered the scene.

A revealing autobiography describes the conversion of a young boy to Islamism. Khaled al Berry grew up in Assyut and joined the Gama'a because so many of his football-playing friends belonged. A charismatic sheikh paid close personal attention to this promising recruit and had an answer to all his questions. There was no sudden, harsh indoctrination but pleasant conversations, and gradually Berry understood that he should no longer watch television and that his cassettes with songs of Arab singers should be destroyed.

During the next three years, al Berry learned the Koran by heart as well as many other religious tracts and became, in his own words, a little replica of Sayed Qutb. He became a leader at school. Though not yet sixteen, he was deemed dangerous enough to be relegated from school and sent to another one, far away. But he remained a militant even as a student of medicine dressed in the uniform of the radicals — a gellaba and the obligatory beard. He felt himself on top of the world, a rebel against bourgeois society, a young person who felt that he was not only virtuous but infallible. He felt at peace with his fellow human beings, who respected him in view of his piety and dedication to his cause.[26] To be a young Islamist in these circles was the fashionable thing to do; it was a rebellious act (against the despised secular government) and at the same time a manifestation of obedience — to religion, to tradition.

Al Berry relates that he spent a great deal of his time in prayer. But how deep did religion go apart from observing the rituals, or was the ritual the religion? They discussed jihad at great length, but did they want to carry out their Islamic revolution merely so that political power should pass into the hands of the religious dignitaries? They were idealists, to be sure, in the same sense that in the 1930s the Romanian fascists of the Legion of Archangel Michael had been idealists. They resented crass social injustice and wanted to alleviate the lot of the poor. They were repelled by corruption in public and private life, and they wanted a society in which decency and justice prevailed.

The fact that large parts of the population — minorities, women, all those who did not accept their beliefs — would be excluded or not given equality was another matter. The Sheikh had assured him that there was no room for false sentimentality. Allah loved only the faithful. Their ideas as to how to shape the ideal society were fuzzy, but the prophet Muhammad and the Koran had outlined everything. Democracy Western-style (or indeed any style) was an alien importation, yet it was not necessary because the principles of justice could be achieved following traditional Islamic ways.

They were enthusiasts like the early Bolsheviks or the Fascists. As in the case of the fascists (and unlike the Communists), they had no need to engage in ideological debates because their spiritual leaders had solved all crucial questions once and forever. Everything had been laid down in the holy books, and their job was simply to obey. They were willing to sacrifice and even to give their lives in the pursuit of their ideals.

But there was also a dark side on which little has been said and less has been written. Khaled ("La terre es plus belle"), who was not physically strong, was never asked to take part in punitive expeditions against deviants and enemies, but he was repelled by the cruelty shown in the maiming and killing of opponents or homosexuals or Copts who had been dating Muslim girls. The lynching of homosexuals among their ranks reminds one of similar practices by the SS in the Nazi era.

Generally speaking, a veil of discretion has been drawn over homosexuality (and sexual practices in general) in the Muslim world. This is not the place to enter a discussion on this subject, even though the role of sexuality among males is not a subject to be suppressed and excluded from the debate on Islamism. It is certainly a topic to be studied; all that can be said with reasonable certainty is that there seems to be a considerable distance between religious commandments, semblance, and reality.[27]

Walid Nafa, the hero in *A quoi revent les loups?*, an Algerian novel about young Islamist terrorists, is sent out to assassinate an intellectual just to find out whether he has what it takes to become a real killer. Later on, a member of Walid's gang stabs Walid's sister to death because her dress was not modest enough. There was certainly more hatred in these young people and their mentors than love of their fellow human beings, even their fellow believers. How to explain the murder of tens of thousand of fellow Muslims, especially in Algeria — children, old people, women who were in no way their enemies?[28] A theological justification was available: the regime was un-Islamic as were the people connected with it, and it could be argued that the masses were equally guilty, so norms of elementary humanity and pity did not apply to them. This was known as *taqfir al gumhur* — the branding of the masses as apostate pagans.[29] If so, everything was permitted as far as their treatment was concerned including, for instance, rape; sexual license coincided with great sexual frustration among young men who were not permitted to mix with the other sex, or, in theory, even to look at women.[30]

It could be argued that Algeria was an extreme case, but many instances of extreme acts of cruelty took place elsewhere: not just murdering the enemy (who often was not an enemy at all) but systematic torture. Cases of dismembering the victims, cutting off his or her genitals, gouging the eyes, and other such practices were reported from Kashmir. The Turkish Hizbullah (also called Ilim) kidnapped their victims in the late 1980s and submitted them to systematic torture — which was videotaped. One of the victims was a Turkish feminist, Konca Kuri, who had pleaded on television that women be permitted to pray alongside men at Muslim funerals. She was tortured for thirty-five hours before being killed, and it was all recorded on videotape. Most of the victims were not even political foes but Muslim businessmen who had discontinued their financial support or even simply innocent bystanders.[31]

Consider another example not atypical for the situation in Algeria in the 1990s. On June 25, 1993, Dr. Hammed Boukhobza was killed by a group of Islamist terrorists in the city of Telemly. He was the head of the national institute of global strategic studies, and there was nothing personal in this attack. It was simply part of the general campaign against intellectuals — physicians, teachers, et al. He was not just killed in his apartment, but his wife and children who wanted to escape were forced to watch how he was literally cut into pieces, his entrails slowly drawn out while he was just barely alive. The terrorists obviously liked to watch the suffering, and they wanted the family to share their enjoyment.[32]

In the winter of 1971, the Japanese "Red Army" purged and killed fourteen of its leading members in a mountain chalet in Northern Japan. What was so remarkable about the murders were not so much the paranoia that had caused them but the fact that the victims had to undergo days of unspeakable tortures.[33] But in retrospect the Nagano murders and the sadism with which they were carried out were not the rule in Japanese terrorism; they caused a shock as far as public opinion was concerned from which the Japanese left would not recover for years.

Why the proclivity toward torture and sadism? It was more than the mere brutalization that occurs in every war. There was the lust of killing, of inflicting pain, of seeing people suffer and slowly die. There was nothing specifically Algerian in such actions; it was frequently said that the Afghan Arabs had been those who had brought along these practices. British tourists who had been kidnapped by Islamic militants in 1994 were told by Ahmed Omar Sheikh, a young British Muslim who had attended the London School of Economics, that they were going to be beheaded, and in the words of the intended victims, "he was laughing, the prospect excited him."[34]

There were reports about similar behavior by terrorists in other places; there were more than a few sadists among them thirsting to "drink the blood of their enemies," eager to kill people and not necessarily in the quickest and least painful way. The underlying motives and urges belong to the realm of psychopathology. The hero (not a Muslim but a pagan Aryan) of *The Turner Diaries*, the bible of American neo-Nazis, certainly belonged to this species; with great relish did he slit the throat of fat Niggers and Jews and also stupid Aryans. Their agony was described lovingly, but *The Turner Diaries* was a book of sick, literary fantasy, not reality.[35]

There were some incidents of sadistic, Charles Manson–style cruelty in Europe (the Balkans) and Latin America, and even more in African civil wars such as in Sierra Leone or in East Africa (God's Army) where rebel groups raped women, amputated the limbs of women and children, and forced young girls to engage in prostitution. But there were far more such incidents in Muslim countries, and the question arises, How could this be squared with the strict Islamic moral code with regard to sexual affairs? Female survivors reported that those raping and later killing their victims (the sabaya sex slaves) would take time off to pray five times daily. They were convinced that everything was permitted to a mujahid, and in any case they were observing the legal niceties such as entering a short-term marriage contract (*zawaj al mutaa* — marriage of pleasure) in conformance with Islamic law for the duration of the rape.[36]

These cases of mass rape, killings, and keeping young girls in sexual slavery seem to have occurred less frequently in other Arab and North African countries. But another aspect of this behavior has been largely overlooked as far as the terrorist mental makeup is concerned: the repressed sexuality traditional in modern Islamic societies, which led quite often to homosexuality (banned by Islam) and, of course, to masturbation (which was also banned).[37] Despite all the admonitions of his Sheikh, young Khaled spent hours at the window of his room trying to catch a glimpse of the Copt girls undressing in the house opposite. This, in turn, led to guilt feelings and greater aggression. An Algerian psychoanalyst (a Jungian) has argued that in Islamic culture the sadist, anal phase is extended over a much longer period than elsewhere; religious individuals invest much of their libido in God, and the importance of the ego shrinks. This is reinforced by a rigid education that puts the stress on the acceptance of established norms, not on the individuum and independent thinking.[38]

Yet another factor remains to be mentioned affecting the conditions that lead to the spread of radical Islamic terrorism: the reaction, and often the ineptitude, of the governments.

Measures taken against the terrorists, especially in the early years by the Egyptian authorities, were harsh and often indiscriminate. Among those arrested, often for years, were not only those whose guilt had been proven but supporters and fellow travelers of the radical Islamic groups. Some of them were tortured; others died in prison from the treatment they had undergone. Prison was a school of radicalization. There is reason to believe that some of those who became terrorists did so because of their experience in prison. For many years there was no attempt on the part of the authorities to reeducate prisoners, to show them that they had been misled by demagogues and that the Islamic lessons they had been taught were by no means the only and the most authoritative interpretation.

If the authorities treated the terrorists harshly, they would face condemnation by human rights organizations and risk having their misdeeds listed in the annual reports on human rights issued by the U.S. Department of State. In response, the Egyptian government would argue that the terrorists had declared a dirty war on them. They were systematically killing prominent and not-so-prominent personalities of government, literature, and the arts. Furthermore, as in Algeria, or Afghanistan, people were abducted or killed at random to terrorize society; in the circumstances the only way to combat this dangerous challenge seemed not to pay too much attention to legal niceties. The onslaught of the terrorists was most ferocious in Algeria where the terrorists tried to kill whole sections of the population (such as the local intelligentsia in small towns); not surprisingly, the response by the Algerian authorities was quite brutal.

The Egyptian response to terrorism was equally brutal and quite effective. In the 1980s there seem to have been at any given time ten thousand radical Muslims, terrorists, or potential terrorists in state prisons or concentration camps. In later years there may have been even more. The Egyptian authorities did not want to add to their numbers, and many of them were therefore permitted (indeed encouraged) to travel to Afghanistan to enlist in the war of the mujahedeen. Among them was Zawahiri and perhaps six thousand to eight thousand other Egyptian radical Muslims. But as the war in Afghanistan ended, many of them tried to return to Egypt where they were anything but welcome, especially if they intended to resume their terrorist activities.

The Egyptian security forces acted harshly against them, and there was a second wave of emigration — some went back to Afghanistan where bin Laden had set up his new organization, others went to the Balkans to fight, and yet others to Western Europe. London became the unofficial capital of Egyptian (and Middle Eastern) terrorism, and Egyptian demands that the ringleaders should be extradited were always refused; for Britain ("Londonistan") these were political refugees, and in any case, even those convicted for murder in their homeland could not be sent back to a country in which they might face capital punishment.[39] In brief, the Egyptian government was certainly guilty of having exported its terrorist problems to both Southeast Asia and Western Europe, and it came to regret this policy years later.

The policy of the Syrian government vis-à-vis local Islamic radicals was equally uncompromising. The history of the Muslim Brotherhood in Syria is long and very complicated in view of endless internal disputes not only between conservative and radical Brothers but also because of splits for other reasons. Suffice it to say that at a time when the Brotherhood was banned in Egypt, it transferred some of its activities to Syria, where even though it was officially banned it seems to have enjoyed greater freedom of action. It had a terrorist wing consisting of groups named Fighters of Hizbullah and Muhammad's Phalanges, headed by Isaac Farhan and Marwan Hadid, which challenged the ruling Ba'ath party in a struggle for power. Ba'ath was secular, extreme nationalist, and in fact semifascist. The Brotherhood was looking for a confrontation through general strikes and riots but also massive terrorist action such as the massacre of cadets at the Aleppo military school in June 1979 and an attempt to assassinate Asad, the Syrian dictator.

The Ba'ath leadership vacillated between a policy of reconciliation, legalizing the Brotherhood and releasing its members from prison, and adopting harsh measures such as killing radical militants quite indiscriminately, including those detained in prison.[40]

Matters came to a head in the northern city of Hama, in the Orontes valley, a traditional stronghold of the Brotherhood. Following a number of terrorist attacks (including the attempt to assassinate Asad), Syrian armed forces tried to enter Hama to arrest leading terrorists and to seize their arms. But the Islamic terrorists were prepared. They declared a jihad and the government forces had to retreat. But they came back in February 1982, systematically flattening the center of the town, killing between five thousand and twenty-five thousand people in the process (some estimates are higher).[41] This was the end for many years of terrorist activities on the part of the radical Islamists in northern Syria. The organization continued to exist, but it no longer constituted a threat to the government. The Hama massacre entered the history books as one of the worst civil rights violations in modern history, but there were no protests in the Arab or Muslim world. Many years later, when Rifa'at, Asad's son, received an American congressional committee soon after September 11, 2001, he introduced his remarks with the words that America had something to learn from the Syrian experience of dealing with terrorists. What he meant was that massive repression worked, whereas half-hearted repression did not.

Terrorism in Egypt ended (for the time being) with the appeal in 1999 by Mustafa Hazan, the leader of the largest still-existing terrorist group, to stop hostilities on Egyptian soil. The sensation of the literary season of 2002 was a four-volume series of books written by the leaders of the Gama'a (most of them still in prison) about their past mistakes.[42] They admitted in retrospect that their extremism had not been in accordance with religious law. It had been wrong to attack politicians and policemen who were, after all, fellow Muslims. The Luxor attack on tourists was condemned because it was wrong to kill civilians; foreigners who had come to Egypt were entitled to safe conduct. They regretted the attacks against Copts who in accordance with the constitution should enjoy equal rights. They conceded that no practicing Muslim should be considered an enemy, and even those who did not observe the religious commandments should be persuaded rather than physically attacked. The Gama'a leaders distanced themselves from bin Laden and al Zawahiri and declared that their members had been forbidden to join al Qa'ida and its front organizations. In a long interview in June 2002 with Egypt's leading illustrated weekly, Karam Zuhdi (serving a life sentence in prison) and other leaders of Al Gama'a, also in prison (some under sentence of death), went one step further and declared that they owed an apology to the Egyptian people.[43]

The Egyptian government was not altogether certain how sincere these admissions of guilt were, but they did not want to miss a chance to reintegrate the ex-terrorists and facilitated their contacts with the media.[44] The ex-terrorists did not forswear jihad and violence altogether, but the real enemy for them was the West and Zionism, not fellow Muslims.

Those who have given up domestic terrorism in Egypt are now in their forties and fifties; whether the radicals in the generation after them will follow in their footsteps remains to be seen. In the meantime, terrorist action had shifted from Egypt to other places, and we turn next to the new forces in radical Islamism.

THREE

Jihad

T ERRORISM BECAME TRULY GLOBAL for the first time in history in the 1990s, as local conflicts turned into a worldwide campaign. The war in Afghanistan had lasted for about ten years; radical Islamists, flush with enthusiasm, thought that it might take only another decade to overthrow the present Arab and Muslim governments and yet another few years to defeat America and the West. For at long last, as they saw it, the young generation in the Muslim world was coming out of its stupor. In the heady days after the Soviet withdrawal (1989), almost anything seemed possible. The fact that Afghanistan entered a period of bitter civil war that led to Taliban rule did not unduly bother the victors. On the contrary, it opened up new possibilities for them, even though Afghanistan was clearly only a sideshow and the main action in years to come would be elsewhere.

There had been cooperation between terrorists in past ages, but by and large it did not go very far. The anarchists were too individualistic and too disorganized to establish an international organization of their own, nor did they need one for limited operations by single individuals. Indian terrorists active early in the twentieth century admired their Russian colleagues and tried to learn from them, and there were connections between various Balkan terrorist groups such as the Macedonian IMRO and the Croatians. But communications were not as yet very developed, and these technical aspects also limited the scope of collaboration.

A change set in after World War II. The German terrorists of the 1970s (Baader-Meinhof and especially their successors, the Revolutionaere Zellen) had connections with comrades-in-arms in other Western European countries. When the situation in Germany grew too uncomfortable, they would move for a while to Holland or France. Above all, they worked closely with the more extreme Palestinian groups such as the various Popular Fronts for the Liberation of Palestine, which at the time subscribed to Marxism-Leninism. German terrorists went to training camps in Jordan and elsewhere in the Arab world, receiving and other help from these quarters and engaging in common operations such as the hijacking of airplanes.[1] They planned to blow up a Jewish meeting in Berlin in commemoration of the Nazi pogrom in November 1938, but this operation failed.

The most important precursor of contemporary international terrorism was Illich Ramirez Sanchez, better known as Carlos the Jackal, a Venezuelan, the son of a millionaire lawyer who began his career with the Popular Front for the Liberation of Palestine. Ramirez Sanchez had contacts in many countries, and his main sponsors were various Arab intelligence services (Syria, Iraq, Libya), for whom he acted as a contract killer — not necessarily of Jews and Israelis. He also had the support of various East European espionage organizations but was a source of exasperation to the East Germans because of his lack of self-discipline and luxurious lifestyle. Ramirez Sanchez had originally become a terrorist because the Communists were not radical enough for him (and because he liked the excitement of life as a hired gun). In later years his support (ideological and financial) came mainly from leading Western European neo-Nazis such as François Genoud.[2] Carlos the Jackal was sentenced to thirty years in prison for multiple murders by a Paris court in 1997, but his international network had disintegrated even earlier.[3]

By and large, such alliances were of short duration and affected few people. A closer parallel to the Muslim International of the 1990s was the International Brigade in the Spanish Civil War. It consisted of antifascists from various countries; there was also a fascist international brigade fighting on Franco's side, but it was much smaller and militarily insignificant. However, the aim of the Interbrigadistas was limited in scope. They wanted to stop the advance of fascism in Spain, hence their slogan *no pasarán* ("they will not get through"). It was defensive in character and it had no ambition of extending the fight to other countries.

Underlying the new globalization of terrorism was the concept of jihad; in its present form, this was a loose federation of terrorist groups that had developed in the 1970s and 1980s. These decades were not a good time for Muslim and, above all, Arab radicals. The Arab countries were ruled by military dictators, and attempts to establish truly Islamic regimes were ruthlessly suppressed precisely in the most militant Arab countries such as Libya and Syria. One light of hope was the overthrow of the Shah and the coming to power of Khomeini and his supporters. Here at long last was a movement that took Islam seriously and introduced a regime based on the religious law, the Sharia, and also actively supported the aspirations of Muslims in other countries. Iran was the most active country at the time as far as the export of violent religion and terrorism was concerned. But it was, alas, the wrong sort of Islam; the differences between Sunnis and Shi'ites were too deeply rooted in history to make close cooperation possible.

Then, with the outbreak of the war in Afghanistan a new window of opportunity suddenly opened up, and militants from all over the Muslim world were not slow to make use of it. The first ideologist and organizer of this new jihad arising out of Afghanistan was Abdulla Azzam, a cleric born in Palestine where he studied agriculture before receiving an Islamic education in Syria and Egypt. He also received a doctorate in Islamic law. He held a lectureship at a Saudi university, but his heart was not in an academic career; while in Egypt he had become a radical Islamist partly, apparently, under the influence of the brother of Sayed

Qutb. Azzam wanted to dedicate his life to jihad, which he considered the duty of every Muslim. He thus decided to move to Pakistan in the early 1980s, where he founded the Bait al Ansar, later called the Maktab el Khadamat (Services bureau) in Peshawar, which for many years served as a liaison office for the recruitment of volunteers from many Muslim countries. Though he had participated in the war of 1967 against Israel, Azzam was not primarily a military leader even though he took part in military actions, but an intellectual and certainly a political leader with a vision. He was a man of boundless energy who traveled near and far trying to mobilize the young generation all over the Muslim world to join the armed struggle against the infidels and to establish Khilafah, God's rule on earth. He was also a very pious person, performing rituals (such as fasting every Monday and Thursday) that were over and above what religious tradition demanded.[4]

As he saw it, the liberation of Afghanistan was not the aim but just the first step in the coming jihad. The real aim was to restore to Muslim rule all the territories that had once been theirs, from Southern Spain to the Philippines, Central Asia, India, parts of Europe and Africa.[5] He believed in something that could be defined as a Muslim Brezhnev doctrine — if the Soviet leader had stated that every country that had become Communist at one time was to remain Communist forever, Azzam argued that all countries that had been occupied by Muslims at one time or another were to be restored to Allah's fold. But why only Spain; why not France, the rest of Europe, America, and Asia? Azzam believed that jihad should continue until Allah alone is worshiped by all mankind. If the Communists had believed in the final and total victory of world revolution, Azzam believed in the final (and near) victory of Islam. Some of his successors, as will be shown, were even more outspoken in this respect.

Azzam's greatest contribution was undoubtedly the creation of a mystique of Muslim invincibility. On one occasion he said that he felt that he was nine years old: seven and a half years in the Afghan Jihad, one and a half years in the Jihad in Palestine, and the rest of the years had no value. The message he preached was that the jihadists, having defeated the strong Soviet army, were bound to triumph over all enemies. As his biographer writes, the gun became his preoccupation and recreation, and his slogan was "no negotiations, no conferences, and no dialogues."[6] If only the Muslims obeyed the command of jihad and would all go to Palestine to do battle for a single week, Palestine would be purified of the Jews forever.[7] Azzad was, however, a practical man and seems to have reached the conclusion that one ought to do one thing at time: first victory in Afghanistan, later the export of the Islamic revolution.

This was the message broadcast at the time in leaflets, audio and video cassettes, and booklets. But they were published in Arabic, and those who supported the recruitment of Muslim volunteers such as the CIA probably did not read Arabic: Pakistanis and the Saudis simply did not care and even welcomed it up to a point. In Peshawar Azzam first met a young Saudi named bin Laden who became his follower and main financial supporter. Azzam was killed, together with two of his sons, in 1989 in circumstances that have not been clarified to this day. His car was blown up outside Peshawar, a short time before there had been another attempt on his life. Who wanted to kill him? According to persistent rumors, bin Laden had been involved but there was no evidence, and bin Laden in later years always referred to the Sheikh with reverence and admiration. His murderers were never found, and apparently there was no great effort to find them.

Who were the volunteers from abroad who came to join the jihad in Afghanistan? They arrived from all parts of the globe, including the United States, Britain, the former Soviet Union, and Australia. But the biggest contingents came from Algeria, Egypt, Saudi Arabia, and Yemen. Some came while the war against the Russian army was still going on and they received their training in the Ansar or Faruq camps in Afghanistan or at a base in Pakistan. The Pakistan Intelligence Service (ISI) was their main sponsor, and among its commanders were leading jihadists such as General Hameed Gul. Other volunteers arrived only after the war had ended to receive training mainly in sabotage operations. Those from the West were quite often recent converts to radical Islam and had been indoctrinated by fiery preachers in their local mosques. There were adventurers among them and unstable young men with psychological problems. But most were earnest idealists who had been told that everywhere in the world Islam was under attack by the infidels and that their persecuted coreligionists had to be helped according to the commandments of the Koran. Those who came from countries like Egypt were often radicals of long standing who were released from prison on condition that they would continue their jihad in Afghanistan rather than nearer to home.[8]

Russia had been the immediate enemy of the Islamists in Afghanistan but once the Russian army withdrew, the strategy was bound to change. The Arab Afghans had no particular wish to become prominently involved in the civil war that ensued after the withdrawal of the Russians, but they owed a debt of gratitude to the Pakistanis. When did America become the great Satan, the chief enemy? After all, the United States had provided decisive help to the Afghan resistance, albeit for reasons of its own. Different answers have been given to this question, but it probably was a gradual process. But also the radical Islamists had always been anti-American and had regarded the alliance as merely tactical in nature.

When the Taliban first appeared and quickly conquered almost the whole country, the foreign volunteers were among their early supporters; the Pakistan ISI encouraged the volunteers. The Arab Afghans' main interest was to gain a secure basis for their future activities, and as far as bin Laden was concerned this was his best bet after the Sudanese government had asked him to leave.

The story of bin Laden is of course very well known and needs to be retold here only in briefest outline.[9] One of the many sons of a leading Saudi entrepreneur, he had not enjoyed an Islamic education but during his student years became converted to radical Islam and volunteered to go to Afghanistan to coordinate

Saudi unofficial help to the jihadis. His family was immensely rich but originating from Hadramaut, considered one of the less savory parts of the kingdom, it was considered socially somewhat inferior; bin Laden certainly did not belong to the inner circle of Saudi policy makers even though he seems to have had powerful protectors such as Prince Turki, head of Saudi intelligence. His resentment against the Saudi establishment was reinforced by the Gulf War; while bin Laden opposed the Iraqis, he thought that inviting American soldiers (including female soldiers) to take part in the defense of Kuwait and Saudi Arabia was quite inexcusable. It was blasphemous, a desecration, and this complaint figured very high in his political agenda. The religious justification was not quite convincing, because it is a moot point whether the Koran makes the whole territory of the Arab peninsula a holy place. True, according to Muslim tradition the prophet is reported to have said on his deathbed: Let there be no two religions in Arabia. But this referred to Mecca, Medina, and the Hejaz in general, and the U.S. forces were stationed far away from these places. Whatever the reason, the presence of infidels certainly became a central motive as far as bin Laden was concerned.

Bin Laden had taken over Azzam's organization and greatly enlarged it. In 1988, al Qa'ida (the base) was founded, according to some sources because the liaison office had been infiltrated by agents of Arab governments and was no longer deemed secure; a more conspirational group was needed. At this time, probably even before the final withdrawal of the Soviet forces from Afghanistan, this group and its allies were planning new attacks against new enemies. Since 1985, when Gorbachev had first mentioned that a diplomatic solution of the Afghanistan problem was desirable, the end of the war in Afghanistan seemed only a question of time. Al Qa'ida was looking for a new base nearer the new targets as the war in Afghanistan drew to its close. They found one in Sudan.

Sudan is one of the poorest African countries and certainly the most backward Arab country; whether it can be considered an Arab country in view of its ethnic composition, especially in the south, is another moot point, but its government certainly participated actively in Arab politics.

In 1989, power in Khartum passed into the hands of military leaders who were fundamentalists, and the power behind the throne was Dr. Hassan Tourabi, an intellectual and one of the most articulate spokesmen of radical Islamism. Tourabi had made it known that the government would be interested in playing host to bin Laden, who was in search of a new base. Some doubts were uttered: Tourabi had studied at the Sorbonne and had been to the United States — could someone like this be trusted since he had been exposed to Western influences?[10] These doubts were interesting inasmuch as the psychology of the radical Islamists were concerned because they remind one of similar misgivings in the Soviet Union in the Stalin era vis-à-vis those who had at one time or another lived in the corrupting climate of the West.

However, the misgivings were overcome, and after a stay in his native Saudi Arabia (where he was not yet *persona non grata*), bin Laden relocated to Sudan together with many of his close collaborators. During the period that followed, he invested heavily in the Sudanese economy, establishing various factories and a bank and helping develop Sudanese agriculture. In conversations in later years, he spoke with great optimism about the economic possibilities that existed for the Sudanese economy; something of the business acumen of his father, who had established a great building empire, seems to have been inherited by him.[11]

At the same time organizational and terrorist preparations continued, the base in Sudan provided considerable advantages — travel to almost any part of the world, money transfer (and laundering), and acquisition of weapons and training camps. Islamic nongovernmental organizations (NGOs) were established, such as the Muslim World League and the International Islamic Relief Organization. There respectable bodies were recognized by the United Nations and given legal status in many countries while serving at the same time as a cover of the jihadists.

From this Sudanese base, various terrorist operations were launched throughout the Middle East and North Africa. The impact of the bin Laden organization was still limited. The base of the group was too narrow, and bin Laden was no more than one player among several on the terrorist scene. Some of the more striking terrorist operations that occurred during this time were launched by independent cells, such as the attempt to blow up the World Trade Center in 1993. Terrorism sponsored by Iran was far more important at the time; bin Laden's main interest was then in the Balkans and in East Africa, and his other plans were long-term.

The Sudanese interlude lasted up to 1996 when Western (and Arab) pressure on the Khartum government to get rid of their dangerous guest had grown too strong. Even Tourabi could no longer help, and thus by May 1996, bin Laden and his retinue were back in Afghanistan where the Taliban, who had come to power, were playing willing hosts. Within the next three years, bin Laden would establish himself as the chief coordinator of the major radical Islamic forces and declare war on the rest of the world.[12]

After Azzam's death, bin Laden had come under the influence of Aiman al Zawahiri, the Egyptian terrorist leader, who had settled in Afghanistan in the 1980s. While Zawahiri in contrast to Azzam was not an ideologue, while he lacked a thorough Islamic education, while his books were not widely read, he was certainly a person of very strong convictions — in brief, a fanatic.[13]

Zawahiri's outlook, which became that of bin Laden, had been formed in Egyptian prisons where the leaders of Gama'a and Jihad had spent years and had sufficient time to work out their basic ideological orientation. In their papers — which later appeared as pamphlets, legal and illegal, both for wide circulation and for a limited circle only — they were dealing with the confrontation with the West. This, as they saw it, was the crucial issue, for there was no chance to build a society based on truly Islamic principles unless the power of the West was broken. The rule of Islam, peace and general well-being, could be established only by means of jihad, of holy war. The crimes of the West, the exploitation and the massacres committed by colonial rule, had to be avenged. But even if there would have been no colonial heritage, the West would still be the main obstacle on the road to the global victory of Islam — Western demoralizing cultural influences as much as Western economic predominance. Clearly this struggle would not be easy, but the jihadists believed that it could and would be won. Many signs pointed to the weakness of the West, particularly the mortal fear of the spiritual superiority of Islam and the unlimited willingness of its believers to fight and to die for Islam's principles.[14] This strategy had to proceed simultaneously on different levels, such as with propaganda (to strengthen the belief of fellow Muslims). Not only should Western power be destroyed, Western ideas and concepts had to be decisively refuted.

These were the basic tenets of the jihadist ideology as formulated first in Egypt and later adopted by the Arab Afghans. They were the basis of the World Islamic Front for Jihad against the crusaders and Jews, which was founded in early 1998. Signatories were bin Laden, Zawahiri on behalf of the Egyptian Jihad, Abu Jasir on behalf of the Egyptian Gama'a, Sheikh Abu Hamza al Misri on behalf of Jamiyat ulama (Pakistan), and Fazlul Rahman, leader of the Jihad movement in Bangladesh.[15] The pillars of the new organization were the Egyptians and bin Laden; it was a loose linkage of several Afghan groups held together by bin Laden's funding.[16] Earlier meetings between leaders of these organizations had taken place during bin Laden's Sudan stay.

One would have expected among the signatories also the Algerian GIA and some smaller Egyptian terrorist organizations, but they were probably not consulted. The presence of the Pakistani Sheikh was needed in order to give religious-legal sanction to the fatwa issued by bin Laden and Zawahiri at the end of the meeting. Neither had sufficient religious standing to make a fatwa on his own. This was a declaration of war on the United States occupying the holiest of territories and plundering its riches; the manifesto also denounced the continued aggression against the Iraqi people. While the purpose of the Americans in these wars was economic and religious, they also served the petty state of the Jews to divert attention from their occupation of Jerusalem and their killing of Muslims in it. In this situation the Islamic religious authorities had ruled that when enemies attack Muslim lands jihad became every Muslim's personal duty. The ruling was therefore to kill Americans and their allies, both civilians and military. This became the individual duty of every able-bodied Muslim until the Al Aqsa Mosque in Jerusalem and the Haram mosque in Mecca were freed from their grip and their armies shattered and broken, until they would depart from all the lands of Islam, incapable to threaten any Muslim.[17] These ideological guidelines were frequently repeated even after the defeat of the Taliban and the dispersal of al Qa'ida. Thus Suleiman Abu Gaith, spokesman for al Qa'ida, writing in June

2002: "America is the head of heresy in our modern world and it leads an infidel democratic regime that is based on separation between religion and state and by ruling the people by the people via legislating laws that are contrary to the way of Allah and permit what Allah has forbidden." Hence the call to subject the whole earth to the rule of Islam, "which was created to be at the center of hegemony," and the affirmation "that we have right to kill (at least) four millions of Americans."[18]

This manifesto was less than sensational for it had been the doctrine of radical Islamists eager to engage in jihad all along. This emerges, for instance, from reading the so-called al Qa'ida Manual, which was composed, probably in installments, between 1989 and 1995.[19] This gives very detailed instructions on how to manufacture bombs and other weapons on the lines of the nineteenth-century *Anarchist Cook Book*. It provides general rules of behavior in conditions of illegality. But sections in this manual also make sense only in the framework of a jihad, such as guidelines on how to treat hostages. It says that religious scholars such as Imam Mosallem have permitted the beating of hostages. Going further, the manual states that it is permitted to strike (torture) the non-Muslim hostage until he reveals the secrets of his people. Killing a hostage is permitted if he insists on withholding information from Moslems — again with reference to the Koran and the Hadith, specifically the Honein attack. (This refers to one of the major battles fought by Muhammad in A.D. 63).) These instructions were composed years before the official declaration of war against the crusaders and the Jews.[20]

What was new was the tactical change. The main enemy for the time being was not the enemy at home (as Sayed Qutb and his disciples had preached) but the crusaders (the Christians) and the Jews. This may not have been easy to accept for Zawahiri, who had always regarded the Egyptian government as the main enemy, but he seems to have reached the conclusion that the struggle at home was considerably less popular than the jihad against outside enemies for which it was far easier to mobilize volunteers.

Among the recruits for the new jihad were first and foremost the Arab Afghans, the veterans who by that time (1998) were dispersed over many countries and who became one of the two main pillars of the Jihad. There are no exact statistics as to how many volunteers from foreign countries had fought in Afghanistan, perhaps twenty to thirty thousand, with a considerable percentage drifting in and out. Many came from neighboring Pakistan and belonged to one of the local tribes. Estimates vary widely — the number of those who came from Algeria was thought to be close to five hundred by some, roughly three thousand by others, and there are similar wide discrepancies in the number of those who came from Yemen and Egypt. They began to leave Afghanistan after the exodus of the Russians and the collapse of the pro-Soviet regime in Kabul (January 1992).[21] On the other hand there was a renewed influx of Muslim terrorists from the Middle East who arrived only after the war against the Soviets was over.

It seems certain that relatively few volunteers were killed during the war, and hardly any were taken prisoner. Some joined al Qa'ida, the majority probably did not; but many were willing to continue their struggle even after their return to their native countries or to the new theaters of war to which they were sent. According to Egyptian statistics, there were toward the end of 1998 some 2,800 fighters in the bin Laden camps in Afghanistan, including some 600 Egyptians, 400 Jordanians, 300 Yemenites, 250 Iraqis, and so on.[22] But more were stationed in Pakistan even though Pakistan had committed itself years earlier to close down the places where the Arab Afghans were staying. When the American offensive against the Taliban regime began in October 2001, there were thought to be 7,000 al Qa'ida fighters on the ground.

Many members of the Arab Afghan units had returned to their countries of origin, some legally, some by way of infiltration. But they weren't welcome anywhere because the governments were afraid of the potential of violence constituted by these veterans, who had been indoctrinated by the gospel of jihad and knew nothing but fighting. Their situation was similar in some ways to that of the militants of the extreme right in Europe after World War I, veterans who did not find, or did not want to find, their way back into society but established free corps in Germany and the Baltic region and the squadristi in Italy, engaging in terrorism. They became the nucleus of the Fascist parties in these countries.[23]

Again, there are only rough estimates regarding the eventual destination of the Arab Afghans. Some disappeared without a trace, while others went on to fight in different parts of the world. It is thought that up to four thousand went to the former Yugoslavia to fight on the side of the Bosnians, and to Kosovo and Albania. The main camp of these mujahedeen was in Zenica, and they engaged in both terrorism and guerrilla warfare against the Serbs. Some seem to have had more ambitious plans, wanting to prepare Bosnia and Kosovo as a new base for al Qa'ida operations in Europe for operations such as attacking Western military installations and embassies in Germany, France, and elsewhere. Many of them were given Bosnian passports, but as the fighting subsided there was growing Western pressure on the Bosnian government to get rid of them. The Bosnians complied up to a point, but several hundred terrorists remained in the country. Some returned to Algeria where they had originally come from and joined the GIA, the most radical terrorist organization responsible for the massacres of the 1990s. One cell relocated to France and Belgium where it engaged in both terrorism and banditry in the vicinity of Roubaix (in northern France) and in Belgium.[24]

Other Arab Afghans had proceeded directly from Pakistan to Algeria where terrorism was rampant and took more victims (at least a hundred thousand) than in any other country at the time. The GIA also established active cells among Algerian emigrants in France and in other European countries. It had more international contacts in Europe than any other Islamic terrorist group, and this infrastructure proved to be of great help to al Qa'ida once it began its operations worldwide. Another sizeable group went to Yemen, where it collaborated with political and tribal groups in opposition to the local government. They were joined by a group of Islamic terrorists from Britain and specialized for a while in kidnapping foreigners to finance their operations.

A considerable number of Arab Afghans went to Egypt, some voluntarily, while others were extradited by Albania, Pakistan, or other countries where they had overstayed their welcome.[25]

The Arab Afghans were involved in many terrorist activities in Egypt up to 1998, when under the influence of bin Laden and Zawahiri there was another change in strategy inasmuch as all the energies were to be devoted from now on to attacking American interests worldwide. In the spectacular attacks against the U.S. embassies in Nairobi and Dar es Salaam, Egyptian terrorists were involved, and the other attackers also had been connected in one way or another with al Qa'ida.

The Egyptian government had taken strong measures against the returning terrorists by staging a number of mass trials. Among those sentenced to capital punishment (mostly in absentia) were Zawahiri, as well as his brother Muhammad, and Istambuli, the brother of the terrorist who had killed Anwar el Sadat. Some interesting facts emerged during the trials about the inner workings of al Qa'ida: the attempts, which were not very successful, to establish closer relations between various terrorist groups; the attempts to expand Islamic terrorist activities to the Caucasus (Chechnya and Dagestan); and internal differences of opinion whether to adhere to a truce with the government in Egypt and Algeria.

What did not emerge from these trials and interrogations were the most ambitious plans engaged in by al Qa'ida: the attacks in the United States in September 2001. This was no accident because those involved in the events of September 11 were not Arab Afghans but were members of another group of recruits who belonged to the Arab diaspora in Europe or had been educated in Europe and America. The Afghan veterans were seasoned fighters, and they were quite capable of continuing the jihad in the Arab world, North Africa, and the Balkans. But for operations in Europe and America, different background and training were needed from the one received in the Pakistani and Afghan camps: a higher education, a working knowledge of languages, and some experience with how to behave in alien societies.

Looking back in 2000 to achievements attained so far, al Qa'ida had some ground for satisfaction. While Western and Arab governments had become aware of its existence and were taking countermeasures, these were as yet not very effective and did not seriously threaten its operations. The fame of bin Laden and his organization had spread through the Muslim world and al Qa'ida had no difficulties attracting new recruits. But on the other hand its potential was as yet limited. It could give only limited help to Muslim brethren in the Balkans and even less to those in the Caucasus (Chechnya and Dagestan). It could not or would not send help to fellow Muslims in Palestine. Most resources were concentrated on the main blow against the great Satan.

European Islam?

If Sudan and Afghanistan were one pillar of the new Islamic revolution, the other was Western Europe where few had suspected it. Not many Muslims lived in Europe prior to World War II, except in the Balkans, which had for centuries been part of the Ottoman Empire. During the 1960s and 1970s, many millions of Muslims streamed to Western Europe to escape the grinding poverty of their homelands and because Europe offered employment as the result of the longest boom in the history of the continent. They came from North Africa (mainly to France, Spain, and Italy), from Turkey (to Germany), and from South Asia (to Britain). By the year 2000, some 4 million Muslims lived in France, some 2.5–3 million in Germany, and less than 2 million in Britain. But there were sizeable colonies even in the smaller countries — more than one million in Holland and Belgium, and even in Sweden Islam had become the second most numerous religion. Many hundreds of thousands lived in Spain and Italy, where even rough estimates were impossible because the number of illegal immigrants was probably much larger than that of the legal residents.

Relations with the host nation were fairly smooth in the early years; most immigrants had come to make money and after a while to return to their native countries. But in the great majority of cases they did not return, partly because they had grown roots in their new homes and had become accustomed to the higher standard of living. True, they were hit hard by the economic downturns of the 1970s and 1980s, but social security payments provided a safety net such as did not exist in their countries of origin. Unemployment, especially among the second generation of immigrants (called *beurres* in France), was certainly considerably higher than among the rest of the population for yet another reason: many immigrants had settled in the centers of the old, traditional industries (especially in Britain and partly also in France), which were in decline and gradually phased out.

The new immigrants were concentrated in quarters of their own in the major cities — the Paris *banlieue*, London, and the Midlands. Such settlement had been the case also with earlier immigration waves, but earlier immigrants, in contrast, had fairly quickly become integrated into local society and had broken out of their ghettoes. Assimilation had been expected from them, and they were only too eager to comply. Such willingness to become integrated did not exist among the Muslim immigration of the post–World War II period, less so even than among the immigrants from India or Africa. They wanted to keep their way of life, which in the new age of multiculturalism was considered perfectly natural.

Cultural assimilation did take place, manifesting itself above all in fluency in the new language, which the second and third generation spoke without an accent, or to be precise with a local accent. As the North African writer Tahar ben Jelloun put it with regard to the second generation of immigrants living in France, they will eat French food, sing French songs, and frequent discotheques, but they would still not feel French. When France played Algeria in a soccer match, the immigrant population would try to drown out the "Marseillaise."[26] Social mingling, let alone intermarriages, occurred only slowly, a little faster in France than in Germany and Britain, which also affected social mobility. Whereas earlier immigration waves had been deeply motivated not just to better themselves but to be well educated, this motivation was not the case with the Islamic immigration after World War II. It was not a matter of class; 25 to 30 percent of the children of French workers went on to higher education, while only 4 percent of the North Africans did. As a result, many of the young people were not just unemployed but considered unemployable. They became or rather remained the new proletariat while only a few made a breakthrough.

Did this happen because of a deliberate intention to keep them down, or should one look for the reasons somewhere else? Naturally there was the inclination among many immigrants to make a "racist" government and society responsible for their misfortune. But this was certainly not the whole truth, or even a half truth. The French government, as many argued, had made greater concessions to the Muslims as a community than to any other religious group.[27] Nor does it explain why members of this radicalized younger generation joined the ranks of the terrorists, for among the recruits were relatively many who were neither poor nor uneducated.

Most of the immigrants to Western Europe had been observant Muslims at home, but not ultraorthodox let alone radical. The Turks who came to Germany were more religious than mainstream Turkish society; they did not come from the major cities, largely secular in character, but from rural Anatolia where Islam was still more deeply rooted. The same was true, *mutatis mutandis,* with regard to the Pakistanis who settled in Britain.

Then, in the 1980s, radicalization set in with the influx of a new generation of young radical preachers paid for mainly by Saudi money. They were pupils of Sayed Qutb and Maulana Mawdoodi; they established new mosques and cultural centers. In Britain alone, fifteen hundred new mosques were built and some five thousand Koran schools established, as well as cultural centers and radical students' associations. They taught their followers that according to Islam they were first and foremost Muslims; they had to fight for Muslim rights and interests everywhere, and they owed no allegiance to the infidel country in which they happened to live. Democracy was an evil political system, and freedom and tolerance were ideals alien to their religion. As Imam Fazazi of the Hamburg mosque was preaching, Christians and Jews should have their throats cut.[28] They established publishing houses such as Azzam in Britain, named after the guru of jihad mentioned earlier. The message was that all Muslims were or should be extremists because the prophet Muhammad had been one; he had, after all, seven hundred Jews in Medina beheaded, and he engaged in constant fighting.

According to the same message, a long war was ahead that would take several years, perhaps decades, but end with the victory of the believers. In this war, Muslims were always right, for their war was a jihad and one must never give any support to the disbelievers fighting the Muslims. Muslims and Islamic organizations which tried to project a moderate image were traitors and apostates: "There is no such thing as a moderate or liberal Muslim."[29]

The British government granted unlimited entry permits to these new religious dignitaries without checking whether their main occupation would be political propaganda rather than religious education. If a neo-Nazi group had called for killing all the blacks in England, they would have run into difficulties under the Race Relations Act, but the Islamist preachers of hate were considered religious dignitaries and therefore immune to prosecution. The Turkish government was certainly not too happy about the political propaganda that was carried out under the cover of religion, but the German authorities thought they could not intervene, for the constitution granted freedom of religion. The attitude of the Algerian government was similarly negative toward the indoctrination to which the Algerian colony in France was exposed. But the British and French governments were not inclined to interfere in what they considered the internal affairs of religious communities, which enjoyed full freedom under existing laws. Even collaboration between Britain and France as far as terrorism was concerned was far from harmonious. Britain steadfastly refused to extradite Rashid Ramda, one of the leaders of a terrorist campaign in France that caused the death of eight and injuries to two hundred. According to Irene Stiller, chief prosecutor in Paris, while cracking down on the IRA, the British were turning a blind eye to terrorist activities on its soil.[30]

The indoctrination would not have been successful but for the fact that the social and psychological conditions were ripe for the growth of extremism. Mention has been made of unemployment among the young, which in turn reinforced already existing trends of alienation from society. Higher education was free in Western Europe, but not many young Muslims availed themselves of these chances; those who did were not exempt from the general radicalization. In one famous case in liberal Sweden in 2002, a young Kurdish woman was killed by her own father for attending a university and thus dishonoring her family. The family had lived in Sweden for many years and was believed to be well integrated.

Many young Muslims came into conflict with the law. Ethnic breakdowns of the prison population were considered politically incorrect and inflammatory and usually not published, but according to many reports the Muslim contingent among young offenders was up to 80 percent in parts of Britain and France. A considerable number of Western European militants of al Qa'ida had been converted to radical Islam while in prison.[31] In France, the correlation between crime, mainly petty crime, and terrorism in the immigrant neighborhoods was even more glaring.[32]

Many signs were pointing to an explosive situation in the Islamic ghettoes all over Western Europe. When Ayatollah Khomeini pronounced his fatwa against Salman Rushdie, calling the faithful to kill the blasphemous writer, not a single Islamic preacher in Britain dared to dissent in public. Some Muslim public figures declared their intention to establish separatist institutions, even a separate parliament in Britain, and young radicals repeated in front of British television what their preachers had told them: that they would not desist from Jihad until their black flag would be hoisted over 10 Downing Street and presumably also on Buckingham Palace. In the summer of 2001, gangs of mainly Pakistani youth were attacking the police in Midland towns such as Oldham, torching shops, and attacking the police as well as Indians and Sikhs in riots which lasted several days and caused massive damage. The far-right British National Front seems to have played a minor part, but most locals believed that tensions were such that they would have led to violence even without any provocation. As an Asian observer commented after interviewing young Muslims in Oldham: "They said Western civilization deserved to be destroyed. Asked where they would start they replied: Everywhere. The riots had no target symbolic or strategic. They did not seem to protest against unemployment. The riots were swagger and mayhem, and the rioters in various towns vied to outdo each other."[33]

The authorities were shocked but by and large saw no reason to take an alarmist view. Only a small percentage of young Muslims had rioted; the majority of mosques were not dominated by the extremists. (It was the same in France — if the imam of the Lyon mosque sympathized with the radicals, the imam of the Marseilles mosque was considered a liberal.) There seemed to be no reason for undue worry in Britain. When a group of young radicals went from Britain to Yemen to take part there in the terrorist struggle, and when they were captured, the British government came to their defense and asked for their release.

In France, violence had occurred even earlier. In 1994–95, armed gangs in the Paris *banlieue* and the north of France had engaged in the robbery of supermarkets and shops, killing a few of their countrymen and also acting as runners for the drug trade as well as smuggling stolen cars from Marseille to the north. Among their leaders were the brothers Chalabi. They were certainly not very religious; all had long criminal records and some were converted to radical Islam in prison. Most had come from North Africa, but some were of Arab origin. The most prominent gang was in Roubaix; it engaged in daring robberies, and its leading members were killed in a shootout with the Belgian police.[34] The experts do not agree to this day whether the criminal element was stronger than the political as far as their motivation was concerned. They had close connections with the Algerian GIA, but they certainly engaged in the robberies also for their own profit.

There was nothing novel in such combinations. Some of the terrorist gangs in France prior to World War I were both anarchists and bandits; in Latin America, according to a time-honored tradition, horse thieves would claim political motivation because thieves would be hanged whereas politicians were not. The section in the French police dealing with them and some of their offshoots was not the political police but BOB, the brigade for the repression of banditry.[35] But some terrorist operations, such as in the Paris metro, were political in character. Altogether several scores of French citizens were killed and wounded in these attacks between 1993 and 1995.

According to some commentators, the violence in the *banlieue* and the great enthusiasm for bin Laden after September 11, 2001, was a revolt against an unjust and racist society.[36] That racism existed is beyond doubt, but it was not a one-sided affair. Angry young people from the Maghreb (northwestern Africa) hated Jews, Gypsies, Africans, and Asians. They burned synagogues and attacked neighbors belonging to other ethnic groups. They felt excluded even though the most popular person in France was Zinedine Zidane, the Algerian soccer star who had decisively helped France win the soccer world championship.[37]

As so often, poverty and social injustice did play a role but did not provide the main key one is looking for. Most of the leading terrorist figures, such as Zacarias Moussaoui (the "twentieth 9/11 hijacker," arrested in the United States), Djemal Beghal, or Kemal Daoudi had no criminal records. They came from middle-class families. Moussaoui became a jihadist only in the course of a long stay in London where he frequented Brixton mosque and became a member of a radical circle. Yet others such as the brothers Courtailler were not of Arab but West Indian origin and had only recently converted to Islam; they too had not grown up in the violent slums. They seemed to be well integrated into French society, but this was an illusion. They had been top students, well adjusted and quiet. After their arrest, their families genuinely refused to believe that their sons or brothers had been involved in terrorist activities.

Who had recruited them? According to close observers of the scene, the recruiters were preying on the psychological weaknesses of bright young men.[38] But there must have been a disposition to move in this direction — perhaps the desire to give their empty life a new meaning or the attraction by adventure and a thirst for action.

Most of the militant cells existing in France were North African by origin, and they collaborated in later years with the al Qa'ida network. But as Judge Bruguyere, the chief of antiterrorism in the DST (the French equivalent of the FBI), pointed out, many of the cells were autonomous and did not get their orders from bin Laden. If, for instance, they planned to blow up the U.S. embassy in Paris and various locations in Strasbourg (including the local Christmas market), it could well have been that bin Laden did not even know about this except perhaps vaguely, and that his participation in the venture was limited to financial help.[39] But there was certainly coordination between the autonomous groups and also mutual help: The group in Milan would be in contact with their friends in Paris and Frankfurt and ask for specific assistance.[40]

The most important base was London, simply because the terrorists enjoyed greater freedom there. Most leading terrorist figures such as Zacarias Moussaoui spent some time in London or frequently visited there. It has been mentioned that Moussaoui became a jihadist only in London; the terrorists could be reasonably certain not to be extradited from England even if in their country of birth they had been sentenced for murder. British security forces were not very well informed about happenings on the terrorist scene, and even if they had known more, they would have been powerless to intervene. London ("Londonistan") had become the center of radical Arab politics in Europe and also of radical Islamic terrorism.

The leading gurus of the jihadists in Britain were Sheikh Omar Bakri, Abu Qatada, and one-eyed and hook-handed Abu Hamza. Bakri was the head of two religious political organizations called Hizb ul Tahrir ("Liberation Party") and Al Muhajirun ("the emigrants," referring to the companions who had gone with Muhammad from Mecca to Medina). These were the most extremist groups outside Afghanistan. In an interview with *Le Monde*, Bakri declared that he and his men would not rest until the flag of Islam would be high over the Elysée and Downing Street.[41] He wanted Britain to be the first country to become truly Islamic, in contrast to some of his colleagues who maintained that the Islamic revolution should begin in countries such as Yemen. Bakri's appeals were not limited to calling for killing the Jews and Christians; he also called for the murder of all the rulers in the Muslim world, who were without exception creatures of the West.[42] In an interview with an Arab language newspaper, Abu Bakri said that the West would be transformed into part of the Islamic world either by invasion from without or through ideological invasion from within: "If an Islamic state arises and invades the West, we will be its army and soldiers from within."[43]

He was not always consistent in his pronouncements. Earlier on he had not attacked Britain and was asked for the reasons of this curious omission. He said he had had in earlier years an understanding with the British authorities, but gradually changed his opinion. In 1998, he was interviewed by the British security forces for having allegedly called for the murder of Prime Minister John Major. (He had said that Major would be a legitimate target if he would visit an Arab or Muslim country; he later said the same about Blair.) He called for jihad against Britain as well, and said that all Jewish and Christian targets were legitimate.

Before September 11, 2001, Bakri had claimed that he was bin Laden's personal representative, but after that date he argued that there was spiritual identification but no organizational ties. He called his fellow clerics in the Muslim world asses and dogs, and said that what mattered was not bookish knowledge but action.

He had posters printed that read "Kill the Jews" and he said that no Muslim was bound by phony British democratic rules which had been passed by monkeys in Parliament. These and other sayings could be found on Bakri's Web site, in brochures on jihad, and in the many interviews he freely gave to the media.

From time to time a question would be raised in Parliament or the press about the inflammatory speeches of the radical propagandists; after all, foreign visitors had been denied entrance to Britain for making far less extreme statements, but the British authorities thought they could not prosecute the Sheikh under existing laws. Perhaps they did not think him sufficiently influential and did not want to make him a martyr. In fact, Bakri's activities were indirectly financed by the state, as he received social welfare payments of about two thousand dollars a month, for himself and his five children. When asked about this by a British newspaper, he replied that it was difficult for him to get a job and that most of the leadership of the Islamic movement in Britain received social security benefits.[44] Mainstream Muslim spokesmen called him a clown and said that he was in no way representative of British Muslims, but most were still reluctant to speak out openly against him.

Some of Bakri's claims regarding his achievements were certainly exaggerated, sometimes grossly so. It was not true that he had recruited many thousands, or even hundreds, of young Muslims in Britain to fight in Afghanistan, Kashmir, Lebanon, Jordan, and other countries. The number of young Muslims who went to fight is not known, but it was certainly quite small; two were killed in Bosnia, one in Chechnya, a handful were taken prisoner in Afghanistan. But there is no doubt that recruitment was going on. Eight British Muslims who had volunteered to fight in Yemen had been sent by Bakri's colleague, Abu Hamza al Misri. There was a division of labor; another Sheikh named Yussef el Qaradawi located in West London was in charge of electronic jihad, raising funds and laundering money. Abdulla el Faisal was a leading speaker, Jamaica-born, and his cassettes were sold in front of many mosques. A central figure was Abu Qatada, located at the Finsbury mosque and several London Islamic cultural centers. Al Qatada did not speak English, and European police forces suspected him rather than el Bakri to be the main figure of al Qa'ida in Europe. He also lived on state support, as did Omar Othman, a cleric originally from Palestine who had been named as accomplice in the U.S. trial against the plotters who had blown up the African embassies in 1998; Othman went to court to have his social benefits reinstated. When the police came to search al Qatada's home, they found several hundred thousand dollars. A few hours before the British parliament passed legislation according to which al Qatada could have been arrested, he disappeared. This raised questions in the media as to whether he had been a MI5 agent all along.[45] Young Muslims were given instruction how to use a Kalashnikov in Finsbury Mosque in north London, while others were sent to farms in the countryside to receive military and sabotage training.[46] Bakri said that the duty of every able-bodied young Muslim over the age of fifteen was to go through such training.

The origins of the Hizb ul Tahrir are discussed elsewhere in our study. Its branch in Britain certainly remained a mystery for friend and foe alike.[47] Other Islamic and Islamist organizations were annoyed that it attracted publicity in the media out of proportion to its numbers. They were said to make false accusations against sincere Muslims. It was said that no one really knew who its leaders were and where they were hiding. Hizb ul Tahrir came under attack for its diversionary tactics in trying to break up the meetings of other Muslim organizations, and suspicions were voiced that it somehow served the interests of the Zionists by its very radicalism.[48] Yet few dared to speak out in public against the jihadists even if these were only a vociferous minority. They had followers not only in London but also in places like Liverpool, Leicester, and Maidenhead; their booklets and cassettes were sold not only in their own mosques but also in front of the London Regents Park mosque. They were attracting hundreds, perhaps thousands of the young and most active Muslims; thus they had access to a formidable reservoir of potential fighters. After September 2001, attacks against capitalism became prominent in Hizb ul Tahrir propaganda, which made British capitalism responsible for, among other things, the horrible sex crimes committed in Britain. What caused this ideological turn is not entirely clear: genuine conviction or the belief that such "anticapitalism" could broaden the appeal of the jihadists.[49]

English authorities were frequently criticized by their European colleagues and the Americans for not collaborating in combating terrorism, London having become the haven of Islamic radicals. The British refused to extradite militants with a terrorist record to countries where they might be condemned to death, but they also refused extradition to other European countries. This situation began to change only after September 2001 when new antiterrorist legislation was adopted.

The German situation differed from the state of affairs in France and Britain inasmuch as it was made very difficult for the immigrants from Turkey to become German citizens. On the other hand, enormous efforts were made by local governments and especially the churches to enter a dialogue with the Muslim communities. The attempts by Catholic as well as Protestant churchmen and women were based on a great deal of naïveté and ignorance about Islam and its attitude to ecumenical initiatives.[50] The church people furthermore concentrated their efforts on the more radical elements among the Turks, such as Milli Guerues, which represented about 3 percent of the Muslims rather than the more moderate elements.[51] The most militant group was the one headed by Metin Kaplan in Cologne, also called the Kalif von Köln, with some eleven hundred members who fought for the restoration of the Khilafah and global power to Islam.[52] These extremists engaged not only in indoctrination but planned terrorist action mainly against the secularists in their native country.

Terrorist organizations from Muslim countries were all represented in Germany; this refers, for instance, to the Algerian, Egyptian, and Palestinian groups. However, there was relatively little violence, except among ethnic groups such as radical Turks and Kurds of the PKK. The militants probably feared that if arrested they might not only lose their considerable social benefits but be expelled from Germany.

Germany was important for the Islamists for the same reason as Britain: as a safe haven and a base of operation in other countries. Several suicide bombers had studied in Germany in cities such as Hamburg. They had been attending the prayers in the local Al Quds mosque but had refrained from engaging in violent action. In fact they had been given instructions not to be politically active so as not to attract the attention of the authorities, thus endangering their terrorist missions. But with all this, the radical Islamists had their mosques, political and cultural centers in which anti-Westernism, anti-Semitism, and the use of violence were preached, and in which the members were taught how to make maximum use of the benefits offered by democratic societies while rejecting the principles such as political freedom, tolerance, and secularism on which these societies were based.

Spain and Italy were also considered "safe havens" by the terrorists. In Spain, a restaurant near an American base had been bombed in 1985 and eighteen Spaniards had been killed there, but since then there had been no such operations. The Spanish police were preoccupied with the struggle against the Basque ETA; they observed Muslim radicals but did not want to open a second front against potential Muslim terrorists. Among the six hundred thousand Muslim immigrants mainly from North Africa, there were thought to be several hundred militants of al Qa'ida, but they came in for closer observation only after September 2001 when several arrests were made.

Many of the Muslims who went illegally to Italy came from Albania; their interest was not primarily in politics but the smuggling of drugs and prostitution. A majority went on to other European countries, and they resented the political activism of some of the North Africans which made all illegals suspect and intensified police control. Italian police did succeed locating and ultimately arresting an important terrorist cell in Milan well before September 2001. This group had connections all over Europe and was scheduled to play a crucial role in the general terrorist offensive that was planned for late 2001, which should have included attacks against American embassies in Paris, Rome, and Tirana (Albania), as well as other targets.

THE HISTORY OF RADICAL ISLAMISM and the terrorist cells in Western Europe remains to be written. While conditions varied from country to country, it appeared that there were greater difficulties as far as the integration of the immigrants from Muslim countries was concerned than with any earlier immigrant group. Many had no wish to become part of society but wanted to maintain their traditional way of life. This stance made their economic and social integration difficult, condemning many of them to a proletarian or subproletarian existence.

The idea that over time a European Islam would develop that was more liberal and open seemed to have been premature at the very least. As a result a new generation grew up who were superficially assimilated and in large part deeply disaffected. Among these sections the preachers of jihad found their followers.

All this is not to say that social and cultural integration was doomed and would never materialize, but that it would take much longer than originally anticipated: three or four generations rather than one. The impact of modernity and the Western way of life was much slower than many had thought, but it was still strong and pervasive. The corruption (as the preachers saw it) was everywhere, and there was no escape except absence of any contact with the outside world, which was, of course, impossible in the long run. These were the sociological prospects; the terrorist leaders, to repeat once again, were not out to attract millions of votes, because they did not believe in democracy and majorities. Their aim was to find a few hundred activists willing to volunteer for jihad and, of course, a much broader section of the Muslim community which, while not actively joining the struggle, would sympathize and extend help in various ways. This reservoir certainly existed and is bound to exist for a considerable time to come.

So far mention has been made of Europe only, but the Afghan alumni and local sympathizers of al Qa'ida have been active in other continents as well, notably in Southeast Asia.[53] They have engaged in propaganda in most Muslim countries and also countries with Muslim minorities, and they have launched terrorist operations in Central Asia as well as the Caucasus, Malaysia, the Philippines, and elsewhere. There have been considerable differences between the various local groups. The Caucasus has seen a mixture of cultural-religious national motives in the fight against the Russians; Chechen gangs in Moscow have been closer to the model of the Mafia than the Koran, and the Abu Sayaf group in the Philippines has specialized in the abduction of foreign tourists for monetary gain rather than in the pursuit of jihad. But other operations such as the unsuccessful attempt by Ramzi Yussef and others to hijack a number of commercial planes from Manila in 1994 were precursors of September 2001.

Should one look for a common denominator? Is there a Muslim (or Islamic) International similar to the Comintern, the Communist International (1919–43)? Or is it merely a conspiracy on an international scale? Having digested so much anti-Semitic propaganda, did they want to take a leaf out of the *Protocols of the Elders of Zion*? Certainly, for the first time in the history of terrorism, an international organization, however loose, has come into being. But there is no central leadership comparable to the Third International, only a common ideology.

Like the Communist International, the bin Laden International operates on a variety of levels. It has been working through legal religious and political associations, as well as an illegal underground apparatus and a variety of groups (NGOs) in between. In some respects, it has been structured on the lines of a multinational corporation, but its branches are under no obligation to provide accounts to a chief executive. Perhaps a comparison with the Second (Socialist) International, which was a loose federation of political parties, would be more to the point, except of course that the Second International strictly rejected terrorism. A comparison with the "leaderless resistance" preached by the militias of the extreme right in the United States could also be made. This is based on the assumption that a group (or a phantom cell) without a visible head would be difficult for the security forces to detect, and if detected, to immobilize. A similar strategy has apparently been adopted by the radical wing of American environmental militants. But it is easier to apply this doctrine in theory than in practice, given the ambitious aims of groups like al Qa'ida on the one hand and the logistic complexities of modern societies on the other. Nor is it certain that the relations between the cells in various countries were as loose as initially assumed; subsequent investigations tended to show a considerable measure of coordination and direction from some central authority.[54]

The practitioners of Jihad have the great advantage in comparison with the Communist International that they could make use of space (mosques and other religious institutions) that in democratic countries were outside the jurisdiction and the supervision of security services and where operations could be planned and prepared without fear of interference. The mosques, the Islamic cultural centers and the schools were the free zones that Sudan had been at one time and later Afghanistan under Taliban rule. As in the Communist International, there is a fairly strict division between legal and illegal work. The terrorists have considerable latitude as far as their behavior among the infidels was concerned; they were sometimes advised to shave so as not to stand out, and they could do things, if need be, that an observing Muslim was forbidden to do; this permission even extended to the consumption of alcohol.

There is no party discipline among them and no monolithic ideology as there had been among the Communists, except in a very general way subscribing to the doctrine of jihad and practicing the various rituals whenever possible. At the same time, they have great freedom of action as far as terrorist initiatives are concerned. All this developed, in all probability, not according to any master plan but spontaneously; a rigid bureaucratic system would not have worked among people from so many countries and different backgrounds. Nor are references to "networking" and "interfacing" of much help; eager to engage in violent action, the conspirators would find like-minded people in clubs and bookshops or somewhere else in the orbit of a mosque known for its radical orientation.

Conspiracy of this kind had been the practice of nineteenth-century secret societies and sects, and not much has changed since except the means of communication. A member of such a society of bygone days, whether European or

Muslim, would find himself at home in this atmosphere except that the earlier conspiracies were usually confined to one country, whereas at present they are more international in character. Radical preachers play a key role because they received their training in the same religious seminars, but radical businessmen or diplomats can also fulfill this function because of their international contacts and activities. Thus, the new radical Islamic International is not particularly sophisticated in its structure. But this is not necessarily a drawback, because their antagonists would have found it easier to understand and combat a modern international organization than a premodern one in the pattern of the nineteenth century.

FOUR

Suicide

S UICIDE BOMBING, one of the most prominent features of contemporary terrorism, has been one of the most difficult to understand for those living in
what is commonly known as the postheroic age. It has led some to believe that
those willing to sacrifice their own life must be supreme idealists and the cause
for which they are willing to make this greatest of all sacrifices must be a just
and noble one. At the same time, it is frequently maintained that suicide attack
is something new in history and specifically Muslim. (At one time, in the 1980s,
it was believed to be specifically Shi'ite.) However, such missions have occurred
over a long time in many countries and cultures. In fact, a review of the history of
terrorism over the ages up to the 1960s shows that in the great majority of cases,
all terrorism was suicide terrorism. The number of attackers who got away from
terrorism was very small. From what we know about their mind-set, it appears
that they did not expect to escape, and in many instances they did not even
try. An attempt to understand the suicide bombers ought to take into account a
great variety of circumstances and motives and should not focus on one specific
group and religion, even if that group happens to figure very prominently at the
present time.

Some have seen the sources of suicide attack in the commandments of religion.
According to the teachings of Islam suicide is forbidden, but martyrdom in the
struggle for Allah is not; on the contrary, it is a religious duty.[1] The term *shahid*
originally meant "witness" (as in a court of law), but as in Christianity it acquired
another meaning — that of a martyr, fighting the infidels and sealing his fate with
death.[2] The *shahid* receives great privileges in paradise nearest the throne of God.
His wounds become red like blood on the day of judgment and shine and smell
like musk. They are the only ones in paradise to have the special privilege of
returning to earth and suffering martyrdom another ten times.[3] True, the longing
to die a martyr's death was not encouraged by orthodox Islamic theology because
this kind of self-sacrifice looked like suicide, which was condemned by Islam. And
in the end, almost anyone who died a violent death was considered a *shahid*.[4]

In our time, various religious dignitaries in Egypt and Saudi Arabia have
opposed suicide terrorism, but others — such as the Mufti of Jerusalem and Palestine — have justified it as *shahada* (martyrdom). Yet others have taken a middle

71

way, regarding attacks against enemy soldiers as permissible, but attacks against civilians are not. Some have favored suicide attacks against the "Zionist occupants" in Palestine but not against fellow Muslims.[5] Sheikh Muhammad Tantawi, head of Al Azhar in Cairo, said on one occasion that all Israelis — men, women, and children — were forces of occupation and therefore legitimate targets of suicide bombers. But on another occasion he said that no Muslim should blow himself up in the midst of children and women but only among aggressors, among soldiers. Yussef el Qaradawi, the TV sheikh of the Al Jezira network, famous in the whole Arab world, also declared suicide terrorism the highest form of jihad and therefore very commendable.

The arguments in favor of such martyrdom are historical, and they usually refer to battles fought in the lifetime of the prophet Muhammad or soon after. Thus Sheikh Sabri, the Mufti of Jerusalem, in a speech justifying suicide attacks, referred to the battle (or campaign) of Mu'tah (629), in which the followers of Muhammad fought a superior Roman (that is to say, Byzantine) army. The leader Said ibn al Halitha was killed early on, and his place was taken by Jafar Ibn Abu Taleb, who continued to fight even after being mortally wounded. According to the chronicler, he had fifty injuries but none in the back because he did not retreat. The prophet named him "Jafar the flyer" because Allah granted him two wings when he entered paradise to replace the two hands that had been cut off in battle. Then a third commander, Abdullah ibn Rawaha, took over until he was martyred. And so it went on until Khaled ibn Walid took command, who, the chronicler reports, developed a brilliant plan for withdrawal and lived to fight another day.[6]

Appeals to go to a battle from which there would be no return are frequent in the Muslim tradition. Thus, al Baraa ibn Malik of the Ansar tribe at the battle of Yamama, said, "Oh Ansar, let not anyone of you think of returning to Madinah. There is no Madinah for you after this day. There is only Allah, and then Paradise." Of Baraa, the tradition says that he died in another battle. He had prayed to God to grant him martyrdom.

As the Mufti of Jerusalem and other contemporary clerics see it, these heroic actions were not suicidal but the obeying of a religious duty such that the martyrs entered paradise directly. They did not have to undergo examination by the "interrogating angels" or pass the purging fires of Islam (Abdul Wahid Hamed, *Companions of the Prophet*, vol. 1). And the Mufti ended his sermon saying that whereas the enemies of Islam love life, Muslims love death and strive for martyrdom.[7]

Such martyrdom is not unique. By a long oral and written tradition, similar legends of heroism and sacrifice are equally frequent in the history of other peoples, cultures, and religions, and many more were reinvented during later romantic ages. A typical example of religious motivation in warfare was ancient Assyria, which in the ninth and eighth centuries B.C. engaged almost continuously in military campaigns. These wars of aggression were by no means imperialist-secular in character (even though they led to the establishment of an Assyrian empire). They were inspired and commanded by the gods, above all the god Assur. Conducting warfare was religious service *ad majorem Dei gloriam,* and the gods justified warfare even if conducted with utmost brutality.[8]

The cult of heroes with a variety of ceremonies on their graves goes back to time immemorial; it can be found in earliest Greek history. The Spartan heroes at the battle of Thermopylae who under King Leonidas fought to the last man did so because law had ordered it and law was sanctioned by the gods. As the author Simonides relates, "Go tell the Spartans, thou who passes by, that here obedient to their laws, we lie."[9] The Jewish zealots who retreated to Massada near the Dead Sea for a last stand that ended in collective suicide were part of the same tradition. The Romans considered all their wars not only just (*bellum justum*) but also pious (*pium*) and there was a quasireligious ritual ceremony for starting such a war: throwing a spear into enemy territory.

The Nordic (Icelandic, Viking, German) sagas deal with little but acts of heroism with the gods of pagan religion playing a prominent role. The heroes who had died in battle were taken to Asgard, the palace of the gods with 540 doors; they were kept there until Ragnarok, the last decisive battle. Their life was described as extremely comfortable. They were eating excellent boar meat and drinking the finest mead. When they were not feasting, the heroes were fighting, cutting themselves to pieces. But when mealtime came their wounds had healed and they returned to Valhalla.[10]

The legends of the early Middle Ages are in a similar vein, with the Chanson de Roland as a prominent example. This is the story of the heroic rear-guard action at Roncevalles of the emperor's army. Roland, the nephew of Charlemagne, and his friend and comrade-in-arms Olivier and thirty other knights were too proud to sound the horn to call for help when faced by an overwhelming troop of Saracens. When they at last blew the horn, it was too late and when help arrived, they were dead on the field of battle. The Chanson says that they fought not only for their country (*la douce France*) but above all for their religion against the pagans.[11] The church regarded them as martyrs, not only those who had died having been persecuted for their belief in Christ. Thus the knights who went to fight in the Crusades were promised not only forgiveness for all their sins but entrance to paradise, just as the Muslim fighters were.

There are countless stories of self-sacrifice in battle, just as the one of Arnold Winkelried, the Swiss who in the battle of Sempach threw himself in the middle of the affray, thus forcing the enemy to concentrate on him and creating a way through their lines for his fellow fighters. Next to Wilhelm Tell, Winkelried became in a later romantic age the central figure in Swiss national mythology. The legend of Ivan Susanin (Glinka's opera "A Life for the Tsar") shows that not only a bogatyr, a knight and professional fighter, but a simple peasant could be a martyr.[12] It is the story of a man who during the Time of Troubles deliberately led the invading Polish army units into the middle of a forest to give the tsar the opportunity to escape. He was killed by the Poles for having misled them and became a national hero invoked by political leaders (including Stalin) up to the present day. It was more than a story of patriotic loyalty because the tsar apart from being the political ruler was also the supreme religious leader.

To write the story of these ages is to a large extent to write about heroes, cults of heroes, and martyrdom. If, during the age of the Enlightenment, these traditions went temporarily out of fashion, they came back with a vengeance during the romantic age, with modern Germany as an obvious example. As Theodor Koerner, the poet of the war of liberation against Napoleon, wrote on the eve of a battle (May 12, 1813): "Happiness lies only in sacrificial death."[13] Koerner did die such a death but a greater poet than Koerner, Friedrich Hoelderlin, not known as an aggressive militarist, had written even earlier (1797) a poem entitled "death for the fatherland" that was in the same vein. The inscription of Horace's *Dulce et decorum est pro patria mori* could be found in the assembly halls of German schools after World War I, and in similar form in Britain and France. This was to commemorate, above all, the heroes of the battle of Langemarck in Flanders (November 1914), when thousands of young students and members of the youth movement (the Wandervogel) had tried to storm the Allied lines singing "Deutschland, Deutschland über alles" — which was not even the national anthem at the time. The fallen symbolized the triumph of youth. They were not really dead but were sleeping in the lap of Christ, according to pictures widely distributed at the time. The graves and cemeteries became shrines of national worship.[14]

The heroes had not died in vain. They lived on in eternal life in the tradition of *Ich hatt einen Kameraden*, Ludwig Uhland's famous poem in memory of the good comrade who was killed in battle. It became a famous popular song, which ended,

> Kann dir die Hand nicht geben
> Bleib du im ew'gen Leben
> (My friend I cannot ease your pain
> in life eternal we'll meet again
> and walk once more as one.)

Under Nazism the heroic tradition involving self-sacrifice was not only continued but became central to the essence of the regime. This fact, perhaps more than anything else, led some contemporaries to interpret Nazism as a political religion. (Some Catholic commentators drew parallels with early Islam.) Up to the outbreak of the war the cult was mainly devoted to those killed in the struggle for the victory of Nazism — that is to say, in the street battles of the early 1930s.[15] The semi-official anthem of the Nazis, the Horst Wessel song devoted to the memory of a Berlin Nazi killed before 1933, clearly states that "comrades killed by the Reds and the reactionaries were still marching in our ranks (*Kameraden die Rotfront und Reaktion erschossen, marschieren im Geist in unseren Reihen mit*).

Later on, Nazi propaganda centered on the victims of the military campaigns in Western and Eastern Europe. Nazi propagandists were given instructions to explain to those who had been bereaved that there was no need to mourn, which was not good for national morale, but they should be grateful that their dearest had been given a chance to sacrifice their life for some higher ideal. They had not to suffer pain but were living in eternity; they were more alive than the rest, having suffered not just a necessary but a noble and beautiful death.[16]

These ideas found their reflection in hundreds of poems written at the time: the fallen were still "living while we were breathing," their death had been a magnificent triumph over death. Another poem related a vision: a miracle had occurred, the fallen had left their graves and had taken their place in the columns marching through town (Holzapfel).[17] It was customary on ritual occasions among German as well as Romanian Nazis that when the list of those present was read out, those who had fallen were included and that someone would say "present" after the names of the dead had been called.

The poems about those who had died a hero's death were written not just by party hacks but by highly respected writers of the time who were not even members of the Nazi Party. One of them was Ernst Bertram, one of the leading Germanists of the time, a member of the George Circle, the aristocracy of the spirit and friend of Thomas Mann (he had proposed to bestow an honorary doctorate on Mann at Bonn University which later became something of an academic scandal). Bertram wrote that only graves were creating Heimat (the beloved homeland), that only the dead were giving us light, that a people came into being through its coffins.[18]

The cult of heroes, and above all the fallen heroes, figured prominently in the ideology and practice of other fascist movements, such as the Romanian Iron Guard (The Legion of Archangel Michael), which was permeated more by religious elements than any other.[19] Many years later an admirer of Codreanu wrote about the "legionnaires":

> In the ethics of the legionnaires' sacrifice, martyrdom, death had a larger than life significance. In the writings of Corneliu Codreanu, Ion Mota and Alexandru Cantacuzino the love for the sacrifice, the faith in death appears like a martial passion, a mysticism akin to the fighting spirit and suicide in the Weltanschauung of the Japanese samurai. In the 20th century one may find something similar only in the auto-da-fes of the kamikaze pilots and the ritual seppuku of the poet Yukio Mishima — the triumph of the will, the triumph of the sacrifice.[20]

Ion Mota was the second-in-command in the Iron Guard and went to fight in the Spanish Civil War on Franco's side; he was killed, and the return of his body to Romania was celebrated by his comrades as the greatest moment in the history of their movement. Another great admirer of Codreanu and his cult of martyrdom and heroic suicide was Giulio Evola, the ideologist of neo-Nazism in Italy, a prominent figure in the war against the West and proponent of a hero's death.[21]

A similar spirit was inculcated in early Spanish fascism by José Antonio Primo de Rivera, the head of the Falange. General Astray, the head of the Spanish Foreign Legion, addressing the students of Salamanca University in October 1936, shouted, "Down with the intellectuals, *viva la muerte!*" expressed something of the Zeitgeist. "The intellectuals" was mainly the great Spanish writer Miguel de Unamuno, who was among the audience. Astray was a brave man, but despite the invocation of death he was not killed on the battlefield but lived to a ripe old age and so, for all we know, did the students who applauded him that day.

SS units wore the skulls-and-bones insignia both on their caps and on their rings, on their daggers and the buckle of their belts. Not only elite units but regular soldiers were expected to undertake missions from which the chances of return were small or nonexistent — for instance, those serving in the German submarine fleet after 1943. Generally speaking, this was true with regard to those on the Eastern front during the last year of the war. In later years, the question was often asked why German soldiers continued to fight when the military situation was altogether hopeless. The consensus reached by the historians was that fear of the Nazi security forces did play a role, as well as fear of the Russians and ideological indoctrination, but that esprit de corps — a feeling of solidarity with fellow soldiers — was probably the single most important motive.

This was, of course, not confined to the German army of the Third Reich; in the Soviet army, the legend of Alexander Matrosov became a shining example for self-sacrifice early on during the war. Matrosov threw himself in front of an enemy machine gun to give his comrades a chance to storm the German positions.

But the closest to contemporary suicide terrorists were the Japanese kamikaze pilots in 1944–45. (*Kami* is the Japanese word for various gods and spirits; *kaze* also refers to a divine figure, a savior in a desperate situation.) The decision to send pilots to crash-dive their planes on American ships was a counsel of despair, not a strategy with any hope for success, and some of the surviving kamikaze admitted in later years the futility of these operations. Several thousand junior officers and cadets volunteered for these missions; there was actually a waiting list of candidates. The attacks took place near Okinawa, in the South China Sea and in the direction of the Philippines and Australia; several dozen American ships were hit, but the campaign had no impact on the outcome of the war.[22]

Who were the volunteers and what motivated them? From the farewell letters of the suicide bombers, from interviews with survivors (who had been chosen but in view of technical failure or other reasons did not proceed with their missions), and from other sources, it is known that religion — in this case, Shinto — played a central part in the psychological decision to volunteer. In the first line of virtually every farewell letter, the emperor, who was considered a god, is invoked. But it was not traditional religion alone (some of the kamikaze were Christians) but the whole Japanese cultural and social tradition, the "Japanese ideology" of the Showa period (1926–45) with its extreme nationalism, its quasi-fascist elements, and its stress on unquestioning obedience to authority that shaped the mentality of these very young people, aged between seventeen and twenty-five. They all believed in the superiority of the Japanese way of life even though many felt the conflict between their patriotic duty in a holy war ("If I had seven lives I would gladly sacrifice them to smite the enemy," one of them wrote) and their duty toward their parents who would miss them. They were equally convinced that there was an afterlife and that they would live on as spirits. The idea that courageous Japanese soldiers would be enshrined at Yasukuni, a site of veneration, may have played a certain role but apparently not a decisive one.

Some kamikaze felt happy that an opportunity had been given to them to die for all that was dear to them. With others the feeling of duty was predominant, and yet others seem to have been reluctant to undertake these futile missions but they were conditioned by their training well before they had joined the army not to question orders. They knew that the appeal for volunteers was a thinly veiled order.[23] The evidence collected many years after the event is contradictory. A fair number of suicide candidates have reported that they were sad and weeping before their missions, that they had no illusions about the outcome of the war even though they had been told that the Americans and the British were devils. They agree that the most important factor was military discipline and peer pressure.[24]

The Readiness to Engage in Suicide Missions

There were suicide missions in postwar armed conflicts such as the war between Iraq and Iran (mainly on the part of young Iranian Islamic guards), in the Korean War, and a few also on the part of the Viet Cong. But these wars took place outside Europe and the Americas and in a postheroic era in which fighting often became a contest of technologies. It was gradually forgotten that in earlier ages, when war was as frequent as peace, the willingness to pay the ultimate price in war had been taken for granted.

A student of the Irish national movement has drawn attention to the tradition of folk heroes such as Cuchulain, the mythological chieftain who sacrificed his life to allow fellow warriors to escape capture and death — themes that were taken up by leading poets of the period such as Yeats. And a line could be drawn from Cuchulain to the Easter Rising of 1916, the crucial date in the history of Irish nationalism, a rebellion that was carried out without virtually any chance of success. The sacrificial motif can be traced even further on to 1981, when ten republican militants starved themselves to death in the Maze prison in Belfast.[25]

An even greater number of militants, some of them terrorists, starved themselves to death in Turkish prisons in 2001–2.

A tradition of suicide terrorism has existed in India and Southeast Asia (Malabar, Pondicherry, Atjeh, the Philippines) which goes back to the arrival of the Spanish and the Portuguese (and their missionaries). For all one knows some of the amok races described by contemporary observers in eighteenth- and nineteenth-century India also occurred on a religious-political background.[26]

The readiness to engage in suicide missions would certainly not have been a source of astonishment to terrorists of a bygone age all over the world. In the rites of passage of many terrorist organizations, the members joining were asked to affirm on oath their readiness to give their lives when needed. It was implied that they had taken leave from life as understood by those around them.

In the pre-dynamite era, with the dagger and the pistol as the main weapons, the chances of terrorists not to get killed in the attempt (or to be apprehended and to be executed) were minimal. Even during the last decades of the nineteenth century, the making of bombs was such a risky business and the bombs produced so unstable that the chances of being blown up during or before the attempt were very high indeed. The danger of getting caught while on missions outside their country remained very high; when two members of the Israeli right-wing underground went to Cairo in 1944 to kill Lord Moyne, the British minister in charge of Middle Eastern affairs, there was no real hope to escape alive. The attack at Lod Airport by members of the Japanese Red Army in 1972 belongs to the same category, even though members of the group survived. Leading members of the Baader-Meinhof gang killed themselves in Stammheim prison using arms that had been smuggled into the building.

The more or less systematic use of suicide missions in our time — usually, but not always, by means of bombing — dates back to 1983. It was applied by a variety of groups primarily in the Middle East but also in Southeast Asia in the Balkans and elsewhere. It was used by a variety of groups Muslim (both Shi'ite and Sunni), non-Muslim (Christian, Sikh, Hindu, Jewish [such as Dr. Baruch Goldstein, who killed a group of praying Arabs in Bethlehem]) and also atheists (the Kurdish PKK, the Lebanese Communist Party, and the various Popular Fronts for the Liberation of Palestine).

The motives of the suicide bombers were complex. The confusion in the West was further aggravated as a result of the fact that attention was almost exclusively focused on certain groups in the Middle East, whereas others were ignored. Hundreds if not thousands of journalists wrote about the suicide bombers of the Palestinian Hamas, about whom there were countless interviews and articles and also academic studies, whereas the Tamil Tigers (LTTE) in Sri Lanka were virtually ignored.

Considering the small number of people involved (the Jaffna Tamil minority in Sri Lanka totals perhaps less than one million) there were proportionally many more suicide attacks in Sri Lanka than in the Middle East. However, the Jaffna Peninsula and nearby places were less familiar to a Western public than Jerusalem or Bethlehem. There was no concentration of the media in Sri Lanka, and it could always be argued that Sri Lankan terrorism was a domestic affair without international repercussions — which was however only partly true, as shown by the murder of Indian prime minister Rajiv Gandhi by members of this group.[27]

Common to suicide bombers is the belief that they were warriors in a just struggle in the best tradition of their religion (or nation), that their group was cruelly oppressed, and that their sacrifice was not just desirable but imperative. Common also was the belief that the collective (the religion, the sect, the nation, the race) was infinitely more important than the individual. Their spiritual imperative was again that of Horace's *Dulce et decorum*: that it was sweet and becoming to die for the fatherland, and to kill in the process as many of the enemy as possible. The feeling of racial or religious superiority and an eternal conflict between their race or religion and that of the enemy also played a role — among the SS, in Sri Lanka, as well as the Islamic terrorists. Common also was the belief not only that their memory would live on forever but that in choosing death they were opting for eternal life in one form or another. The promises varied with the nature of the religious-political character of the group to which they belonged.

Contemporary suicide terrorism began in Lebanon in April 1983 and in Sri Lanka in December of that year. The attacks in the Middle East were mainly directed against the United Nations. Forces stationed in Beirut (U.S. and French) were spectacular and eminently successful. Hundreds were killed in these attacks, which resulted in the evacuation of the foreign forces (except the Syrians) from the country. The U.S. embassy in Beirut was also attacked as were Israeli military installations. These activities were carried out by a little-known Shi'ite organization named Hizbullah, which acted under Iranian sponsorship and with substantial material help from Teheran.

In the years that followed, more attacks took place in Lebanon. Altogether there were about sixty between 1983 and the present day, but they were on a relatively small scale. The most deadly ones took place in Argentina (1992 and again in 1994) and were directed against local Jewish institutions.

In the meantime, suicide missions were directed by other radical Islamic groups against Muslim leaders, against Emir al Sabah, the ruler of Kuwait (1985), against Anwar Sadat of Egypt (1981), and against Lebanese Prime Minister Bashir Gemayel (1982). It later appeared that the assassination of Sadat was to be part of a general insurrection in Egypt which, however, never materialized.[28] Prominent Muslim personalities were killed in suicide attacks in Algeria and the former Yugoslavia as well as Egypt and Pakistan, as was General Ahmed Shah Masoud, the commander of the Northern Alliance in Afghanistan (September 2001). The first suicide mission in Israel took place only in 1993, but before analyzing in greater detail this new strategy in the Arab and Muslim world, where initially it was practiced only sporadically, we ought to deal with the other main theater of such missions: Sri Lanka, where for years suicide missions became more or less standard procedure.

Sri Lanka (formerly Ceylon), the island south of the Indian subcontinent, has been ruled since independence by an elected, more or less democratic government in which the Sinhalese majority prevailed. Relations between the ethnic groups were less than cordial; the Tamil concentrated in the north of country felt oppressed and discriminated against. Whether this feeling was justified in reality is a separate question; the Sinhalese certainly argued that the Tamils got more than their fair share in every walk of life.

The Tamil fight for greater independence was at first political and nonviolent, but with the advent of a new, younger, and more militant generation, it turned to armed struggle. Race riots in 1983, in which allegedly some three thousand Tamils were killed, aggravated the situation. Many Tamils felt helpless, and the belief among the younger generation gained ground that only military action could restore their dignity and ultimately bring them independence.

This attitude led to the emergence of a number of activist groups consisting mainly of left-wing students of which the Tamil Tigers of Eelam (LTTE) became the most important by far, having eliminated their competitors, often by violent means. The LTTE was headed by Prabhakaran, who has remained its political and military leader from the beginning in 1975 to the present day. Prabhakaran's personal position was absolutely central, comparable only to the position of the leaders of the dictatorships in Europe in the 1930s.

He led the LTTE from very modest beginnings, when it was a small gang engaging in robberies to acquire the means to conduct both guerrilla warfare and terrorism, to greater importance and glories when it could maintain a little flotilla of its own, both to attack the government forces and to maintain contact with the much larger Tamil community in South India. It also temporarily established "liberated zones" primarily on the Jaffna Peninsula. Support for the LTTE on the part of the 70 million Tamils in South India was limited, but there was a great deal of help on the part of the eight hundred thousand Tamils living abroad, in Canada, Australia, and elsewhere. Money was collected — according to some estimates, up to $150 million annually — to finance the armed struggle of the LTTE. During the two decades of terrorist and guerilla attacks, about sixty-five thousand citizens of Sri Lanka were killed (more than thirty-seven hundred in the year 2000). In between there have been armistices and negotiations but a decisive breakthrough toward peace came only in early 2002.

A search for the deeper causes of the conflict and its particular bitterness is not easy because there is a wide distance between facts and perception. The Tamil wish to establish a state of their own is based on historical claim, but there never was a Tamil kingdom in Sri Lanka. The Sinhalese majority and the Tamil coexisted for many centuries more or less in peace. When the British withdrew, there was no claim for Tamil autonomy. The Tamil has been represented in the government administration over and above their percentage of the population. Under the British and in the decades after, Tamil had been appointed to key positions in every walk of life, such as the army, the police, and the Supreme Court, and they played a leading role in the cultural life of the country and the universities. Nor did religion play a central role, the Sinhalese being Buddhist, the Tamils predominantly Hindu. The Tamil separatist movement did not make an appeal to religious motives in its propaganda, partly, no doubt, in order not to alienate the 15 percent of Tamils who were Christian. To the extent that Hinduism was rooted among Tamils, it was an upper-class phenomenon, whereas the Tamil Tigers were based predominantly on the less wealthy sections (but not the poor) of the population. Tamil separatism, in other words, is secular, and its leadership is atheist. At the same time, the leaders have used a symbolism going back to ancient Tamil history — the tiger being the symbol of Murugan, one of the favorite Tamil gods. There is among the Tamils the concept of honor after death and the brave mother sacrificing the family for the sake of liberation. The idea of martyrdom and the cult of the martyrs (a "martyr's week" is celebrated in November) also plays a central role in Tamil propaganda.[29]

Given that they are not religious believers, how does one explain the religious fervor of the Tamil Tigers? Some have tried to account for it as a civic religion or as a hysterical mass cult.[30] But all this does not satisfactorily explain the total alienation of the radical Tamils, the fanaticism and the persistence of their struggle. Measured by objective standards, the position of the Tamils in the country had been considerably better than that of most minorities elsewhere in Asia and Africa. Nevertheless the perception of being persecuted and tormented was very real and led to the outbreak of the violent struggle and its continuation over many years. Nor was there a historical propensity toward violence and in particular toward suicide missions.

Hinduism on the other hand has a strong element of nonviolence (*ahimsa* and *satyagraha*), even though Hindus have not always lived up to the prescription of their religion. Furthermore, the radicalization and the terrorism were by no means shared by all Tamils, above all not by the Tamils in the south of Sri Lanka and the Tamil intelligentsia. There had been a tradition of political radicalism in Ceylon with the south gravitating more to a lumpen Marxism (as the critics called it — Ceylon was perhaps the only country in the world with a sizeable Trotskyite party), whereas the inclination in the Tamil north was more toward chauvinism and racism bordering on fascist ideas (to quote the critics). But this radicalism had seldom manifested itself in systematic violent action prior to the 1970s.[31]

Furthermore, the Sinhalese government, taught by bitter experience, has made several far-reaching offers of autonomy over the years to the Tamils, which have been rejected. Nor was the economic factor of any decisive importance. The statist economic policy (Sri Lanka is called a socialist republic to this day) led to stagnation and unemployment. But young enterprising Tamils could have easily joined those of their countrymen and women who went looking for their fortune outside their country (as many did with much success) rather than engaging in suicide missions. In any case, social issues virtually never figured in their political program.

If so, there remains no other explanation than the antipathy between different national or religious groups in multinational societies, which for some unfathomable reasons seem to be even stronger on islands such as Ireland, Sri Lanka, or Cyprus. There is a deep-seated unwillingness to share a common country and the desire to have a state of their own at any price. The Sinhalese government did show insensitivity with regard to the minorities, for instance, as far as the language issue was concerned. The Sinhalese radicals thought that the English language was the root of all evil and wanted to replace it with their own language, and among the Tamils there was a similar reaction. There were fights among the communities and victims, but a feverish imagination was needed to believe (as their propaganda claimed) that the government and the Sinhalese majority aimed at the genocide of the Tamils.

Tamil terrorism specifically conducted a campaign which combined elements of guerrilla warfare (that is to say, liberation of territories and establishing an alternative administration) and terrorism. The Sri Lankan army was weak, and the Tamils — who did not lack monetary resources — had modern weapons such as SA 7 ground-to-air missiles; on frequent occasions they were better equipped than the forces opposing them. Thus they succeeded in making life so uncomfortable for the Indian peacekeeping force that the Indians withdrew their units after a few years. Generally speaking, the Tamils showed not only enormous persistence but also great inventiveness. While unlike the Palestinian resistance they had no neighboring countries sympathetic to their cause, providing supplies and a safe haven, their speedboats plying between India and Sri Lanka gave them the opportunity to carry weapons (and fighters and drugs) almost freely.

Suicide terrorism carried out by the Tamil Tigers was quite indiscriminate; it was certainly spectacular as far as the number of victims and the success of their missions were concerned. They assassinated not only an Indian president but also President Premadasa of Sri Lanka, and they killed or injured many government ministers, military commanders, and also Sinhalese (and occasionally Muslim) peasants and other citizens who had the misfortune of belonging to the wrong ethnic minority. The Tigers had a reputation of honesty and lack of corruption; at the same time, they murdered without compunction not only non-Tamils but also those among their own community who were considered rivals or insufficiently enthusiastic to their cause. Politically the impact of suicide terrorism was less impressive since it did not bring about a decision in the struggle. A variety of pressures induced the LTTE to declare an armistice in February 2002: the general world situation in which there was little sympathy for terrorist groups, whatever their aims; declining financial support from Tamils abroad; and the opening of a new front with the Muslim inhabitants of northern Sri Lanka.[32]

Among the Tigers engaging in suicide missions there was a fairly high percentage of women (about 30 percent), very much in contrast to Muslim suicide terrorism. The LTTE began the systematic indoctrination of its fighters at school level; fourteen-year-old cadres wrapped in explosives were used in many a mission. Very often they were given the honor of having a last meal with the leader of the Tigers on the eve of their mission. According to popular belief, they carried cyanide pills with them so as not to fall alive into the hand of the enemy. But this seems to be a legend, at least in part, for Tamil Tigers have been taken prisoners, and only some of them are known to have carried poison with them.

In the final analysis, the most important single factor in Tamil suicide terrorism could well be the personality of the leader — similar to the central role of Hitler and Mussolini in European fascism — and also the feeling of racial incompatibility between the two groups. It is certainly far more important than in most other terrorist groups. That the Tamils of India do not show the same propensity toward violence is certainly interesting. Their attitude toward the Tamil Tigers is similar to that of the Irish of Eire to the IRA of Northern Ireland: a vague sympathy but no solidarity with their terrorist campaign.

Other important features are the esprit de corps, the feeling of obligation not to let down the commander and the comrades-in-arms. Also of significance is the ancient cult of martyrs that the LTTE leadership has revived. This veneration takes various forms, such as ancestor rituals, special cemeteries (like those in Europe for the fallen in both world wars), and "hero stones." According to LTTE doctrine, the hero belongs to the collective, the public, not just his or her own next of kin. Mention has been made of the celebration of Great Heroes Week (November 21–27), which happens to be close to the birthday of Prabhakaran, the leader.

Thus the Tamil Tigers are in important respects a unique phenomenon. As far as their ruthlessness is concerned, they have been compared with Nazism and Pol Pot's movement in Cambodia.

History and cultural heritage are of limited help only in explaining the fanaticism and endurance of the LTTE. The central role of the leader resembles a cult in which the members blindly follow the leader. The content of his message is of importance but apparently less so than the free-floating thirst for action underlying it.

Suicide terrorism has occurred at all times, but at certain times far more often than others. The main scene in the 1980s was Sri Lanka and Lebanon, where the main perpetrators were Shi'ite groups. In later years, the scene of action shifted to Israel, Turkey, and the Indian subcontinent, as well as attacks against American targets in various parts of the world. Some sixteen groups have been identified as engaging in suicide terrorism. Such figures are bound to be imprecise, however, for some of these groups engaged in a few such attacks only and then disappeared; in other cases, one and the same attack was claimed by several terrorist organizations. Certain suicide attacks were carried out by individuals with the help of an organization but not necessarily under their direct control. Groups changed their names, character, and mode of operation. Thus Harakat al Ansar in Kashmir and Pakistan became Harakat ul Mujahideen and eventually Jaish-e-Mohammad — all this within a period of five years. A group such as al Qa'ida founded by bin Laden and al Zawahiri came into being as the result of the merger of several radical groups from a variety of countries, closely cooperating with each other but not necessarily always under strict control from one center. Some of the most striking political assassinations and terrorist acts in the 1990s were carried out by individuals (the murder of Yizhak Rabin, Oklahoma City, etc.).

The suicide terrorism scene has been very much in flux all through its existence, but with all these reservations it is easy to identify the groups that have been most active.[33] Above all, the Tamil Tigers conducted some two hundred such attacks to their credit, while the Shi'ite Hizbullah and Amal (as well as some secular nationalist groups) in Lebanon in the 1980s committed fifty some such attacks. Hamas and Islamic Jihad in Israel in the 1990s are attributed with perhaps seventy to eighty suicide attacks over the years. To this, one should add the Kurdish workers party PKK, which over a number of years engaged in some twenty suicide attacks. These groups have tended to exaggerate their strength to frighten the enemy; Islamic Jihad at one stage boasted that it had four thousand volunteers waiting eagerly to die a martyr's death. But since the beginning of the second Intifada and with the lull in fighting in Sri Lanka, the greatest number by far of suicide bombings have been they work of members of various Palestinian groups.

Figures of suicide bombings are bound to be approximate at best, for one does not know about the attempts that were planned but aborted for technical reasons, or about the cases in which the perpetrators decided for whatever reason not to go through with their plans. According to some estimates, only every other Palestinian suicide attack has succeeded; according to others the figure is only one in five.[34] Nor do figures tell the whole story. There is an obvious difference between the massive al Qa'ida attacks which caused international crises (the African embassies; the attack on the USS *Cole* in 2000; September 11, 2001) and attacks that took place in some distant Turkish or Kashmir village which caused only a few casualties and were not even reported by the media.

However, even an incomplete survey of suicide terrorism shows that while many, perhaps most, suicide attacks were carried out by groups that were secular in character, those that were the most effective — causing the most victims and attracting the most attention — were engineered by Islamist groups. To these groups we turn next.

Following the spectacular attacks by Hamas and al Qa'ida, there were endless discussions among Muslims and outside students of Islam whether there was anything inherent in this religion conducive to suicide terrorism. A consensus holds that the Koran says that suicide is a sin, and that those who commit it will not enter paradise. But there is also general agreement that those fighting in defense of Islam are engaging in jihad — that is to say, holy war — that they are heroes acting in accordance with one of the most basic commandments of their religion: "Do not say that those who are killed in the cause of God are dead: for they are alive although you do not perceive that." These are the same words we have encountered in ancient and medieval mythology, in German poetry of the last century, as well as in the poetry of other countries.

The martyrs are those who are killed in God's cause, and in God's cause alone — not in the name of king, nation, or for an ethnic cause, or for fame or glory. Jihad, like many other Islamic concepts, has been interpreted in various ways by different Muslim commentators.[35] Does it mean war, or does it refer to a moral struggle in which the individual tries to overcome his or her base instincts, as the Sufi school claims?

In the most influential of Hadith collections (al Bukhari), there are 199 references to jihad and each assumes that it means warfare. However, medieval Islamic jurists weakened somewhat the original implications of jihad, which would have meant uninterrupted struggle against all non-Muslim societies and states up to the final, worldwide victory of Islam over the nonbelievers. They pointed to the fact that the prophet himself had established temporary truces with his enemies.

This moderate interpretation, however, was by no means accepted by all. The most prominent representative of an aggressive interpretation was Ibn Taimiyah (1268–1328), who maintained that jihad as warfare was an elementary duty of every Muslim and that those rulers who did not accept this principle had to be considered nonbelievers or apostates.[36] His key text is from the Koran: "Prescribed for you is fighting though it be hateful to you" (Surah 2, 216). The Ibn Taimiyah tradition continued throughout the ages and with the emergence of radical Islamism became official ideology of an important segment of Muslim thought and politics. In an updated form it provides the doctrine of Islamic terrorism in the 1990s. The Ibn Taimiyah approach is based on the assumption that peace and a just social order will only prevail in the world once Islam has been victorious worldwide, for all other religions and ideologies want to persecute the true believers and aim at the defeat and downfall of Islam. (With all this, radical Muslims have their problems even with Ibn Taimiyah, who denied that Jerusalem was one of the holy places of Islam).

As for the question of afterlife, Islam teaches that the martyrs should not be mourned by their friends and loved ones, for there is no real sense of loss in their death. They continue to live, enjoying the hospitality of their Lord. The similarity with what the Nazi cult of death was saying about excessive mourning is striking as is the idea that the martyrs do not experience any pain at the time of their death. All their sins are forgiven, and they have the privilege of intervening on behalf of members of their family or clan to enable them also to enter paradise. There are detailed descriptions of paradise — wonderful gardens, streams with clean water, and above it a jeweled dome of pearls and rubies extending roughly from Damascus to Southern Yemen. The martyrs will recline on thrones and eat and drink meat and fruit with happiness. Some seventy thousand servants will wait on the martyrs and seventy black-eyed women, all of them fair virgins, young and full-breasted with wide lovely eyes, will be at their call.

Such luxurious conditions in the next life have been considered something of an embarrassment by some of the Koran commentators and radical Muslims in general. They have argued that for a young man from Gaza or Jenin preparing to be a *shahid* (martyr), Israeli occupation and the resistance against it are the decisive motives, not the lust for sexual gratification. This may well be the case, but the rewards are still promised and the act of martyrdom is, in fact, often described as a "wedding." After the suicide bombing committed in a Jerusalem suburb by Ayat al Akhras, an eighteen-year-old Palestinian girl, her three-year-old niece was reported saying, "I want to join my aunt in paradise."[37] Such a reaction was hardly the result of deep intellectual reflection or a profound emotional shock, not even peer pressure. It must have appeared to the little girl as the most natural thing to do in accordance with what she had learned from her elders.

Others have maintained that these descriptions of the joys of paradise belong to the less authoritative commentators and are not to be taken quite literally. However, many descriptions appear in the Koran more than once; the story of the virgins, for instance, appears in Koran Surat Waqiah, Surat At Tur, Surat An Naba, and is also repeated in the more authoritative Hadith.

Whether aspirants for martyrdom believe all the attractive details about life in paradise is yet another question. The fact that there are rivers with pure waters would clearly have impressed a seventh-century desert dweller much more than a contemporary young Arab accustomed to running water everywhere. The issue of the virgins has become a matter of considerable contention in societies in which sexual repression is common. Some translators of the Koran and the Hadith have used the term "angels" instead of virgins, but this did not make sense in the context. One of the most respected commentators, the Egyptian Jalal al Din al Suyuti (1445–1505), living in a less repressive age, described the sexual joys in most explicit terms. The martyrs, he wrote, would have a permanent erection and their penis would never soften; the sensation they feel will be so enormous that if one would experience it on earth one would faint. As for the women, always willing, they would have appetizing vaginas.[38]

A recent revisionist Western commentator has argued on the other hand that many parts of the Koran remain obscure if read in Arabic but become clearer if read in Syrian-Aramaic. According to his version, the virgins become "raisins of crystal clarity." But there are major problems with the discoveries of Dr. Christoph Luxenberg — the fact that crystal-clear raisins await them in paradise would not be that much of an attraction even for desert dwellers. Arab fundamentalists in any case will never accept such far-reaching revisions of the interpretation of the holy texts. And those indoctrinated about afterlife were told about virgins and not about Dr. Luxenberg's raisins.[39]

Suicide Terrorism — When and Where

Having briefly dealt with the geopolitics of suicide terrorism, the questions of the identity, the social background, and the motives of the perpetrators remain to be discussed. The most detailed breakdown in existence covers Israel. Altogether one hundred missions were undertaken up to July 2001 inside Israel and the occupied territories, which does not take into account the attacks carried out inside Lebanon during the occupation. Of these one hundred, thirty were launched during 2000–2001. Seventy-five terrorists were killed, twenty-five were intercepted before carrying out the attacks or captured because the explosives failed to detonate. (Between July 2001 and August 2002, ninety-eight suicide bombers went on their missions; thirty-five were intercepted or they failed to blow themselves up.[40]) Two-thirds belonged to Hamas, one-third to Islamic Jihad. Later on, such missions were organized by other groups such as the Al Aqsa Martyrs Brigade. Two-thirds of the "martyrs" were under the age of twenty-three and there was hardly anyone over the age of thirty. The majority came from Gaza (54 percent), 45 percent from the West Bank and one (the oldest) was an Israeli Arab. Twenty-three percent had an elementary education; the rest were high school graduates or had a higher education. Eighty-six were bachelors and fourteen were married. Of the 605 victims of suicide bombers (through August 2002), about 75 percent were civilians, including citizens of countries other than Israel.

Virtually all suicide bombers came from large families with many brothers and sisters; Hamas and Islamic Jihad announced that they would not select single children to engage in suicide missions. Some parents expressed great pride following the death of their children; others said that they would have prevented them from engaging in a suicide mission and that they were not willing to sacrifice more of their children. The young women among them were all unmarried; one of them had been divorced by her husband because she was infertile.

According to a survey by the Israeli security services in July 2002, details of which have not been published, a significant percentage of Palestinian suicide bombers suffered from an advanced form of serious diseases, organic or mental. Because this report was not scheduled to be published, propagandistic intentions were unlikely to be involved. Judgment will have to be suspended as long as the statistical details are not available.[41]

Islamic Jihad used, on the whole, younger bombers (aged seventeen or eighteen) who had received little training, and their attacks were frequently more primitive and caused fewer fatalities.[42] As the fighting against the Israelis continued in 2002, more women were among those who went to blow themselves up, as well as children aged thirteen and fourteen. After the death in April 2002 of two suicide bombers aged thirteen (Ismail Abu Nada and Anwar Hamduna), the Hamas leadership in Gaza came out against the use of children in such missions. A family of the Palestinian Authority said that the media were indirectly responsible because they daily broadcast programs glorifying martyrdom. A member of a family of one of these very young suicide bombers said in an interview that the decision to blow himself up could not possibly have been his.[43]

A Palestinian feminist (Sumaya Farhat Nasser) said in an interview that the suicide bombings were part of general brutalization in Palestinian society manifesting itself in violence within families, aggressivity in schools, and mental disease. According to her evidence, half the children were hyperactive and could not sit still for more than ten minutes.[44] On the other hand, interviews were published and documentaries shown in which mothers and fathers of the bombers expressed their total identification with their martyr-children, encouraging them and claiming that the day they killed themselves was the happiest day in their lives (Um Nidal about her son Muhammad).[45]

In comparison with the activities of the Palestinians, the (much fewer) international operations of al Qa'ida were planned a long time ahead, and those who took part in them came from a very different background. Some were Egyptians, some North Africans (mainly Algerians), but the majority came from Saudi Arabia. Their background was middle class or upper middle class; many came from professional families. The Saudis mainly originated from certain regions of the south, the Asir, and within these regions from certain tribes and clans. An astute Saudi observer noted that most of the suicide bombers came from a part of the country which had made enormous progress within the last three decades. This region was well-off and had become a center of tourism for the rest of the country. In view of these facts, the participation of the southerners had nothing to do with poverty but with certain indirect consequences of urbanization. The intellectual development had not proceeded at the same rate as technical progress. Southerners were trustworthy, God-fearing, and naïve people who tended to believe whatever the preachers told them, and certain preachers had used religion as a cover behind which to disseminate their venom. In brief, "they believe everything they are told. They listened more attentively than they should have done regardless of who stood in the preachers' pulpit."[46]

The majority of the Saudi suicide bombers had a higher education, but according to all the evidence their education was not exactly well rounded; it was almost exclusively technical. Their general knowledge was limited, and they were certainly not intellectuals in any meaningful sense of the word. Nor were many of the suicide bombers well versed in their own religion. They had frequently been to the mosque and said the ritual prayers, but how much they understood of Islam is yet another question. Mention has been made of the interesting fact that in one of the trials against Egyptian terrorist groups, offshoots of the Muslim Brotherhood, it emerged that the leader did not know a single verse from the Koran by heart and that this was by no means a unique case. In the farewell letter written by Muhammad Atta, the leader and coordinator of the group, to his comrades on the eve of September 11, there are not only elementary mistakes in Arabic, his native language (it might have been written in a hurry), but whenever he quotes the Koran (which he does frequently) he missed the obligatory invocation "the Almighty is right," which no pious Muslim would do.[47] Thus, the religious education of the suicide bombers is limited on the whole to some elementary quotations and incantations they heard from their preachers.

All this does not perhaps come as a particular surprise because the al Qa'ida operations were carried out in foreign countries, and those chosen or volunteering for them had to have certain knowledge of the outside world. The ability to move freely in Europe and America without attracting too much attention was more important than a thorough religious education. Such knowledge of the modern world could not be acquired in Pakistani religious schools or Palestinian refugee camps. But the lack of a thorough knowledge of so many of them of their own religion still shed interesting light on their motivation.

Within the radical Muslim International, there were considerable differences between those who had grown up in the Middle East and others who were enlisted in Western Europe. Among the latter were recent converts to radical Islam, petty criminals, drug smugglers, and quite often unstable characters who were chosen for terrorist missions because they had been to British, French, or German schools, were street-wise, and had the required technical and linguistic faculties.

A typical example for those recruited in Western Europe was Nizar Trabelsi, a North African who emigrated to Belgium and had a disappointing career as a footballer in Germany. He drank heavily, was later arrested for drug dealing, served a prison term in Germany, and then drifted into the al Qa'ida orbit. For him, as for others, radical religion seems to have been a way out of a dead-end existence, giving him a set of beliefs and perhaps a little hope, and above all allowing him to become part of a group of like-minded comrades. At the same time it led him to a life of action rather than resignation. Another such character was Richard Reid, born in England to a West Indian father (who spent the better part of his life in prison) and a British mother. He smuggled explosives in his shoes on board of an aircraft and (unsuccessfully) tried to ignite them. He was a dropout at school, was arrested for a string of minor crimes, and was converted to Islam by a radical Muslim preacher who took care of the inmates of a prison for juvenile offenders outside London.[48] Another al Qa'ida operator belongs to the same category; he tried to smuggle explosives from Canada to Seattle but was arrested owing to the watchfulness of a border guard near Vancouver. He too had a record of criminal offenses in Canada.

There are also the stories of the young Australian, enterprising but exceedingly moody, who became a drifter and ended up in Afghanistan; of a young Scotsman from a family of academics who dropped out at university, underwent psychiatric treatment, and also converted to Islam, ending up doing what he thought was his religious duty in Afghanistan. Another story concerns a boy from Marin County, California, a not atypical product of the ultra-permissive way of life of middle-class suburbia with all its confusions, who went to Afghanistan to be taken prisoner by his fellow countrymen. But these foreign volunteers joined the Taliban rather than al Qa'ida, nor do the stories imply that most suicide bombers were drifters or mentally unstable and/or had a record of crime. Professor Ariel Merari, a Tel Aviv University psychologist who has studied the phenomenon of Palestinian suicide terrorism probably more closely than anyone else, noted on the basis of many interviews that he did not find a single psychotic among the candidates for terrorism suicide. But according to some evidence, a great many had a weak ego, were unstable and were looking for a spiritual anchor and a sense of certainties and community in a bewildering world.

Suicide bombing in its most recent form appeared first in Lebanon in 1982–83 and was carried out by members of Hizbullah and Jihad al Islami, Shi'ite organizations trained, financed, and equipped by the Iranians. Initially many observers gained the impression that suicide terrorism was somehow a specific Shi'ite characteristic. They saw the origins of this phenomenon in the particular virulent character of the Shi'ia, the self-destructive and self-punishing elements (such as self-flagellation), in a movement which had received enormous fresh impetus as the result of the Khomeini revolution in Iran. As contemporary observers saw it, the Shi'ite suicide bombers were marching to their death as Husein, Muhammad's nephew, had done at the battle of Kerbela (632).

It should have been clear, however, at least from 1985 on, that suicide missions were by no means a Shi'ite monopoly; about half of the attacks in Lebanon were carried out by members of nationalist and left-wing organizations (including the Communist Party).[49] The latter were less effective than the Hizbullah operations, partly perhaps because the latter were less well organized and prepared than Hizbullah, which had Iranian instructors and money. Women were among the secular suicide bombers in Lebanon, whereas it would have been unthinkable for a radical Islamic organization to send anyone but a young man on such missions.

The part of women among the Tamil Tigers' suicide bombers has been noted, and it was even higher among the PKK suicide bombers in the 1990s. The PKK was a Kurdish militant group established by several students of Marxist-Leninist persuasion who demanded freedom for Kurdistan. However, the nationalist-separatist inspiration was infinitely stronger than the Marxist impulse, which became less and less prominent over time. The role of the leader, Abdallah

Ocalan, was preeminent (as it was among the Tamil Tigers), and it is significant that only one of the PKK suicide bombers had volunteered for the mission, while all others were selected.

Sixteen PKK suicide attacks altogether took place between 1994 and 1998, when the campaign petered out; there were eleven young women among the suicide bombers.[50] Most of these attacks caused relatively little damage or loss of life, primarily because of insufficient training and technical preparation. However, in the present context it is not success or failure that count but above all the decision to opt for suicide missions and the motives underlying it. The high percentage of PKK women among the terrorists has been explained against the background of the lower social standing of women in Kurdish society, mainly in the countryside where most of the support of the PKK came from, and their suffering. But this is not wholly convincing because the status of women in Muslim society was even lower, whereas in Tamil society women did not suffer from discrimination, which did not, however, prevent their participation in the terrorist struggle.

There is no need to enumerate every terrorist movement which has engaged in suicide missions to find common features and differences among them. Suicide missions have been chosen as a strategy for a variety of reasons. They frequently cause many victims and attract greater media attention than other terrorist attacks. They generate fear, even panic among the victims. They are relatively easy to plan because no route of escape is needed, and once a suicide terrorist is on his way, it is difficult to stop him; even if he does not succeed reaching his target, he will still be able in most cases to inflict some damage on the enemy while being apprehended.

If terrorism in general has attracted attention out of proportion to its intrinsic political importance in view of its sudden and mysterious character, the fact that seemingly everybody anywhere could be a target of suicide terrorism has had an even greater psychological impact.

The suicide terrorist is only the last link in a chain. There is no spontaneous suicide terrorism. The candidates are chosen by those in charge in the organization. The suicide terrorists are indoctrinated and trained — receiving intelligence information to guide them — and eventually are given the arms and explosives to carry out their mission. The people who guide the suicide terrorists have their political agenda. They organize the missions not as a purposeless manifestation of despair but to attain a certain political aim. While the suicide terrorist may be unstoppable, those behind him are certainly not; they can be deterred by inflicting unacceptable damage on them. Thus the leadership of the Lebanese Hizbullah after years of suicide terrorism discontinued these operations realizing that they were no longer very effective. Among Palestinians too, support for suicide terrorism vacillated. During Intifada Two, such support was high, but it declined following Israeli military counterblows. Enthusiasm for suicide terrorism seems to be confined to members of a certain generation. Once it is realized that the martyrdom of these young people does not bring the desired goal any nearer, the readiness to sacrifice one's life is bound to wane.

The motivation of the religious suicide terrorists is in many ways easier to explain than the secular. The radical Muslim has been promised various rewards such as life in paradise, his family will be taken care of, he knows he will not really be dead but continue another and much richer existence in the future. Support for the families of martyrs is an important consideration, as is the religious obligation to repay one's debts prior to the suicide mission — hence the financial help (amounting to about twenty-five thousand dollars) given to the families of suicide bombers by Iran and Iraq, as well as other Arab countries and Muslim foundations. In comparison, the families of those killed in open combat with the Israelis were paid merely two thousand dollars. Saudi Arabia provides a trip to Mecca for the members of the family of the suicide bomber, as well as other fringe benefits, such as housing. If in Sri Lanka the candidates for suicide had their last supper with the leader, there has been a thorough ritual in Lebanon and Palestine for the suicide terrorist to be photographed on the eve of his scheduled mission, to give his mission a solemn, quasi-religious character.

The secular suicide terrorist cannot have such expectations. But the differences between religious and secular motivation could be less wide than often assumed, for the underlying motives might be quite similar. There is the feeling of doing one's duty (religious, patriotic, or a mixture of the two) and of hate of the enemy, the infidel, the occupant. There are social and psychological pressures to engage in suicide missions. The readiness to sacrifice one's life is generated through a process of indoctrination — in orthodox religious schools or conspirational circles. Religious or ideological indoctrination needs some rootedness in an objective situation; the rage and the hate of the enemy have to be perceived as obvious. But in some cases the personality of the leader is sufficient to play the decisive role in committing acts that otherwise are incomprehensible, such as the collective suicide of groups of sectarians (Jonestown).

An analysis of the cult of suicide terrorism in Sri Lanka, which is not at all religious in character, shows far-reaching similarities with the Muslim cult. There is, in the words of a close student of the LTTE, an elaborate symbolism of death and resurrection and a sacrificial commitment to the nation, a demand for blind faith, a mysticism of blood, and an intimate communion of brotherhood: "The LTTE has divided the year into the veneration of martyrs on five fixed recurrent occasions."[51] The leadership of the Tamil Tigers claims to be "beyond religion," but in fact the concept of martyrdom is deeply religious even though (as a historian of the LTTE says) they are not aware of it. It is a political movement with religious sources and religious aspirations, and the same is true for the radical Muslim groups in the Middle East. Common to both is the concept of absolute obedience also mentioned in Muhammad Atta's last instructions to his comrades;

as Ignatius of Loyola, the founder of the order of the Jesuits, put it in his "Constitutiones," the members of the order have to obey God and their superiors *perinde ac si cadaver essent* — as if they were corpses.

But there are also certain important differences between the suicide terrorists of the LTTE and the Muslim bombers. The LTTE assassinated a fair number of leading enemy political figures, and most of their attacks were directed against military and police targets. They proudly counted the number of suicide attacks in order to commemorate them, but the attacks against civilian targets were not included in their count. The Tigers considered attacks against civilian aims "terrorist" in character, and even if they committed such acts they wanted to be remembered as soldiers in a national liberation army. This was much in contrast to the doctrine of such organizations as Hamas and Islamic Jihad but also al Qa'ida, which believed that the concept of jihad gave them a priori permission to use all and any targets in their holy war.

A variety of psychological explanations, analytical and from the field of orthodox psychiatry, have been adduced to explain suicide terrorism, including the concept of "overvalued ideas" — that is to say, the obsessive belief in an idea, or ideology or set of values.[52] This might account for a fanaticism which includes the willingness to sacrifice one's own life but also for those who are sending the suicide bombers on their mission. But it is doubtful whether complex explanations are apposite; the motives are almost always rooted in the general historical, cultural, and social context, in the society in which the future suicide bombers are growing up.

This is a closed society with the emphasis on obeisance; a critical attitude, so dear to the West in modern times, is wholly absent. Into this society the suicide terrorist is born — or he opts for it in his search for spiritual certainties; converts become more easily fanatics than others. It is doubtful whether the content of the indoctrination is of decisive importance. It could be a firm religious belief, or extreme nationalism or another ideology appealing to deep-seated urges. Dr. Eyad Serraj, a Gaza psychiatrist, has argued that in every case of suicide bombing there has been a personal trauma or tragedy, such as the killing of a friend or close relation by the Israeli occupants.[53] But this explanation does not apply to the Saudi suicide bombers of September 11, none of whom lived under Israeli occupation, nor, if true, is it of any relevance to suicide bombers in Lebanon, Kashmir, or other parts of the world. Algerian psychiatrists have pointed to the central importance of the appeal to *khulud* (immortality), *shahid* (martyr), and *al adhiya* (sacrifice), as well as the cult of death in the indoctrination of the Algerian radical preachers in the indoctrination of youth. But Algeria has been free for decades. The occupation of the country by foreigners cannot have been an issue.[54]

Arab psychiatrists have pointed out that suicide bombers tend to be introverted, but this like some other observations remains to be investigated. Akio

Namimura, a member of the Aum sect which carried out the attack on the Tokyo underground, told an interviewer that when he graduated from school he faced two alternatives: become a monk or commit suicide. He also said that the pre-dictions of Nostradamus had a great influence on his generation.[55] But it is not certain that this case was typical for many of his generation in Japan, let alone in other cultures and civilizations.

How does one account for the fact that, as in the cases of the Manhattan and Pentagon bombers, the indoctrination survived years of exposure to the tempta-tions of Western civilization? We are dealing with a relatively small group, and it is not at all certain that, in the long run, the majority of those exposed to the temptations are not bound to be corrupted. As for the minority who will remain impervious, they physically live in Western society but their hearts and minds are still at home with the gurus of their formative years. In a very few cases, al Qa'ida members (such as the shoe bomber from London or a young Arab of Swedish nationality with a Finnish mother) were actually born in Europe; for them, the excitement of belonging to a conspiracy may have been the single most powerful motive.

The great majority has, however, come from the Middle East. They lived together even in London, Paris, and Hamburg; they prayed and spent most of their free time in a small circle of like-minded people. Far from being absorbed by the customs and manners of this civilization, they may feel pushed into the defensive, alienated by what is (or what they consider to be) the sinful way of life to which they are exposed. When Sayed Qutb, the ideologist of radical Islam, went to America in the late 1940s, a drunken woman allegedly tried to seduce him on ship. This incident played an important role in turning him decisively against the West. We have only Qutb's word for it, and it is known that he always had problems with the opposite sex, but as so often is the case, the perception counts; it is the story of Joseph and Potiphar's wife, and the temptations of the flesh to which some Christian martyrs were exposed.

The psychology of the closed mind has not been studied so far very thoroughly. The fact that the suicide terrorist may have acquired a technical education in the West does not mean that he has understood (let alone shares) Western val-ues. The indoctrination begins at a very early age; signs on the walls of Hamas kindergartens in the occupied territories in Palestine read "the children are the holy martyrs of tomorrow." According to Dr. Huda Zakaria, an Egyptian soci-ologist who has studied the suicide terrorist phenomenon, the terrorist group is different from the previous group (such as the family); it does not plant its values gradually through childhood and youth toward a constructive aim but prepares him for destruction and death: "The person who plants such ideas in the mind of a youngster turns him into a loose cannon after his personality has been reshaped in the interests of the new group.... It activates rapid indoctrination by the most sacred means for the soul such as religious belief." In the words of the Egyptian sociologist, the candidate for suicide terrorism is activated by remote control and can explode at any moment. In at least one case in Palestinian suicide terrorism, the detonation was effected not by the bomber but by remote control — a phone call.

Indoctrination is the central factor, but it is not unique or new. It can be found throughout history in the psychological preparation of many young people prepared for military elite units, in various secret societies — the Janissaries in the Turkish empire, for instance, or the SS in their *Ordensburgen* — and in other places. The suicide terrorist no longer thinks; he finds his inspiration and refuge in prayer, as outlined in Mohammed Atta's letter to his comrades before the attack of September 11, 2001.[56] There should be a ritual washing and shaving, and the night is to be spent in prayer trying to forget the world. Then there should be further prayers, and after this Atta advises the others, "Smile and feel secure. For God is with the believers and the angels are guarding him without him feeling it." We do not know, however, whether all or any of the suicide bombers did indeed spend the last night praying; some reportedly spent it in a bar or a night club.

Once the terrorist is seated in the plane, there is more prayer. He is to keep busy with repeated invocations of God and the travel prayer should be recited, because the terrorist is traveling straight to God. His heart is now purified and he is entitled to slaughter like cattle anyone resisting him and also hostages who do not resist. Slaughtering is an offering on behalf of God, as well as his parents; it is an act of grace conferred on the terrorist by Allah.[57]

These, in brief outline, are some of the features of the psychology of the suicide terrorist motivated by religion or quasi-religious creeds. The subject is exceedingly difficult to investigate. Just as there are various terrorisms, the character and the motivation of suicide terrorists differ from country to country. Only very few of those who feel intensely motivated about politics or religion are willing to sacrifice their lives. In other words, while indoctrination is crucial, a psychological predisposition ought to exist too. But since the candidates for such missions are unlikely to submit to tests and discussions about their motives (of which, in any case, they may not be fully aware), the issue will remain to a large extent the subject of speculation.

The issue of indoctrination (or brainwashing) has figured prominently in connection with the activities of some of the new religious cults (and sects) in Europe and America. In several Western European countries, brainwashing has been made a crime, and much effort has been invested in finding effective ways of "deprogramming" those affected. The American Psychological Association has commented on mind control; the cults and sects affected have violently protested against any attempt to restrict what they consider freedom of religious practice.[58] Some of these sects have induced their members to commit collective suicide. If it is possible to persuade hundreds of people to commit suicide, it stands to reason that it is possible with equal ease to make them engage in suicide terrorism.

Muslim terrorist groups, but also others engaging in suicide terrorism, have argued that indoctrination is of no importance, that jihad is a religious obligation, and that more volunteers apply for action than they can use for such missions. But the evidence shows that wherever suicide terrorism occurs, preachers (or nationalist propagandists) play a crucial role in creating a climate conducive to such action. As for the psychological disposition, it has emerged from interviews with suicide bombers who were caught or failed in their missions that, when asked for their motives, they repeated, usually verbatim, what they had been told by their spiritual teachers. Obviously, one would look in vain for critical spirits or independent thinkers among them.

Suicide terrorism has appeared incomprehensible to people living in secular societies in which, by and large, ideological passion was a spent force and fanaticism had become a phenomenon restricted to marginal groups. It seemed not only mysterious but also invincible, for how could anyone resist enemies willing to sacrifice their lives? Suicide terrorism can spread panic, at least momentarily, among the "enemy"; it can cause substantial financial damage to the enemy, as in the case of Israel.

It is also a useful tool in the battle for public opinion outside the country directly involved. With all this there has been a tendency to overrate the importance of suicide terrorism. It has been tried in a dozen countries and it has been discontinued in most — even by the Lebanese Hizbullah and the Tamil Tigers, who were the most prominent suicide bombers at the time. The economic damage caused has not been fatal; a handful of dishonest heads of corporations in the United States have caused more damage to the stock markets and the reputation of the capitalist system than all terrorists taken together.

As far as the frequency of suicide bombing is concerned, in recent years Israel has been the exception, partly because of the considerable number of those volunteering for suicide missions but mainly because of the mistakes of the Israeli governments: political mistakes such as the desire to hold on to all the territories occupied in 1967, tactical mistakes rooted in ideological obstinacy. Israel has the most effective and sophisticated technology to combat terrorism, but it has refused for a long time to apply it because of the unwillingness to give up territories or to divide Jerusalem. Walls and other physical obstacles are not a panacea; they cannot, for instance, prevent cross-border artillery duels as in Kashmir. But they are bound to reduce suicide missions to a large degree.

Suicide terrorism is asymmetric warfare par excellence: It knows no rules. The martyrs are permitted to use even the most devastating weapons, concentrating attacks against civilians, for they seem people driven to despair by lack of hope. The state, in contrast, is not permitted to retaliate effectively; it has to stick to rules and conventions. It is curious that there has been so much emphasis on the elements of despair and lack of hope among Western commentators; they probably played a role in some cases but not in many others. The young Saudis who hijacked the planes on September 11, to give but one example, were certainly not driven by lack of hope, and in any case those motivated by religious belief are certain to enter paradise upon blowing themselves up. In other words, they are full of hope, rather than despair.

As for the invincibility of the suicide bombers, we have it on the authority of Tertullian (A.D. 160–225) that the blood of the martyrs is the seed of the church.[59] But a Christian martyr in the early pacifist tradition is not really comparable to a believer in jihad, and seen in historical perspective, Islam expanded as the result of its military campaigns, not because of turning the other cheek.

Suicide terrorism is not a sporadic phenomenon. It needs not only people willing to become martyrs but also organizers and coordinators. This is where suicide terrorism is most vulnerable, and it is also doubtful whether there is an unlimited reservoir of candidates for such missions. Suicide terrorism has been a more effective weapon than other terrorist strategies, but only when those targeted have adopted the wrong political and military countermeasures.[60]

Enthusiasm for martyrdom persists as long as there is a reasonable chance that it will lead to victory. Sacrifice must have a purpose.[61] It can prevent reconciliation and even trigger a war. But what if, after years of such missions and hundreds of martyrs, the suicide bombers and their dispatchers feel no nearer to their target? Or what if the militants prevail in their campaign, as they did in the case of Algeria fighting France — and if the political system that emerges is the opposite of what the militants had hoped for? Prabhakaran, the chief guru of the Tamil Tigers, once remarked that his ethnic group would achieve independence in a hundred years in any case but that terrorism would shorten the process. With remarkable persistence and ingenuity, the Tamil Tigers engaged in a terrorist campaign which lasted almost twenty years and resulted in few achievements and a great deal of ruin. Among the Palestinians too, intellectuals began to ask questions in the summer of 2002 not so much about the morality of suicide bombing inside Israel but about its efficacity. The majority of the Palestinians still believed that it was their most effective weapon. But how to keep up the momentum in the long run? This is the dilemma bound to face campaigns of suicide bombing sooner or later.

FIVE

Israel and the Palestinians

THE CONFLICT BETWEEN Israelis and Palestinians, a struggle between two peoples over one country, has manifested itself over the years in every possible form of political violence: regular warfare and civil war, guerrilla warfare and terrorism, civil disobedience, and even warfare by proxy. Our concern is not with the conflict per se but only with the terrorist element which, as so often, is not easy to separate, because it frequently appears in combination with other forms of political violence.

Terrorism did play a major role in the conflict: Some of the leading actors in the drama, such as King Abdullah of Jordan, Anwar el Sadat, and Prime Minister Rabin, were killed by terrorists. True, Abdullah's heirs continued his policy, and the same is true, *grosso modo,* for Mubarak, who succeeded Sadat. Had Rabin lived, he would have faced the same difficulties on the road to peace which confronted those who came after him. But with all this, terrorism greatly influenced public opinion, and it certainly made a most difficult political problem even more impossible to solve.

The Arab riots of 1920 and 1929 were violent attacks in the major cities against the Jews, who were considered invaders by the Palestinian Arabs. In 1929, it was believed by many Arabs that the Jews wanted to infringe on the religious rights of the Muslims in the Old City. But even then the issue at stake was not only Jerusalem and Zionism; the Jewish community of Hebron, which had been there for centuries and was anything but Zionist, was virtually wiped out in a massacre.

The riots of 1936 also spread to the countryside; it was at one and the same time a popular rebellion and a settling of scores (more Arabs were killed by Arabs than Jews and Englishmen) and it was in part guerrilla warfare. To what extent was it successful? The riots of 1936 certainly had an impact on British policy inasmuch as Jewish immigration was drastically cut. But there is much reason to believe that the British would have engaged on a policy of this kind in any case; war clouds were on the horizon, and for the British the good will of the Arabs was far more important than that of the Jews, who were much fewer and whose support against Hitler could be taken for granted. Furthermore, the restrictions of immigration were carried out already in 1936 at the very beginning of the Arab uprising or even before.

The end of World War II and the postwar years witnessed the emergence of Jewish terrorism, of Irgun and the Stern gang. They were urban in character and directed against the British Mandatory government. They and their sympathizers have argued ever since that their terrorism played a decisive role in getting the British out of Palestine and the establishment of a Jewish state. But this is far from certain. Once the British had decided to give up India, there was no strategic reason to hold on to the Middle East bases — which had always been intended to serve as a bridge to the British possessions in South and Southeast Asia. In other words, the British would have given up their League of Nations Mandate in any case, just as they withdrew from Egypt and other bases. At most it could be argued that but for the activities of the Zionist terrorists they might have withdrawn a bit later; in this case the political constellation would have been less auspicious from a Zionist point of view, for in the meantime the Cold War would have started and there might not have been a majority in the United Nations in favor of establishing a Jewish and a Palestinian state. But it is still likely that a Jewish state would have come into being sooner or later anyway.

The Palestinians rejected the UN resolution of November 1947 and with it the right to have a state of their own, which, in retrospect, was a major mistake, however unsatisfactory a solution this was from their point of view. As a result what should have been a Palestinian state became part of Jordan. The Jewish state that came into being was not accepted by its Arab neighbors. There was a considerable amount of violence, mainly crossing of the border by armed Arab refugees. But there were also acts of terror committed by politically motivated *fidayin*, forerunners of the terrorists of the 1970s and 1980s who had the support of the Egyptian and sometimes also the Jordanian army. This led to Israeli retaliation and thus began the long spiral of action and reaction. It was not quite a guerrilla war, but rather cross-border hit-and-run raids of short duration. Israel was a small country and there was nowhere to hide. Conditions for guerrilla warfare simply did not exist. But the raids were still a major nuisance. As an Israeli report put it at the time, "It disturbs the peace, engenders an atmosphere of war and harms the economy both directly and indirectly and by necessitating extensive security measures."[1]

The Six-Day War (1967) ended in a stunning Israeli victory, with all the territory that should have been the original Palestinian state now under Israeli control. It is difficult to argue that the Israelis missed opportunities to make peace with the Arabs before 1967; the country was too small and its image too feeble, and it could make no further territorial concessions. In any case, most Arabs thought that Israel would not survive.

This changed decisively in 1967. True, the Arab governments still declared that they would never make peace with Israel, but the image of the Jewish state had been transformed. It was now able to act from a position of strength. But instead of actively pursuing a policy of defusing the conflict, it waited for Arab initiatives that never came.[2] Instead of giving up voluntarily the territories that had been occupied, many settlements were established, frequently by national-religious settlers who believed that the whole of historical Palestine was theirs by right. Jews settled not only in the outskirts of Jerusalem but also in Hebron and in outlaying places far away from other Jewish settlements and very near to Arab towns and villages. These prestige settlements had to be heavily subsidized on a permanent basis; it should also have been clear that from a security point of view these settlements constituted a nightmare.

It could, of course, be argued that it was not at all certain that surrender would have led to peace with the Arabs. But it is still clear in retrospect that most of the territories should have been given up unilaterally, simply because Israel was not in a position to hold on to them indefinitely as the price was too high. The Arab population was too large to be incorporated into Israel, and the settlement policy — far from making the country more secure — created borders that were difficult or impossible to defend.

A nationalist-religious mythology developed after 1967 which made it difficult for Israeli governments to conduct a rational policy; the same was true with regard to Jerusalem. The aim of Zionism prior to 1967 had not been the physical possession of the whole city and the control of all the holy sites. In fact, the attitude of Zionist leaders toward Jerusalem had been ambiguous at best; they did not like the city, which embodied much that was negative in Jewish history and from which the Zionists wanted to dissociate themselves. The ministers and the members of the Knesset came to the sessions in Jerusalem, but most continued to live in Tel Aviv. As the result of the insistence on Israeli rule on an undivided Jerusalem, the conflict between Israelis and Palestinians turned a territorial conflict into a religious confrontation with the whole Muslim world. The failure to take decisive action after 1967 was a colossal mistake. The longer the occupation lasted, the more difficult it became to maintain it and the more intractable the conflict became.

Fatah, which in later years became the main antagonist of Israel, was founded in the early 1960s by a group of ex-Palestinians studying in Cairo, among them Yasir Arafat.[3] At about the same time (1964), the Palestine Liberation Organization (PLO) was founded following a resolution by the major Arab states to set up a organization uniting the various Palestinian groups existing at the time. Fatah was the most active of these groups, and within a short time it took over the PLO and launched terrorist operations inside Israel. These were, in the early days (1964–86), small scale, such as an attempt to blow up a section of the Israel main water carrier.[4]

Terrorism on a massive scale began only after the Six-Day War. The first such spectacular attack was the hijacking of an El Al flight from Rome, forcing it to land in Algiers. This was followed in September 1970 by a mass hijacking of three American and one Swiss airliners, which were later blown up on the ground in

Dawson's Field, Jordan. The most spectacular attack was the massacre of eleven Israeli athletes at the Munich Olympic Games. The hijackings were carried out by a group called the Popular Front of the Liberation of Palestine.

Fatah had been originally close to the Muslim Brotherhood in Egypt, but under Nasser the Brotherhood was no longer *persona grata*, and Fatah without difficulty adapted itself to the then-prevailing ideology of radical pan-Arab nationalism. The aim was the return to Palestine, and the only means to achieve this was "armed struggle." Fatah also invoked in its manifestoes a concept of the Palestinian revolution leading to a world revolution liberating the world from colonialism and imperialism. But this concession to the Zeitgeist was not taken too seriously and later on tacitly dropped.

The strategy of Fatah at the time was to launch a guerrilla war in the West Bank and Gaza, but this was bound to fail because the West Bank unlike the countries in which guerrilla war had been successful, had no jungles and desolate mountain areas; there was nowhere to hide. Thus the activities of Fatah consisted at the time mainly of attacks across the border, mainly from Jordan and Lebanon. This involved the organization from an early date in a military confrontation with the Jordan and Lebanese governments, which had to suffer the consequences in the form of Israeli counterblows for which they were not prepared. This in turn led to major fighting in Jordan ("Black September"), as the result of which Fatah was thrown out of that country. Later on, there was a similar confrontation in Lebanon, where Fatah clashed with the Christian militias and for a while also with the Shi'ites in the south of the country.

The Popular Front for the Liberation of Palestine was founded only after the Six-Day War. It was based on a number of political groups which had been in existence since the late 1940s, and most prominent among its leaders was a Christian Arab physician, Dr. George Habash. Its ideology at the time was Marxist-Leninist, which it regarded as a "scientific guide to revolutionary action." In the global struggle between communism and imperialism, it saw its place firmly in the camp of Cuba, Vietnam, North Korea, and the left-wing terrorist forces in Western Europe with which it cooperated. It also regarded the Arab bourgeoisie an "objective ally of Zionism" against which war should be waged.[5]

PFLP carried out some fifteen spectacular attacks between 1968 and 1972, which attracted worldwide attention, such as the hijacking of airplanes and attacks on embassies, but there was nothing specifically Marxist-Leninist in its strategy nor did it enhance in any way its aim to establish a revolutionary party or to battle the Arab bourgeoisie. Such a political doctrine helped them get assistance from the Soviet Union and other Communist countries, even though there were doubts in Moscow early on concerning the depth of their ideological commitment, which indeed became weaker and weaker over the time. The PFLP was weakened furthermore by the secession in 1969 of the Popular Democratic Front for the Liberation of Palestine headed by Naif Hawatme, also a Christian Arab, a native of Jordan, which in turn also split in two.

Like the PFLP, the PDFLP belonged in later years to the "rejectionist front," those opposing peace negotiations with Israel under any circumstances.[6]

The followers of Hawatme gradually weakened in their opposition, however, and began to cooperate with Arafat. They engaged in several cross-border attacks against Israel, most notably the raid on a school in northern Israel (Ma'alot) in which twenty-seven schoolchildren were killed, and attacks in Bet Shean and Jerusalem. But on the whole, the PDFLP put greater stress on political work than on what it defined as the "romanticism of terrorism" of the PFLP. It was originally supported by Syria and Libya, but this was later discontinued as the number of its members shrank and some joined the PLO.

Around 1973 (and partly as the result of the Yom Kippur War that year), the major Palestinian groups decided to engage no longer in international terrorist attacks (e.g., hijacking of planes) which had given them diminishing returns; those that took place thereafter (such as the Mogadishu hijacking, Entebbe, the Achille Lauro affair, etc.) were undertaken by small renegade factions. The new Fatah strategy was to gain a firm foothold in southern Lebanon, which was to be used as a springboard against Israel. But this involved Fatah in the Lebanese civil war, which led to the Israeli invasion in 1982. Fatah became involved in internecine struggle with other Arab regimes; one of the original reasons of Syrian invasion into Lebanon was to reduce the influence of Arafat. Following the siege of Beirut by the Israelis, Arafat and the PLO leadership had to be evacuated to Tunis (1982).

The Israeli invasion of Lebanon and the establishment of a security zone in the south of that country, which was maintained up to the year 2000, provided security for residents of Northern Palestine against cross-border attacks, but a price had to be paid. Israeli forces had been welcomed at first by the Shi'ites in South Lebanon but as the result of the prolonged occupation, the Shi'ites turned against Israel. Their political military organizations, Amal, and above all Hizbullah, became stronger and with the support of Iran and Syria constituted a formidable threat. About eight hundred Israeli soldiers and those of its allies, the SLA Christian militia, were killed — over a period of fifteen years.[7]

The irregular Palestinian forces fighting Israel changed their strategy several times over the years in accordance with the general world situation and the state of affairs in the Middle East. Originally the emphasis had been on spectacular attacks in various parts of the world, above all the hijacking of the planes. But these exploits did Fatah more harm than good; meanwhile the PLO had been recognized diplomatically by many countries as the representative of the Palestinian people, and the hijackings were considered unbecoming a player on the international scene.

In 1988, a state of Palestine was officially declared, and the year after, at the Madrid conference, the peace process began slowly.

Terrorist attacks did occur in the following years, but they were carried out mostly not by Fatah but by small "independent" terrorist groups such as Abu Nidal (a Syrian-sponsored organization) or by the Iranian secret service (in Argentina). In the measure that Fatah became a "state on the way," it had to conform to established rules. It could not give up terrorist activities altogether to boost morale on the West Bank; at the same time it could no longer devote most of its energies to this pursuit, nor could it afford to endanger its international standing by attacks that would bring it negative publicity.

Altogether it is estimated that about 80 percent of the attacks between 1970 and 2000 were directed against Israeli civilians, the rest against various sorts of military targets. According to Israeli sources, about 45 percent of the attacks consisted of explosive bombs, 28 percent fire bombs, 14 percent shelling of Israeli settlements from across the border, and 5 percent other forms of armed assault. Among the more spectacular forms of terrorist attacks were hostage takings (about eighteen) and suicide bombing. During the first Intifada, about half of the attacks were thought to be spontaneous, but since its end the great majority of attacks were planned and carried out by one of the major terrorist organizations. Not included in these statistics are attacks against Israeli or Jewish targets outside Israel.

The outbreak of the Intifada in December 1987 seemed to point a way out of this dilemma, even though there is no evidence that this campaign had been planned in detail by the PLO leadership. The immediate occasion was a traffic accident in the Gaza strip in which Arabs were killed by an Israeli truck, but there was so much tension that an outbreak could have occurred at any time. A spontaneous civil resistance campaign began with strikes and commercial shutdowns accompanied by violent (though unarmed) demonstrations against the occupying forces. The stone and occasionally the Molotov cocktail and the knife were the weapons, not guns and bombs.[8] Those in the forefront of the struggle were young boys, and the image of mere children throwing stones at Israeli tanks and heavily armed soldiers did the Palestinian cause a world of good — it was certainly asymmetric warfare — David against Goliath, anything but terrorism, a popular uprising.

Fatah had little control over the Intifada in the beginning. Its leadership was still in faraway Tunis, and the moving spirits on the West Bank and Gaza were leaders of Hamas (more below) or Islamist sympathizers. This assessment has been disputed by the PFLP, which argued that for the first three months of the Intifada, the Hamas leadership stood aside. The initial tactics in the Intifada were those of civil disobedience — nonpayment of taxes, noncooperation with the Israeli authorities. But almost from the beginning there was an element of terrorist violence, which grew as time went on. One was the killing of Arab "collaborators"; these included some who had indeed acted as informers or had helped the Israelis in other ways. But there were also killings of people who were wholly innocent of these charges but who became victims of a mass hysteria. Some score-settling between families and clans also took place. It is thought that between three hundred and four hundred such people were killed by mobs, sometimes to the embarrassment of the leadership.

The Intifada militants also began more or less systematically to burn fields, orchards, and forests which were Jewish property; no lives were lost, but considerable damage was caused. Lastly there were clashes in which groups of schoolchildren hikers were stoned and injured. Then there was the Temple Mount riot in October 1990, when masses of Arab worshipers attacked the police and then Jews who were praying nearby. Eighteen Arabs were killed and many Arabs and Jews were injured. There is no reason to assume that this incident was planned. It was the rush of many thousands of people congregating in a narrow space, of pushing and shoving and stone throwing and the presence of an insufficient number of policemen.

The (first) Intifada caused Israel considerable economic losses, and some eighty Israelis were killed. The number of Arabs killed during the first three years was much higher — between four hundred (Israeli estimates) and seven hundred (Arab estimates). The Intifada caused political polarization among the Jews of Israel and affected the morale of the army. On the Arab side the economic damage was enormous, and the radicalization of the younger generation became a major political factor. The Intifada lasted for six years and was called off at the time of the first Oslo agreement in 1993. But terrorist operations, though they took place, were only an incidental element in the course of the Intifada. It was a popular, and in the beginning mainly spontaneous, uprising.[9] The typical terrorist operations which took place in the latter part of the Intifada, and especially during the year thereafter, were planned and carried out by a new player: Hamas, to which we turn next.

Hamas

Hamas (*Harakat al muqawamah al Islamiyah*, "Islamic resistance movement") was originally a branch of the Muslim Brotherhood in Palestine. It had been active as a religious and cultural organization for many years and, like the Egyptian Brotherhood, provided social assistance to the needy.[10] The Brotherhood (or Islamic Trend, as it was often referred to) had taken a modest part in the riots of 1936–38. It had an office in Jerusalem and was active in the organization of Arab resistance in 1947–48, and it continued to exist under Jordanian rule when it took part in parliamentary elections.

After the Six-Day War, the Brotherhood was active above all in the Gaza district, where it even enjoyed a certain amount of patronage on the part of the

Israeli authorities, which may have regarded it as a counterweight against Fatah. Hamas was legally registered in Israel in 1979 (as yet under a different name) as an organization engaging in religious education, the building of mosques, the establishment of social clubs, and social work. It was headed by Sheikh Ahmed Yassin, who had been paralyzed ever since an accident in his younger years.

The politicization and radicalization of Hamas occurred in 1987–88 as the result of a number of circumstances. It was part of the general trend of radicalization that occurred in the Muslim world at the time. The economic conditions in Gaza, the fortress of Hamas, added fuel, and there was also the competition with Fatah and PLO, which were much less orthodox Islamic in outlook. In later years, Hamas engaged in self-criticism, noting that during the earlier phase of its activities it had been guilty of neglecting jihad, which made it possible for nationalist and communist organizations to outflank it. These "leftist organizations" (according to Hamas) had been brainwashing the young generation simply because Hamas had not played an active role in the national struggle.[11]

The turn to jihad manifested itself in the Hamas charter published in 1987, which said that the aim of the Islamic movement was holy war: Since the land of Palestine had been entrusted to the Muslims until judgment day, no Arab state and not even all Arab states together were entitled to give up any part of it.[12] Jihad against the Christians and Jews was an individual religious duty for every Muslim. The Palestinian cause was a religious obligation, and the young generation had to be trained to engage in this struggle. Even Muslim women had the right to engage in jihad, without the permission of their husbands if need be, just as slaves had the right to go on jihad without asking their masters.

According to the Hamas charter, there was no room for a peaceful solution and international conferences to resolve the Palestine conflict. These were merely games for children, and the people of Palestine were too noble to engage in such maneuvers. The only purpose of negotiations was to establish the rule of unbelievers in the land of the Muslims — and as the Koran says, Christians and Jews will never be pleased unless Muslims accept their religion. In its English language publications, Hamas claims that the jihad was not directed against Jews as followers of a religion. But this is difficult to combine with the anti-Semitic references made at the same time in Hamas propaganda to Nazi "documents" such as the *Protocols of the Elders of Zion*.[13]

This uncompromising Jihad doctrine involved Hamas in certain contradictions. The Muslim Brotherhood and the other radical Islamists had always rejected nationalism as an alien Western importation. This had been the core of their struggle against Nasser, Sadat, and the Syrian rulers. Hamas tried to find a way around this doctrinal problem by declaring that Arab nationalism was not bad, provided it considered itself part and parcel of the Islamic ideology. In other words, other nationalisms were materialistic and secular, whereas the Hamas Palestinian nationalism was Islamic and had a "divine banner." This provided the ideological justification for collaboration with other Palestinian nationalist groups that were secular, or in any case did not share its radical Islamic orientation.

The Hamas leadership stated that it would be only too happy to collaborate with nationalist groups that it regarded with respect and appreciation. Only those of the Marxist left were excluded because they were loyal to the Communist East (or groups whose loyalty was with the Crusading West). Hamas declared that it felt closer to the PLO and Fatah than to any other organizations — how could one turn a cold shoulder to family or close friends? "We have but one homeland, one affliction, one shared destiny." The charter went on issuing stern warnings against the Freemasons, Rotarians, and Lions; these clubs were dens of spies for the benefit and guidance of the Zionists, who were also behind the alcohol and drug trade. The charter refers specifically to the *Protocols of the Elders of Zion,* the famous nineteenth-century forgery purporting to be the blueprint for Jewish domination of the world. In brief, in basic respects Hamas followed the doctrine of the extreme right in Europe and of Nazism; there was no fashionable nonsense about anti-imperialism or anti-colonialism, let alone postmodernism.

The only doctrinal concession made was a declaration toward the end of this programmatic document that Hamas was a humanist movement which would never attack followers of other religions. It was perfectly possible for Christians and Jews to live in peace and harmony with Muslims — in the shade of Islam and under its rule. The term used is *dhimmi,* meaning second-class citizens, paying a tax to the Muslims for protecting them. There was criticism of Egypt and other countries who had dropped out of the jihad. Hamas regarded this as high treason.

The charter may have provided a solution for a variety of doctrinal problems on the theoretical level, but it did not always work out in practice. There were tensions from the beginning with Fatah and the PLO. Fatah was surprised by the sudden emergence of Hamas as a strong competitor in the struggle for power. Hamas had a substantial infrastructure, above all in the Gaza district but also on the West Bank, through its clubs and other grassroots organizations, stronger perhaps than Fatah. Fatah was afraid that Hamas would outflank it as the more radical and militant organization. Hamas also had considerable financial support from Saudi Arabia, the Gulf states, and Islamist organizations elsewhere. Furthermore, Hamas was undermining the position of the PLO as the future government of Palestine; how could the PLO engage in negotiations with other countries if it was not in full control? Fatah did not, of course, oppose terrorism per se, but it wanted to use it in support of its political initiatives, and the activities of Hamas made this impossible.

Coexistence between Fatah and Hamas was thus uneasy from the very beginning. Hamas published anti-Fatah leaflets as early as 1987, accusing its leader both of cowardice and corruption. There were violent clashes between followers of the two camps, culminating in fighting in Gaza in 1994 when eighteen Palestinians were killed and more were injured.[14]

This clash was followed by peace negotiations and periods of close collabora-tion, but quite often the old conflicts would again come out in the open. Hamas was too strong to be ignored or suppressed by the PLO. According to public opinion polls carried out by the Palestinian Center for Studies and Research in Nablus, support for Hamas was about 20 percent in 1993–95, but it was higher among university students and in Gaza. Thus Fatah had to take measures against their rivals from time to time if it did not want to lose face altogether. True, Hamas, with all its extremist slogans, was willing to make tactical concessions. It would declare a truce from time to time — one lasting almost a year. It would cooperate with the secular PFLP in the "rejection front" against the PLO. It would meet American diplomats and engage in political activities and fund raising in the United States. Sheikh Yasin would remain its spiritual leader, but political power passed into other hands, most notably Dr. Musa Marzuq, who was born in a refugee camp, had graduated in engineering in Egypt, and later, for more than ten years, lived in the United States. He acted as chief negotiator with the PLO and also with the Iranian government, the main supporters of Hamas.

Terrorist activities of Hamas began in 1988–89, soon after the outbreak of the first Intifada. Its military arm was the Izz a Din Kassem squad (or battalion or brigade), named after a sheikh who had been fighting the British in Palestine in 1935. The first operations were directed against fellow Arabs, but from 1989 there were several cases of anti-Israeli attacks, two Jews were stabbed to death in Gaza, two Israeli soldiers were killed, and three workers employed in a Jaffa factory were stabbed to death. Generally speaking, the knife was the favorite weapon during the early years of jihad, although in one case (October 1991), Israeli civilians were run over at a hitchhiking station near Tel Aviv. In another case (June 1992), a civilian was attacked by an axe-wielding assailant. Another favorite approach was to offer a lift to soldiers waiting in a queue and to kill them once inside a car (the cars had Israeli license plates and the attackers chosen were fluent in Hebrew). Lastly there were occasional shootings from speeding cars. Almost all the terrorists came from Gaza and vicinity.[15] Only rarely was an attempt made to enlist Israeli Arabs for terrorist operations.

There was not yet great sophistication in the use of explosives, nor had candi-dates been trained for suicide missions. This began to change in 1993–94 when Hamas had enlisted experts for bomb making, and the first suicide bombers went into action. Some of the very early operations aborted. The first successful suicide bomb attack occurred in the Jordan valley in October 1993. The first bus attack happened in Afula in northern Israel in April 1994, which was followed by sui-cide attacks in Tel Aviv in October of that year in which twenty-one people were killed, in January 1995 (Netanya with nineteen victims), February 1996 (Jerusa-lem, twenty-six fatalities), March 1996 (another suicide bomber in a Jerusalem bus, 19 fatalities), to mention only the most deadly operations.

The timing of the operations was not random; the more promising the peace negotiations, the greater were Hamas's efforts to sabotage them. The attacks reached a height after the murder of Prime Minister Rabin. It is generally believed that the Labor Party lost the elections of 1996 — and Netanyahu, leader of Likud, came to power — as the result of the bomb attacks in Jerusalem and Tel Aviv. It is also surmised that this strategy originated in Teheran, although Hamas may not have needed much persuasion to accept it; there had been no change in its opposition to the peace process. Its overall aim remained, as repeated on many occasions, the expulsion of the Jews from all parts of historical Palestine.

The attacks of 1995–96 caused strong Israeli reactions as a result of which many Hamas terrorists were arrested and their chief bomb makers assassinated. The PA (Palestinian Authority) also adopted measures against Hamas as a result of which Hamas militants were detained by the Palestinian authorities. There was a considerable decline in Hamas terrorism in 1997–99, with only one or two suicide bombings (Mahane Yehuda market in Jerusalem, July 1997, and Ben Yehuda Street, Jerusalem, September 1997) and a few ambushes. The military leadership of Hamas was arrested or escaped to other Arab countries (mainly Syria) and to Iran. Hamas leaders interviewed by Arab newspapers said that while they welcomed the cover provided by Syria and the "Islamic support" extended by Iran, resistance in Israel had become very difficult with immense pressures and challenges. The jails were full with the sons of Hamas, some of whom had made confessions revealing military secrets. The terrorist struggle waged by Hamas was the target of distortion, fabrications, and dirty psychological warfare waged by the proponents of Oslo peace accords.[16] Part of the blame was put on the CIA, which was reported to coordinate the exchange of intelligence information between the Israelis and the Palestinian Authority.

Suicide terrorism has been discussed elsewhere in our study. In Israel prior to 2002, the majority of suicide bombers came from Hamas and had graduated from Islamist educational centers. Later on, a substantial number of suicide bombers belonged to the military wing of Fatah and the PFLP, and candidates for such missions would occasionally move from one organization to another. They were young, unmarried, and had apparently been influenced by the example of the Lebanese Hizbullah, who had pioneered suicide terrorism in the previous decade. Some of those arrested before they could carry out their missions said that they were also motivated by the wish to revenge the death of relations or friends, but the predominant motive was religious fanaticism.[17]

Hamas gradually recovered from the setback suffered earlier in the 1990s and resumed its activities, mainly suicide bombing, after the second Intifada had broken out. Its first targets were military installations and settlements in the areas conquered by Israel. But they soon realized that military bases were too difficult a target, and in the case of the settlers only a few victims would result since there were hardly any major concentrations on the West Bank. Therefore, beginning in November 2000, places in Israel proper were targeted — in Jerusalem, near Tel Aviv, Hadera, Netanya, and other places. In most of these incidents, the bombers were killed; in some cases the explosives did not work, and in a considerable number of cases the terrorists were intercepted before they could carry out their operations. However, even in these circumstances it is estimated that Hamas was responsible in the year 2000 for twice as many attacks as all other terrorist groups combined.

The military effect of these attacks was negligible, but the psychological impact was considerable. It created a climate of insecurity among the civilian population in Israel, and it also helped to radicalize large sections of the population, who came to believe that far harsher measures had to be taken against the residents of Gaza and the West Bank — leading, if need be, to the expulsion of the inhabitants. In brief the conflict escalated. Some outside observers argued that one should not overrate the Hamas radicalism, quoting an Arab saying that all fundamentalists were opportunists (*kul al wusuliyin-usuliyin*). Of course true Hamas, like other such groups, had to make concessions to realities in its activities, in contrast to its ideological pronouncements, which remained unchanged.[18] But Western observers were more often erring in the opposite direction, underrating the intensity of hate and fanaticism in the motivation of the radical Islamic groups.

Mention has been made so far only of Hamas, but other terrorist groups were also operating, such as the Palestinian Islamic Jihad (PIJ — *Harakat al Jihad al Islami al Filastini*). This group had been founded in Egypt in 1979 by Dr. Fathi Shiqaqi, Bashir Musa, and Dr. Ramadan Shalah, Palestinian intellectuals who were expelled from Egypt because of activities considered subversive by the government. Shiqaqi was killed in Malta in 1995, probably by Israeli counterterrorism agents. Shalah, like other leaders of the extremist groups, had lived for years in the United States. The group had a following of a few hundred only, but owing to the material support it received, mainly from Iran, it succeeded in staging several major terrorist operations. Unlike Hamas, it did not engage in religious and social activities, but instead concentrated on terrorism. Its ideology was largely identical to that of Hamas: dissatisfaction with the Muslim Brotherhood in Egypt, which they thought too tame and moderate. Jihad's overriding aim was the construction of one great Islamic state reaching from the Atlantic to the Pacific.[19]

There was, however, one important doctrinal difference: For Hamas, being devout Sunni Muslims, Khomeini's revolution in Iran could not possibly be an ideal pattern to be emulated, because the Shi'ite religion was considered a deviation from true Islam, and to collaborate with it was considered almost as bad as a Protestant fundamentalist accepting the authority of the pope. However, the Jihad intellectuals were deeply influenced by the Iranian example and tried to emulate it. Jihad was particularly impressed by the activities of Hizbullah in Lebanon, which had played an important role in compelling the Israeli forces to withdraw. The Iranian government reciprocated by extending financial and military help. The Jihad leaders openly advocated a pro-Iranian and pro-Syrian orientation; Shiqaqi wrote a book entitled *Khomeini, the Alternative and the Islamic Solution.*

Jihad had a few protectors within Fatah ("Abu Jihad"), but at the same time there was bitter competition with Fatah and also with Hamas about positions of influence in institutions in Gaza and the West Bank. At one time there were violent clashes, particularly in Gaza, and closer cooperation between the various groups was established only with the outbreak of the second Intifada in September 2000.

The military (terrorist) arm of Islamic Jihad consisted of two relatively small groups. Among the major attacks launched by them were bombings in the Gaza district in 1993, in Tel Aviv in March 1996 (with twenty persons killed), two attacks in Jerusalem in 1998, again one in Jerusalem in March 2001, and in Hadera and Binyamina (in July and August 2001, respectively). It is difficult to single out responsibility in each case, because on a number of occasions one and the same operation was claimed by more than one organization, and on some occasions, when a mishap had occurred, no one claimed it.

The mode of operation in virtually every instance was a car bomb or a suicide bomber blowing himself up in a public place, such as a pizzeria, an outdoor market, or a bus stop. The Jihad attacks were not particularly innovative; more interesting was their ideological motivation. They were all practicing Muslims, and some (such as Sheikh Tamimi of Hebron) were well-known clerics. But they had constructed their own private interpretation of Islam, in the same way as some of the Egyptian jihadists had done. They refused to accept the authority of the Islamic legal authorities of the last thousand years (let alone those of the present generation) and accepted only the version of the prophet and his immediate successors. Their close cooperation with the Iranian Shi'ites throws additional doubts on their Islamic orthodoxy. They were certainly radicals, but sectarians rather than true fundamentalists.

While Hamas, Jihad, and the PFLP were active, Fatah also strengthened its military potential as a Palestinian Authority was set up in Ramallah. Tanzim ought to be mentioned first and foremost in this context. It was established in 1995 by the Palestinian Authority, partly as a counterweight against the Islamic armed groups but in the main as the army of the future Palestinian state. It received its budget and its equipment from the Palestinian Authority. Tanzim was distinct from the Palestinian police even though it would collaborate with it. Its commander was Marvan Barghouti, who came from a well-known Ramallah family and had been a student militant. Most of its officer corps consisted of former Fatah activists who had been detained in Israeli prisons.[20] While under the authority of Yasir Arafat, Tanzim kept a certain distance from the PA political organizations and had an image of certain independence, even though it had no ideology of its own. Tanzim took part in attacks against Israeli forces — shooting attacks against

Israeli soldiers at border crossings but also the use of roadside bombings after the outbreak of the second (Al Aqsa) Intifada. Tanzim was stronger on the West Bank than in the Gaza district. While Hamas and Islamic Jihad had carried out twice as many armed attacks against Israeli targets during the two years prior to the outbreak of Intifada II, Tanzim's activity changed after September 2000 when Tanzim and Force 17, the Palestine Authority elite unit, and above all Al Aqsa Martyrs Brigade were responsible for many more attacks than the Islamist groups.[21] The second Intifada broke out following a visit by Ariel Sharon, at the time leader of the opposition, on the Temple Mount. This visit was considered unwise, if not an outright provocation, by many; on the other hand, tensions were such that it seems most likely that a new outbreak of mass violence would have occurred in any case sooner or later.

The history of Force 17, Arafat's personal security force, goes back to the 1970s. When the PLO leadership was evacuated to Tunis, Force 17 followed. It changed its name and organizational structure several times (Special Security Force, Presidential Security Unit). It counted several hundred members, and eventually (in 2001) it numbered three thousand. Its early commanders had been involved in the attack on the Israeli athletes at the Munich Olympic Games, and these leaders were systematically hunted down and killed by Israeli counterintelligence. In later years, Force 17 engaged in both terrorist and intelligence activities from bases in Jordan and also in Europe. Among its victims were Arab critics and enemies of Fatah and the PLO. After the outbreak of Intifada II, Force 17 was involved in shooting and mortar attacks against Israelis both on the West Bank and in the Gaza district. Many of these attacks were carried out under the umbrella of the Fatah Al Aqsa Martyrs Brigade, yet another new organization consisting of Tanzim and Force 17 fighters. Lastly, the Lebanese Shi'ite Hizbullah, the Party of God, played a notable role in the 1980s and 1990s in the Lebanese civil war and later in the fight against the Israelis. Hizbullah was as much a guerrilla organization as a terrorist group, and it also engaged in political and social activities.[22] It was wholly supported and equipped by Iran and Syria; this gave it safe bases and many other advantages, but it also limited its freedom of action. Its early activities in Lebanon, which have been frequently described, included the bombing of foreign embassies and hostage taking. Later on, it concentrated its operations on guerrilla-style attacks against the Israelis. After the withdrawal of Israeli forces in 2000, Hizbullah was in virtual control of southern Lebanon and continued to engage in occasional cross-border attacks, even though the Lebanese government had some token representation in the area. At the same time, it established itself as a political party with representatives in the Lebanese Parliament.

IF WE ANALYZE the course of the Israeli-Palestinian conflict, it emerges that terrorism did play a significant role from the very beginning, but that the terrorists always aimed at greater, more ambitious things. The main Jewish terrorist group of the 1930s and 1940s was called IZL (National Military Organization), and it used the Irish rebels as an example. The Palestinian militants in the late 1960s wanted to emulate the Algerians and the Vietnamese in a struggle for national liberation in which individual terrorism did play a role, but a subordinate one. But a small country such as Palestine was not suitable for guerrilla warfare Algerian- or Vietnamese-style. True, much later the first Intifada began, a national insurgency in which violent demonstrations rather than ambushes and suicide bombing were at first the most prominent feature. But this changed after a while. The demonstrations ceased, and the stone throwing was replaced by terrorist attacks; the same was true with regard to the second Intifada which, in addition, involved both the Israeli army and the armed forces of the PA as well as the terrorist organizations of yesteryear such as Hamas. In brief, there was terrorism but also elements of a civil war. Reality is always more complicated than doctrines and agreed-upon strategies.

As in other national and ethnic conflicts, the question arises why terrorism occurred in the first place and whether it could have been prevented. For the IZL in the 1930s, it was the only way to fight, and the same is true of the Palestinian resistance. If in retrospect the cardinal mistake of the Palestinians was to reject the UN plan of 1947, which would have given them a state of their own, the basic mistake of Israeli governments was to hold on to the territories conquered in 1967. If Israel had been a superpower, such an occupation would have been forgotten if not forgiven. But Israel was merely a small country, and it faced restraints unlike a superpower. Though opposed in principle to a binational state, it pursued after 1967 a policy which in fact brought about such a situation, except that the other nation, the Palestinians, were bitterly opposed to Israeli rule.

Israel did so for two reasons. First, it argued that the borders of 1948 had been indefensible. But more important yet was another circumstance: the nationalist-religious mystique about the right of the people of Israel to rule all of historical Palestine. For the same reason it was argued that Jerusalem must forever remain undivided in Israeli hands, the capital of the state of Israel and of no other country.[23] Israeli occupation was moderate in the early years. Israelis did not really want to interfere in internal Arab affairs, but even the gentlest occupation is still rule by foreigners and generates resistance, and resistance leads to harsher rule; this pattern is what emerged over the years.

The rest of the country of Israel became the hostage of religious nationalist settlers with messianic visions. Far from defending the rest of the country, the settlements became a political provocation (such as the presence of settlers in Hebron), a financial incubus, and a military nightmare. A significant part of the Israeli army was tied down defending distant, small settlements and the roads leading toward them. In these conditions of warfare, the Israelis were always on the defensive and could never bring into action their technological superiority.

Cross-border attacks would probably have continued even if Israel had returned to the old borders. But infiltration could have been made far more difficult through physical obstacles, and if it would have come to a military conflict, it would have been one between states and in most respects easier to conduct (and to win) for Israel.

In the terrorist campaign, the Palestinians had a number of great advantages over the Israelis, even if the Israelis had all kinds of sophisticated weaponry. They had, above all, the active support of other Arab states — political, financial, the supply of weapons, and safe havens. Palestinian terrorism became more sophisticated and more daring as time went by. The wave of Islamism produced scores of candidates for suicide terrorism. It has often been argued that there was no defense against suicide terrorism, but this is of course not true. Suicide terrorism can be thwarted by radical measures such as taking the families of the bombers hostage and executing them, or by destroying whole villages and expelling the rebellious population. Fire can be fought by fire, but only at a heavy price which small countries dependent on the goodwill of at least part of the world community cannot afford. This was the dilemma facing Israel, and this is why most Palestinians reached the conclusion that at long last they had found a weapon against which the Zionist enemy had no defense.[24] Russia could have solved its Chechen problems in the way Stalin tackled such problems: by simply ordering a forcible evacuation and expelling all the people belonging to a certain ethnic group. But even Putin's Russia could not take such measures. Israel had no Arctic Circle or Central Asia where those expelled could have been resettled. One can easily imagine how world popular opinion which had turned against Israel in any case would have reacted had Israel adopted even more drastic measures.

There were narrow limits to what Israel could do. The refugee camps had become virtually no-go zones for the Israeli security forces; these were the places where terrorists were trained, where the bomb factories were located, and where terrorists could hide after an operation. But if the Israeli forces would try to enter a refugee camp in hot pursuit, there would be a storm of indignation, for it meant Israeli soldiers frightening women and children, breaking into miserable dwellings, and sometimes destroying them. Terrorists were hiding behind women, children, and elderly people, but this was a perfectly legitimate tactic in contemporary terrorist warfare. Terrorists engage in operations that the security forces of a state are not allowed to use. Israel was bitterly attacked for the systematic assassination of key figures among the terrorist groups, which became its policy in the second Intifada.

According to the rules of asymmetric warfare, the terrorist has a legitimate right to opt for all and any weapons and strategies, whereas a state has not. It is said that terrorism is the operational mode of the weak, but on the other hand the weak have privileges which the other side does not have: they are entitled to kill civilians, women, and children, whereas the security forces of a state according to existing norms must not execute anyone without due process. This had not been the doctrine of nineteenth-century terrorism, which considered it cowardly to hide behind women and children or, generally speaking, to launch indiscriminate attacks. But such restraints belonged to another time and another continent and civilization.

However, the norms of asymmetric warfare applied only as long as a terrorist threat was no more than an irritant, even a major one. The moment a terrorist threat would turn into a danger threatening the very existence of a state, the situation is bound to change and many former restrictions no longer exist. States do not commit suicide voluntarily; if faced by a major threat, once its very survival is endangered, a state is bound to disregard legal and public relations considerations, however important, and bring into action all the measures and all the weapons at its disposal.

There was always the danger that terrorist leaders would forget this obvious lesson. Terrorism according to historical experience can be effective against a state only up to a point. Even a weak state is stronger than a strong terrorist movement once the weak state's core interests are at risk.

Jewish Terrorism

A review of terrorism in Israel would not be complete without at least a brief mentioning of the nationalist-religious underground which came into being after the Six-Day War. These extremist groups appeared on the margins of certain religious schools (*yeshivot*) and settlements beyond the Green line, such as Kiryat Arba, and they were part of the general fundamentalist revival. The ultra-orthodox Jews had always been anti-Zionist. Some of them did not even recognize the existence of the state of Israel and as far as they were concerned it did not matter in the least who was in physical control of historical Palestine and the holy sites. The national religious on the other hand regarded it as their sacred duty never to give up a single inch of the country that God had promised them in the Bible and restored to them as the result of the Six-Day War.

There had been a few attacks and at least one assassination (Dr. Rudolf Kastner) even before 1967; Kastner had been head of the Jewish wartime rescue committee in Budapest and was accused of negotiating with the Nazis in an attempt to save a few lives while sacrificing others. But this murder was carried out by a small group of secular conspirators, whereas the political violence after 1967 was rooted in a certain messianic interpretation of Judaism not less intransigent than the Islamists, but for the fact that its ambitions were limited to one country — namely, Israel/Palestine. This terrorism consisted of various groups whose aims and motivation were by no means identical. One group engaged in sporadic vigilante terrorism, attacks on mayors of Arab cities on the West Bank such as Bassam Shaka of Nablus, and killings of individual Arabs from neighboring villages, mainly in revenge for attacks against Jewish settlers and perhaps also as an attempt to frighten the Arabs and induce them to leave. Later on, members of this group and some new adherents, believing that it was their mission to bring about the kingdom of Israel and its redemption, established new underground cells. According to their doctrine, the temple had to be rebuilt on the Temple Mount and the Al Aqsa mosque destroyed; four attempts were made to set fire to the mosque, but they were not well prepared and did not come close to succeeding. However, potentially, this group was extremely dangerous because Al Aqsa was, after the Kaaba in Mecca, one of the holiest places of Islam, and any attempt to destroy it might have triggered a religious war not just with the Palestinians but the whole Muslim world — similar to the destruction of the Ayyodya Mosque in India, which led to major riots and remains a bone of contention to this day. These terrorists envisaged a final, decisive struggle between the forces of good and evil and regarded it as their sacred duty to bring about this confrontation as soon as possible by an act of provocation.

Some of the Jewish terrorist attacks were the actions of individuals who had persuaded themselves that it was their personal obligation to engage in jihad in the hope that their action would inspire others or at least put a stop to what they regarded as the fatal process of surrendering land that belonged by divine right to the Jews. This was, as far as can be established, the motivation of Baruch Goldstein, a American physician and member of a nationalist settlement who went to a Hebron mosque in February 1994 and shot Arabs praying there, only to be killed himself eventually. According to a state investigation committee, Goldstein was haunted by a siege mentality, seeing a danger for the survival of the Jewish people, and reached the conclusion that only an extreme act would stop the rut. Goldstein and his fellow believers were deeply depressed by the Oslo accords which, as they saw it, were a further major step in the wrong direction.[25] Goldstein's grave became a place of pilgrimage for like-minded zealots.[26] A number of Israeli extremists who had planned to blow up an Arab girls school in Jerusalem were arrested in April 2002. There was a small but dangerous terrorist underground among the Jewish community, and given the explosive situation, even a minor attack could have far-reaching repercussions.[27]

The murder of Prime Minister Yizhak Rabin was carried out not by a settler but a twenty-five-year old student of computer science, Yigal Amir of a Yemenite lower-middle-class background. It was the action of an individual, but it did not take place in a spiritual or organizational vacuum. For many months before, the right-wing parties had denounced Rabin as a traitor willing to give up not only Hebron but also other places in Jewish hands. Amir had in fact inquired with leading rabbis whether *din mosser* and *din rodef* applied to contemporary traitors. These were medieval Jewish religious pronouncements concerning the possible use of violence against enemies who were either informing on Jews or actively persecuting them. The rabbis for their part had told Israeli army soldiers to disobey orders to evacuate Jewish settlements.

About a month before Rabin's murder on November 4, 1995, a group of extremists had assembled in front of the prime minister's home in Jerusalem and pronounced the *Pulsa di Nur,* an ancient (mystical rather than Jewish orthodox) ceremony in which the death curse is pronounced ("Angels of destruction will hit him, he is damned wherever he goes, his soul will instantly leave his body," etc.).[28] In brief, there was a great deal of incitement to violence in the air, in small meetings as well as in mass demonstrations, and it was in retrospect only a question of time until someone from the radical camp would commit an act of violence against those whom they considered traitors. Yigal Amir's action was in the tradition of the Zealots who had also been proponents of violence two thousand years earlier, but it is doubtful whether there was anything specifically Jewish about his motivation. His ideology was almost indistinguishable from that of the killers of Anwar Sadat, who believed — like him — that personal jihad, the killing of the head of state (or prime minister) was a divine order.

Lastly, mention should be made of Rabbi Meir Kahane and his Jewish Defense League, which landed itself on the list of terrorist organizations published annually by the U.S. Department of State. The group certainly committed acts of violence, but it aimed at the impossible — at one and the same time to operate as a terrorist group and as a political party in Israel. As a result it did not succeed much in either capacity. The JDL was founded in 1968 in Brooklyn and has been active, albeit in a diminished form, to the present day; Meir Kahane went to Israel in 1971, where he had a second career. He came from a family of rabbis, but in his youth did not live according to the Orthodox canon, and in his later years too, his nationalism was far more pronounced than his religious orthodoxy. He was certainly not a religious fundamentalist; his group both in America and Israel gravitated toward demonstrative violent actions.

In America his group announced that it would protect defenseless Jews in New York against physical attacks. They also abused and sometimes attacked Soviet diplomatic representatives in the United States to draw attention to the plight of Soviet Jewry. He was extreme in his opposition to mixed marriages, and in Israel he became the leading proponent for the eviction of the Palestinians from Israel and the occupied territory. He thrived on publicity, and while he was a gifted rabble-rouser, he knew that only violent speeches and gestures would get him the publicity he needed. He was arrested, as were other members of his organization, for illegal possession of arms, ammunition, and explosives. His followers committed a number of terrorist actions in the United States in the 1970s, such as placing a bomb in the office of Sol Hurok, the theater promoter who was also active in Soviet-American cultural exchanges.

In Israel his followers burned cars that belonged to Arabs and fired on Arab buses. When asked for his comments, Kahane said that he wholly supported them:

"as long as they (the Arabs) are here, we are lost."[29] At first Kahane found the going in Israel difficult because there was much competition on the extreme right, but in the course of time he developed a small following and was elected to the Knesset, the Israeli parliament. However, Kahanism became an embarrassment to the Israeli government and society, and it was outlawed. Kahane was killed in November 1990 by a member of an Arab terrorist group, who, it later emerged, belonged to the circle of those involved in the first (1993) attempt to blow up the World Trade Center. His son, daughter-in-law, and some of his grandchildren were killed when Arab terrorists attacked their car on a road in the West Bank territories.

Thus, Kahanism was not much of a success. For the very orthodox, it was too secular. For left-wing intellectuals who found often extenuating circumstances for terrorism if it was rooted in left-wing ideology, Kahanism was an abomination. Even a right-wing ex-terrorist such as Yizhak Shamir, prime minister of Israel and once a leader of the Stern gang, did not think highly of him: "Kahane a terrorist?" he said. "He was a second-rate terrorist, all bluster, symbolism and rhetoric with almost no real action. He had no concept of underground militarism and camaraderie."[30]

Terrorism in most other countries is a domestic problem or at most a conflict between two neighboring countries, such as over Kashmir. But the political repercussions of Arab terrorism in Israel/Palestine were far wider. The cause of the Palestinian Arabs has always had supporters in the Arab world, and to a lesser extent in the Muslim world. Even during the riots of 1936–39, the Egyptian Muslim Brotherhood dispatched some volunteers to fight, and when the Jewish state was founded in 1948, the Arab and Muslim countries actively opposed it. Sympathy with and support for Palestinian political ambitions and terrorism became stronger rather than weaker as time went by. Every evening, Arab television stations featured programs in which brutal Israeli soldiers were shown threatening and killing Palestinian refugee children and women. The achievements of Palestinian terrorism didn't gain the support of the Arab world, but their defeats and weaknesses did. This created an enormous amount of rage, and as a wave of Islamism swept the Arab and Muslim world, Israel became one of the main targets of jihad. Jerusalem (and Palestine) were places holy to every believing Muslim. The very presence of Jews desecrated them and was an offense before God: the "Zionist entity" had to be eradicated. As a Moroccan sociologist (Nadira Barkali) put it, Palestine became for many of them a place for the projection of those of their dreams which could not be realized in their own countries, with their repression and lack of hope. Against this psychological background, Palestinian resistance appeared as something magic and sacred: Heroic fighters who did not bow to superior force. And thus the biggest demonstration in the history of Morocco with five hundred thousand people participating took place in September 2000 with the outbreak of the second Intifada.[31]

The policy of Israeli governments concerning Jerusalem and the territories after 1967 played into the hands of the Islamists. Israelis could argue a thousand times that Mecca and Medina were far more sacred places for the Muslims than Jerusalem and that Jerusalem hardly ever appeared in the Koran. From an Islamist point of view, this argument was wholly irrelevant; what counted was not what was written in the holy books but what the present generation of Islamists was feeling. It was the perception that counted, not the facts. They felt that Jerusalem should be theirs and the Jews killed or forced to leave, and this result was the only thing that mattered.

Thus Israel became one of the main catalysts of Muslim rage. It was not the cause, certainly not the main cause, of Muslim rage; the Palestinian issue came to figure (to give but one example) only late in the day on bin Laden's agenda. If Israel had not existed, Muslim frustration and rage would have found another outlet. But it did exist and found itself at the receiving end of so much hostile emotion and hatred.

Terrorism in Israel became a factor of international importance. Thus, the growing conviction in many places that, all other considerations apart, Israel should be forced to make far-reaching concessions to reduce Arab and Muslim resentment came as no surprise. Whether these concessions would be sufficient to pacify Islamist feelings was not certain; whether even the most far-reaching concessions would affect the roots of Muslim rage was doubtful, given the desire of the radical Islamists to destroy the Jewish state. Israeli unwillingness to compromise with regard to the holy places and its continued occupation of all the territories seized in the war of 1967 weakened its position in international affairs. It also made an effective defense against terrorist attacks very difficult. Whether the conflict could have been prevented is more than doubtful. But it would probably not have become an issue of such crucial importance for the Muslim world (and thus in world affairs) if ideology and emotion had not prevailed over common sense and realism in Israeli thinking. It would have remained a regional conflict and not become a religious war.

SIX

Intelligence Failure?

M USLIM RULE IN SPAIN came to an end with the defeat of its army in 1492. What allegedly happened next is described in a ballad ("Al Puhara") by the Polish national poet Adam Mickiewicz.[1] Almansur, the king of the Muslims, went to the Spanish camp and asked that his life be spared, declaring his willingness to serve the Christian God and their prophets. He wanted (in his words) to become a brother of the victors, and to give further emphasis to his good intentions, he embraced the leaders of the Spanish army and kissed them on the mouth. Then suddenly he weakened and became very pale, shouting, "Look at me, oh infidels, I brought you the plague, I put the poison in your midst. You will suffer the same way." With a hellish laughter he died. The Spaniards fell very silent and tried to escape, but the plague followed them and all the army died.

The affair of Almansur is pure poetic license — that is to say, invention. Nor should it be read as a denunciation of Muslim perfidy. Treason (on behalf of a patriotic cause) is the main theme of *Konrad Wallenrod*, the cycle of which "Ballada" is a part, and the poet's attitude is a very complicated one, justifying treason, at least by implication.

If the story were true, it would raise a number of interesting questions for students of military intelligence: Why did this surprise attack succeed? Why did the Spaniards know so little about Almansur's true intentions? Was it naïveté or an exaggerated feeling of security or perhaps the failure to understand the psychology of the enemy? Was it known to them that the plague was raging in the enemy camp?

The issues of surprise attack and intelligence failure have featured very prominently after September 11, perhaps for the first time in the history of terrorism. Terrorist groups have virtually never kept their existence and their intentions secret; that they did not make it known when and where the next blow would fall was a different question. The British police was well informed about the activities of the Irish Fenians. The Russian police knew even more about their terrorists; they had deeply penetrated their ranks with spies and agents provocateurs. All European police forces were aware of the Anarchist danger. If the terrorists nevertheless succeeded in assassinating a variety of kings, prime ministers, and other

119

notables, this was because the most dangerous attempts were made by individuals or small groups which could not be penetrated by the security forces.

September 11 was believed to be, rightly or wrongly, an intelligence failure on the scale of Pearl Harbor, Hitler's attack on the Soviet Union in June 1941, the breakup of the Soviet Union, or Saddam's invasion of Kuwait.[2] But is such a comparison fair? Is it realistic to compare a terrorist attack with a major military operation involving massive troop concentrations and other preparations that can be detected through a variety of channels?

Psychologically the attack of September 2001 came as a shock and enormous surprise, and the question arises why this should have been the case. Were there indications of the shape of things to come? Were they ignored, and if so, for what reason? These questions will probably be dealt with by a variety of investigation committees in the years to come. However, such examinations should not be restricted to government intelligence agencies, simply because these agencies have no monopoly for gathering intelligence and the assessment of the political situation in foreign parts. The role of the media should also be investigated, as well as the information and the opinions of the area experts, especially those concentrating on the Middle East and South and Central Asia. Nor should one ignore the views of the academic experts who have studied terrorism over the years.

The media and the specialists create a climate of opinion. What they say has an impact on the public and indirectly also the intelligence agencies. Then there is the question of access: Every student of intelligence knows that the fact that certain information has been obtained means very little per se unless those in charge of the intelligence agencies can communicate their findings to their bosses — the president, the secretaries of defense and of state and so on — and that the bosses trust the findings.[3] But it is only proper that any investigation of the intelligence failure should start with the CIA and the other agencies in charge of national security. The same applies to the security services of the other countries in which members of al Qa'ida and related groups were active.

The CIA was founded soon after World War II, and its main task was the defense of the security of the United States during the Cold War. According to a general consensus, the CIA was effective and innovative as far as the technical means of observation were concerned — electronic and photographic intelligence — but not as good in the field of Humint, that is to say, human intelligence received from agents on the ground who could supply reliable and timely intelligence. It is, of course, infinitely easier to conduct espionage in an open society such as the United States than in a tightly controlled police state. Furthermore the CIA labored under various handicaps: Following the revelation of a number of scandals in the 1970s, it was bitterly criticized and frequently termed a "rogue elephant." As the result of various purges, the imposition of strict controls, and reforms that were of doubtful value, the CIA had little freedom of action. Having been taken to task for exceeding its powers, it became more bureaucratic as the first more highly motivated and more experienced generation of CIA officials was replaced by a second and third generation which had learned the bitter way that risk taking was not rewarded in their organization.

During the Cold War, terrorism certainly did not figure highly on the CIA agenda. In the 1960s and 1970s, CIA publications did not betray a great deal of insight and sophistication; it was not unusual to be told that perceptions of terrorism varied from country to country and that while violent people were regarded as terrorists by some, they were seen as fighters for national (or social) liberation by others.

The state of affairs as far as the FBI was concerned was not different. There were only a very few cases of terrorism in the United States, and in accordance with government instructions the FBI considered terrorists criminals.[4] This classification was perhaps necessary from an administrative point of view but it did not help much to understand the motives of the terrorists and their political aims. The FBI was more preoccupied with bank robberies than counterterrorism; in the words of a senior FBI official, the general feeling twenty-five years ago was that the FBI was out of control and had to be tamed down,[5] hence the "paralytical fear of risk taking" in later years both among agents in the field and at headquarters. In the 1990s when the Sudan government offered specific information about bin Laden and his followers, the FBI was not interested.

Once the Cold War had ended, many argued that there was no reason to maintain intelligence on the same relatively high level of expenditure and manpower because the main threats to the United States, such as nuclear war, had virtually disappeared. This estimate was not shared by the CIA. As a former director of the CIA, James Woolsey, stated in evidence before a congressional committee: The dragon had been replaced by a jungle full of poisonous snakes.[6] But this line of argument was accepted only in part; budget allocations were cut, stations were closed, and other savings made.

The CIA was not very well prepared for dealing with the snakes. The technical means were of much less help once the identity of the enemy had changed. It was no longer a great military machine; monitoring and decoding were not of great help when dealing with relatively small terrorist groups. If it had not been easy to train agents with a fluent knowledge of Russian, with a knowledge of Eastern European countries and mentality, how much more difficult was it to find "assets" speaking Middle Eastern or Asian languages. If such people were found, chances were that they had relations living in countries considered hostile and to get security clearance necessary for their employment would be difficult if not impossible.

Nor was the general climate of opinion auspicious; the CIA would look for recruits in colleges and universities where attitudes toward the CIA were often hostile. Many students had been told by their teachers that it was dishonorable to serve in the spy service of an imperialist country. Even popular thriller writers

such as John Le Carré were telling their readers that there was not really much
to choose between one side in the present conflicts and the other; their message
was one of moral equivalence. Those who joined the intelligence agencies in the
1970s and 1980s were by necessity the product of the Zeitgeist, and the climate on
campus was not very patriotic. The emphasis in higher education was on being
"critical" (which was often a synonym for negative), more on theory than the
realities of world affairs.

All this did not contribute to high morale and high-quality intelligence. The
CIA was aware that dangers to U.S. security were brewing in foreign countries.
The attempt to blow up the World Trade Center in New York in 1993 had been a
warning sign, but it had been a bumbling, amateurish attempt ending in miserable
failure, and the idea that terrorists might learn from their mistakes and that next
time attacks would be far more dangerous seems not to have occurred to many
in the FBI and CIA. Furthermore, according to the division of labor between the
intelligence agencies, the FBI and the Department of Justice were dealing with
the New York events, with the inevitable result that not all the material that
came to light was passed on and closely studied for leads by the CIA.

The CIA was aware of the existence of Osama bin Laden; a short profile was
published in 1996 entitled "Islamic Extremist Financier," in which he was named
as one of the most significant financial sponsors of Islamic extremist activities,
which was perfectly true.[7] But it was only the less important part of the truth,
for he was more than mere financier. The word "terrorism" is notably absent in
the 1996 profile (which was also published by the Department of State). And
the statement had nothing to say about the motivation, aims, or activities of al
Qa'ida outside the Middle East. Nor were the bin Laden financial assets included
in official U.S. lists of terrorist resources, with the result that no attempt was
made to seize them.

As time went by, more and more warning signs appeared on the horizon. There
were, to mention but the most important ones, the attacks on the Khobar bar-
racks in Saudi Arabia, the bombing of the embassies in East Africa, and lastly the
attack on an American warship, the USS *Cole*, in Aden. In addition, information
was received about further plans, probably on U.S. territory, possibly using unconventional weapons. A congressional investigation in 2002 reached the conclusion
that there was a modest but relatively steady stream of intelligence indicating the
possibility of terrorist attacks inside the United States, including plans to use
aircraft. The director of Central Intelligence announced in December 1998 that
terrorist action seemed inevitable and that its scope could be larger than previously experienced.[8] George Tenet, head of the CIA, wrote that "we must now
enter a new phase in our effort against bin Laden. . . . We are at war. . . . I want no
resources or people spared in this effort."[9] But these instructions were either not
followed up (there were only five analysts in CIA dealing with al Qa'ida, only
one in the FBI), or they failed to have an impact on the president and his close

aides. Above all, U.S. intelligence seems not to have been aware of the worldwide character of al Qa'ida and allied groups, which might be in part the result of the negligence of European intelligence services which also failed to pay attention to the conspiracies afoot in their countries.

Some of the information came from informants who belonged to bin Laden's inner circle, but for one reason or another had decided to collaborate with their interrogators. One of them was Ahmed al Fadl, a "walk-in" in intelligence language, who appeared as a witness in August 1998 in the trial concerning the bombings of the African embassies. He reported that the bin Laden group was experimenting with chemical weapons in Sudan, where the group had been located prior to its expulsion. This evidence was by no means kept secret. It was published at the time in the American media. It should have set the alarm bells ringing and led to the bombing of a factory (al Shifa) near Khartum. This was denounced almost immediately as a terrible American intelligence failure, for the factory in question (it was argued), far from producing poison gas, was manufacturing medical drugs.

This is not the place to review U.S. counterintelligence efforts over the years, but merely to establish why warnings were not heeded. But often it is impossible to discuss the one in isolation from the other, for a counterintelligence failure would have far-reaching consequences in every respect. This was the case in the al Shifa incident as in the bombing of what were thought to be bin Laden's quarters in Afghanistan when the terrorist had left the place a few hours before. The fact that the Monica Lewinsky affair reached its climax at the time and that President Clinton was accused of trying to divert attention from his own personal predicaments by sensational strikes against putative terrorists did not help.

In retrospect it appears that even if no chemical weapons such as VX nerve gas were produced at the factory in question, there is every reason to believe that something dangerous went on in the immediate neighborhood.[10] And in any case, by the strange paradoxical logic often prevailing in the history of terrorism and counterterrorism, even if a wrong target was hit, the long-term results were beneficial, for the Sudanese government — afraid of further American action (and suffering badly from the embargo that had been imposed on it) — broke its ties with the terrorists and even began to collaborate with Western governments.

What were the expectations of the leading figures of U.S. intelligence during the months and years prior to September 11? The evidence is contradictory. Chiefs of intelligence know that it does not pay to show too much confidence, because there is always the danger of unpleasant surprise, big or small. Thus George Tenet, head of the CIA, in an interview given less than a month before the disaster, was musing about a major disaster: "Then the country will want to know why we did not make those investments, why we did not pay the price, why we did not develop the capability."[11] A briefing paper circulated among senior government officials in July 2001 announced that Osama bin Laden would launch a significant terrorist attack against U.S. facilities or interests within the next few weeks, that it would be spectacular and scheduled to cause mass casualties, that preparations for the attack had been made, and that it would occur with little or no warning.[12]

But on other occasions Mr. Tenet and his colleagues were showing optimism; their feeling was that they kept bin Laden on the run and that the terrorists in their caves in Afghanistan were worrying where America would strike next. In fact, the terrorists were not impressed by the ineffective U.S. reactions after their attacks in Africa and Aden, and this might have helped to persuade them that the risk of an even greater attack could be accepted.

While all this went on, a number of blue-ribbon official committees were deliberating on what to do about future terrorist threats. Among them were military commissions, such as the one investigating the attack on the USS *Cole*. Like many before and after, it reached the conclusion that the Department of Defense did not allocate sufficient resources to intelligence analysis and collection in support of combating terrorism. And it asked the secretary of defense to give greater priority to these issues, mentioning specifically "the development of language skills that support combating terrorism analysis and collection."[13] But this recommendation was just one of many, and it came by no means on top of the list of priorities.

Most of the work of the committees was defensive in character, considering various ideas and proposals as to what should be done following an attack with weapons of mass destruction. This is true, for instance, with regard to the Gilmore report which was submitted to the vice president.[14] Two other commissions, Hart-Rudman and the National Commission on Terrorism, were more directly concerned with issues of intelligence. Hart and Rudman are former senators, whereas Paul Bremer III, heading the national commission, had been for years terrorism coordinator in the State Department.

These committees consulted experts inside and outside the government, and their analysis and recommendations were much to the point. Thus the Bremer report correctly noted that international terrorism was changing, that it had become far more dangerous, and that its aim now was to kill as many people as possible. It specifically singled out al Qa'ida and noted that some of the most dangerous terrorist groups were also operating inside the United States. It emphasized that good intelligence was the best weapon against international terrorism, but that there were significant obstacles to the collection and distribution of information on terrorism, obstacles that must be removed. The committee noted that while recruiting clandestine sources (assets) to obtain information was encouraged in theory, it was discouraged in practice.[15]

The CIA was not aggressive enough, however. If it wanted to recruit new assets, it had to follow guidelines which virtually excluded contacts with people who had committed (or were suspected of committing) terrorist acts or related crimes or even been involved in human rights violations. However, since information about terrorist groups was likely to come only from people who had been associated in one form or another with such groups, the CIA was virtually reduced to rely on secondhand information obtained from other intelligence services facing fewer bureaucratic obstacles and having fewer scruples.[16]

The commission was also critical of the FBI, which was said to "to have suffered from bureaucratic and culture obstacles to obtain terrorism information"; in other words, it had no people with linguistic skills and knowledge of foreign countries and mentalities. About the Department of Justice it was said that it applied electronic surveillance and physical searches of international terrorists "in a cumbersome and overly cautious manner."

In addition to proposing a more aggressive policy of intelligence collecting, there were specific recommendations such as allocating money for state-of-the-art technology in the electronics and computer fields. Closer attention should be paid to the more than five hundred thousand foreign students present in the United States; it was rightly suspected that many thousands were in the country illegally, having outstayed their visa, and some of them were suspected of terrorist intentions or activities. This recommendation encountered the resistance of universities afraid of losing income or infringements upon academic freedom, or both.

When the commission handed in its weighty reports, having consulted many experts and visited twenty-five countries (in the case of Hart-Rudman), gratitude was expressed for its dedicated work. But the recommendations were ignored, despite massive lobbying during spring 2001 with, among others, Secretary of State Colin Powell and Secretary of Defense Donald Rumsfeld.

The Bush administration had its own agenda with regard to terrorism, which did not figure highly. The vice president was to be in charge of counterterrorism (together with many other tasks), and FEMA (the Federal Emergency Management Agency) was to take the lead. When ex-Senator Hart watched the news on television, he felt not only shock and horror but frustration: "I sat tearing my hairs out."[17]

The reaction of Ambassador Bremer was similar. Several months after September 11 he was asked whether the September attacks could have been avoided. Perhaps, he said, if "the U.S. government had better and more aggressive intelligence and law enforcement, if we had moved earlier to shut down the terrorist bases in Afghanistan, if we had established better controls over our borders and if our leaders had paid more attention to the real dangers of mass casualty terrorism inside the United States."[18]

The United States is the most open society in the world with some 3.5 million people and 380,000 cars daily crossing its borders. There is, of course, no certainty whatsoever that the attacks could have been prevented, even if all these recommendations had been accepted and carried out. It could certainly not have been prevented by those in charge of border control. It would have been highly desirable if the FBI would have had supercomputers at their disposal, which because of financial stringencies they did not have. But the best computers are not of much use if there is no information to feed them.

The task of intelligence begins, of course, well before a terrorist campaign has been launched, and the question arises why the relevant agencies were not aware of a conspiracy that involved not a handful of people, but many hundreds, possibly a few thousand. The answer usually given is that it is very difficult if not impossible to infiltrate small cells in faraway countries, that foreigners trying to do so would have immediately attracted unwelcome attention.

But even if the conspiracy was hatched in Afghanistan (which is not certain), it was not carried out there. The recruits came from a variety of countries; they had been enlisted, often many years earlier, in Western Europe and probably also in North America; they had been trained in part in Afghanistan but they had communicated with the center and with each other in various ways; and they had received some of their arms in Western Europe. In brief, it had been an almost open conspiracy involving at least a dozen countries. Even if the place and the date of the planned attacks were known only to a very few terrorists, there should have been no secret about their general intentions (to attack in the United States), and the identity of some of the participants should also have been known. When the Senate Intelligence Committee had its hearings about the events leading to September 11, Republican Senator Arlen Specter commented that the various warning signs amounted to a virtual blueprint for an attack. There is no doubt that major mistakes were committed.[19]

Whether it was enough to forestall September 11 is another question, for there are almost always warning signs and not all of them can be followed up. If a day before the attack messages were intercepted to the effect that the match is about to begin and "tomorrow is zero hour," this could have meant a great many different things. But it is still true that not enough priority was given to the designs of the Islamic terrorists, and that, if there had been a feeling of greater urgency, chances would have been greater that more warning signs would have been received, greater attention would have been paid, and that this might have led to effective counteraction.

European police forces were also hamstrung. The militants were recruited and trained in mosques and Islamic cultural centers, and there was reluctance (and often explicit bans) about tampering with places of worship or even closely observing them. In addition, the British and the German security agencies seem not to have had sufficient personnel with the linguistic and the other skills needed, nor did they have sources of information inside the terrorist groups. Lastly, the growth of the militant Islamic groups went largely unnoticed at first also in Russia, in the Caucasus, and in the Central Asian republics.

If the various agencies, American and European, were not in a position to forestall an attack, they at least could have made life much more difficult for the terrorists. In view of the enormous damage caused by the attacks of 9/11 and the total surprise, almost superhuman sophistication and cunning has been attributed to those who organized it. But this seems to be a great exaggeration, for the terrorists had few obstacles to overcome in societies as open as the Western. If one of them was caught, it was either because of an accident (like the would-be bomber from Vancouver on his way to cause havoc in Seattle) such as the particular vigilance of a border guard, or by uncommon stupidity, such as Moussaoui, who made it known that he wanted to learn flying but pointed out that he was not interested in either taking off or landing. Robert Baer, a legendary CIA operative, is quoted as having said with regard to those who carried out the attack of September 11, "These people are so damned good."[20] But since no one was after them, since no one was aware what they were up to, since ethnic profiling was strictly forbidden, there is a reasonable chance that even a group of village idiots would have succeeded.

To summarize the reasons for the intelligence failure: The so-called "scrub order" of 1995, according to which a person with a criminal or human rights record could not be recruited unless a committee or committees had approved the action, made it next to impossible to penetrate the terrorist groups. But intelligence initiatives had been deficient even before this order; for decades there had been no premium on risk taking, and it was taken for granted that it was always preferable, both as far as the agency was concerned and one's own career, to err on the side of caution. This is the way bureaucracies operate, but for an intelligence agency it is a prescription for failure. But even if there had been greater readiness to take greater risks, where would the people have come from who had the necessary qualifications to serve in the field?

It could be argued that such a reservoir of people able and willing to serve in the field simply did not exist. Some of the leading old-timers had resigned from the CIA during the year prior to 9/11, and in the circumstances the United States was dependent on the intelligence services of other countries. This was, of course, done, and it is apparently true that most of the operational intelligence that was received in Langley originated in other countries — European, Middle Eastern, and South Asian. The problem was, of course, that these agencies were not necessarily willing to share their most valuable secrets with the Americans, and that some of these agencies (such as Pakistani intelligence) were sympathizing with the terrorists or even actively supporting them.

The United States still had one weapon that could have been used but was not used sufficiently: money. When Allen Dulles arrived in Switzerland late in 1942, there was virtually no American espionage network and he had to start from scratch. Dulles made it known that he had considerable means and was in the market for purchasing information.[21] He did receive a considerable amount of information, good, bad, and indifferent, correct and false. Chances are that much of the intelligence the United States would have received for money would have been unimportant or false, but among it there would almost certainly have been some nuggets of considerable, perhaps decisive, importance.

But there was no willingness to invest heavily in the purchase of intelligence, the easiest and the laziest way to operate because there seemed to be no particular urgency to do so. The psychological-political climate was not conducive: The United States had prevailed in the Cold War, and it appeared almost invincible. It seemed far-fetched, to say the least, that a bunch of fanatic mullahs from deepest Afghanistan were engaged in a major conspiracy that could inflict great harm on the United States. True, they had shown both aggressive spirit and competence in the attacks in East Africa and Yemen. But East Africa and Yemen were far away and an attack on mainland America still seemed unlikely, except to a few experts who greatly worried but had no access to the president, the vice president, or the secretaries of state and defense. (President Clinton preferred to receive his intelligence briefings in writing; President Bush meets the CIA director most mornings.) And even if they would have had access, who would have listened? So many other important issues needed to be discussed, and everyone was in need of some rest, especially during the summer holidays. And so it came to pass that during the late spring and summer of 2001, the various working groups on terrorism and the principal actors in Washington did not meet, even though there had been more and more information to the effect that al Qa'ida planned an attack in the United States and that there might have been an attempt to assassinate the president while at the Genoa summit.[22]

Following investigations after the event, a variety of warnings came to light that had not been followed up at the time. On August 6, 2001, a memorandum had been submitted to President Bush according to which bin Laden and his followers intended to bring the fight to America. Various possibilities had been mentioned on this and earlier occasions, including the hijacking of planes and crashing them into the White House, Pentagon, and CIA headquarters. There had been a similar report in 1999, and according to a message from an FBI agent in Phoenix, Arizona, there was suspicious activity at American flying schools involving militant Muslims. Even earlier in 1996, Abdul Hakim Murad, a Pakistani pilot with links to al Qa'ida who had been arrested in the Philippines, had confessed that his groups intended to crash planes loaded with explosives into prominent federal buildings on mainland United States. But five years had passed and no attack had taken place; obviously vigilance had slackened. There had been warnings from British, Egyptian, French, and Israeli intelligence as well as from agents in the field, but most of this information had not been specific. There were no hard facts and dates, and it was not clear whether the attacks would take place in a week or a month or a year or whether these were just fantasies. True, some items should have been followed up but were not, whether because these were just drops in an ocean of information, or because of bureaucratic difficulties created by the central administration, or because of the fear of being considered politically incorrect. "Ethnic profiling" was thought to be a cardinal sin.

The CIA did not have agents inside al Qa'ida except perhaps one operative who was not very high up in the hierarchy. Given bin Laden's propensity to play his cards close to his chest and the fact that the cells in various countries kept only close links with the center, infiltration was exceedingly difficult. What could the administration have done facing these reports? It could have allocated far greater resources to the intelligence agencies and kept watch that these were put to good use. But it could not have grounded all civilian aircraft for an indefinite period.[23]

The Media and the Terrorist Threat

Postmortems on intelligence failure usually focus on agencies such as the CIA. But intelligence agencies are seldom the only bodies engaged in collecting of information on current events and their evaluation. While it is unlikely that the U.S. media would have been able to send investigative reporters to join bin Laden in Afghanistan, or that an assistant professor of Islamic studies would have spent his sabbatical with al Qa'ida, journalists and academics both have (or should have had) an interest in these movements. In fact, several journalists did see and interview bin Laden in the 1990s, whereas the CIA apparently did not. While the academics were not in a position to monitor the communications between bin Laden and his underlings, they should have been at least as well equipped as the CIA experts to assess radical Islamism.

Any investigation of an intelligence failure which ignores this part of the story — the information that came in or should have come in by channels other than intelligence — is therefore incomplete and might be unfair and misleading.

The failure of the American media to realize the importance of terrorism is in part the story of deficient coverage of the outside world in general. There were in the 1990s far fewer foreign correspondents than forty or fifty years earlier. It was estimated that keeping a foreign correspondent abroad cost about three hundred thousand dollars, and thus it came as no surprise that of the one hundred leading newspapers in the United States, three-quarters had no foreign correspondents at all. In the 1960s up to 40 percent of the news time on television was dedicated to foreign news.[24] Thirty years later this percentage had shrunk to 10 percent or less. Of the correspondents stationed abroad, some 35 percent were in the Middle East, or to be precise in and around Israel, because the conflict between Israel and the Palestinians was thought to be of greatest interest to readers. But by and large, editors believed, rightly or wrongly, that most of their readers had only a limited interest in foreign affairs, unless these affairs had a direct and visible impact on their life. According to the common wisdom, prominently featuring foreign news stories meant a drop of 25 percent or more in newsstand sales.

There was no systematic coverage in the American media about the outside world in contrast to, for instance, the leading European newspapers; if a dramatic event would occur in Sarajevo or Mogadishu, journalists and camera operators would be dispatched in great numbers and there would be for days or weeks very extensive coverage. But then the journalists would depart, and for months or even years these exotic places would not be mentioned even once.

After September 11, the same editors who had been reluctant to put foreign stories on the cover were lamenting that they had failed their readers as far as terrorism is concerned and that it was even possible that this failure had played a certain part in the lack of national preparedness.

There were other, deeper problems; journalists operating in democratic countries can move more or less freely and function more or less normally, but most of the Middle Eastern and Asian countries are not democracies. Journalists asking questions that are too sensitive or those too critical in their coverage can find themselves cut off from vital access to sources one way or another or can be compelled to leave. Foreign journalists were ambushed and kidnapped, and some of them were killed. Being subject to pressures and blackmail, direct and indirect, journalists tried to be "objective" or neutral in their coverage, which also expressed itself in the terms used. Sometimes the word *terrorist* was put in quotation marks, while very often other terms were used, such as "urban guerrillas," "militants," or "activists." A spade could be called an agricultural implement in many ways. It is understandable that journalists in the field unwilling to offend terrorists used such practices. It was more disturbing when heads of news agencies and editors in home offices behaved in a similar manner.

The general weakness in reporting and analyzing foreign affairs quite apart, there was no great eagerness to cover in depth either terrorism or radical Islamism. True, terrorism on a grand scale is always of interest to the media, but it all depended on where it happened. A reader would have looked in vain for any satisfactory treatment of, for instance, the issue of suicide bombing in Sri Lanka, which happened to be the *locus classicus* of such operations. He would have found even less about the activities of radical Muslim organizations in various parts of the world engaging in violent actions, their traditions, ideological inspiration, international connections, and ultimate aims. The issue was, of course, not totally ignored and there was no embargo; there were several television documentaries, but these were few and far between. They were considered controversial and probably detrimental to good relations with ethnic or religious minorities.

There were some obvious indications reflecting the general lack of interest in terrorism prior to September 11, 2001. One is the magnitude of the rewards for the capture of the terrorists considered most dangerous (they went up from a few hundred thousand dollars to $5 million over a period of ten years), and this even after major terrorist attacks had occurred. The other is the circulation in Washington of the two journals specializing in the field of terrorism. Outside the Library of Congress, those interested would have found it virtually impossible to find a copy of these publications in a major library. They were considered of little interest, a luxury at a time when libraries faced (as always) financial stringencies. Books about terrorism or radical Islam fared a little better but not very much so. They would sell a few thousand copies. Most of them were published by university presses, and only rarely would they be reviewed in leading newspapers in a prominent place.[25] In brief, just as the politicians did not think that terrorism was a very important issue, publishers and newspaper and TV editors seemed to agree with them.

Moreover, there was a certain bias against intelligence agencies and, to a certain degree, also with regard to those writing about terrorism. The aversion to the CIA goes back to the 1960s and 1970s, to Vietnam and the period when the intelligence agencies had come in for massive attack on the domestic scene. Ironically, after September 11, 2001, a great many articles appeared in the American media with titles such as "What went wrong?" or "The trouble with the CIA," asking some pertinent questions such as why the CIA and the other agencies did not have agents on the ground fluent in local languages, why the CIA had become increasingly unwilling to take risks, why it had reduced its reliance on overseas human intelligence, and generally speaking, why it had not been up to the job.[26]

The irony was that twenty-five and thirty years earlier articles with the same titles had appeared, sometimes written by the same authors who had argued that the CIA was taking too many risks and that it had contacts with very unsavory characters and engaged in dubious activities. There had been an anti-CIA bias in much of the media; intelligence agents in movies and television plays were usually depicted as villains. Justified or not, these attacks on the CIA created a negative climate. They were bound to lead to substantial cuts in intelligence budgets and induced those employed by these agencies not to engage in any activities that might expose them to new attacks. In other words, the people who complained in 2001 about insufficient risk taking by the CIA had made a major contribution to the development of this mind-set in bygone years.

Terrorism and the Academic Experts

Conflict resolution had appeared on the American academic scene decades earlier, but terrorism as a subject of research and comment virtually did not exist before September 11. This changed radically with a veritable explosion of comment, particularly on the part of social scientists. The Social Science Research Council (SSRC) published essays almost daily by sociologists, political scientists, and anthropologists, which were subsequently published as books.[27] The intention was to provide in-depth background information in contrast to the clichés and the superficial writing in the media. However, it soon appeared that most of the comments had little to contribute to an understanding of terrorism in general and the events leading to September 11 in particular. One would have expected some interesting contributions from psychologists, but there were no psychologists among those invited, and there might have been good reasons for this apparent oversight. Instead, there was the same inclination as in the media to parade hobbyhorses, except that in contrast to the media they were not carried away by emotions of patriotism; in a majority of cases postcolonial studies, American imperialism, the new world order, the liberalism of fear, and antiglobalism featured far more prominently than terrorism. On the other hand, advice was liberally offered to the authorities on what to do, and what not to do, about terrorism.

Two groups of experts remain to be mentioned who had (or should have had) an important impact on public opinion. There were many hundreds of Middle Eastern and South Asian specialists in American universities and also many students of Islam, ancient and modern. America had greatly benefited from the influx of leading scholars from Europe after World War II, with Philip Hitti teaching in Princeton, Josef Schacht at Columbia, H. A. R. Gibbs at Harvard, and Gustav von Gruenebaum at UCLA. American academe had become second-to-none in this field. True, most of these experts had only limited interest in contemporary affairs (except in their capacity as private citizens), but they helped to establish a solid tradition of scholarship. Their many students were to take leading positions in the fields in later years.

Inevitably perhaps these fields became much more politicized in the late 1960s and the 1970s. Edward Said, a well-known professor of comparative literature at Columbia, of Egyptian-Palestinian origin, published a book entitled *Orientalism*, which became the bible of the new critical thinking.[28] As he saw it, traditional Orientalists (many of them of Jewish origin) had adopted a patronizing attitude toward Islam and the Arab peoples, insufficiently appreciating their contribution to world culture and firmly believing in the superiority of Western civilization. According to Said, classic academic Orientalism was inspired by the spirit of imperialism and colonialism.

The Said thesis generated many critical reactions, and it is probably accurate to say that it met with a lack of acceptance from any serious scholar. But it still won much acclaim on the political level, for it coincided with a shift to what was commonly called the left in this field of studies and also the influx of newcomers — young lecturers of Arab origin. Furthermore, there was the impact of certain new intellectual fashions such as postmodernism and postcolonial studies which, strictly speaking, had little in common with Marxism but served as an up-to-date manifestation of free-floating radicalism.

All this had a bearing on mainstream academic attitudes. Also a wider public existed for the views expressed by representatives of the new orthodoxy that were echoed in the media. Graduates from these "post-Orientalist" study centers and departments would later join government agencies, and the academic experts would be called in for consultation by Washington. A similar process, albeit not necessarily for the same reasons, took place in other Western countries.

The post-Orientalist mainstream views were perhaps most authoritatively expressed by Professor John L. Esposito of Georgetown University, not an extreme exponent of this school. Esposito's main text is entitled *The Islamic Threat: Myth or Reality?* and it voiced his belief that the threat was largely or perhaps entirely a figment of imagination.[29] As he saw it, "Islamic fundamentalism" (a term he more often than not put in quotation marks) was largely a liberating force, even though there were some regrettable lapses and excesses. Many millions of Muslims throughout the Middle East, North Africa, Central Asia, and South Asia were aspiring to greater political liberalization and democratization, and most Islamic movements were not anti-Western.

In Esposito's view, Islam and the Arabs had been unfairly demonized, and Western policies had too often backed the wrong horse, meaning traditional Arab regimes rather than the progressive Islamists whose doctrines were in many ways less important than their (progressive/populist) social roots and motives. Most Western students of Islam (and politicians) were secular in approach and therefore incapable of understanding the subject of their study. Islam was regarded by them as something fixed and seen as reluctant to accept change.

Esposito believed that Islam (and Islamism) was not a threat to the West but a challenge to the complacency of Western societies. Esposito did not accept the view that mixing religion and politics necessarily led to fanaticism and extremism, only a threat to entrenched elites and rulers.[30] The West should not see Islamization programs as a danger, because these would lead sooner or later to the emergence of civil societies.

Esposito also dealt with bin Laden and his comrades-in-arms. American policy makers regarded him as a dangerous terrorist, but in fact there was no real hard evidence that he had committed or sponsored acts of terrorism. Instead, Esposito claimed, bin Laden was a champion of popular causes. Esposito did not think that one could give a clear answer to the question of "Who is a terrorist?" given that the definition of legitimate and illegitimate force is a contentious and subjective one. In some ways, he echoed Pontius Pilate asking, "What is extremism? What is terrorism? Often the answer depends upon where one stands."[31] True, later on Esposito had fewer doubts about terrorism and the terrorists, and he admonished mainstream Muslims to address more aggressively the threat to Islam from religious extremists. But this was well after September 11, 2001.[32]

If Esposito warned against focusing on Osama bin Laden and catapulting him to center stage, some of his colleagues went further and considered any preoccupation with Islamic terrorism positively unhealthy. As Professor Fawaz Gerges wrote:

> Should not observers and academics keep skeptical about the U.S. Government's assessment of the terrorist threat? To what extent do terrorist "experts" indirectly perpetrate the irrational fear of terrorism by focusing too much on farfetched horrible scenarios? Does the terrorist industry, consciously or unconsciously, exaggerate the nature and degree of the terrorist threat to American citizens?[33]

The post-Orientalist students were genuinely worried about those who were misleading, deliberately or not, public opinion about the real essence of Islam. The main culprit was the British historian Bernard Lewis, who had settled in the United States and whose essay "The Roots of Muslim Rage" was widely read when it was published a decade earlier.[34] It was Lewis's contention that the struggle between Islam and the West — having lasted fourteen centuries, after a long series of jihads and crusades, attacks and counterattacks — was again seized by an intense and violent resentment of the West. Esposito did not dispute the roots as discussed by Lewis (of Islamic countries falling behind) but he thought it false and irresponsible to generalize; after all, no one would dare to talk about Jewish or Christian rage. Readers of Lewis, as Esposito saw it, would logically conclude that Muslims have a historical propensity to violence against and hatred for the West, or else that Muslims are emotional, irrational, and prone to war.

Esposito believed that this was far from the truth because it did not differentiate between a variety of groups; the majority of fundamentalist organizations were led by well-educated leaders who may criticize and reject the West but were by no means violent in character.

If Esposito wrote on the whole in measured, almost statesmanlike terms, this same assessment cannot be made of Edward Said, the well-known literary scholar. While of Christian descent and a secularist, he felt it his duty to defend Islam against its detractors. He had likewise been provoked by Lewis and attacked him in terms seldom found in academic discourse.[35] Lewis was not only strident and reductionist, his practices were fraudulent, bogus, antihuman, and arrogant, and his thesis was devoid of historical truth and indeed rational argument. But the issue was not only Professor Bernard Lewis; he had strongly influenced Samuel Huntington, the Harvard professor whose book on the clash of civilizations was very widely read; he had also influenced journalists, and perhaps some people in government.

According to Said, these perfervid anti-Muslims making extravagant claims suggested that all or almost all Muslims were fundamentalists and that all fundamentalists were terrorists. Most of what the media reported about Islam and Muslims was simply hostile propaganda sponsored by Jewish, pro-Zionist writers. Even in Hollywood and in television, where in an earlier period the sheikh had been an exotic figure of charm and romance, Muslims had now become uniformly violent and evil.

In reality, according to Said, Muslims and in particular Arabs were not more violent than other people, except if they had been provoked beyond endurance by Western imperialists and Zionists. The prevailing trend in the Muslim world was not toward the adoption of reactionary medieval attitudes. By and large, in the contest between the Islamists and the overwhelming majority of the (peaceful and reform-minded) Muslims, the former had lost the battle. Political Islam had failed.[36]

Paradoxically, Said did not deal in his book with the problem of Islamism; he must have thought radical Islam of little importance and was greatly surprised and somewhat dismayed when the Islamists welcomed his book as one of their main weapons against secularists — such as Said.[37] To summarize the views of Esposito and Said, American public opinion had been misled about the real mood and the real state of affairs in the Muslim and Arab world.

But was it really true that anti-Islamic views prevailed among the (often Jewish) experts who had conjured up a nonexisting threat? Martin Kramer, writing just before September 11, certainly did not think so. In a review of Middle Eastern studies in America, which caused great annoyance among those whom he had targeted, he showed on the basis of much factual material that while in the 1960s and 1970s there had been great enthusiasm among American students of the Middle East for the liberating, progressive force of Arab nationalism, this had been replaced by a similar faith in Islamism, which took the place of Arab nationalism as "the irresistible force for liberation, the motor of reform, the fulcrum of civil society."

As time went by, Islamism would reveal itself to be none of these things, but instead retrograde reading of Islam.[38] Nevertheless, those who had been singing its praises in American universities went from strength to strength. The post-Orientalists had taken over the Middle East centers in the universities, the foundation panels which allocated study grants, as well as MESA, the professional organization of students of the Middle East. And they were, in Kramer's words, waiting for the Middle East to catch up with them, but it never did. Nothing unfolded according to their theory and expectations:

> Weaned on the certainty of change from below, the new generation (of post-colonial, post-Orientalist scholars) had to interpret decade after decade of immobility and economic stagnation, the empowerment of the state and the demobilization of society. Even worse, they tried to play their deuces as if they were aces, destroying their credibility in the process. Over time they forfeited the trust of government, the public, the foundations, and even their own departments.[39]

Among the reasons for the intelligence failure of the post-Orientalists, Kramer mentioned one that had little to do with ideological blinkers, which of course also played a role — the heavy emphasis on "theoretical relevance" that had been preached by the leaders in the field and the fact that theories were considered to be far more important than Middle East realities: In such a climate there is a strong incentive to put theoretical commitment before empirical observation. Even though this had been the source of repeated error, breaking out of this ideological circle was to run the risk of being denounced as a disciplinary naïf or a latent Orientalist.[40]

Kramer's report on the state of Middle Eastern studies inevitably caused great resentment and bitter attacks, and it was suggested that his criticism had been informed by the fact that he was Jewish and made his home in Israel. It is indeed likely that his Tel Aviv vantage point had influenced his assessment and sharpened his senses, but in the final analysis this question did not pertain to the sociology of knowledge. It was not really decisive whether those criticizing the mainstream thinkers in the field were Arab, Jewish, or Patagonians. The crucial issue was who had been right and who had erred in assessing trends in the Middle East and the Muslim world?[41] And it was difficult to deny that the post-Orientalists had erred, not just by *suggestio falsi* but also by *repressio veri*. When Osama bin Laden had published his famous fatwa of 1998 calling for the indiscriminate murder of Americans, not one of the members of the post-Orientalist fraternity had thought it necessary to draw attention to this fact. There was one notable exception, Bernard Lewis, the symbol of all that was reactionary and hateful in old Orientalism. Lewis published the text of the fatwa in *Foreign Affairs*, and he was virtually the only one to draw attention to this ominous event.[42]

Kramer was charged by a colleague with exaggeration. Was it not true that a Georgetown professor had published a book in 1999 which included a long chapter about "Osama bin Laden and the Advice and Reform Committee?" The author had indeed spent two years in Saudi Arabia and his book contained many interesting details together with the usual genuflections to the age of postmodernism, Foucault, Baudrillard, and postcolonial studies.[43] The book, according to its cover, was a significant contribution to the theoretical debate about domination and resistance and other postcolonial concepts. There was a great deal about the launching of the "Advice and Reform Committee," but not much about terrorism and the Afghan International Brigade. Bin Laden, he wrote, amounted to little in the Saudi context; most Saudi princes had more money than he had. The author overlooked the fact that bin Laden did not seek his political future in the Saudi context.

When a critic of Kramer wrote that it was not ignorance of bin Laden that explains the tragedy of September 11, but a failure of imagination on the part of all concerned regarding the specific forms such an attack might take, this was only part of the truth. For the search for Osama bin Laden, his sympathizers and their activities had been thought of little importance and had, in fact, been discouraged. Another critic of Kramer argued that the academics had not failed but that the politicians subordinating political to economic reform had ignored their recommendations; in reality, U.S. policy makers had little influence promoting either.[44]

Not all the ideas and suggestions of the mainstream post-Orientalists had been wrong and unhelpful. They had been right in stressing the need for a constructive dialogue with the reform-minded democratic forces in the Islamic world in an attempt to reduce the danger of a clash between civilizations which the radicals had conjured up and indeed tried to provoke. But their cardinal mistakes were wishful thinking and harboring illusions about prevailing trends in the Muslim world. And even if they had been right asserting that the radical groups advocating violence against the West were a small and declining minority (which it certainly was not), the idea should have occurred to them that there was room for apprehension, because to conduct a terrorist campaign one did not need the participation of hundreds of millions.

No critic had argued that Islam was an aggressive religion *tout court* and that all strands of thought within Islam aimed at permanent jihad. The apologists, on the other hand, must have been perfectly aware that the jihadists were active and influential, but they thought that to publicize this was politically unwise. Thus it was only after September 11 that it was conceded that "one must come to terms with the fact that supremacist Puritanism in contemporary Islam is dismissive of all moral norms or ethical values.... Their prime and nearly singular concern is power and its symbols."[45]

Kramer's argument was open to criticism for other reasons. If, as he argued, mainstream American Orientalists had lost credibility with the government, how could they be made responsible, even in part, for the intelligence failure of September 2001? He had probably exaggerated somewhat their loss of credibility, and furthermore they could always argue that the main reason for Arab rage was Israel and that they had always warned against American support for the Jewish state. This was not altogether persuasive, for they had denied the existence of the rage earlier on, and Israel had hardly ever appeared in bin Laden's propaganda prior to 2001. But there were many critics of Israel in Washington and on the campuses, and such arguments helped at least to limit the damage.[46]

To summarize — the mainstream of American students of Middle East and Islam had been wrong as far as their assessment of contemporary trends in the Arab world had been concerned. True, they had never had a decisive influence on the making of U.S. foreign policy in that region. But their views, directly or indirectly, did have a certain impact both on policy makers and on public opinion, and they were certainly not preparing the non-experts for the shape of things to come.

What of the state of Middle Eastern and Islamic studies in countries such as Britain, Germany, or France? This is only of limited relevance in the present context because outside experts had traditionally not played any significant role in the policy making of these countries, and their outreach on public opinion was limited. (In France, they had been a little more influential.) The majority of Islamic and Middle Eastern scholars had been critical of the West for not being more forthcoming toward the Muslims and Islam, and an even greater majority had regarded Israel as an alien intruder in this part of the world. An earlier generation of French Orientalists, such as Massignon and Bercque, had been greatly enamored of all things Islamic, so much so that many Muslims thought that they had converted to Islam. But the ideological bias of their successors had been tempered by greater realism; by the 1990s, they had few illusions about the liberating, democratic mission of radical Islamism. A few, such as Bassam Tibi, a Syrian scholar teaching at a German university, were warning against the dangers he saw; others, like the French Gilles Kepel and Olivier Roy, also devoted books and articles to the violent young men preaching jihad, but they thought that the wave had crested and that political Islam was in quick decline.[47] They did not foresee the events of September 2001, nor had they claimed that the study of terrorist groups in the Muslim world was a taboo subject.

Precisely a year after the events of September 11, 2001, the first world Oriental Congress opened in Mainz, Germany, and was attended by two thousand guests. The keynote speakers made it clear that the Muslims were wholly misunderstood by others, that the West had no interest as far as Middle Eastern realities were concerned, and that U.S. policy was all along radically wrong. Edward Said, who received the award of the Congress, declared that it was not the task of Islamic and Middle Eastern experts to issue warnings with regard to terrorists, this was the job of secret services: "Why do we pay taxes?"[48] While outside observers commenting on the Congress referred to the bankruptcy of the discipline, the majority expressed satisfaction and confidence as far as their performance was concerned.

Studying Terrorism

The discipline of the study of terrorism is a recent development; it goes back no further than the early 1970s. It was almost entirely limited to the United States and Britain; while there was a great deal of terrorism in Western Europe and Latin America, there was no systematic study in these countries, except, of course, monographs dealing with local terrorist groups.[49] The history of the discipline remains to be written; in the present context only certain of its aspects are of relevance, above all the question to what extent did it help to understand the coming of the "new terrorism" of 2001 and what impact did it have on policy makers, the media, and the public at large.

Among those who made important contributions during the early stage were David Fromkin, the author of a seminal article in *Foreign Affairs* in 1975; Martha Crenshaw, then a young professor who became interested in the field as the result of her study of the Algerian insurrection against the French; Brian Jenkins at Rand who had been a captain in the Green Berets in Vietnam earlier on and also a painter; J. Bowyer Bell, a student of the Ulster conflict; and Paul Wilkinson, then a lecturer at University College, Cardiff, with his main interest in terrorism and the liberal state. Walter Reich, a Washington-based psychiatrist, was attracted to the study of terrorism as the result of his interest in the psychological roots of violence, and the writer of the present lines came to the field following work on the history of guerrilla warfare.[50] There had been a few earlier writers such as E. V. Walter, an anthropologist, and Th. P. Thornton, who back in 1964 had noted that terrorism was above all a symbolic act.[51] But Walter and Thornton had been writing well before the resurgence of terrorism after World War II, and while they were often quoted by those who came after them, their real impact on the development of the discipline was limited.

Not all of those present at the creation of the discipline stayed with it. Fromkin, who had been among the first to emphasize that nationalist-separatist terrorists had greater support than those belonging to the extreme left or right, turned to the study of Middle East and Balkan diplomacy; my own work during most of the 1980s and early 1990s was in fields other than terrorism. Thornton worked for some time in the National Security Council while Alex Schmid, Dutch by origin, joined the staff of the United Nations.

The assignment considered most urgent in the early days of the study was to find a definition, for how was it possible to study a topic without agreement as to what it was? My own feeling was skeptical, not that it was not highly desirable to agree on a definition but the difficulties in finding an all-comprehensive definition seemed (and actually were) insurmountable. The character of terrorism tended to change in time and space. What was true for one terrorism movement in a certain country during a given period did not necessarily apply to a group in another country, at another time, heir to different politics and traditions.[52] To give but one example: When Paul Wilkinson wrote his early book (*Political Terrorism,* New York, 1974), his preoccupation was solely with revolutionary terrorism, which was only natural because it was the prevailing mode at the time. Ten years later the situation had changed, and with it the emphasis on other forms of terrorism. But in the early days a great deal of time and effort was invested in the endeavor finding a comprehensive definition; many definitions were produced, some of them helpful, others less so. The magic, elusive formula has not been found to this day.[53]

With all this there was certainly agreement about certain features common to the terrorism of the 1970s and 1980s, such as the fact that terrorism was the weapon of the weak, that it killed relatively few people, but that it had a considerable propagandistic impact — terrorism as propaganda by deed as the nineteenth-century anarchists had claimed.[54]

Other assertions were only partly true even at the time, such as the thesis that terrorism was the weapon of the poor and downtrodden or that terrorists were revolutionaries mostly (or always) of a left-wing persuasion. Poverty was sometimes a contributing factor, and very wealthy people and societies seldom engage in terrorism, but there have been exceptions even in this respect. This thesis was factually untrue and it underrated the ideological motivation of the terrorists. Those who believed that terrorists were left-wing revolutionaries were greatly shocked and surprised when they had to face increasingly terrorist campaigns that were anything but left-wing in inspiration.

There was also the neoanarchist school whose best-known spokesman was Noam Chomsky, famous student of linguistics, according to which it was wrong to study substate political violence (i.e., terrorism) in isolation. For was it not true that states, and especially imperialist states such as the United States, had been instrumental in the murder of many more people than the relatively small and uninfluential terrorist groups? The political motives of this approach were obvious, based on the tacit assumption that most (if not all) violence from below was justified whereas a state, and in particular a great and powerful state, was a priori evil since it was based on repression.

This approach would have made the study of terrorism impossible, for it would have included not only U.S. foreign policy, but also Hitler and Stalin and eventually the whole history of mankind which, after all, had been replete with wars, civil wars, and repression of many kinds. It was a manifestly absurd approach, and few among the terrorism experts would seriously consider it. But it had a certain impact on sections of the wider public; Chomsky was a well-known intellectual, and through his many books, articles, interviews, and the Internet he reached an audience larger than the terrorism experts did with their specialized publications.[55]

Once the issue of the definition had been bypassed, the terrorism experts engaged in a search for a theory, or theories, to explain and if possible to predict terrorism. Everyone agreed that without a theory terrorism studies were a rudderless ship, but where could the compass be found? Some believed that the relative deprivation model, which took several forms, was most promising. Terrorism was thought to have been caused by misery and oppression, but the leaders usually consisted of educated, middle-class people. However, these theories could never satisfactorily explain why terrorism did not usually occur in the most oppressed and poorest countries, and after a number of years their influence waned. In later years, new concepts emerged such as "asymmetric warfare" and "networking" (with special reference to terrorism), but these were generally new terms for old and well-known realities.

Other students of terrorism looked to clinical psychology for guidance: could one establish perhaps a psychological profile of a terrorist? They were offered a variety of theories, some helpful, some abstruse. Some experts had discovered certain personality traits among the terrorists, while others had failed to do so and a few even claimed that terrorists were perfectly normal people. But this was not very helpful either, for if they were indeed people "like you and me," how to explain that the great majority of mankind did not engage in terrorism?[56]

It would be difficult to point to major theoretical breakthroughs in the field of terrorism studies, but even if new terms appeared such as "asymmetric warfare" or "networking," these referred usually to trends and facts that had been known for a long time; in the case of "networking," it was the existence of loosely connected cells of terrorists. One expert complained that statistical analysis was uncommon in terrorism research; as Galton had advised his contemporaries a long time ago: Whenever you can, count. But such advice was tempered by the admission that people were usually extremely complex and their behavior often erratic and confusing, and it was by no means always clear what factors were important and should be counted and compared.[57]

Terrorist studies had taken off in the late 1970s, and while there still was no intention to establish departments or centers at universities dealing with these topics, conferences took place and seminars, national and international, and journals were founded devoted to this specific kind of political violence. A great body of knowledge was assembled, not as the result of breathtaking theoretical breakthroughs or the Newtonian discovery of a model that would give an answer to the many remaining questions, but as a consequence of the diligent study of specific aspects of terrorism and individual movements from Sendero Luminoso in Peru to the Palestinian Hamas, from the radical Islamic groups in Egypt to the IRA and the Basque ETA.

There were still many unsolved problems. There was no denying that terrorism was carried out by people who felt oppressed; contented and happy people seldom commit acts of violence and even less often acts of indiscriminate violence. But it was equally obvious, as noted more than once earlier on, that precisely in the most oppressive regimes in modern times — such as the fascist states or Stalin's Russia — there had been no terrorism, and even old-fashioned dictatorships such as Franco's Spain or Syria under Hafez el Asad had made short shrift with terrorism. This did suggest that terrorism could operate and flourish only in certain conditions.

It also became increasingly clear that the terrorism of the 1970s and 1980s was by no means a monopoly of the extreme left as many had originally believed, but that it was waged also by the violent fringe of the extreme right in many countries and that the theories about the "revolutionary" character of terrorism were one-sided and misleading. At most, it could be argued that terrorism often was, or pretended to be, "populist" and that populism could with equal ease turn left and right. But accepting the obvious did not lead very far.

A second fact became more or less accepted. Terrorism, in contrast to the guerrilla warfare of World War II and the early postwar period (with Yugoslavia, China, but also Vietnam and Cuba as the obvious examples), had not been very successful. While many of the guerrilla movements emerged victorious, few if any of the terrorist groups did. By the 1960s the era of decolonization had more or less ended, and what remained were a variety of relatively small terrorist groups, some left-wing in inspiration, others right-wing, yet others nationalist-separatist. They caused difficulties, sometimes serious difficulties, to the governments in power, but they were not remotely as important a political factor as the guerrilla movements had been.

It seemed therefore only obvious that most terrorism experts should reach the conclusion that all in all there was no "steady growth" of terrorism, as popular media sometimes announced, and that the then-existing terrorist groups were unlikely to attain their goals.[58] But leading students of terrorism also stressed that it seemed quite likely that this perspective was bound to change, and that as weapons of mass destruction (WMD) would be used by terrorists they would sooner or later be able to inflict infinitely greater damage on society.

But would the then-existing terrorist groups use weapons of mass destructions? The Gilmore committee in its report of 1999 recalled some of the early predictions of terrorism experts. Brian Jenkins had written that terrorists want a lot of people watching and a lot of people listening but not a lot of people dead: "Scenarios involving the deliberate dispersal of toxic radioactive material do not appear to fit the pattern of any terrorist actions carried out so far. It has not been the style of terrorists to kill hundreds or thousands. To make hundreds or thousands of people terminally ill would be even more out of character." However, writing almost twenty-five years later, Jenkins reconsidered his position and reached the conclusion that both the change in terrorist mind and the increased accessibility to nuclear material had made nuclear terrorism more likely.[59]

J. Bowyer Bell, the expert on the IRA, wrote in a similar vein that there was no evidence that terrorists have any interest in killing large numbers of people.[60] My own writings (from 1977) were quoted by the Gilmore committee to the effect that the terrorist groups existing at present will not use this option, either as a matter of political principle or because it would defeat their purpose. But I added, "Some groups might well opt for the weapons of super violence because their aim is not political change but the total destruction of the enemy." Writing ten years later I sounded slightly more cautious — groups such as the German, Italian, French, Turkish, or Latin American terrorists were unlikely to use nuclear, chemical, or bacteriological weapons assuming that they have any political sense at all — an assumption that cannot always be taken for granted: "They claim to act on behalf of the people, they aspire to popular support, and clearly the use of arms of mass destruction would not add to their popularity."[61]

In retrospect, our assessments were correct with regard to the terrorist groups that existed at the time. But in the 1990s new groups of a very different character came into being on which the restraints of an earlier period no longer applied. Not only did access to the means of mass destruction become easier, fanaticism became far more pronounced than before. This trend, especially the growth of religiously motivated terrorism, was noticed by students of terrorism early on.[62] Bruce Hoffman, to give but one example, noted that religious-motivated terrorism was unconstrained by the political, moral, and practical constraints that affected other (secular) terrorists, and he also observed that religious terrorism had a constituency different from the secular.[63] Most students of terrorism realized that the new terrorism differed in essential aspects from the old. Establishing who first used the term "new terrorism" is difficult now, but by the end of the decade it was in common usage. My own book entitled *The New Terrorism: Fanaticism and the Arms of Mass Destruction* (1999) ended with the following words:

Diderot once noted that the transition from fanaticism to barbarism was but one step, and if present trends continue there is every reason for grim forebodings. . . . The consequences of aggressive madness in the age of high technology and the era of weapons of mass destruction may well be beyond our imagination. Megaterrorism could well become what Florus, a Roman historian, wrote about a contemporary *fax et turbo sequentis centuri* — the incendiary torch and the devastating storm of the coming century.[64]

Similar forebodings were often voiced in the media, as presidents and political leaders frequently referred to terrorism as one of the great dangers facing mankind. Television networks devoted much of their prime time to news of terrorist operations. There was even some hyperbole when publicists referred to terrorism as the cancer of the modern world, growing inexorably until it poisoned and engulfed the society on which it fed. But there was a curious discrepancy between the rhetoric and the action that was taken. When the Swedish prime minister was killed in 1986, the Swedish government offered an award equal to the monthly salary of a popular entertainer or investment banker for information leading to the apprehension of the killer. The West German government offered some fifty thousand dollars for their most dangerous terrorists and the French about the same. The United States offered at the time up to five hundred thousand dollars, not an overwhelming sum considering the frequency of the speeches on terrorism and the intensity of the rhetoric. The U.S. government devoted $20–30 million annually to the development of technological means to preempt and combat terrorism; this sum greatly increased in the 1990s, and $10 billion was allocated for the struggle against terrorism in fiscal year 2000. This presented a marked change in attitudes vis-à-vis terrorism. But in the 1980s, the sums allocated for this purpose were still small by any standard.

Senators, congressmen, and the media would question from time to time (especially when a few months had passed without a major terrorist attack) whether this expenditure was really necessary.[65] Brian Jenkins compared government support for terrorism research at the time to the electrocardiogram of a healthy person — spikes followed by flat lines. There would be a sudden overwhelming focus followed by terrorism research being virtually ignored. Bruce Hoffman reports that when he left RAND for an academic position, one of the reasons was that the Cold War had ended and everyone in official Washington was saying that terrorism was going to disappear. There was no terrorism funding despite the World Trade Center bombing in 1993, which was viewed as an aberration, not a harbinger.[66] During the Cold War, various working groups dealt with surprise attack, but after 1990 these dissolved or faded out.

In retrospect, most terrorism experts did not pay sufficient attention to the bin Laden conspiracy which, after all, had been many years in the making and affected many countries in all continents. They expected instead a wave of terrorist outbursts at the end of the millennium committed by various Christian (and pagan) sects, and when the events that had been feared did not happen, there was a feeling of relief and a lowering of vigilance. As one observer wrote: "Whatever the historical significance of the millennium idea in some Christian movements, round numbered dates were apparently not more likely to be tied to violence than others. While the millennium as an idea remained alive, it was divorced from action."[67]

Few terrorism experts had been trained in Middle Eastern and Islamic studies and followed events in the Muslim world with close attention, and they were certainly not alerted by their post-Orientalist colleagues who derided the few politically incorrect outsiders pointing to certain acute danger signs. Those who were trying to alert governments and a wider public of the dangers ahead were either written off as alarmists or accused of being hopelessly prejudiced against one of the world's great religions or having some vested interest in barking up the wrong tree.

Other circumstances also tended to mislead students of terrorism, such as the fixation on the impending use of the weapons of mass destruction. Primary here was the impact of the 1995 Tokyo subway attack by members of Aum, a Japanese sect which had used poison gas. Aum Shinrikyo, with assets of hundreds of millions of dollars, had purchased helicopters from Russia, had experimented with all kinds of chemical substances, and tried to purchase weapons from half a dozen countries. It was not a terrorist organization comparable to those of an earlier age, and the attack, even though comparatively unsuccessful, was considered by many a turning point in the history of terrorism. It led to certain measures being adopted by the U.S. government (such as the Defense Against Weapons of Mass Destruction Act of 1996 as well as several presidential directives), and for a while it heightened awareness of the dangers of a new age of terrorism. But when a number of years passed without any further and more effective attacks, a widespread feeling existed that the danger had, after all, been exaggerated.[68] Obviously, terrorists had great technical difficulties to overcome launching a successful attack using WMD, which they seemingly had not yet mastered. The idea that terrorists might learn from the Aum failure in Tokyo, just as Muslim radicals might learn from the failure to bring down the World Trade Center in 1993, found some adherents, but more seem to have believed that the threat was not at hand. At the same time, the danger of using more sophisticated and deadly conventional approaches was not given sufficient attention.

A debate began among the experts well before September 11, 2001, concerning the essence of the "new terrorism."[69] Simon and Benjamin, who had served in government, argued that a new period had dawned with the attempted bombing in 1993 of the World Trade Center, Oklahoma City, the attacks against the U.S. embassies in Africa, and the Aum attacks in Tokyo. While there was no disagreement in principle, other experts registered certain reservations. Reuven Paz pointed out that terrorism sponsored by radical Islamic groups went back several decades, whereas Olivier Roy believed that Iran had no longer a terrorist government; he had been among those who had pronounced Islamism dead (or at any rate dying, ten years earlier). Ehud Sprinzak, an Israeli professor, derided the "overheated rhetoric" and the "widespread hysteria" over terrorists acquiring weapons of mass destruction. Benjamin and Simon, on the other hand, having worked in the 1990s in the National Security Council, were more apprehensive and warned against belittling the threat. Whether this specific danger was close or as yet remote, there was almost general agreement that religiously motivated terrorism was to remain a threat for many years to come and that bin Laden had marshaled a network of operatives in more than fifty countries.[70] The insights gained by students of terrorism in recent decades had a certain impact on the thinking of governments, but much less so on academics and the media. It was a little depressing to be confronted time and again by statements or concepts that had no foundation in reality.

Mention has been made of the fact that those who downplayed the specific danger of major terrorist attacks were mostly students of Islam and of the Middle East. They feared that generalizations about Islam would antagonize the majority of peaceful Muslims. Others among them, subscribing to radical politics and secular in their outlook, were bound to underrate the religious fervor of radical Islam. As they saw it, fundamentalism was something like a "false consciousness," the ideological superstructure (in Marxist terms) of economic grievances. There was the belief, at least among some of them, that "militants" of the bin Laden type were somehow objectively fulfilling a revolutionary mission in their struggle against imperialist America.

If there was an intelligence failure in September 2001, it had many reasons: Western intelligence services had not succeeded in infiltrating the ranks of the conspirators, and their doctrine and their determination as well as their growing technical sophistication were not taken seriously enough. Not enough attention was paid to the international character of the conspiracy, the fact that it had spread to many countries. Or, to be precise, there was perhaps a growing realization that somehow a major attack was prepared, but it was no more than a vague feeling and there was no sense of urgency. In a similar way, the authorities were aware of the vulnerability of modern Western societies, but there was no acute apprehension and the feeling that in these circumstances anything could or should be done about it. In the media, terrorism did not figure prominently, and the majority of Islamic and Middle Eastern experts (especially the postcolonialists among them) for ideological reasons thought it wrong to give it much publicity. Those specializing in the field of terrorism studies were aware that terrorism had changed and that its potential had greatly increased, but they did not have any information as to when and where it would strike.

What if any lessons for the future can be drawn from the intelligence failure of September 2001? The obvious lessons are that intelligence is the key, and that it is always dangerous to underrate a foe. To obtain intelligence is difficult in the circumstances, especially when dealing with small groups of people operating in distant countries or in closed religious or ethnic communities in the West. But obtaining intelligence even in totalitarian regimes has been possible despite their effective apparatus of control and repression. Obvious preconditions are the presence of capable intelligence agents and the availability of sufficient funds; various reports prior to September 11, 2001, noted that this was not the case. Greater efforts have been made since then, but only time will tell whether these efforts are sufficient. When asked why journalists succeeded in obtaining in Afghanistan intelligence material (video film about Taliban preparations for the use of poisons) which the CIA received, the CIA spokesman answered, "There are more of them than of us and they are better paid."[71] Surprise is even more important in terrorism than in war: there are no massive troop concentrations, no major logistic preparations, and surprise attacks can come from unexpected quarters and through unexpected tactics. Deception plays a role in terrorist planning and so does innovation.

If counterterrorists learn from mistakes committed in the past, so do terrorists.

SEVEN

The Far Right

ERRORISM HAS ALWAYS provoked violent and often diametrically opposed reactions among a public baffled and shocked by sudden attacks. When the anarchists appeared on the European scene at the end of the nineteenth century, the prevailing attitude was one of panic and consternation. Joseph Conrad wrote about the banality of evil, and Henry James did not know at all (*Princess Casamassima*) what to make of the violent men attacking heads of state but also innocent bystanders. The reaction of the majority of the public was not different. But there were also some sympathizers, mainly among the avant-garde artists of the day, impressed by the aesthetics of terrorism. Even in his Paris prison Carlos ("the Jackal") had his admirers — among his correspondents was Hugo Chavez, the president of Venezuela. Timothy McVeigh, the bomber of Oklahoma City, counted among his pen pals Gore Vidal, the bestselling American writer.

Quite often the motives of the terrorists were obvious and there was substantial public support. When Vera Zasulich was acquitted by a Russian court for having shot a police general who had given orders to torture a member of her revolutionary group, students were waiting at the courthouse to honor and celebrate her action. There was support, moral and financial, in Russian liberal society for the daring of the social revolutionaries challenging a tyrannical regime. The Fenians, the Irish militants of the nineteenth and early twentieth centuries, had considerable sympathies among British liberals and also Irish Protestants; the assassins of Walther Rathenau, the Jewish foreign minister of the Weimar Republic, had well-wishers among the extreme right, the precursors of the Nazi Party. When Stalin sent his emissaries to kill Leon Trotsky, the murder was widely welcomed by Communist party members who had been told that the victim was an agent of Nazism and Western imperialism.

The early Latin American terrorists such as the Montoneros had their well-wishers on the left, and the same is true with regard to the Baader-Meinhof gang in Germany and the Red Brigades in Italy, as well as the Weathermen on American campuses. True, these fellow travelers were limited in numbers because the German and postwar Italian republics, with all the justified criticism that could be made against them, were the freest that these countries had ever known in their history, and the assertions by the terrorists that these were fascist, or at least potentially fascist, repressive regimes seemed far-fetched to the overwhelming majority.

The history of terrorist movements shows that those motivated by nationalism always had a greater reservoir of sympathy than those of the extreme left or right. The Jewish Irgun and the Stern gang had moral support among sections of the Jewish community in Palestine and in the United States. The Tamil Tigers could always count on support, moral and material, on the part of the Sri Lankan diaspora, the Armenians on assistance by fellow Armenians abroad, and the Palestinians on support by fellow Arabs. While not all their attacks were necessarily approved by their well-wishers, the feeling was that the heart and the instincts of the terrorists were in the right place, and that excess of patriotism in the struggle against the hated oppressor was never a sin. Even the Algerian radical Islamists slaughtering tens of thousands of their fellow countrymen found some sympathizers among North Africans in France. But as terrorism became more brutal and indiscriminate (and quite often self-defeating) in the choice of its targets, the terrorists quite often maneuvered themselves into isolation. The Japanese Aum spraying poison gas in the Tokyo underground did not have well-wishers outside their ranks.

Reactions vis-à-vis the attacks of September 2001 are of interest for a variety of reasons — because they ranged from total outrage and the burning wish to punish the evildoers to understanding for their motives and even identification with them. Surprisingly similar views were expressed on seemingly opposed sides of the political spectrum — the extreme right and the far left — and the events presented a field day to believers in conspiracy theories and paranoiacs of every kind. Lastly, the reactions showed great confusion with regard to the meaning of what had happened.

Inevitably the media would ask for their opinion virtually every person of fame or notoriety — philosophers and ballet dancers, pop stars and theologians, politicians, poets, and occasionally even some of those who had studied terrorism in its various manifestations. The media could certainly not be accused of casting their net too narrowly; on the first anniversary of September 11, the *New York Times* invited comments from twelve well-known Americans. They included three novelists, two law professors, two former politicians, one judge, one former heavyweight champion boxer, one playwright, one philosophy professor, and one senator.[1] The number of terrorism experts had been very small, but it increased a thousandfold within a few weeks, all of them giving interviews, providing interpretations, and making predictions. Everyone who had ever been near Afghanistan became an authority, as did many of those who had only recently acquired knowledge about the difference between Shi'ia and Sharia, between jihad and *zakat*.

The results were predictable. Karl Heinz Stockhausen, the famous composer, had to spend weeks and months explaining that he had not really meant what he said when he declared that the attacks on Manhattan had been the greatest work of art of all times. It was not really the fault of the philosophers, pop stars, and poets who as concerned citizens had felt it only their duty to express their views on issues of such vital importance. Less obvious was why the media should feel that soliciting their opinions was essential.

Comments of this kind reflected surprise and emotional shock, but they hardly shed new light on the deeper reasons for the terrorist actions. There was general agreement that one should not be satisfied with superficial explanations for what happened but instead to try to examine the roots. But those who had believed before that it was the fault of homosexuals and abortionists, or of the Jews, or the fact that the United States had killed hundreds of thousands of Iraqi children, or of poverty and oppression in the third world, or of relentless, cruel globalism, continued to believe that they had been correct all along. Those who had been convinced that Western societies were rotten (*le nous est haissable*) naturally were looking for extenuating circumstances for the terrorists. There was considerable psychological resistance against accepting new information that came to light about the origins of the new terrorism, about motives and ideology, about the identity and the background of its practitioners.

Some took it for granted that the terrorist attacks were the expression of the accumulated burning hatred of millions, if not billions, of people who had been exploited, oppressed, and mistreated. True, as time went by it appeared that the hatred was greater among the literary essayists than among the masses of people in Asia, Africa, and the Middle East who did not take up arms, who did not even demonstrate their rage in the streets.

The Extreme Right

Jerry Falwell, well-known American fundamentalist preacher, spoke harshly about the terrorists in an interview two days after their great attack, but in a discussion that followed he added that God may have allowed these deeds because of the moral decay of American society. He listed the ACLU, abortionists, feminists, gays, and others in the context and said they had much for which to repent.[2]

However, the following day there was an apology. Falwell said that the terrorists alone were to blame, even though theologically the groups which had worked to secularize America had helped to remove the nation from its spiritual foundation. Pat Robertson, who had been present at the interview, added that he had thought even at the time that Falwell's comment — a political statement attributing blame — totally inappropriate.[3]

Falwell and Robertson were spokesmen of the fundamentalist, conservative right; a spokesman for some the neo-Nazi groups, on the other hand, had no compunction justifying the terrorist action and even to express envy. Thus Billy Roper, deputy membership coordinator of the National Alliance, said, "Anyone who is willing to drive a plane into a building to kill Jews is all right by me. . . . I wish our members had half as much testicular fortitude."[4] Similar statements were attributed to Tom Metzger of WAR (White Aryan Resistance): September 11 had been an example of victory of Walhalla; the enemy of our enemy (i.e., bin Laden) was our friend. He wished that his comrades had at least half as much fortitude as the suicide pilots.[5] Rocky Suhaida, chairman of the American Nazi party, Eastpointe, Michigan, was quoted to the effect that one had to accept the fact that a handful of very brave people were willing to die for whatever they believed, and that it was a disgrace that among 150 million white Aryan Americans so few were willing to do the same.[6]

Martin Lindstedt, director of political warfare for the 7th Missouri Militia, Granby, Missouri, declared that he wished that the Arabs had stolen a couple of hundred jumbo jets full of "Talmudic khazar mamzers," criminal regimeist whiggers, niggers, gooks, beaners, etc., and crashed them into the Supreme Court, Congress, the FBI building, all fifty state capitols and television stations"; he would have called it a damned good start.[7]

Many dozens of similar statements were made and distributed during the weeks after 9/11, and they showed that a profound change had taken place; whereas in the era of George Rockwell and the neo-Nazi groups of an earlier period their orientation had been super-patriotic, more recently they had become antipatriotic (the enemy of our enemy is our friend), and since Washington was the enemy, even non-Aryan Arabs became allies. As William Pierce, author of the notorious *Turner Diaries* and head of the National Alliance, put it: Anthrax attacks would have been inconceivable fifty or sixty years earlier. But the much greater corruption and irresponsibility of government and the government's greater intrusion into the life of law-abiding citizens had caused an enormously greater degree of alienation and hatred.[8] Pierce explained that the terrorists who had carried out the attacks had a sense of pride, not caring about money and being comfortable but wanting to keep their independence and way of life. He also found a way around the "Semitic obstacle": not all the people in Afghanistan were greasy, black-haired, swarthy, and hook-nosed. Some of these people were of Aryan origin, following the Aryan conquests and colonization in Central Asia thirty-five hundred years ago. (He overlooked the fact that the terrorist attacks were not organized and carried out by Aryan Afghans but by what he called swarthy Middle Eastern types.)[9]

There was not total unanimity among the extreme right, and some of the militias were offering their help to the government. Some of these organizations published headlines such as "Dirty Rotten Arabs and Muslims" (Council of Conservative Citizens), claiming that Arab treachery and deviousness have been a scourge since biblical times. Some groups published advertisements featuring side-by-side photographs of Osama bin Laden and former U.S. Senator Spencer

Abraham, a Republican from Michigan (Federation for American Immigration Reform).[10]

The Holocaust deniers, such as Robert Faurisson (France) and David Irving (England), tried to use the opportunity to plead that they had been right all along. Irving compared the killing of innocents in New York ("by nineteen intelligent and virile young Muslims") to the killing of innocents by the Allies bombing German cities in World War II. Like Faurisson, he believed that it was all the fault of Israel with an "imaginary holocaust leading to a real one" (Faurisson). He also praised the brave "terrorists" engaging in a suicide mission; the real terrorists, he claimed, was the United States, or to be precise, Judeo-American power.[11] Roger Garaudy, on the other hand, once a member of the Politburo of the French Communist Party who had moved to the far right, argued that the Jews had been involved, as shown by the absence of the four thousand on the morning of the event as well as by the great profits made by Jews through stock market deals on the basis of foreknowledge.[12]

The majority of the American neo-Nazis, or at least the great majority of their spokesmen, took the position that the terrorists had been right, the U.S. government was the guilty party, and the neo-Nazis welcomed the attacks. This stance did not come as a great surprise to people who had observed their move over the years from extreme nationalism to nihilism. The enemy was not just Washington but the American people, because the majority was too stupid or too lazy to share the ideas and the program of the National Alliance and similar such extreme sects. Their primary loyalty was not to their country and certainly not to places like New York and Washington but to their doctrine. Furthermore, some of the extreme fringe groups had dabbled in terrorism, and there was a good deal of envy that the Arabs had done something of which they had only dreamed. As Tom Metzger and William Pierce were saying, they did not love Arabs but opposed the campaign against terrorism because it was only complicating the struggle of the American neo-Nazis. The war was good for the Jews, but it was not good for the neo-Nazis because the government would use the September 11 tragedy to stamp out freedom altogether.[13]

Pierce believed that the danger of terrorism had become real only because government policy had made it real through its foreign policy. Other militia leaders, such as Paul Mullet in Minnesota, a local leader of the Aryan Nation in St. Paul, thought on the contrary that events in New York City had caused him to activate his unit and that they were preparing to strike in Minnesota.[14] Only time will tell whether the attack by the Islamists gave encouragement to the latent terrorism of the American neo-Nazis and spurred them into action.

Some of this camp refused to take the terrorists as a model. Pastor Dave Barley said that he sympathized neither with Zionists nor Muslims, but that allowing Muslims to remain in the United States was some kind of warped, self-imposed national death threat. The Vanguard News Network in Missouri argued that while Muslims were not quite as bad as Jews, they were not American by race or mentality and therefore had to leave.

Many of the neo-Nazis were believers in conspiracy theories, hence their conviction that there was overwhelming evidence that the 9/11 events were a mere smokescreen for the true intentions of the globalists to impose the New World Order: the main bugbear of the extreme right.[15] The *Aryan Loyalist* magazine hailed the New York attacks as a splendid demonstration of Nazi-style Blitzkrieg, mentioning Otto Skorzeny. (Otto Skorzeny had been commander of Hitler's Leibstandarte and led a variety of raids, such as the liberation of Mussolini from captivity.) Those among the neo-Nazis who condemned the war in Afghanistan as a war of invasion were in the majority.

Some spokesmen of this camp realized that they had much in common with the extreme left in their rejection of the war against terrorism and propagated a policy that they claimed was neither left nor right but represented an "International Third Position." They doubted that the attacks had been carried out by bin Laden and his group in the first place. The overlapping between left and right took strange forms: An American novelist writing in the *Frankfurter Allgemeine Zeitung* reported that many of her friends got up in the morning one hour earlier than usual to read European newspapers because the patriotic American press could not be trusted. The same argument was found among the writers of the extreme right: the media were deliberately misleading the American people. Expert observers of the extreme right-wing scene in the United States noted that one had often to dig deeply to establish whether a certain piece of anti-antiterrorism comment had emanated from the far left or from the extreme right.

The line taken by the neo-Nazi and extreme right-wing groups in the United States and their European comrades was similar in many respects. They had always been anti-American and, of course, anti-Semitic. A study of the German *National Zeitung* and similar publications in other European countries showed that they thought that the terrorist attacks had been America's fault. True, they had also for years attacked immigration into Western Europe, in particular from Africa and Muslim countries, and they had no wish to appear as advocates of the bin Laden cause. They evaded this dilemma by adopting a neutralist position — let America and the fanatical Muslims fight it out somewhere, but let Western Europe stay out of this conflict, showing for once a courageous independent line.

However, far more radical pro-terrorist proclamations of German neo-Nazis justified the attacks of September 2001 as legitimate national resistance. The Pentagon was, after all, the center of worldwide mass murder, and the World Trade Center was the symbol of international exploitation and globalization. In brief, the United States had to swallow for the first time a bit of its own medicine. Whoever supported America supported multiculturalism, international capitalism, and globalism.[16]

The basic attitude toward America was deeply hostile on the far right; this emerged perhaps most clearly from the doctrinal writings of Horst Mahler, a lawyer who had been one of the pillars of the Baader-Meinhof group and had been sentenced to a long prison term for terrorist activities. Out of prison he veered to a new radical right-wing ideology and became one of the gurus of neo-fascism in Germany. From a manifesto published after September 11, Mahler apparently still believed in an anticapitalist world revolution and regarded the New York attack as the long overdue attack against Judeo-American barbarism. The Jews had no right to have a state of their own, nor had the Americans. There was no such thing as an American people, only a crude, immoral, violent mass which had produced nothing but corruption, pseudo-democracy, the bloodiest imperialism in history, censorship, robbery, bigotry, the dumbing down of the population, and the export of smut to the rest of the world. Mahler's register of American and Jewish sins is actually longer, but those we listed should be sufficient to give a general idea of his views. For these reasons all and any blows against America and its collaborators are perfectly legal under international military law.[17]

The similarity between anti-Americanism of the extreme left and the pro-fascist right is striking. In his earlier years Mahler would not have put such an emphasis on anti-Semitism, nor would he have been singing the praise of the values of the "Christian Occident." But otherwise the opposition to America (and the justification of terrorism) had not undergone a basic change. Nor was Mahler a lonely figure in his long march from the extreme left to the far right. He was in the company of some leaders of the revolt of 1968 such as Rabehl and Roehl, which leads to the question whether it was right (as Rabehl argued) that the origins of that rebellion (as of the Baader-Meinhof terrorism) had been in patriotic anti-Westernism and anti-Americanism rather than in Marxism-Leninism.

Of considerable interest was the position taken by the radical right in Russia. There was, on one hand, the secret (and often not so secret) joy that America had been humiliated and defeated (just as Russia had been humiliated and defeated), but there was also the fear that if America would retaliate, it might become a serious rival for influence in Central Asia. Above all, Russia was fighting a war against radical Islam in the Caucasus (the Wahabis) which constituted a real threat in Central Asia and even inside Russia.

What was the correct line to be adopted by a Russian patriot in these complicated circumstances?

The voice most often and most loudly heard was that of Alexander Dugin. Dugin had appeared first on the Moscow scene in the early years of perestroika as a proponent of a strange ideological mixture — Russian patriotism, Soviet power, doctrines of the French and Italian neo-fascist thinkers, and German geopolitics of the 1920s. In the general ideological confusion prevailing in Russia after 1989, many people were quite willing to listen to a farrago of nonsense of this kind; since Dugin was very critical of the West and Western democracy, sections of the new establishment — above all, the army general staff — welcomed his ideas and supported him. Dugin also advocated a new kind of Eurasianism, a Russian policy orientated in the future not toward the West but toward Asia.[18] This school of thought did have adherents among Russian émigrés in the 1920s, but at that time it was mainly philosophical in character whereas Dugin and some of his co-thinkers, such as Fyodor Girenok and Alexander Panarin, professors at Moscow University, were thinking both in spiritual terms and of Realpolitik. They never made it quite clear what Asians they had in mind as Russia's prospective allies — it could not be China or Japan, or Afghanistan or even radical Islam.

But it was obvious, as Girenok said at a meeting in October 2001, that when they watched the planes smashing the World Trade Center towers, emotionally they were not on America's side.[19] They recalled that America had dismembered the Soviet Union (and was now doing the same to China), that it had bombed Belgrade, that it had tried to intervene in Chechnya. As they saw it, it was not at all clear whether the radical Islamists under bin Laden had really been the attackers or whether the American establishment and the intelligence services had instigated and carried it out. America was systematically destroying Russia from a spiritual point of view, thus preparing a new world war. American calls for freedom and democracy were hypocritical and misleading and should not be believed for a moment. The terrorist attacks had given Russia a wonderful opportunity to resist the aggressor (America) and to line up Germany and the rest of Europe to prevent a new world war. But this unique opportunity had been squandered by the Russian leaders, who were little better than lackeys of Washington. American policy as they saw it was made by Russophobes such as Zbigniew Brzezinski, and this situation would not change in the foreseeable future.

There was, in brief, a great deal of hostility and resentment mainly among the Russian right, but there were doubts even among former liberals about whether the country should join the war against terrorism. Konstantin Zatulin, a leader of the Otechestvo party, argued that while he was not in principle anti-American, the attack in 2001 had been a blow to America and therefore in the Russian interest because it would weaken America's position as the only remaining super-power. For the same reason it would be against the Russian interest if America would win the war against terrorism. Mikhail Delyagin, head of the Institute on the Problems of Globalism, went further: America was a terrorist state just as NATO was a terrorist organization, and Russian cooperation in the war against terrorism was therefore ruled out.

However, given the realities facing Russia in its foreign policy, the anti-Americanism and the sneaking sympathies with the terrorists could not amount to very much in practice. The real enemy at the gate was not Brzezinski and Amer-ican materialism but Chechnya, the Jihadis in Central Asia, and even Muslim separatist trends inside Russia. It could be argued that precisely for this reason, to neutralize the Islamist opposition at home, Russia should try to be on good terms with some leading Muslim countries such as Iran and Iraq. Perhaps their goodwill and support for Russian policy in Chechnya and elsewhere could be bought by Russian support against Washington. However, this policy had been tried before and had not been very successful.

Conspiracy Theories

Terrorism has always given rise to conspiracy theories, and September 11, 2001, generated a wave of such theories almost unprecedented in history. They came from the extreme left and the far right, but also from the very big army of lovers of conspiracy theories. Some invoked the quatrains of Nostradamus, whose astrological predictions have been a bestseller ever since they were first made public in the sixteenth century. Admirers of Nostradamus claim that he wrote that "In the city of God there will be great thunder" or that two metal bits would "crash into two tall statues in the new city and the world will end soon after" or "two sleek birds will fall from the sky on the metropolis. The sky will burn at forty-five degrees latitude," and so on in a similar vein. According to another quotation, "The year 1999, seventh month, from the sky will come a great King of Terror."

Most of these quotations were made up. They refer to texts that do not exist. At best they are embellished and improved versions of quatrains which are so general in character that they can be made to fit, with small changes, every possible situation that will ever arise in human history.

Others invoked the Bible: Ezekiel 38 was often quoted by aficionados of this genre after September 11. This is the prophecy about Gog and Magog with plague and bloodshed and torrents of rain, hailstone and burning sulfur and so on.

Others preferred the book of Revelation, which specializes in the description of disasters.

The belief in conspiracy theory is much more widespread than generally assumed. It is usually present in paranoia — the assumption that there is a pattern (usually negative or hostile) in random events. Nothing in the world happens by chance; obvious motives of other persons are rejected, and in severe cases this mental attitude leads to vengeful attitudes and violent confrontation. There is a close connection between terrorism (and the interpretation of terrorism) and conspiracy theory. There were and are terrorist groups in history that were more or less free of such symptoms. But they were certainly present in terrorist movements of the extreme right; the murderers of Rathenau (the German foreign minister) believed that he was one of the Elders of Zion; the doctrines of the American far right are constituted almost entirely of conspiracies against patriots — by the United Nations, by Freemasons, the Illuminati, and of course, Zionists as well as a hundred other evil forces. The same is true with regard to the ideology of the lunatic fringe of the Russian right.

Conspiracy theories appear among groups of the extreme left, but these prefer their conspiracies in a pseudo-rational or even pseudo-scientific guise. For them Hitler was a creature of Wall Street and particularly the house of Morgan. Or, to give a more recent example, the American campaign in Afghanistan was described not as part of the war against terrorism, but as an imperialist cabal to control Central Asian oil. No major oil fields exist in Afghanistan, but any reference to oil imperialism sounds plausible to a certain public, and one could always bring in pipelines in the absence of oil fields.[20] Why was it that Bush launched his campaign against terrorism just at the time that the United States was moving into recession? No doubt, to save the American economy which otherwise might have collapsed.

Extreme right-wing German conspiracy experts published many explanations for the true meaning of the events of September 11 which, as they claimed, could be understood only on the basis of a knowledge of Masonic-kabbalistic symbols. To give but one example: Why was the war in Afghanistan started on October 8, 2001? Because on October 8, 1571, the naval battle of Lepanto took place which, the authors claim, was of decisive importance in the relations between Christianity and Islam. The authors then argue that the Vatican aims to relocate in Jerusalem with Israeli permission and note that the number 8 in kabbalistic tests means ritual slaughter, and they then proceed to present various figures such as 08101571 (the date of Lepanto), 7811638 (5+7=12=3), 692792, and so on.[21]

Such ravings can be found in every possible variation, and they are mentioned here mainly to show that while paranoia and the belief in conspiracy theories are particularly strong in religiously motivated terrorism, no political or religious trend has a monopoly in this respect. A bestselling book published in France proved that no airplane had ever crashed into the Pentagon, that this had been a mere figment of imagination, or to be precise a deliberate piece of misinformation. Such fantasies emanated neither from Islamists nor the extreme right, but from Thierry Meyssan, an author of the left who argued that it had been an inside job, an attempted coup by the military-industrial complex.[22]

Another bestseller entitled *Ben Laden; la verité interdite* by Jean-Charles Brisard and Guillaume Dasquie did not deny that an attack had taken place but argued that bin Laden and al Qa'ida were creatures of the American government and U.S. oil interests. This book appeared in the United States under auspices of *The Nation* books; according to Lyndon LaRouche, a grand master in the field of conspiracy theory, bin Laden was a British agent, whereas for others on the extreme right he was a Jewish or Zionist agent acting on behalf of Wall Street. A study of certain medieval Christian texts, about witches, the devil, and related subjects could be as good an introduction as any for the understanding of such contemporary conspiracy theorists.

In the Muslim world the belief in giant conspiracies can be found in the basic writings of the jihadists such as Sayed Qutb: Jews and Christians have everywhere and at all times been fighting Islam with the wish to destroy it. They are afraid of Islam and the Muslim's zeal for their religion, and while there have been domestic disputes between capitalism, communism, Zionism, etc., they always have a common cause against Islam. Thus all Christians and Jews are deceivers and treacherous, and their diabolical intrigues will be defeated only when Islam prevails all over the world.[23]

The same belief in the utter corruption of the West and all non-Muslim societies can be found in Mawdoodi, the other precursor of modern radical Islamism, as well as Khomeini and his followers among the Shi'ites. It appears in the publications of the Egyptian jihadists, al Qa'ida, and virtually every interview given by Osama bin Laden.

The paranoid element in religiously motivated terrorism (Jewish extremist sects not being an exception) is blatantly obvious, but it has not yet been systematically investigated. It can be found in virtually every society and at every time, but in some civilizations it is far more pronounced than in others, in fact, it has been the prevailing mode of thought. The world map of political paranoia shows that in the West it is now the belief system of a lunatic fringe, whereas elsewhere it remains frequently part of the mainstream consensus. This is true in particular for Arab societies, and it came to the fore after the events of September 11.

Arab Reactions

Most Arab media and many Arab officials argued after September 11 that Arabs could not possibly have been involved because they lacked the sophistication to carry out such a highly complex attack. They recalled that in the first hours after the bombing at Oklahoma City, Arabs had been suspected even though they had not been involved at all. Who were the most likely culprits? The American secret services or Mossad, Israeli Intelligence? Was it by mere accident that four thousand Israelis normally working at the World Trade Center had not appeared at work that morning? Zionists had engaged in terrorism before; why should they not have been responsible this time too? They were the ones to benefit most from the attack.

But how would they profit? On this point there were conflicting versions. Most commentators argued that only Mossad was capable of breaking into the American security apparatus. Others maintained that it was a matter of profit and greed: Jews were huge stockholders in the airlines and insurance companies, they had sold their shares at the highest possible prices in Europe ten days earlier. When the stock market began to function again on September 17 they competed among themselves to buy the shares back at the lowest possible price.[24] Many commentators invoked the granddaddy of all modern conspiracy theories: the *Protocols of the Elders of Zion*: The Jews had been bitterly disappointed that their candidates, the Democrats Gore and Lieberman, had been defeated, and they used therefore the attacks on Manhattan to regain their influence to Judaize the White House. Many newspapers published these versions with absolute certainty, others were more cautious: We are not placing blame without clear-cut proof, they said. But it is at the very least a possibility which must be considered by the Americans, who should not accuse the Arabs and bin Laden without clear-cut proof.[25] But another well-known columnist claimed that, on the contrary, the attacks had been launched not by the Democrats but by President Bush who was elected by the smallest majority ever in American history ("not enough to head a village council position in Southern Egypt"). Some writers conjured up apocalyptic scenarios: Why not assume that Zionist organizations perpetrated this dastardly act so that Israel could destroy the Al Aqsa Mosque while the world was preoccupied with what happened in America?[26]

The allegation that there was no proof was repeated time and again. The papers that had been found and published by the American authorities, such as Muhammad Atta's last instructions to his comrades, were obviously forged. Others borrowed their scenario from science fiction: The planes had not been hijacked at all but redirected by remote control. (This theme was also taken up by the largest Iranian paper, *Keyhan*.)

However, the Jews were by no means the only suspects as far as the Arab media were concerned. Among other possibilities considered or stated as certainties were the following: It was the revenge of the Japanese for Hiroshima and Nagasaki. It had been carried out by the enemies of globalism. It was instigated by those opposed to the missile defense system. It was carried out by the CIA and FBI. Those behind it were American dissidents from the right, such as the militias. The attack was carried out by an extremist religious sect believing that the coming is near of the Messiah who aspired to purify America of its crimes.[27]

The list could be prolonged. Among the players participating in the game were not just journalists but public figures such as Syrian minister of defense Mustafa Tlas, Saudi princes, heads of centers of strategic studies, ambassadors, a former head of the Pakistani intelligence service writing in *Al Ahram*, leading religious figures, prominent professors, and other important personalities.[28]

Was all this domestic propaganda or was it scheduled for foreign consumption? This question is impossible to answer with any certainty. For foreign consumption these stories were quite unsuitable because Western believers in conspiracy theories did not need Arab help for the construction of their versions of contemporary history, and the rest of the Western public would only doubt the sanity of those spreading disinformation of this kind.

Given the propensity of the Arab and Muslim world for believing conspiracy theories, it would be wrong to rule out that the writings were not genuine, meaning that the writers did not believe in what they wrote. Nor was it a case of what is known among the Shi'ites as *Taqiyyah*, denying obvious facts in a dangerous situation to defend the interests of Islam. The main problem was, of course, how to combine two sets of belief that were mutually exclusive — that the Jews had carried out the attacks and that the Muslim world was proud that America had been humiliated and defeated?

As time went by it became clear that the attacks had indeed been launched by members of al Qa'ida or an allied group; some of its spokesmen such as Obed al Qurashi said so.[29]

Even early on some Arab journalists in Kuwait, Lebanon, and Saudi Arabia had been critical of people in their countries spreading the conspiracy theories — mainly Islamists from Egypt — pointing out that Arabs, after all, had tried to blow up the World Trade Center in 1993, that Arabs knew how to fly, and that they had hijacked planes more than once. Nor was it logical to argue at one and the same time that the attacks had served America right, that it had been attacked because of its pro-Israeli policy, and that the Mossad had been the prime culprit.[30] One Saudi journalist pointed out that no serious person believed any longer in the authenticity of the *Protocols of the Elders of Zion.*

Such criticism became more frequent, and even some Islamist writers suggested that inanities of this kind were only spreading confusion in the Arab street. They were certainly detrimental as far as the prestige of al Qa'ida was concerned — its achievement could certainly not be fully appreciated if the martyrs who had committed the heroic acts had been Mossad agents. However, some of these versions continued to be believed not only among the less educated sections of society but also among intellectuals. At the very least, it was believed that the whole truth was not known.

But even a year after the event, many Arab public opinion makers continued to argue that al Qa'ida was not responsible for the attacks, despite the fact that al Qa'ida leaders had in the meantime given interviews in which they related in some detail how they had prepared the attacks of September 11.[31] When the American ambassador in Egypt drew the attention of the local journalists to this fact, the result was a demand that he should be declared *persona non grata.*[32]

Anti-Semitism

There was an upsurge of anti-Semitic incidents after September 2001, which manifested itself, for instance, in attacks against synagogues such as in Djerba, Tunisia (in which nineteen foreign tourists were killed), and in France. It was correctly pointed out that criticism of the policy of Israeli governments was not a synonym for anti-Semitism, but the new anti-Semitic wave had not just to do with Middle East politics. It was propagated by groups, mainly from the far left, that had previously shown only limited interest in the Palestinian-Israeli conflict.[33] Open anti-Semitic propaganda made its appearance among students on American and European campuses, under the auspices of the antiglobalist movement — among them Trotskyites, Anarchists, and other sects.[34] A Nobel

Prize winner in literature accused the Jews (not just the Sharon government) of committing atrocities comparable to Auschwitz, and a leading figure of the antiglobalism movement noted that whenever she logged in to an "activist news" broadcast by her comrades-in-arms, she was confronted with a string of Jewish conspiracy theories and excerpts from the *Protocols of the Elders of Zion*.[35]

If Nazism had believed in "Jewish capitalism," the far left developed the concept of "Jewish imperialism." These developments among sections of the left gave hope to the neo-Nazi gurus in the United States and to erstwhile leaders of the German terrorists such as Horst Mahler that a "third position," a synthesis of anti-Imperialism, anti-Americanism, and anti-Semitism of the far left and the extreme right in alliance with Muslim terrorism was potentially a formidable political force, perhaps the wave of the future. Given the very specific and exclusive religious doctrine of al Qa'ida International, it was more than doubtful whether any such alliance with Western infidels, however sympathetic to their cause, could be of lasting importance. But it certainly did not prevent Western well-wishers from offering their political and propagandistic services, just as twenty-five years earlier they had welcomed and supported the "Khomeini revolution."

EIGHT

Anti-Americanism

"**W**HY DO THEY HATE US SO MUCH?**" This was one of the main questions asked following the events of September 2001, but was it the right question? Or was America perhaps attacked because it had not retaliated forcefully for many years against earlier terrorist attacks, because it was considered weak, indecisive and therefore a not very risky target?[1] Nations are seldom loved, great powers even less so. Neither Russia nor China, neither Great Britain nor the Spanish nor the Ottoman empires, neither India nor Germany nor France at the height of their power were loved; at most they were respected, very often feared. The reasons were obvious: a big power often tends to disregard the legitimate interests of its smaller neighbors and other countries or to impose its will, be it intentionally or unthinkingly. Its culture and its economy have an enormous impact on smaller countries; a Mexican proverb expressed these fears: "so far from God, so near to the United States."

To be hated is a consequence of being great and powerful. It can be remedied not by becoming gentler, only by becoming weaker. Smaller countries may be pitied or despised but are seldom hated. Is the United States more an object of hate than other superpowers in history? There is no evidence other than anecdotal to this effect. The many reports on global public attitudes toward the United States presented by USIA in the 1990s on the basis of countless public opinion polls assert that increased political and economic ties have not caused negative reactions to American culture where the question was asked.[2] According to the same report, the United States is valued as provider of economic assistance, and majorities endorse a U.S. role in safeguarding regional security.

Perhaps these reports have painted too rosy a picture. Undoubtedly groups in many countries bitterly opposed America, and its overwhelming military strength after the end of the Cold War, when it emerged as the only superpower. Some were angry with America because its survival as a superpower had been contrary to their predictions of America's inevitable decline. Others resented the egoistic pursuance of America's economic interests, the disregard of ecological concerns, the pervasive influence of its cultural exports. It is certainly true that Washington should have shown more consideration to the desires and feelings of other countries during the months after September 11, but is it really true that, as one

American commentator put it, "with a few small adjustments in tone and policy much more good will and popularity could have been bought."[3] If America had joined wholeheartedly the campaign against global warming and the international criminal court and accepted similar undertakings, would there have been more international support for the pursuit of the terrorists?

Up to the middle 1990s there were few terrorist attacks against American interests by foreign terrorists, and but for the attacks in Beirut in 1983 there had been hardly any at all. If so, had there been a sudden and dramatic deterioration in the situation during the late 1990s under the Clinton administration which had certainly been more moderate and more popular outside the United States than its predecessors? Or was it perhaps that there was no dramatic change in attitudes but that the anti-American militants had become more aggressive because they had realized that America could be provoked with impunity? Osama bin Laden, the leaders of Hamas, and other spokesmen for the terrorists had declared on many occasions that America and the West in general were paper tigers; there was no reason to be afraid of them. Their young people above all wanted to live, whereas the young jihadists were longing to sacrifice their lives. There is much evidence to the effect that contempt for America played a greater role in the large-scale attacks than any other motive; however much they may hate them, terrorists seldom attack enemies whom they fear.

These questions will be debated by politicians and by students of international affairs for many years to come, but these are not the central issues pertaining to our subject. The reactions by politicians, the media, and the general public after September 11 in the United States and abroad are of relevance only inasmuch as they reflect the understanding of and attitudes toward the new terrorism that suddenly confronted America and other countries. Reactions inside America and outside it have to be considered separately because motives and circumstances were different.

America after September 11

The instinctive reaction of the American public and its political class was one of showing spontaneous solidarity and to rally behind the administration. The administration was new and the president inexperienced in foreign affairs; he had yet to prove whether he was capable of coping with a crisis of such magnitude. But there were few dissenting voices for many months. This was not considered the time for protest; with parts of Manhattan in ruins, the political climate was not conducive to the spread of anti-antiterrorism. The attitude of the media was similar; there were legitimate discussions about questions such as whether the army was the agency best prepared to take the leading part in the war against terrorism. One could argue that "war" was perhaps not the most appropriate term to use for fighting terrorism. One could claim that Afghanistan, all things considered, was not the decisive battlefield in the campaign against terrorism. But these were tactical questions, not issues of principle. With regard to the urgent necessity to take countermeasures against terrorism and to prevent a recurrence there was virtual unanimity.[4]

But there were, as usual, some exceptions. Individuals and small groups were rejoicing; reference has been made to the neo-Nazi groups. Bobby Fischer, at the time in the Philippines, was reported as having said that this was wonderful news. It was high time to finish off the United States once and for all.[5] However, the ex-chess champion of the world had not been in the best of mental health for a long time and no one thought it necessary to comment and react. There were other voices condemning the attacks against innocents but at the same time finding a variety of reasons to justify them. They came from university campuses and from artists and writers. Frequently, they were not as a matter of surprise. Noam Chomsky, the distinguished theorist of linguistics, had consistently opposed American foreign policy, which had always been wrong and evil. It was therefore not surprising that he should predict that America was about to kill between 3 million and 4 million Afghans.[6]

Oliver Stone, the movie director and one of the giants in the field of conspiratology, called the attacks a rebellion against globalization and Hollywood. Susan Sontag attributed most of the blame to American policy, such as the murder of Iraqi children (she later modified her views). Norman Mailer declared that the World Trade Center was a monstrosity that had to be destroyed. Eric Foner, a New York professor, wrote that he did not know whether to be more frightened by the horror that had engulfed New York or the apocalyptic rhetoric emanating daily from the White House.[7] Another professor at Rutgers University said that the ultimate cause of the attack was the fascism of U.S. foreign policy. One of his colleagues at the University of New Mexico announced that anyone who could blow up the Pentagon would get his vote. Louis Farrakhan commented on the events as did Professor Edward Said. Kathe Pollitt wrote in The *Nation* that the American flag stood for jingoism and vengeance.[8] At Amherst, two American flags were burned during a teach-in (or a demonstration).

On the various Internet sites providing antiwar information, propaganda for Rudolf Hess, the late deputy of Adolf Hitler, appeared side-by-side with the views expressed by left-wing anti-Americans.

Some reactions were not according to past form. Christopher Hitchens, a stalwart of the extreme left who had called Mother Teresa a fascist and demanded the prosecution of Henry Kissinger as a war criminal, wrote in The *Nation* that he was apprehensive from the first moment about the sort of masochistic e-mail traffic that might start circulating from the Chomsky-Zinn-Finkelstein quarter. He was not to be disappointed. For him the bombers of Manhattan represented fascism with an Islamic face; what they abominated about the West was not what Western liberals don't like but what they do like and must defend.[9] Michael

Walzer, a guru of the mainstream left, wrote that those who were expressing *schadenfreude* (secret joy) were not simply making excuses for the terrorists; they had joined the ranks of the terrorist supporters. "The only political response to ideological fanatics and suicidal holy warriors was implacable opposition."[10]

When some of the more provocative utterances of the opponents of the war against terrorism were given wider publicity by their critics, there was a pained outcry that the anti-American quotations had been taken out of context. A new wave of McCarthyism was engulfing the country; freedom of speech and academic freedom were in danger. But since it was technically impossible to reproduce whole speeches, all quotations were by definition taken out of context. On the other hand, people in favor of what they considered a just war complained that American campuses had been indoctrinated for years by the enemies of American values and democracy, that only politically correct candidates had been hired, that the outbursts after September 11 were merely a reflection of these trends.[11]

The impression was certainly gained that the hard-core left and radical chic were convinced even after the terrorist attacks that patriotism was bad since it served American imperialism and even fascism. This, in turn, generated a lot of anger on the part of the defenders of traditional American values. The "patriots" were accused by the antipatriots for taking advantage of the national crisis to reverse the trend the latter had presided over and make patriotism again fashionable.[12]

These debates, however intrinsically interesting, are not the central subject of our study. While great publicity was given by the media to these declarations and manifestations, they doubtful had much political impact. It is true that some of the leading academic associations were dominated by people deeply inimical to what the majority considered American values. But it is doubtful whether in the stormy meetings on campus reported from Stanford to City College in New York even 1 percent of the student body participated, and in most instances there were considerably less.[13] Teach-ins of this kind were always frequented and dominated by spokespersons and militants of extremist political groups. Their outreach was limited to a very small section of students from departments such as English literature or sociology and in some cases theology. As Professor Eric Foner of Harvard, of whom mention has already been made, put it, polls at his university had shown that there was firm support for the war against terrorism on the campuses: "If our aim is to indoctrinate students with unpatriotic beliefs, we're obviously doing a very poor job of it."[14]

It may not have been for want of trying but the happenings on the campuses were quite unrepresentative of the feelings and the opinions of the great majority of Americans. Once the anger about American patriotism and the rapid victory in Afghanistan had somewhat abated, Israel became the butt of attack on some campuses. Since the new culprits were, however, more often than not sympathizers with the Israeli peace party rather than with Prime Minister Sharon, more than a few observers of the radical scene on the campuses maintained that the underlying cause was anti-Semitism rather than anti-Zionism.

It was, however, quite unlikely that those who had expressed sympathy for the terrorists, such as Bobby Fischer or the professors from New Mexico and Rutgers, would join them in their struggle as the left had supported the Republicans in the Spanish Civil War. If they were truly serious, they ought to have given them not just rhetorical support but also more concrete assistance. But somehow they lacked the courage of their convictions. There was always the chance that one individual or another would join al Qa'ida, but they were unlikely to come from the groves of academe. Support from these quarters was purely platonic; the most al Qa'ida could hope for was "critical support."

If these debates (or shouting matches) are of some relevance in the present context, it is mainly because they revealed a substantial deficit of knowledge as far as terrorism was concerned and also an unwillingness to learn. True, some sensible proposals were made to offer more courses in the universities about issues such as political violence, but there were even more suggestions that seemed far-fetched, to put it cautiously.

In the age of anarchist terrorism, those eager to learn more about the motives of the terrorists would have studied the doctrine of anarchism. Those who wanted to know more about the Russian Social Revolutionaries or the Irish militants would have studied recent Russian and Irish history. The attacks of September 2001 were carried out by members of al Qa'ida and related groups, and universities promised to enlighten their students about the background of these attacks. But one would have looked in vain for many courses on the nature of jihad or fanaticism or similar aspects of terrorism. These continued to be "controversial" subjects. Scholars of Islam in American universities did speak out against terrorism and published manifestoes in which they stressed that the grief and the rage against the attackers were completely understandable and shared by all, but that the anger must not be directed against individuals utterly innocent of these terrible crimes.[15] They pointed out that Islam was a peaceful and tolerant religion, and that verbal and physical attacks against Muslims (and people who were thought to be Muslims) were particularly distressing because many American Muslims had fled to the United States seeking refuge from intolerant regimes.[16] Universities recommended the study of selected passages from the Koran, and some made such lectures mandatory. Such declarations showed a sense of decency and humanity, and they were also wise from a political point of view: If the terrorists had aimed to widen the distance and the misunderstandings between the civilizations (for which Samuel Huntington was made responsible), it was the duty of those in favor of peaceful coexistence between the communities to build bridges and to prevent a further increase in tension — hence the decision to publicize the statements of leading American Muslim organizations denouncing the terrorist attacks, ignoring other groups that had done so only reluctantly or not at all. At times of crisis, a case can be made for not making the whole truth known because it could be considered inflammatory.

But with all the calls for a peaceful solution of the present conflicts, there should have been the readiness to have a new and harder look at the beliefs and aims of those who had prepared and carried out the attacks, and, for all one knew, were only too eager to continue their activities. Was it just a matter of a few radical outsiders who had hijacked a great religion? How much support was there for their doctrine? What were their demands and how could they be satisfied? There was little enthusiasm to confront these issues.

In brief, while the great majority of Americans reacted more or less instinc-tively — having been attacked, one was obliged to defend oneself and hit back — there was on the campuses and among the literary intelligentsia a school of thought, not perhaps large in numbers but loud and aggressive, that if there had been such an attack, America had had it coming and it must have been its own fault. As the focus shifted in 2002 from war against terrorism to war against Iraq, the opposition movement received a great uplift; there had been a certain oppo-sition to the campaign to remove the Taliban from Afghanistan, but the idea to depose Saddam Hussein generated far greater resistance.[17] One of the arguments most frequently heard was that the connection between Osama bin Laden–type terrorism and the dictatorship in Baghdad had not been proven. It could well be that the danger emanating from Iraq — weapons of mass destruction in the hands of an aggressive "rogue state" — was a greater danger than the actions of small groups of jihadists, but there had been a sudden change in the transition from one target to another without sufficient explanation at home and abroad, and this shift caused confusion and resistance.

Terrorism and Anti-Americanism in Europe

European attitudes toward America have been ambivalent for a long time. There was sympathy for America and even enthusiasm — Goethe's *Amerika, du hast es besser als unser Kontinent*. But there had also been a tradition of cultural anti-Americanism going back at least two hundred years. Mr. Trollope's mother, Frances, poked fun in a famous book about the bad manners of the uncouth Americans spitting chewing gum on the floor on every possible occasion.[18] Amer-ican literature was mostly trash, its newspapers unreliable, the children dull, the women looked like hedgehogs, and they disliked the British. The American people had no refinement and no loyalty. Charles Dickens ridiculed what the Americans had made of the English language — the famous department of circumlocution.

To look down on Americans was de rigueur in English literature and politics throughout the nineteenth century. America was too egalitarian, too plebeian, and too nouveau riche at the same time. While for many, America was too demo-cratic, for some it was not democratic enough. In Germany, there was a whole literature about the unfortunate emigrants who had gone to America with so many expectations and illusions only to end in bitter despair. The best known was a novel by Ferdinand Kuernberger, *Der Amerikamuede* (1855).[19] This anti-Utopia is the story of Dr. Moorfeld, a young and idealistic German émigré who hopes to find in the new continent the realization of his dreams. But all he encounters are crass materialism, fraud, greed, brutishness, lack of culture, and in the end even anti-German pogroms. He returns to Europe a wiser and much sadder man. Whereas Mrs. Trollope's book was a caricature based on personal experience and elements of truth, Kuernberger's work belonged to a different genre. He had been no more to America than Dante had been to hell. A French wit noted that it would have been preferable if America had never been discovered, for it was the only country that had proceeded from infantilism to senility without passing through the stage of maturity.

Anti-Americanism in the nineteenth century was cultural; politically America did not count prior to World War I. This began to change, but not for the better, in the 1920s and 1930s. The Nazis were anti-American because of America's inferior culture and dismal racial mixture; Hitler said that any one of Beethoven's symphonies had been a greater contribution to world culture than anything Britain had ever produced, and his contempt for America was even greater. For the Communists and their fellow travelers, America was the main obstacle to revolution and a better world. They knew from Maxim Gorky, who had visited America in 1906, that dirt and boredom impregnated everything in the city of the Yellow Devil (New York), that the American mob was a horrifying beast, and that children there were scavenging the dustbins for a piece of moldy bread. Wall Street was threatening the world with nuclear war. In Paris in the late 1940s, there were great demonstrations against America's role in the Korean War ("Ridgeway *la peste*"), later on, at the time of the Vietnam War and the students' revolt, there were even greater protest demonstrations against cold-warish America in Germany. The correct position of large sections of the European intelligentsia during the Cold War was neutralism and equidistance. America was dangerous and too aggressive. American mass culture was demeaning and a threat to all that had been created in Europe over centuries.

But there was a curious dichotomy between attitudes of the intelligentsia on the one hand and the political class as well as the majority of the population on the other. With rare exceptions, the politicians, while not necessarily admiring America, favored an alliance, and those who did not, such as de Gaulle, were motivated by power politics, and he disliked the British even more.

But the great majority was barely influenced by the anti-Americanism of the intelligentsia. Despite all the books and speeches uttering dire warnings, many millions of Germans emigrated to the New World during the nineteenth century, and many more millions from other European countries. Despite all the attacks (often justified) against American kitsch, inferior movies, and pop music — not to mention Coca-Cola, McDonald's and other such imported abominations — this had no great impact on the taste of the majority of Europeans. This, in briefest outline, was the background to European reactions after September 11. Whereas the political leadership and the majority of the population were broadly speaking supporting Washington, albeit with caution, large sections of the media and the intelligentsia were critical or hostile. This was intriguing because many of the political leaders of France, Britain, and West Germany had, after all, come from the same stable; they had been revolutionary socialists or even Trotskyites thirty years earlier. The reasons were not difficult to fathom: The politicians had to deal with problems confronting them in the real world, while the media and sections of the intelligentsia faced no such unpleasant constraints. They could ignore the dangers, they could be negative and freely criticize — it was, after all, not their job to come up with solutions.

There were, of course, differences from country to country. This trend was most marked in Germany and Sweden, and it was also palpably felt in Britain, France, and Italy but to a lesser degree; to be precise, the countervailing forces were stronger there.

Within a day or two after September 11, as most of the victims were still buried under the ruins of the World Trade Center, prominent German intellectuals came on record saying that the main danger was not terrorism but American overreaction; to quote the title of a famous novel by Franz Werfel, not the murderer, the victim was guilty. Günter Grass announced that Afghanistan would be America's second Vietnam, the answer to terrorism was economic justice, and he was very critical of Chancellor Schroeder declaring solidarity with Washington. Adrienne Goehler, Berlin's senator for cultural affairs, compared the World Trade Center towers with two giant phalluses, and since Ms. Goehler belonged to the Green party and was a feminist, this comment was not meant to be a compliment. The writer Botho Strauss, who belonged to the right, talked about the war of evil against evil. Sloterdijk, a philosopher, went further and called the United States a rogue state.[20]

German television commentators and professors of comparative literature claimed that the West had not understood the deeper reasons of the terrorist attacks and maintained that the mental structures (*Denkstrukturen*) of Osama bin Laden and President Bush were the same.[21] The majority of prominent German writers, whether left-wing or nationalist in inspiration, were critical or hostile of America and found at most a few words of regret about the victims. Their explanations for the root causes of terrorism were always the same: It was the protest of the poor and exploited against the rich countries, which did not care about their misery.

The comments in Germany by the far left on the terrorist attacks changed with time. At first, immediately after the bombing of the World Trade Center, the ex-Communist *Neues Deutschland* wrote that nothing could justify this mass murder, and even the ultra-left *Autonome* called the attacks "fascistoid" (para-fascist) and anti-Semitic, which had nothing to do with left-wing militancy — there was nothing in common with the terrorists. But as time passed and measures were taken to combat terrorism, these were condemned as manifestations of militarism, imperialism, and NATO hysteria.[22]

Western experts on radical Islamism — admittedly there were not many of them, as this specialization was not favored by the profession — had repeated a thousand times that fundamentalism was not a protest against being poor. As a leading specialist in the field put it: "To think so is simply unsophisticated. Nevertheless, the tenacity of the unsophisticated approach does great honor to the intellectual influence of Marxism, but people do not turn fundamentalists because they are destitute. Poverty cannot cause fundamentalism, property cannot cure it."[23] The reference to Marxism was probably exaggerated; the syndrome was mainly a manifestation of intellectual laziness and of the unwillingness to accept unwelcome facts. For not only had Western specialists expressed doubts about the poverty argument, the radical fundamentalists themselves had denied it countless times, not to mention Western sympathizers with their cause such as the British journalist Robert Fisk. It was not primarily a matter of poverty, but refuting these deeply engrained ideas seemed a hopeless cause.

One hundred German experts on Islamic and Arab affairs also published a manifesto sharply critical of the United States. They claimed that European countries had nothing to fear, since for the radical Islamists America — more specifically American policy in the Middle East — was the enemy, not Western civilization.[24]

This was true to the extent that the terrorists would be careful not to endanger their bases in countries such as Germany, Britain, or France as long as they could use them for staging operations against the United States. (The argument was not quite correct because the terrorists had also planned to attack targets in Europe, particularly in France, but these plans never materialized.) But the German experts' reasoning was still faulty; it amounted to claiming that they knew better than the Islamists what the Islamists themselves wanted. They refused to take seriously the Islamist doctrine which had always stressed that while America was the Great Satan, Western civilization being secular and therefore anti-Islamic was also a perennial enemy. They also ignored the fact that among the many millions of Muslims in Europe were groups wanting to establish Islamic rule (*Khilafah*) wherever Muslims lived.

In Britain, the *London Review of Books* was the first to ask a score of intellectuals for their comments, and almost without exception they were anti-American to a larger or lesser degree; a symposium by the periodical *Granta* showed similar results, except that in the case of *Granta* many of the comments came from Muslim writers. As Mary Beard, an expert on ancient Roman religions, put it: however tactfully you dress it up, the United States had it coming.[25] Similar views were expressed in the *Guardian*, which together with the *Independent* became the main pillars of anti-Americanism. As Seamus Milne, a *Guardian* editor, wrote, Americans were simply too obtuse to understand the situation. There was no glimmer of recognition that they were once again reaping a dragon's teeth harvest that they themselves had sowed.[26] BBC television collected an audience of young Muslims in the radical mosques of London to shout down in a talk show a former U.S. ambassador, but this kind of program did not go down very well with a fair-minded British public.[27]

Tempers were running high. It was suggested that the *Guardian* should be renamed the "Daily Terrorist," whereas the *Guardian* and the *Independent* claimed that people who did not agree with their brand of anti-Americanism were blood-thirsty boneheads. The *Guardian* quoted a Ms. Tricker to the effect that "now they felt how the Iraqis feel," and a Mr. Pritchard who thought that if the attacks resulted in defeating America's overweening ego as the world's sole remaining superpower, this will have been a highly productive achievement.[28]

There was, as a leading commentator in the *London Times* put it, a surprising amount of defeatist misinformation, morally dubious self-flagellation, and exaggerations of the enemy's invincibility on the part of what was once known as the left-wing intelligentsia, advocating a spineless policy that could prove almost as dangerous and destructive to humanitarian values as the appeasement of the 1930s.[29] The line taken by the anti-Americans was at first to warn against immediate, indiscriminate attack on the part of Washington eager to engage in a new war. When this did not happen, the emphasis was put on the enormous dangers looming: Afghanistan had been the graveyard of all invaders and America would face the same fate. The Taliban fighters were utterly fearless, and the American ground forces were no match for them. The war against terrorism was too expensive, America simply could not afford it, it would be ruined by it. Similar arguments emerged concerning World War II and the Cold War.

This, as subsequent events showed, was not quite true either, and the stress shifted again. The Taliban and al Qa'ida became victims; they were said to be slaughtered by the millions. At the end of two months, anti-American attitudes in these circles had not basically changed, but the confidence with which they were uttered was no longer the same, and some daring spirits even suggested they might have been mistaken.

Brian Appleyard wrote that anti-Americanism had never been right and that he was sick of his generation's whining ingratitude, its willful, infantile loathing of the nation that "has so often saved us from ourselves."[30] But was it really the story of a whole generation or perhaps only of some of the most vociferous and loudest among them? Their influence in the media was infinitely stronger than in the country at large. In the streets of London and even of Bradford, there were no mass demonstrations; no one was willing to go on the barricades except a handful of young al Qa'ida sympathizers shouting and waving in front of the television cameras.

How to explain these differences in outlook? Were the critics of America the only ones farsighted and caring? Or was it perhaps another manifestation of a syndrome that had frequently appeared in Europe after World War II: the copying of American intellectual, sartorial, and culinary fashions, usually with some delay, ranging from jeans and T-shirts to hamburgers, pop, and postcolonial studies? In other words, was European anti-Americanism merely a rehash of the American anti-Americanism fashionable in some circles in the United States?

France has been for many decades the country spearheading anti-Americanism in Europe, but on this occasion there was less of it among the intellectuals than in either Germany or Britain. *Le Monde* had never been known for its warm feelings toward America, but it did announce immediately after the attacks "nous sommes tous Américains." The spirit of solidarity did not persist for very long. Soon after, a hundred or so intellectuals published a manifesto putting most of the blame on America, but there was hardly anyone of rank among them. The French Orientalists who had announced for a long time the impending demise of radical Islam continued to maintain that they had been right all along. But they were reminded that their third-world sympathies had affected their judgment — the idea that the West had always been more culpable than the Orient, Israel more than the Palestinians, the Algerian colonels more than the Algerian terrorists.[31]

Maitre Isabelle Coutant-Peyre, who defended Zaharia Moussaoui — arrested in the United States as the suspected twentieth suicide bomber — made it known that she was to marry Carlos the Jackal, whom she had also defended and who was spending a life sentence in a French prison for a series of murders. Once a communist, he had over the years moved toward fascism.[32] But these were the actions of eccentrics that can be found at any time and in almost any place, and are in no way typical of French public opinion.

Among the many long and passionate comments published during the weeks after September 11, a few should be singled out because they stood in different ways for the opinions of segments of the intelligentsia. One was by an Indian woman writer, Arundhati Roy, who had gained greater attention in Britain, Germany, and France than in her native country.[33] Ms. Roy, daughter of an Arab mother and a Bengali father, originally an actor and subsequently the winner of the prestigious Booker Prize, had taken an active part in Indian domestic politics, participating in demonstrations against the construction of dams. Her articles were written with great anger and reminded one of similar polemics, before and after World War II, by writers such as Louis Ferdinand Celine and Jean Paul Sartre. For her, President Bush was no more than a sinister doppelganger (alter ego) of Osama bin Laden; America was responsible for the attacks; terrorism was merely a manifestation of a much deeper malaise; Bush just wanted to use these events to fire workers and suppress freedom; there was no proof that al Qa'ida

had committed the attacks, and in any case the coalition against terror was paying homage to a cult of violence, much worse than anything the Taliban had
ever done.[34]

Ms. Roy was introduced in the European press as the authentic voice of India,
an assessment that was not shared by many of her fellow countrymen and women;
"Ms. Roy is a stupendously vain, preening egotistical self-publicist seeking the
limelight," was one comment; "sanctimonious tone," "lack of intellectual pro-
bity and judgment," and "champagne socialist" were some other epithets used by
her Indian critics. Ms. Roy's essay was interesting in the present context mainly
because of the fact that so many leading newspapers in the West published it
and misrepresented the public standing of its author.[35] In India, preoccupied with
Kashmir, it passed almost unnoticed. Indians worried mainly about Pakistan, and
if there was criticism of Washington, it had mainly to do with the fact that the
Americans were too soft vis-à-vis Pakistan and radical Islamic terrorism.

A less strident Indian voice was that of Salman Rushdie, not an expert on how
to make friends and influence people in the Muslim world, warning Americans of
the depth of the anti-American feelings in Europe (meaning Britain). He focused
on what he heard in Europe on American patriotism, American obesity, emotional
centeredness, and so on. Rushdie said he did not share these petulant attacks but
advised the Americans to take them seriously. Nor was it entirely clear where
he had heard all this criticism, what was meant by "public conversation" and
"segments of the population" — certain literary salons — or political parties, the
working class, the middle class, or the House of Lords.[36] V. S. Naipaul, the Nobel
Prize winner, was the least compromising of the Indian authors; his comment was
that "I had no idea that madness in the Islamic world had gone so far."[37]

A French philosophical contribution to the debate came in the form of a long
article by Jean Baudrillard, a postmodernist quite well known in France but taken
more seriously and even admired on American campuses. For him the spirit of
terrorism was a product of globalization. He knew what bothered bin Laden and
was certainly more adept at putting it in more obscure language than the Saudi
entrepreneur and terrorist. The West had put itself in God's position of divine
omnipotence, become suicidal, and declared war on itself. Baudrillard's style is not
of crystal clarity, but the following sentences give a general idea of his sentiments:
"When the situation is thus monopolized by the world power, when one deals with
this formidable condensation of all functions by technocratic machinery and one
way of thinking, what other way is there other than a terrorist transfer of the
situation? It was the system itself which created the objective conditions for this
brutal retaliation. By picking up all the cards, it forces the other to change the
rules."[38] It is doubtful whether bin Laden and al Qa'ida would have recognized
themselves in this picture.

French intellectuals were not awestruck by Baudrillard's arguments (as some
Germans were by Ms. Roy). Alain Minc noted that Baudrillard's attack reminded

one of communist antihumanism which had disguised itself as anti-Americanism and which one had thought had disappeared with the Cold War. Jacques Juillard went several steps further and recalled that there had been in France a long tradition of intellectuals who, opposed to freedom and democracy, had made common cause first with fascism and later with Stalinism.[39]

A more enlightening contribution to this discussion came from an unexpected quarter: Julia Kristeva, a psychoanalyst and specialist in semiotics and also a leading figure on the Paris intellectual scene. She made the sensible point that time had come to show less naïveté, "to reconsider our simple belief in progress." Out of fear of adding fuel to religious wars, commentators were refraining from mentioning negative features of religion, singling out only the positive ones as if there was no connection between a religion and the fundamentalism it produced: "Religions which exorcised evil and mentioned hell had been less naïve than some of our contemporaries." Ms. Kristeva reached the sad conclusion that much educational work still lay ahead.[40]

These then were a few of the countless comments made in Europe after September 11, but the one which had the greatest immediate impact was written in a very different spirit. It was the longest and the most violent in language (even more so than Ms. Roy). It was written by Oriana Fallaci, a leading Italian journalist (but well known all over Europe) who had retired about ten years earlier and had lived in virtual seclusion in New York. It was highly emotional and in parts quite vulgar, replete with the Italian equivalent of four-letter words, not befitting a lady of a certain age belonging to the upper strata of Italian society. But if in the case of Ms. Roy and Baudrillard one could not be entirely certain how much of it was genuine and how much was posturing and the desire to provoke and to reach a big audience, there could be no doubt in the case of Fallaci. For her the terrorists and the radical Islamists backing them were barbarians to be defeated at all cost, and the Westerners refusing their own culture and values were masochists. She praised American patriotism — there was a world of difference between a country in which the flag is waved only by hooligans in a football field and a country where it is raised by the entire population: She was not speaking to the "laughing hyenas" enjoying seeing images of wreckage and snickering — it serves the Americans right.

> I am speaking to those who neither stupid nor evil are wallowing in prudence and doubt. And to them I say — wake up people, wake up. . . . You don't understand or don't want to understand that a reverse crusade is in progress. Accustomed as you are to the double cross, blinded as you are by myopia you don't understand or don't want to understand that a war of religion is in progress. Desired and declared by a fringe of that religion perhaps, but a war of religion nonetheless. A war which they call Jihad, a holy war.

Oriana Fallaci's essay "La rabbia e l'Orgoglio" ("Anger and pride")[41] was widely commented upon in measured terms by Umberto Eco, and violently by other intellectuals such as Dacia Maraini and Eugenio Scalfari, of *La Repubblica*.[42] Eco noted the general bewilderment: The defense of Western values had become the banner for the right, whereas the left was usually pro-Islamic.[43] Some critics of Fallaci asked how a self-respecting newspaper could have published such an aggressive and vulgar article. But as far as popular acclaim was concerned, Fallaci carried the day. Published as a little book, *La rabbia e l'orgoglio* became number one on Italy's bestseller list, selling a million copies in a few weeks. There was a movement afoot to ban the publication of the Fallaci book in France, but it did not succeed; it became number two on the French list of bestsellers in the summer of 2002 and also reached the top of the bestseller list in Germany.

So much then about the reaction of some of the sections of the European intelligentsia toward America and the new wave of terrorism. Following President Bush's "axis of evil" speech and his call to destroy Saddam Hussein's weapons of mass destruction, attacks against U.S. policy became far more frequent and intense. Anti-American criticism was frequently accompanied by anti-Israeli comments. After the major raids in April 2002 of the Sharon government culminating in the temporary occupation of major Palestinian cities and refugee camps, anti-Israelism replaced at least temporarily anti-Americanism. As far as these circles were concerned Washington–Tel Aviv was the "axis of evil." This was not surprising because even though the Palestinian issue was not the central one in radical fundamentalist doctrine and propaganda, it certainly did play an important part — hence the frequent appeal to America to restore peace by desisting from its one-sided approach in the Middle East conflict, always assuming that the West European attitude was not one-sided. At the same time, the more realistic of the critics admitted that such a change in U.S. policy would by no means bring an end to terrorism, for even the liquidation of the Jewish state was only one of the aims of the radical Islamists and their supporters. Criticism of the policy of the Sharon government was certainly legitimate, coming from inside Israel as well as from outside. But was it just criticism of Israeli policy or were other elements involved?[44]

Perhaps it was mere accident that the same individuals and media in Germany and England, who were most prominent in the anti-American campaign and its condemnation of Israel had also been sympathetic vis-à-vis left-wing Holocaust revisionism (such as the Norman Finkelstein affair) and had taken a hostile stand on other issues involving Jews. There was the feeling that the Jews had talked too long and too loudly about their sufferings during the Holocaust (as if only they had suffered . . .) and that the time had come to hear less about Auschwitz. This was also the line taken by Martin Walser and others in Germany a few years earlier. There was more to the anti-Israeli line taken by sections of the European left than just the revulsion generated by Israeli occupation of the West Bank.[45]

It is only fair to reiterate that while most of the anti-Americanism in the media came from the left, the contribution of the extreme right and the European neo-Nazis, as mentioned earlier on, was considerable. True, some sections of the extreme right in Europe were even more Islamophobic than anti-Semitic, and since the political problem facing them was immigration by Muslims rather than Jews, their ire was directed against the former. But the majority of the neo-Nazis and other such groups still came out against America. Thus, to give but a few examples, the Danish neo-Nazi movement (DMSB) sharply opposed "dancing to the American tune"; the Hungarian leader of the far right, Istvan Csurka, called the attacks "a not-unexpected reaction from the oppressed people of the world against globalization and the deliberate genocide taking place in Palestine." In Germany Horst Mahler, once one of the leading figures of the Baader-Meinhof gang, declared that the attacks were justified and eminently effective, and blamed them on the Jews and their "Yahweh cult." Also in Germany (in Stralsund) an American flag was burned by members of the far-right NPD, and in Frankfurt (Oder) young neo-Nazis marched under the slogan "USA — international center of genocide." In France, the Unité Radicale declared that "this war was not our war" and hailed the end of the American empire. The National Socialist Front (NSF) in Sweden announced that the terrorist attacks were an attack on the New World Order — "democracy kills and one must not be surprised if its victims hit back."[46] The publications in the media overwhelmingly came from the left, while the protests in the street were almost all sponsored by radical Muslims and the neo-Nazis.

The evidence showed that a significant part of the European intelligentsia was critical of America, but this was hardly a new phenomenon, even though it tended to emerge more strongly at a time of crisis. But it was difficult to discover the universal, burning, all-pervasive hatred of America which had allegedly penetrated every corner of the globe. It certainly could not be found in China or Russia, not in Japan or India, not in Africa, not even in Indochina, where one might have expected it. There was resentment and envy but not really much deep hatred. The media and the individuals who were so negative about the war against terrorism were tirelessly stressing that they were not anti-American and that there was much about America they admired, from Jefferson and Lincoln to the leading contemporary American critics of America. This was much in contrast to the anti-Americanism of the extreme right which did not make such fine differences.

The picture was not even that clear in the Middle East. While a Palestinian poet stressed that he hated America as the Jews had hated the Nazis, such voices were not very frequent in other Arab countries, except if they were commanded by the government. On the contrary, Arab writers took great pains to stress that despite U.S. policy in the Middle East, which they detested, they did like Americans and American culture. Ms. Roy, the outspoken Indian critic of America, made it known that there were certain American writers whom she admired and also the landscape and to call her and those sharing her views "anti-American" was therefore wicked and misleading. An Arab intellectual wrote: "We continue to be fascinated by them, we eat their food, we wear their clothes. When we travel abroad we go West not East."[47] Even if this is painting too rosy a picture of Arab attitudes, it seems still true that the universal hatred of America, if examined more closely, was limited to part of the population of countries in the Middle East. Forty years earlier, Frantz Fanon had genuinely believed that his writings expressed the views and feelings of the poor and oppressed in the third world, whereas in fact his appeal had been limited to some left-wing intellectuals in the West. The anti-American articles published after September 11 were in many ways a replay of Fanon and Sartre. When the anti-Americans complained about globalism, they did not really mean globalism and for the friends of Osama bin Laden the "crusaders" were the great enemy. Globalism was the least of their worries.

But the central subject of our investigation, to repeat once again, is not primarily the prevalence and the causes of anti-Americanism. It is this question: to what extent did reactions to September 11 contribute to a deeper, more realistic understanding of the nature and the roots of contemporary terrorism? And in this respect, anti-Americanism has not been very helpful. The new terrorism has not been about poverty and not primarily about Israel.[48] What it was about can be read in the writings of Sayed Qutb and the interviews of Osama bin Laden, the autobiography of al Zawahiri and the manifestoes, legal and illegal, of the various radical Islamic groups.

But these explanations might have been too simplistic for the advocates of anti-Americanism, from right and left who have a different political agenda. In some cases it might be the deep-seated political naïveté about which Mrs. Kristeva has been writing. Or, as Andre Glucksman believed, the blindness vis-à-vis terrorism was conscious, not involuntary, and it reached its peak with the belief that it was a manifestation of higher morality: One does not want to dirty one's hands but in reality it is only the cowardice to confront evil.[49]

Whatever the reasons, conscious or unconscious, there was strong resistance against taking effective action against terrorism. The belief that American bellicosity was more to fear than Islamic terrorism was not shared by Western European governments, at least not until the issue of Saddam Hussein's weapons of mass destruction came up and opposition to American policies became more widespread and pronounced. This despite the well-known fact that the German, French, and British governments at the time largely consisted of ministers who had originally come from the same ideological stable as the anti-American critics of the far left. Was it just the fact that those in official positions had access to information which the other side lacked, or was it because those in official positions were subject to constraints and responsibilities which the critics, deriding

Bush and finding mitigating circumstances for Osama bin Laden and Saddam Hussein, could ignore?

First-year students are taught that, contrary to popular belief, history never repeats itself. But there are recurrent patterns in history and there are similarities between the attitudes of sections of the intelligentsia of the left as well as of the right in Western Europe in the 1930s toward fascism and contemporary attitudes toward radical Islamic terrorism. Historical fascism with its mass parties is, of course, a thing of the past, but there are other typical aspects of fascism which persist in contemporary terrorism: the brutality, the fanaticism, and the hatred of individual freedom, democracy, and Western values in general. Mitigating circumstances were found at the time for the emergence of Nazism, such as the unjust peace treaty of Versailles. Sixty years later, other mitigating circumstances were invoked to explain the actions of those who had declared war on the West: "Islamophobia" and the ideological hostility allegedly prevailing in the West, which was poisoning relations with the Islamists.

NINE

Battlefields of the Future 1: India and Central Asia

Political violence has been endemic on the Indian subcontinent for a long time but it attracted little outside attention largely because it was considered a normal part of the tensions between different communities. Ethnic tensions quite apart, terrorism has been endemic for a long time in parts on the subcontinent such as Bengal and Assam. In some ways such benign neglect was justified; while three major and many minor Indian leaders were killed by terrorists (Mahatma Gandhi, Indira and Rajiv Gandhi, the latter two prime ministers at the time), these actions did not seriously destabilize the government and society. Furthermore, old-fashioned dacoity (banditry) has also been endemic in India and Pakistan, and it was not always easy to differentiate between political terrorism, robbery, and kidnapping for material gain.

Over the last decade, the situation has become more dangerous; both India and Pakistan have become nuclear powers. There is the danger that terrorism may trigger off a nuclear war and that, furthermore, as a result of a deliberate policy or of political chaos, weapons of mass destruction may fall into the hands of terrorists.[1]

Furthermore, there has been a transformation of the conflict between India and Pakistan, and also within these two countries, as a result of the rise of religious fundamentalism (Islamism and Hindutva). To a territorial conflict a religious dimension has been added, and the spillover of events in Afghanistan added fuel to a situation which had become explosive even before.

Both India and Pakistan were founded as secular states, but in the 1970s, particularly under General Mohammed Zia ul Haq, a great boost was given to the Islamization of Pakistan as a counterweight against political parties and also to provide a new sense of unity after disastrous military defeats and the loss of East Pakistan. The country was swamped with weapons of every kind, and a veritable culture of jihad developed. Thousands of *medresset* (or *madressas* — religious schools) were set up in which youngsters between the age of six and sixteen were taught the Koran by heart and a few other essentials about Islam. They were indoctrinated in the spirit of jihad and were trained in the use of weapons. These training grounds were usually located in a mosque and were sponsored by religious political parties and Middle Eastern governments, mainly Saudi Arabia, but also by local businessmen. The pupils came from the poorer sections of the population, and it was from among these people that the Taliban movement arose and that the terrorist groups drew their footfolk. As a commentator put it: They were less centers of spiritual development than mainly breeding grounds for sectarian intolerance and hatred, leading to terrorism.[2] Altogether about 1 million pupils were or are trained in perhaps ten thousand *medresset*. One, named Dar al Ulum al Haqqaniah, located south of Peshawar, is the biggest of these training centers, and it also played a central role in the history of the Taliban movement.

They belonged to a variety of schools, the most influential of them the Deobandi movement, which originated in a town in India in the middle of the nineteenth century. It was meant to educate young men in a spirit of Islamic orthodoxy, largely to stem the tide of Islamic modernism. The Indian *madrassa* still exists; during the last decade its position has been politically delicate. It has supported the Taliban, but stressing that this support was purely spiritual and that its Indian patriotism was second to none. It has made slight concessions to the modern world; radio and newspapers are permitted but television is banned, the computer is accepted, but not the Internet. Women are not given access but outside the campus a school for women has been established. The Pakistani government, belatedly realizing the political danger inherent in these institutions, has tried to supervise the teaching, but it is not clear whether it will be able to impose its authority.[3]

The spirit of jihad manifested itself in the fighting in Afghanistan as well as greater militancy in the struggle against India but also on the domestic front. Among the victims were the Shi'ite minority in Pakistan, about 15 percent of the population, which in turn caused the growth of militant groups among the Shi'ites which, inspired by the Khomeini revolution in neighboring Iran, also wanted to bring about the imposition of Islamic law — but not of the Sunni variety.

A second target of the *madrassa* graduates were the militants of rival religious schools; the Sunnis were divided into various factions such as the Deobandi, the Barlevi, and others. Finally, there was a general movement afoot to destabilize the country by systematically killing (as in Algeria) members of the free professions and intelligentsia such as physicians, teachers, and journalists.

There was a great deal of urban violence, mainly in Karachi, to a lesser extent in Hyderabad, and other cities. Karachi, a medium-sized city of about four hundred thousand when Pakistan came into being, houses today more than ten million, largely in slums, squatting quarters, and other temporary abodes. The population was swelled first by millions of refugees from India (Mohajirs) who soon outnumbered the natives, later by Biharis from Eastern Bengal, refugees form Afghanistan, and so on. It was a struggle of all against all in which ideology hardly played a role, but crime and a turf war a great deal.

In a bad year hundreds of people were killed in shootouts between rival groups every month. The hitmen usually appeared in groups of two, three, or four; many were college dropouts or even graduates who had chosen this kind of life because there were few chances to find other jobs. Kidnapping was a favorite mode of operations; it is estimated that in the struggle for power over the control of Karachi in 1990 there were some two hundred kidnappings. According to reports many victims were inhumanely tortured.[4]

Another favorite mode of operation by the terrorist groups was to attack mosques of other parties, usually at prayer time, which guaranteed a maximum of victims. Churches, needless to say, were also attacked. The Pakistani army played a double role. On one hand Pakistan Army Intelligence was the patron of the Taliban fighting in Afghanistan which was given all possible help. At the same time the army was used by the government to restore law and order if and when fighting between various armed groups inside Pakistan such as Sind province got out of hand.

Two major and many minor terrorist groups are active at the present time in Pakistan. The leading ones are Lashkar-e-Taiba (the Army of the Pure) and Jaish-e-Mohammad (the Army of Mohammad).

The former resembles the Muslim Brotherhood in Egypt and Hamas in Palestine inasmuch as its political wing (named Markaz Dawa al Irshad) engaged in social and political activities, and is running schools as well as publishing houses.[5] Bin Laden, who was the main source of financial support, addressed in years past the annual meetings of the Markaz over the telephone from Sudan and Afghanistan.

The ideology of Markaz and Lashkar was originally Wahhabi, but gradually it distanced itself from Saudi Arabia, arguing that there was not as yet one truly Islamic state in the world. The one closest to it was the Taliban in Afghanistan, hence their support. It opposed any concession in Kashmir and saw its aim in the liberation of all Muslims in India and eventually the establishment of Islamic rule all over the world. At the same time they have not been averse to entering tactical alliances with anti-Indian groups in South India and, according to Indian reports, they have been flirting with the Tamil Tigers even though the Tigers have pursued a consistent anti-Muslim policy in Sri Lanka, engaging in ethnic cleansing of all non-Tamils.

The main mode of operation of the Lashkar in Kashmir (about which more below) has been hit-and-run operations against the Indian army and Indian civilians, but it has also increasingly engaged in terrorist operations.[6]

The other main terrorist group, Jaish-e-Mohammad, is the successor organization of Harakat ul Mujahideen, later Harakat ul Ansar; its origin was in the multitude of the humanitarian relief and military organizations mushrooming in Lahore and Peshawar during the war in Afghanistan. These groups under their leader, Maulana Masood Azhar, were also part of the bin Laden conglomerate.

Azhar had established contact with bin Laden early on, fought in Yemen and Somalia, but was arrested by the Indians and released only in December 1999 following an exchange of prisoners after his organization had hijacked an Air India plane. The traditional main targets of Jaish-e-Mohammad are India, the Shi'ites in Pakistan, and the United States. However, more recently attacks against Christian churches as well as hospitals and churches run by missionaries have also figured prominently.[7] They were responsible for the attack on the local Kashmir parliament in October 2001 and subsequently the attack against the Indian parliament in New Delhi. The ideological differences between them and the Lashkar are difficult to discover with the naked eye but there is rivalry between them over funding and political influence.

Sunni terrorism against Shi'ites in Pakistan provoked counteractions on the part of the Shi'ites carried out by terrorist groups like the TJP, the SMP, and various offshoots. Some of their leaders were Iranian-trained clerics, and their ranks were swelled by thousands of Hazaras; a major Afghan Shi'ite tribe which had been defeated by the Taliban escaped to Pakistan and had sworn revenge. The scene in Pakistan resembled a jungle in which everyone was fighting at times everyone else. The terrorists were making money by drug trafficking and gun running, so they were heavily armed. Their operations endangered the very existence of the state, and no one could estimate even remotely how many people had been killed in this permanent fighting.

India

The murder of Mahatma Gandhi in 1948 shocked not only India but the world at large: Gandhi had been the apostle of nonviolence, and India had been thought to be the most tolerant of nations. Insufficient attention had been paid to the fact that when nationalism arose in India in the nineteenth century it was not only directed against the colonial power but drew its inspiration from a Hindu ideology (*Hindutva*) based on the belief of Hindu and Aryan supremacy. Their gurus believed that Hindus were a nation by themselves, representing a civilization all of their own.[8] What room was there for non-Hindus or for the Untouchables in an India in which blood and religion were to play a central role? True, many leaders of the Indian national movement tried from the beginning to reach an understanding with the leadership of the Muslim community, but there was also a more aggressive (and militarist) trend which saw its main task in defending Hindu rather than Indian interests. They were influenced to a certain extent by European fascism, opposed the "Gandhi-Muslim conspiracy," and emphasized that a Muslim could not really be a true national of India and a loyal citizen. From among these circles, Nathuram Godse, Gandhi's murderer, emerged. But the very fact that these extremists had assassinated a beloved leader caused a major backlash from which they did not truly recover for many years. The organization was banned and thousands of its members arrested.

But the seeds for a nationalist, even racialist revival existed, and its main instrument was the RSS (Rashtriya Swayamsewak Sangh), which had been founded in the 1920s. In some ways it resembled the Muslim Brotherhood, for initially it saw education and religious work as its main assignment. It undertook social work, mainly among the Hindu refugees from Pakistan in 1948–49. But it also had a military wing with its uniforms (saffron or khaki shirts) and its training in martial arts and weapons. Its commitment to democracy and above all to secularism was somewhat dubious from the very beginning, but its political role was limited for many years to local politics in certain areas of Northern India. The BJP (Bharatiya Janata Party) also stood initially for the reunification of India, but later on more realistic counsel prevailed. The presence of a sizeable Muslim minority in India presented major problems in any case, without adding to it a hundred or more million unwilling Pakistani citizens. However, from the 1970s the BJP, the political party which served as the cover organization for these circles, got a major uplift as the result of two separate developments — one was the decline of Congress, which had ruled India from independence. The BJP (again like the Muslim Brotherhood) appeared as the apostle of honesty and unselfishness vis-à-vis the corruption of Congress. At the same time, a wave of religious fundamentalism swept India as well as other countries. Congress had become outwardly at least more respectful of the Hindu religion, whereas, ironically, the BJP declared in its manifesto that Hindus and Muslims were really blood brothers because racially the Muslims of India had also been Aryans.

However, the old tensions between the communities persisted, and the continuing conflict with Pakistan, with which India had been fighting several wars, was bound to have ideological repercussions. Sometimes a conflagration would be the result of a deliberate provocation, such as the destruction in December 1992 of a sixteenth-century mosque in Ayodya by a big mob of Hindu militants and the attempt to build a Hindu temple there.[9] A few thousand people all over India were killed in the riots that ensued. But on other occasions a mere accident or an isolated random attack would trigger off a major massacre, such as when in December 1990 in Hyderabad in south India, an auto rickshaw driver was stabbed by two young Hindus. Muslims retaliated and in the riots that followed, which lasted ten weeks, more than three hundred were killed and more than one thousand injured.[10] In the riots in Bombay in 1992–93, some seven hundred people were killed, most of them Muslims, following the simultaneous bombing of seven major buildings by Muslim terrorists and the incitement of an extreme right-wing group, the Shiv Sena, led by a political cartoonist named Bal Thackeray. In this outbreak the Bombay underworld (the Dawood gang) seems to have been prominently involved; peace was restored following elaborate negotiations. The masterminds behind the bombing, Dawood Ibrahim and

Ibrahim Abdul Razaq, escaped to Pakistan and later to Dubai when their presence became too embarrassing for the Pakistani government. But Bombay was by no means an exception. In some northern states such as Assam, terrorism was more or less endemic. Christian churches were systematically attacked, and tribal people chose terrorist operations in their fight for greater independence.

There has been a great deal of research into the roots of this communal violence. About the basic causes there is little dispute: the fear of the minority Muslims to be swamped and the suspicions of the Hindus of their alien neighbors.[11] But the communal violence is usually carried out by a small minority of fighters, and the question has arisen whether they are motivated more by aggression and even bloodlust or by a sense of competition like in a cricket match. As one militant put it: "You have to score at least one more run than the opposing team. The whole honor of your nation is at stake on not scoring less than the other team."[12]

The communal riots, often recurring annually, greatly contributed to the rise of Hindu fundamentalism and explains in great part its rise to power in 1999. Many of the leaders of the BJP had belonged earlier to the RSS, the military wing of the movement. Once in power they had to moderate their politics, if only because the Muslims constituted an electoral factor that could not be ignored. But the BJP still pursued their agenda, for instance in the field of education, introducing school curricula that put great emphasis on *Hindutva*. Not only the writing of history was affected, mathematics was to be based on the Veda and departments of astrology established at universities.

While Muslims in the Arab East have traditionally regarded Zionism and the West as invaders, the situation in India was different, for the main historical complaint of the Hindus was the Muslim invasion of India and Mogul rule for many centuries and the destruction of Hindu civilization. The great contribution of Muslims to Indian culture symbolized by the Taj Mahal made little impression on radical Hindus. There were other, topical irritations, such as the conversion of the Dalits (the Untouchables) to Islam as a way out from their inferior status in Hindu society; this was considered an unpardonable sin by radical Hindus. But the most evident bone of contention was, of course, Kashmir.

Kashmir in the far north of India is one of the most beautiful and fertile parts of the subcontinent, but it has also been for more than fifty years the most embattled. When India was partitioned in 1948, the ruling maharaja decided after long hesitation to join India, even though the great majority of his people were Muslim; in adjacent Jammu, also under his rule, about two-thirds of the population was Hindu.[13] About one-third of Kashmir came under Pakistani rule; the situation was further complicated as a result of the fact that probably the majority of the population would have preferred independence rather than belonging to either India or Kashmir. (But neither India nor Pakistan wanted an independent

Kashmir.) There have been many rounds of negotiations and United Nations resolutions, but much of the time there has been fighting of every kind ranging from full-scale war (in 1965 and 1971 as well as in 1999), to cross-border raids of small and not-so-small units, as well as almost constant terrorist acts.[14]

Indian rule in Kashmir has been brutal, and there have been many human rights violations, as are bound to happen in any occupation facing a hostile population. Indian sources claimed that four hundred thousand Kashmiri Pandits had been forcibly pushed out of the Valley by the terrorists. Muslim sources talked about tens of thousands of their coreligionists who had been killed, not to mention an even greater number of arrests, rapes, etc. The Islamists supported by Pakistan on the other hand have declared a jihad and tried to turn a national liberation insurgence into a religious campaign.[15] Thus the struggle against the Indian occupation in Kashmir turned into a call to destroy India altogether. As the head of the Markaz (the political arm of the Lashkar-e-Taiba) declared in November 1999, "Today I announce the break-up of India, Inshallah. We will not rest until the whole of India is dissolved into Pakistan." Another leader called on the same occasion for "wiping out India altogether."[16] This kind of inflammatory talk at a time when both India and Pakistan had acquired nuclear power status created a very dangerous situation, and ever since 1989 there has been the threat of an explosion. Pakistani governments encouraging terrorist groups were no longer in full control.

The confrontation came to a head with the attack by five members (probably of Jaish-e-Mohammad) on the Indian parliament in New Delhi on December 13, 2001. Thirteen people were killed in the shootout, which lasted almost an hour. The intention had been to kill or to take hostage the prime minister of India and other leaders.[17] This led to a major outcry in India to teach Pakistan a lesson, and only owing to the intervention of the United States and other countries was a major conflagration prevented. But the incident showed how dangerous the situation had become and how easily a major terrorist attack could have led to war with incalculable consequences.[18]

Kashmir was not the only territorial conflict facing the Indian government. For years there had been terrorism in Punjab among radical Sikhs fighting for an independent state — Khalistan. But the Sikhs were a relatively small minority, they were not Muslims, and they did not have the full support of a foreign power. As a result, terrorism in the Punjab sharply declined in the late 1990s.

The declaration of jihad against India had a limited appeal in the Muslim world. While in the case of Israel there was an enormous outcry from Indonesia to Morocco, mass demonstrations, and offers of help, and in the case of Afghanistan many thousands had volunteered to fight for the liberation of their Muslim brethren from infidel yoke, there was virtually no response in the case of the Pakistan-Indian conflict, even though the number of Muslims killed was infinitely larger. Was it because the fate of Muslims on the subcontinent was of marginal interest only to the rest of the Muslim world? Or was it perhaps the fact that India (like China, also having to deal with a Muslim minority) had a population in excess of a billion and no Muslim group outside Pakistan, however radical, wanted to tackle a state of this size? On the contrary, following the riots of 2002 and the aggravation of the situation in Kashmir, Arab governments turned to India with the request to play a more active role in Middle Eastern politics.

The same was true with regard to China: The Uighurs, a Muslim minority in the westernmost province of China, had bitterly complained for years that the Chinese authorities had systematically persecuted them to the extent of even banning the observation of Ramadan. According to these sources, some sixty thousand Uighurs had been arrested and some six hundred had died while detained. These figures were almost certainly greatly exaggerated, but there was little doubt that the Chinese were in no mood to make concessions to the separatists. But no one in the Muslim world even dreamed of declaring a jihad against China. On the contrary, the Beijing government was requested to intervene in Middle East politics.

Terrorism in the Caucasus

The Russian-Chechen conflict has attracted international attention for a decade. It has taken a variety of forms, from full-scale war to guerrilla warfare and terrorism, and only this specific aspect is of relevance in the present context. But it is difficult, often impossible, to differentiate between terrorism and other manifestations of violence, just as it is next to impossible to differentiate between the various components in the motivation of the highlanders of the Caucasus resisting the Russians. There have been in history very few instances of urban guerrilla warfare, but the fighting in Grozny in 1995 and again in 2000 have certainly been among them, with small groups of three to five fighters launching attacks against the Russian forces. Even after the fall of Grozny, there was urban fighting in towns such as Komsomolskoye, which had been believed "cleaned" of Chechnyans. Sporadic terrorist attacks took place even after the defeat of the Chechens, and it is impossible to draw a clear line in these conditions between guerrilla warfare and terrorist operations.

The Caucasus contains an enormous variety of peoples, ethnic groups, languages, and religions, and there is a very long history of conflict between them, not necessarily always along religious lines. Russian attempts to subdue the Caucasus beginning in the 1770s took almost a century. The legendary Imam Shamyl, an Avar from Dagestan, was the leader and became the symbol of native resistance. Eventually the Russians prevailed. The Chechen, one group of many among the native Caucasians and by no means the largest, were among the resistants and suffered badly; many were killed, others expelled. During the Soviet period they fared neither better nor worse than other minorities. During World War II, they were deported to Central Asia as elements that could not be trusted, together with the Ingush, their neighbors with whom they did not, however, politically have much in common. (Together they counted at the time about half a million.)

When the Soviet Union broke up, an independence movement developed in Chechnya pressing a variety of demands — religious and cultural as well as environmental. A national congress was formed, headed by Jokhar Dudayev, a former Soviet air force general. Dudayev declared Chechnya's independence from Russia in June 1990; the Ingush on the other hand seceded from Chechnya and declared themselves an autonomous republic within the framework of the Russian Federation. Chechnya's declaration of independence was, in retrospect, an unwise step, but it was made in a period in which everything seemed possible in view of the general chaos then prevailing in Moscow. A wholly independent state of Chechnya was not really viable; furthermore, the vital Russian economic interests should have been taken into account, such as the oil pipe leading from the Caspian Sea to the west.

Russia's decision to invade Chechnya in 1994 was equally unwise. Russia could have granted many Chechen demands while preserving its own vital stakes. The decisive consideration in Moscow for going to war was in all probability emotional rather than rational; having lost so much of their empire, those in power may have thought that a line had to be drawn somewhere, and the Northern Caucasus seemed an obvious place to do so. But all other considerations apart, the Russian army was very much weakened and had hardly any experience coping with guerrilla warfare since the Basmatchi rising in Central Asia in the early 1920s.

The first Chechen war lasted two years. Russian superiority especially in the air was total. Grozny was heavily bombed and partly destroyed. In May 1996 Yeltsin visited the Chechen capital and declared that the war had been won and all the bandit gangs destroyed. But during the months that followed, insurgent Chechen units gradually forced the Russians to leave Grozny. The Russian forces suffered heavily and in late August a cease fire was arranged. The truce amounted to a Russian defeat but it left the Chechen too weak to assert their independence.[19]

In December 1999, Russia invaded Chechnya a second time and during the next few months occupied Grozny as well as all other cities without, however, being able to impose their authority entirely.[20] Small-scale Chechen attacks continued. Armed Chechen gangs retreated first to the south, to the Argun valley and when defeated there, they retreated into the Panisi valley in Georgia.

Russia has argued all along that the Chechen rising was part of a general radical Islamic conspiracy promoting terrorism. This is true in part but does not provide the whole picture. Islam was a latecomer to the Caucasus, and inasmuch as there was an Islamic underground in the Caucasus during the Soviet period it was mainly Sufi in character. (The Sufi are one of the more quiet, mystical trends in Islam.) After the breakup of the Soviet Union there was an invasion of what the Russians call Wahhabism, meaning the radical fundamentalist trend; those belonging to this camp prefer to be called Salafists.

Saudi Arabia gave a great deal of money for the building of mosques and cultural centers which often, but not always, became training centers for militant cadres. Young Muslims went to Saudi Arabia to receive religious training, but more went to the Asian republics where underground *madrassas* had existed even during the late Soviet period, in addition to the two legal Islamic religious seminaries. But the Islamic tradition in the Caucasus had not been on the whole one of Muslim fanaticism. Islam was part of the national tradition and it was greatly influenced and modified by local customs that were in no way consonant with orthodox Islam. Most people would declare themselves religious persons, but this did not mean that they would carry out most religious duties. Their religion was a mixture of Islamic, national, and folkloristic elements. If they were fighting against the Russians or other foreigners, this had more to do with general xenophobia or distrust of anyone who did not belong to their group than with a firm theological belief in jihad.

A few military commanders were Arabs, such as Omar ibn Khattab, a native of Jordan who had come to join the Chechen in their struggle against the infidels, but these foreigners were not an essential part. The Chechen wars would have taken place even without them. It is also true that after the first Chechen war, all kinds of ideological elements made their appearance, which had been hitherto unknown such as anti-Semitism. This kind of propaganda was all the more grotesque because there were no Jews in Chechnya or among the forces opposing them. But it did not prevent some of the Chechen media from engaging in propaganda along the lines of the *Protocols of the Elders of Zion.* Arbi Barayev, one of the main gang leaders and kidnapers, declared that he and his men would kill every Jew they would meet, a statement of academic significance only but it strengthened suspicion that at least some of the Chechen militants had fallen under the influence of the bin Ladin–type jihadists.[21]

Chechen fighters engaged in a variety of terrorist operations ranging from attacks on Russian army units to the kidnapping of foreigners and locals to the murder of collaborators with the Russians as well as Muslim religious dignitaries who were not sufficiently radical to their taste.

Some of these activities belong to the realm of crime rather than terrorism as commonly understood. This refers for instance to the frequent kidnappings. An ear or a finger would be cut from the body of the victim; the action would be videotaped and sent to his family with a demand of ransom. The ransom asked was sometimes $1.5 million, but the kidnappers are known to have accepted a mere fifty thousand. In the case of five Stavropol building workers who were kidnapped, one was beheaded, the scene was filmed, and the cassette sent to the families of the other four.[22]

Many of these activities took place between the two Chechen wars; the power of the then-Chechen government headed by President Maskhadov was exceedingly limited. When Maskhadov proclaimed the closure of three terrorist training camps installed by Khattab, this order was simply ignored.[23]

The Chechen militants carried out some of their terrorist attacks outside their own region. This refers to the raids into Dagestan and the attacks in the resorts of Northern Caucausus such as Pyatigorsk and Mineralnye Vody. It has not become clear to this day whether the bombing of housing estates in Moscow, Volgodonsk, and Buinaksk in which more than three hundred people were killed were carried out by Chechens or others. By and large the strong (and very patriotic) Chechen mafia in Moscow has been careful not to mix business and politics. They have made a notable financial contribution to Chechen independence but steered clear of carrying the war into the Russian capital. According to court investigations, the attack in Moscow was carried out by three jihadists from Northern Caucasus (but not Chechnya), and natives of Dagestan are suspected of the Buinaksk bombing. All of them were said to be emissaries of Khatib, the Jordanian alleged to be bin Laden's man in the Caucasus. Later on in 2002, there were allegations that some of the defeated fighters from Afghanistan had fled to the Caucasus and were hiding there.

Chechnya was by no means the only region in the Caucasus in which terrorism appeared in the post-Soviet period. Some of the most spectacular terrorist operations occurred between rivaling parties in one and the same country such as in Georgia and Armenia. This refers, for instance, to the attempt on the life of Eduard Shevardnadze, president of Georgia and the attack inside the Armenian parliament. More often, attacks were sponsored by radical Islamic groups. One of their main targets was Dagestan, to the north of Chechnya. Khatab and Basaev, one of the main guerrilla and terrorist leaders, wanted to establish a Caucasian jihad legion, and in August 1999 they invaded Dagestan, seizing several regions. But far from strengthening the local Dagestan Islamists, this raid compromised and weakened them, and the invaders were defeated.[24] Political leaders in Dagestan were opposed to Wahhabism, and religious leaders gave it only lukewarm support. They argued, like president R. Aushev of Ingushetia, that Wahhabism was a harmful, unacceptable trend, distorting Islamic teaching and dividing the Muslim community. The general council of Russian muftis announced in 2000 that Wahhabism should be combated because it was a deviation from the true teachings of the Islam. It meant, among other things, a denial of folk customs deeply rooted in Russian Islam.[25] The Russian muftis were less happy about the American (and indirectly the Russian) intervention in Afghanistan, but this did not affect their aversion to the radicals in their midst.

Western Caucasian regions were on the whole more moderate than those in the East. In the Kabardino Balkar region, some three to four hundred radicals planned at one stage to overthrow the local government, but the religious establishment opposed them. A fair number of these insurgents had been trained in Khatab's Chechen camps, others were mere brigands.

With all this, it is less than certain whether the authorities are in full control as the jihadist propaganda mainly directed toward the young generation con-tinues. While the elders of the communities argued that jihad in the Caucasus was a foreign importation, the mood of the younger generation is said to be more militant.[26]

In Azerbaijan jihadism was certainly considered a foreign importation. This emerged from the trial against members of the Hizb ul Tahrir in Baku in early 2002. An Uzbek militant named Abdulrasul Abdulrahimov had been dispatched to Azerbaijan and found a number of like-minded radicals, not all Azerbaijanis. They decided to stage a coup and to establish a radical Islamic regime based on the Sharia. They called their group *Hizb ul Tahrir* (Liberation Party) and regarded it the successor organization to one of the same name which had been founded in Jerusalem (then part of Jordan) in the 1950s. They engaged both in political propaganda and the preparation of explosives and drew up lists of people to be removed. But as their organization spread, the state security organs became aware of their activities. It ended up in the court of serious crimes in Baku, where all the leading figures were among the accused except the Uzbek who had absconded in time.[27]

Hizb ul Tahrir was founded by a Palestinian teacher named Taqi ad Din al Nabhani in the 1950s in Jerusalem. Its ideology was close to the Muslim Brother-hood and the ideas of Sayed Qutb, but it stressed more than the Brotherhood the specific Arab character of Islam and also established close relations with the pan-Arab Ba'ath party, which was secular in character. A very aggressive anti-Western and anti-Jewish party, it preached the use of violence but, with one exception, Jordan, never attained much influence in the Middle East. On the other hand, having undergone various organizational and ideological adjustments, it did take root in Central Asia and also in Britain.

The prospects of radical Islamic terrorism in the Caucasus remain uncertain; the urban regions are probably too secular and too socially developed to provide good prospects for the jihadists, but their long-term chances in the more backward rural regions could be better. Much depends, of course, on general political, social, and economic developments in the region.

Islamic Terrorism in Central Asia

The progress of radical Islamism in former Soviet Central Asia largely escaped the attention of the rest of the world when it took place after the breakup of the Soviet Union; this began to change only when Taliban rule in Afghanistan became a major issue on the international agenda. There were several reasons for this lack of attention; the radicals appeared without much fanfare, first in rural regions such as the Ferghana valley where there had always been an Islamist presence, underground in the Soviet period. The warnings of the Russians and the local authorities were dismissed as exaggerations at best, because they were believed to have a vested interest in playing up this danger to justify the presence of Russian military forces. This was perfectly correct, and it was also true that the danger served to perpetuate the rule of the old elites to run their countries with (to put it cautiously) less than democratic methods.

However, with all this the danger of jihadism was not wholly imaginary but a very real and growing threat. A civil war in which fifty thousand people were killed raged in Tajikistan between 1992 and 1996, and in later years terrorist gangs were active in virtually all Central Asian republics. Their most spectacular exploit was the bombing at one and the same time of five buildings in Tashkent in February 1999, including the ministry of finance, the National Bank, the Ministry of Interior, and the National Security Service. About 250 people were said to have been involved in the preparation of these attacks, of whom 128 were jailed and 19 executed.[28]

Radical Islamism appeared in Central Asia during the last years of the Soviet period, but it was only during the perestroika interregnum that it could act more or less freely when thousands of "unofficial" mosques were built. The rulers in the five republics such as Karimov and Akayev followed a policy of carrot and stick vis-à-vis Islam; they accepted it as part of the national tradition and identity, but they bitterly opposed political Islam as a rival to their rule. They wanted to establish secular regimes on the pattern of Kemalist Turkey.

Islam had historically not played a central role in Turkmenistan, Kirgizia, and Kazakhstan, the north of which was more Russian than Kazakh. But it was a major factor in Uzbekistan and predominantly Shi'ite and Persian-speaking Tajikistan, and it was in these two countries that most of the confrontations occurred.

True, the readiness of the population to accept radical Islam was subject to great regional variations even in these two republics. It was stronger, paradox-ically, in urban areas than in the countryside (except the golden valley) — in Ferghana, especially the Andijan and Namangan districts. The valley in which about one-third of the population of Uzbekistan lived was the most fertile but also the most embattled region of Central Asia. During the Soviet period, it had been subject to various economic experiments which had failed, leaving behind a legacy of poverty and ruin in a potentially rich area.

The valley became the main base of Islamism in Central Asia. Many of the leaders and rank-and-file of the terrorist movement which developed are natives of the Ferghana valley. Other strong points were the mountainous regions of Tajikistan. Militant Islamism was paradoxically weak in traditional religious cen-ters such as Bukhara, perhaps because Sufism, a nonviolent trend of Islam, was deeply rooted there, which made the terrorists less than welcome.[29]

Radical Islam and the terrorist movement received their main impetus from the war in Afghanistan, in which many soldiers from Soviet Central Asia took part but hardly with great enthusiasm. The Khomeini revolution in Iran had had a certain impact on Tajikistan even earlier on, and Teheran wanted to gain influence there.[30] But Iran was still far away, whereas Afghanistan was very near and many Tadzhiks lived there across the border. Later on with the victory of the Taliban, the main terrorist organization, the IMU, received an enormous uplift. Afghanistan, and in particular al Qa'ida, became their main supplier of arms, their combatants were trained there, and if they were pursued they could always find a safe haven across the border. They could launch annual incursions from there into Uzbekistan and Kirgizia, and for a while it appeared that these raids were on a larger scale every year.[31]

IMU (Islamic Movement of Uzbekistan) was the strongest by far of the armed groups; originally there had been others, such as Tauba (Repentance) and Adolat (Justice). IMU was the armed wing of Hizb ul Tahrir but they enjoyed a great deal of independence. Mention has already been made of this party, which was founded sixty years earlier in the Middle East — never attaining great importance there — but which somehow found its way to Central Asia, where it became a considerable political force.[32] Together with the Islamic Renaissance party in Tajikistan, it threatened the hold of the political regimes.[33] But whereas the latter, which was somewhat more moderate, came to share power after the Tadzhik civil war, the Hizb ul Tahrir was banned in Uzbekistan.

Was this ban inevitable? In the doctrine of Hizb ul Tahrir as stated in its books and pamphlets, there is little room for compromise. It calls for coercion and force to establish a radical Islamic political and social system, and that all physical obstacles should be removed to spread Islam across the world.[34] The Caliphate should be restored; their appeal is, in the words of an Uzbek political scientist to young academics and students, of "highly emotional people, socially and politically inactive but with uncontrolled destructive instincts, with an absence of faith and rational thinking."[35]

The founders of the IMU (Islamic Movement of Uzbekistan) were two young men from the Ferghana valley, Tohir Yuldeshev, the chief ideologist, and Juma Khoyaev, better known as "Namangani," who became its military leader. The story of the IMU and its leaders has been told elsewhere.[36] All that need be mentioned in the present context are the essential facts — that they established links with like-minded groups in the Caucasus, throughout the Middle East, and, above all, Afghanistan. They received financial support from Islamic international organizations, but some of it was procured locally; it was reported that they and allied groups controlled some 70 percent of the drug traffic.[37] They seem to have followed the practice of Maoist guerrillas in the 1930s of paying the locals for food and other services so as not to antagonize the population. It grew from a few dozen militants to about two to three thousand fighters whose families were evacuated to Afghanistan. Discipline was strictly enforced; once having joined the organization, there was no way of leaving it. In 1999, nineteen young men who had tried to break ranks were found decapitated.[38] The incident happened near the village of Chikhaza. The men were part of a group of thirty-six fighters who wanted to lay down arms to be pardoned under an amnesty. Their equipment was superior to that of the government forces, and their fighting spirit was high; they had the reputation of fighting to the end if there was no escape.[39] In the Ferghana valley, to give but one example, they would not just behead a police captain serving the Karimov regime, but display his head in front of his station. The government, needless to say, would react equally harshly and in good measure would lump all the opposition together, so that many oppositionists who had little if anything to do with the radical Islamists would still be branded as such.

The IMU annual raids, usually by relatively small groups in various directions from across the border, threatened the Central Asian governments, and there seemed a reasonable chance that they would wear the governments down. But they were too dependent on the Taliban, and once they had lost their base in Afghanistan (and their leader Namangani, who was killed in fighting there) they were seriously weakened. They appealed not only to the middle-class intelligentsia but to the poor and suffering in Uzbekistan. Given the record of the governments there — which was negative, by and large — they should have had more success. Many of the allegations made against these governments of autocratic practices, corruption, mass arrests, and so on were correct. Karimov's policy was heavy-handed, to say the least; he made no attempt to integrate the moderate Islamists. Whether such an attempt would have succeeded is not certain, but it was not even tried.

If so, what inhibited the Islamists from reaping greater successes? The reasons were to a large part the same that made it so difficult to establish stable, prosperous and reasonably free societies in the Caucasus and Central Asia. There was a great reservoir of enmity and aggression, but it was not necessarily along religious lines such as in the conflict between Armenia and Azerbaijan, and even in this case it was as much a national as a religious conflict.

The conflicts were as often as not between ethnic groups that were Muslim — between Lesghians and Azeris, between Avars and Azeris, between Persian and Turkish Azeris in the Caucasus, to mention only a few; between Uzbek and Kirgiz, between Uzbek and Meskhet Turks; between various Tadzik Tribes, north and south, to mention but a few. Tribal loyalties, language (or dialect), and the place where a person was born were often more important than religious solidarity. If the IMU identified itself too closely with one ethnic group it more or less automatically antagonize another. Hizb ul Tahrir and IMU would try to overcome these obstacles by emphasizing the universal appeal of radical Islam. But they did not succeed more than the Taliban in Afghanistan, for their kind of Islam was too splenetic to have a universal appeal, and while it might appeal to young intellectuals it was too remote from local traditions and customs in which Central Asian Islam had developed over the centuries.

But it would be too early to write off these guerrilla and terrorist groups even if they lost their safe bases in Afghanistan. They will not be cut off from their financial sources; they have considerable fighting experience; the region, sparsely populated, mountainous, accessible only with difficulty, is ideal guerrilla country. In these circumstances it will mainly depend on the strength of the governments and the success of their policies whether political violence as exercised by radical Islamic groups will remain a marginal phenomenon or whether it will continue to be a serious threat to the existing governments. It will also depend on the global strength of radical Islamism, of which the Central Asian variant is one segment.

TEN

Battlefields of the Future 2: The International Brigade

The danger zones in the years to come in world politics and the world economy are not shrouded in secrecy, but there is no similar certainty with regard to global terrorism. Those who engage in terrorism are counted not in millions but in thousands. Given the easier access to very effective weapons, traditional and weapons of mass destruction, it is perfectly possible that the terrorism of the future will be carried out by even fewer, a mere handful of people. The appearance of political mass movements in history is thought to be related to "objective trends," to tensions, trends, and ideologies. In contrast, the appearance of small fringe groups at the margins of politics and society is unpredictable. They can appear at any time and in any place. The decisive factor is not the objective situation, the reality, but the individual perception. Terrorists could be motivated by feelings of rage or frustration or hate, the reasons of which might be a matter of or no little concern to the overwhelming majority of their fellow citizens. These militants might be religious sectarians or antiglobalists or animal rights activists or strongly believe in a cause of which most of mankind is not even aware. They also could have private grievances. In the past, acts of violence carried out by such small groups were not very important because their destructive potential was limited. But this will no longer be true in the future.

With all these reservations, there still is the probability that terrorism is more likely to occur in certain parts of the world than in others, and at the margins of certain radical political or social movements. We deal with these movements in this chapter.

Terror from the Extreme Right

Among the consistently underrated and ignored sources of terrorism in the past and also in the present has been the violence emanating from the extreme right and neofascist groups. This situation exists for a number of reasons. Some observers have persuaded themselves that true terrorism is always, or almost always, left-wing ("progressive" or "revolutionary") in inspiration — a revolt

against an intolerable and unjust political and social order. This belief is difficult to eradicate; when faced with realities which contradict these notions, it will
be argued that these are exceptions, deviations from the norm. There is deep psychological resistance against accepting the fact that terrorism is not an ideology,
and not a manifestation of a certain ideology but a mode of operation, a strategy
that can be adopted by almost any group within the political spectrum and a few
outside it.

There are yet other reasons for this neglect. The voices of the extreme right and
the neofascists are not loudly heard in the mainstream media. Their spokesmen
are not intellectuals; they do not participate in the public discourse on politics or
culture or social questions, and it is only too easy to forget about their existence.
They have their own journals and assemblies, their own Internet lists, their own
videos, and even their own pop music. In brief, there is a neofascist subculture
hidden from view but nonetheless very real. Part of this subculture is the use of
terrorism.

Terrorism from below played a subordinate role in historical fascism, not
because the Fascist and Nazi Parties had any compunction to use it, but because
they believed in another strategy. They were confident that they would conquer
the street with their paramilitary formations, and they also thought that they
would gain power through political action — that is to say, mass parties. They did
in the early phase of their history kill individual political opponents — the murder
of Giacomo Matteotti by the Italian fascists in 1924 was an obvious example, but
in later years the violence they used was state terror, terror from above — mainly
through the political police, arrests, concentration camps, and executions.

The neofascists, on the other hand, have no conceivable hope of gaining political power through either elections or a show of open force as the Nazis and the
Italian fascists did, and it is exactly this feeling of weakness which makes terrorism an attractive alternative. They feel politically isolated and racially in a
minority, swamped by aliens and other enemies. The masses, far from listening to
their message, are too indifferent and stupid even to understand their message,
and in these circumstances the only way to make themselves heard is by shock
therapy, destabilizing state and society by way of terrorism. Those familiar with
the doctrine and literature of neo-Nazism in the United States know that this
strategy, as outlined for instance in William Pierce's *The Turner Diaries*, envisages
a battle against the American people in which tens of millions of people will be
killed by means of weapons of mass destruction.[1] As these strategists envisage
it, attacks against the "system" are bound to produce general lawlessness, a dis-
ruption of public services, and a breakdown in public order, as well as a major
economic crisis. In this situation, the masses will be confused and lose confidence
in the authorities, and there will be a political awakening of broad sections of the
population who will join those aiming at establishing a new Nazi order.

During the last two decades, there have been assassinations of individual citizens by terrorists from the far right, but on the whole there have not been many such attacks. Oklahoma City has remained an isolated incident. But this could change within a very short time, and there have been reports over the years that militants of the extreme right have been trying to obtain weapons of mass destruction, or, to be precise, the raw materials from which such weapons can be produced. The extreme right is a house divided. There is not one party, let alone one leader. Some factions are single-issue hate groups, such as antiabortionists, Holocaust deniers, neo-Confederates, or believers in alternative Christianity who have little in common with the proponents of neo-Nazism or such pagan cults as Odinism. Not all neo-Nazis believe in terrorism by means of weapons of mass destruction.[2]

These splits are by no means a source of weakness, since the extreme right does not, in any case, believe in political action, in democracy, or in change of the system by peaceful, reformist means. On the contrary, part of the strategy of the militants is "leaderless resistance," a principle quite similar to the organizational structure of the bin Laden conglomerate. Small groups of activists operate independently from each other in such a way that even if members of one cell are arrested, they are not in a position to know about other groups whose survival will not be jeopardized. In the past, this form of loose organization had its limitations, but in the age of weapons of mass destruction, small groups of people could be sufficient to create havoc and panic.

There has been a certain amount of national and international cooperation between these groups of militants, but not very much; essentially, they remain confined to one region or one state. Their status has been one of semilegality, but if they were to engage in terrorism in earnest they would have to opt for going into deep illegality, which so far they have hesitated to do. The great danger facing them has been infiltration on all levels from the leadership down to the rank-and-file; the smaller the terrorist group, the more difficult it is to infiltrate. Small may well be beautiful and certainly less risky as far as the terrorism of the future is concerned.

In view of recent history, more attention has been paid to neofascist and neo-Nazi terrorism in Germany and Italy than in other countries. Following the decline of the left in Italy, a government came to power which included the successor party of the Fascists. The party and especially its leader, Fini, very much moderated their stance in order to acquire respectability, much to the dismay of their more radical supporters. But on the other hand they may have found it difficult to attack a government (Berlusconi) which, all things considered, was closer to them than the previous ones. Italian right-wing terrorists had been responsible for some of the bloodiest attacks in Europe (at the Piazza della Loggia in Brescia, at the Bologna railway station, and the Piazza Fontana in Milano), and they had also developed the most elaborate strategy of the systematic destabilization of the government. But by and large they have shown less activity than their German comrades.

The extreme right and the neo-Nazis in Germany have been split into more than a hundred groups, among them some who have given their members systematic military training. Every year since 1998, German police discovered caches of weapons containing not only automatic weapons, but also shells and mortars, machine guns and hand grenades.[3] According to police estimates, the number of "violence prone" members of the extreme right is estimated at nine to ten thousand. Their main target at the present time is immigrants (asylum seekers) from Asia, Africa, and the Middle East, of which Germany has more than any other European country. But the neo-Nazis have also become more active on the margins of the antiglobalism movement: they protested against German participation in the war against Serbia and the support of the American war against terrorism.

A potential of neo-Nazi terrorist attacks existed also in Britain and Sweden. In Britain the movement was very much influenced by their comrades in the United States — they read the same books, such as *The Turner Diaries*, and used the same names for their cells (such as "Commando 18"). However, by and large these attacks (almost always against new immigrants) were the work of individuals who were not core members of any group.[4]

Neo-Nazi terrorism in Sweden is largely homegrown; among its victims were policemen, an investigative journalist, and a trade union organizer. Little is known about the social background of the members of these groups. The generally prevailing idea of unemployed young workers being the main recruiting ground of extreme right-wing militants seems not be borne out by the known facts, according to which the offspring of middle-class families was at least equally involved.

In recent years, relations between the extreme, neo-Nazi right in Europe and Islamist and Arab terrorist groups which existed for a long time have become more intensive, especially in the field of business transactions. These shadowy deals, which on occasion also involved the Mafia, have seldom been reported in the media.[5]

Ultra-Left Terrorism

Those on the political left demanded strong government action against the terrorists from the right, but such appeals involved them in contradictions; they feared that an antiterrorist legislation would be used also against the violent militants of the left. Some of the most sensational assassinations in Europe, such as in Nanterre and the Netherlands, had, after all, not been carried out by neofascists but sympathizers with the left. Terrorism from the far left has been down in Europe but by no means out. The obvious example is the 17th of November organization in Greece, which has over the years targeted American and British diplomats and NATO officials, but seldom if ever Greek citizens. In its statements it professed Marxism-Leninism and a revolutionary strategy, but at the same time it has advocated a fanatical, uncompromising nationalism. It is putting far more stress on Greek national interests than on social revolutionary change.[6]

Since no member of this organization has been apprehended by the police in twenty-five years, Greek governments have been accused of either abysmal inefficiency or of the presence of sympathizers in its ranks. In July 2002, a member of the group fell into the hands of the police since he was injured while trying to place a bomb in Athens harbor. As a result the leading members of this small group were arrested. It appeared that its origins had been in one of the Trotskyite sects of the 1960s. When the colonels established a dictatorship in Greece in 1968, the Trotskyites split into a political and a terrorist wing. But while the dictatorship lasted, these "activists" were hardly in appearance. They began their actions only in 1975 when democracy had been restored in Greece. There is a striking similarly with the Basque ETA, which had also been Marxist-Leninist in the beginning but later veered toward integral nationalism. As in Greece, terrorism began in earnest only after the overthrow of the dictatorship; terrorist groups need a minimum of freedom to prosper. ETA was far more active than the Greek comrades because its basis was ethnic and it could rest on a broader base. (ETA killed some eight hundred, while the Greek terrorists murdered only twenty-two over roughly the same period.)

But the Greeks were by no means the last left-wing revolutionary terrorists in Western Europe, as claimed by some authors. This was shown by the murder of two academics advising the Italian ministry of labor, Massimo D'Antona in Rome and Marco Biagi in Bologna.[7] On the occasion of the murder of Biagi, the Red Brigades, believed to have been dormant if not dead, published a long manifesto explaining their action. The one innovation in addition to the usual key words used in the past (revolutionary struggle, strategy of the armed struggle, imperialist counterrevolution, working-class militancy), was the attempt to connect their terrorism with that of bin Laden; the attacks in New York and Washington had shown the vulnerability of world capitalism. The ultra-communist Italian terrorists saw themselves in a common front with radical Islamism.[8]

Such collaboration with religious obscurantist forces under the banner of anti-imperialism may seem grotesque. But cooperation, direct or indirect, between Islamic terrorism and the ultra-left was by no means limited to Italy. The case of Algeria is significant. The Communists were sharply critical of the terrorists, be it only because the declared aim of the latter was "to kill ten thousand Communists" even though there weren't ten thousand Communists in the whole of Algeria, but the Trotskyites had less compunction in this respect. They declared their support from the very beginning for the Islamist insurrection (the strike of June 1991) and continued their "critical support" in the following years. They were not very influential inside Algeria but they had sympathizers among British journalists and French Orientalists and were active among those suggesting that most of the terrorism was carried out and sponsored not by the Islamic terrorists but by the military government.[9]

As a sympathizer of Louisa Hanoune, the leader of the Trotskyites (also called the Algerian La Pasionaria), put it, "Here was a woman beautiful like a princess out of Arabian Nights who talked perfect Arabic and who said things on television which only the Islamists in their mosques dared to say."[10] How to explain that a spokesmen of the ultra-left was proud to say the same things the Islamists were saying in their mosques? An Algerian commentator noted that the Trotskyites were wedded to the old anarchist theories of the nineteenth century that the world could be rebuilt only if it had been reduced to chaos earlier on.[11]

At this point the hopes and expectations of the neofascists and the ultra-left met, but for the fact that their ideas of the world to be rebuilt after the coming revolution were different. However, for the time being, Islamic terrorism had to be considered an ally because "objectively" it was taking a politically correct position. This was also the line taken by various French groups and groupuscules of the far left.

Algeria became in the 1990s the bloodiest battlefield of terrorism, and for its well-wishers the most embarrassing. The victims — their number is esti- mated between 100,000 and 150,000 — were not colonial oppressors or wealthy exploiters but for the majority simple poor people, more often than not killed at random. True, certain groups were singled out — women and professional people such as teachers, students, and journalists. More than seven hundred schools were destroyed, the underlying assumption being that these schools corrupted the youth. A few hundred Islamic preachers deemed undesirable by the extremists were killed, not to mention Christian clerics, monks, and nuns.

Algeria

Algeria became independent following a bloody and protracted fight against France, the colonial power, and the tradition of violence had of course much to do with the giant massacres of the 1990s. In addition, Algeria produced an ide- ology which not only justified violence but declared it absolutely essential. This refers to Frantz Fanon and his cult of "cleansing violence" as a means of self- affirmation.[12] Violence seen by Fanon was a liberating force, binding the rebels together. True, toward the end of his life, Fanon began to realize the corrupting influence of the barbarism that ensued; this should have occurred to a trained psychoanalyst earlier on, but ideology proved stronger than clinical knowledge and experience.

But Fanon was not the sorcerer's apprentice who let the genie out of the bottle. He was not a native Algerian; his fame was greater among European and American intellectuals, and it is doubtful whether more than a handful of Algerian rebels ever read him. The breakdown in the 1990s had to do with the abysmal performance of postliberation Algerian governments. First Ahmed Ben Bella managed within a few years through harebrained state socialist schemes to ruin the economy of a country which as a major oil producer should have been relatively well off. He was followed by General Abdelaziz Bouteflika, whose economic policy was equally disastrous and who encouraged in every possible way the Islamists to combat the influence of the leftist elements in the country. The situation was aggravated by a very high birth rate and very high youth unemployment. Lastly, there was the return to Algeria of several hundreds of militants from Afghanistan, sworn to seize power by means of a bloody struggle.[13] They joined the FIS (Front Islamique de Salut, the main Islamist movement) and later the even more radical GIA (Groupe Islamique Armée).

The civil war began with a mass strike declared by the opposition in June 1991 and escalated the year after when the military government cancelled the results of the elections when it appeared that the Islamists of the FIS were about to win. This dictatorial act was widely criticized; the generals in power argued that if the Islamists had won, these would have been the last elections in Algeria. Their dilemma was that of the government of Weimar Germany in 1932–33 facing the upsurge of Nazism, and they did not want to commit the same mistake. But the historical parallel was less than perfect: the generals were not simon-pure democrats, and the Islamists were not a monolithic camp. The rulers should have tried to negotiate with the more moderate among them.

The next years witnessed countless massacres throughout the country and even in the capital and its suburbs.[14] Thousands were slaughtered every month, and the crimes were so bestial that the propaganda of those who claimed that no faithful Muslim could be guilty of them fell on fertile ground. The Algerian terrorists were giving terrorism and Islamism a bad name. Thus a campaign of disinformation began that did not have much of an impact inside Algeria, for Algerians knew from bitter experience what was happening in their country and who the villains were. But in Europe and America, the Algerian government came under considerable pressure. Countless committees and many individuals visited the country in an attempt to establish the truth.

There is every reason to assume that the government fought back with equal ruthlessness, that in all probability hundreds, if not thousands, were killed without a trial or disappeared without a trace, murdered by the army or the police. This syndrome was not new. It had happened before in Argentina, Uruguay, and other countries — in fact, in every country in which terrorism threatened the very existence of the state and society. Once terrorism had passed a certain stage, terrorists could not expect any mercy from their opponents. Legal restraints were off and many innocent people perished in the process. But it was still true that the overwhelming number of attacks in Algeria (and also in France) were carried out by the radical Islamists, especially the GIA who claimed credit for them, and even distributed video training films in which the mass murder of army recruits was shown.

The terrorists and their sympathizers argued that the government was responsible for the mass murder because it had infiltrated (and somehow manipulated) the GIA, the most radical terrorist group, because it had given arms to local militias and in other of ways. But all this could not explain the fact that many thousands of Algerian soldiers and policemen had been killed; furthermore the GIA made no secret of their attacks but claimed credit, and the more moderate Islamists of the FIS denounced their barbaric acts. Furthermore, there was ample evidence that the GIA and other ultra-extremist forces consisted to a considerable extent of criminal elements.[15]

The military government came under international pressure to open a dialogue with the FIS; partly as the result of this pressure, the civil concord which was reached, and a general amnesty in 1999 — but also as the result of war weariness on the part of the FIS — there was a substantial decline, especially in the cities, in the number of attacks and victims in 2000.[16]

But the GIA and some new small group — acting autonomously such as a Salafist group (GSPC), which seems to have been directly connected with bin Laden — continued to fight. Their number was estimated at three thousand, possibly more. It seems safe to say that by this time the element of banditry had become preeminent and the religious motivation was no longer of decisive importance.[17]

The situation in Algeria is important because the country continues to be a breeding ground for terrorism. True, a great part of the population, not only the intelligentsia and the middle class, have been deeply antagonized by the brutal slaughter, and many, especially among the rural population, have taken active part in the battle against the "monster," as terrorist Islamism is frequently called. True, Algeria is not nearer to democracy than ten years ago, but no Middle Eastern country is, and the preconditions in Algeria are worse than elsewhere. More decisive is the fact that social and economic conditions have not improved, and that so many young people are still unemployed. The fact that Algerians have been exposed to such an extent of barbarism has generated counterforces and perhaps a certain degree of immunity against the forces of violence. But even if radical Islamism has caused widespread revulsion, terrorism in Algeria is not necessarily bound to disappear.

The Balkans

The wars in the Balkans seem not to belong to a survey of terrorism, present and future. When Yugoslavia broke up in the 1990s and Croatia and Slovenia declared their independence (1991), the separation from Serbia did not proceed without violent conflict and painful consequences such as killings and ethnic cleansing. This was even more palpably felt in the case of Bosnia, when two hundred thousand people were killed and many more lost their homes. The war in Bosnia was ended by the Dayton peace accords in November 1995. Next came the struggle for Kosovo, a province of Yugoslavia populated mainly by Albanians but historically important for Serbia. A guerrilla war led to full-scale NATO intervention (March 1999). Once this war was over, the Albanians took the offensive both in Kosovo trying to expel the Serbians living there and also in independent Macedonia, which has a significant Albanian minority. The West, and above all America, had intervened to protect the Muslims in the Balkans, but this action earned them little gratitude in the Muslim world.

These events are still relevant in the present context for a number of reasons. As in the Balkans before and after World War I, many ethnic groups' national aspirations have not been fully satisfied (and indeed cannot be fulfilled without harming others), and they wish to prolong the conflict. One of the means to do so is guerrilla warfare; the other is terrorist operations.

In the armed conflicts of the 1990s, terrorism played only a subordinate role. It is difficult to think of more than one or two leading political figures who were killed as the result of a terrorist action. In the process of ethnic cleansing, a great deal of individual killing did take place, but it was more on the pattern of a guerrilla war than on terrorism as commonly understood.

However, the Balkans have a long tradition of terrorism in which the Macedonian Revolutionary Organization (IMRO) played a leading role as well as the Croat Ustasha. Nor should it be forgotten that World War I was triggered by the attack of members of a Serbian terrorist organization against the Austrian heir to the throne in Sarajevo. There certainly is the danger that dissatisfied nationalist groups in the former Yugoslavia, of which there are a great many, will use terrorism as a means to destabilize their neighbors and thus achieve their aspirations. The presence of UN observers and forces makes a war or a guerrilla war unlikely because it would be easy to trace, whereas terrorism in these circumstances could be the most likely mode of operation chosen.

Second, the Balkan wars, specifically the war in Bosnia and Kosovo, gave Islamic terrorists from the Middle East and South Asia a foothold. Many Afghan veterans came to Bosnia and Kosovo to fight and establish their bases there. If this help would have been limited to participation in local fighting, it would not have been of great consequence except to the states directly affected. However, there was growing evidence that the veterans of al Qa'ida and allied groups used their bases for smuggling arms, laundering money, getting false papers, and, generally speaking, for planning terrorist operations in Europe and America. Eventually, more than a dozen European and Middle Eastern countries (including Italy, France, Britain, Turkey, Egypt, and Algeria) were asking for the extradition of Muslim terrorists.

This caused more than a little embarrassment for the governments in Albania and Kosovo. On one hand, they felt a debt of gratitude to the people who had helped them in their hour of need, and they reciprocated by assisting them in various ways, mainly through logistic assistance. But on the other hand, the guests had been outstaying their welcome and they did not wish to invite foreign political sanctions — especially after September 11, 2001. Consequently, most of the mujahedeen were asked to leave, and some were extradited from Albania to other countries such as Egypt.

However, there were also other reasons for the growing weariness of the host countries. The mujahedeen had not come to the Balkans to help the local Muslims establish secular states. They thought that unless strictly Islamic governments were installed, the whole fighting had been in vain. But the majority of Kosovars and Albanians did not want a society run along the Sharia, which was one more reason that the local governments saw the volunteers leave without too much regret. However, there is evidence to the effect that not all of them departed; some became holders of Bosnian and Albanian passports, and some married local women and stayed on. In the words of a former Czech foreign minister, Jiri Dienstbier, neither the United Nations nor NATO succeeded in defeating the alliance of terrorism and organized crime in Kosovo, which based on the inner circle of the Albanian KLA is responsible for about 70 percent of the smuggling of heroin to Central Europe and Scandinavia.[18] The Balkans will remain, at least for some time to come, a potential base for terrorists.

Terrorism and Banditry

While terrorism in Algeria was clearly ideologically inspired in its initial phase, the element of banditry became progressively stronger, and it was difficult to draw with any certainty a clear dividing line between these two elements. The same is true, *mutatis mutandis*, with regard to terrorist groups in other countries, for instance in the Philippines and in Colombia. It was also true with regard to the ex-Trotskyite terrorists in Greece who took to bank robberies in the 1990s to improve their financial situation both as a group and as individuals.

The history of the Abu Sayaf (bearer of the sword) group goes back to an earlier national resistance movement, the Moro National Liberation Front (MNLF) located in the centers of the Muslim population, which constitute about 5 percent of the total in the Philippines, mostly in parts of the island of Mindanao and the islands offshore. The Muslims felt themselves discriminated against and for religious as well as cultural reasons wanted a state of their own. They armed themselves, and in a guerrilla war against the authorities thousands were killed on both sides and many more lost their homes. MNLF received the support of Libya and later of Iran, but all things considered it was not one of the most extreme movements, and eventually peace negotiations began, resulting in the Tripoli agreement (1976) in which some of the demands of the MNLF were accepted. The agreement did not give the separatists full satisfaction, but from this stage on their emphasis was on nonviolent resistance.[19]

The transition to a peaceful struggle was not welcomed by Muslim radicals, some of whom had fought with bin Laden in Afghanistan, so they split away from the main movement. The group was small, totaling no more than about two hundred terrorists, with perhaps a few more sympathizers mainly concentrated on the Sulu archipelago. What it lacked in numbers it compensated for with hectic activity and public relations. Little is known about its ideology; religious fanaticism seems not to be particularly strongly developed among its members. They do want, however, full independence rather than mere autonomy, which they received according to the various agreements with the government. Its operations have included attacks against Christian churches and bookshops; in one attack against the Christian city of Ipil there were fifty-three victims. Their favorite mode of killing was by beheading. They financed their operations by kidnapping tourists (mainly foreigners), piracy, smuggling, and robbery — always arguing that such activities were in accordance with the principles of jihad.[20] These operations generated resistance among the mainstream nationalist Moro groups, which accused Abu Sayaf of dragging Islam into criminal acts. They argued, above all, that kidnapping for profit was not in the spirit of the Koran. Embarrassed by the Abu Sayaf criminal actions, the mainstream groups offered their assistance to the Manila government after September 11, 2001. But the Abu Sayaf militants, having amassed tens of millions of dollars in ransom money, did not greatly worry about theological niceties and the interpretation of Islam. For them, crime had become a way of life and income. Some of this money seems to have trickled down to the inhabitants of the islands, who are their main supporters, and this as well as complaints about the neglect of the central government assures them a political base.[21]

The political element in the motivation of Colombian terrorism, the main focus of terrorism in Latin America at the present time, is considerably greater than in the Philippines: A struggle is taking place both for political power and for control of the drug business. FARC (Revolutionary Armed Forces of Colombia), the biggest of the three Colombian terrorist organizations (not counting the AUC, United Self-Defense Forces, the paramilitary group of the right), came into being in the 1960s. Its original name was M 19. It was sponsored at the time by the local Communist Party and was meant to be active in the cities. Such activity proved to be very difficult both in view of limited political support and the greater ease with which the police could trace and break up terrorist cells in the cities. The FARC and the ELP (fashioned after the Che Guevara model) transferred their activities to the countryside, where the government was weak and they had a natural constituency in the farming communities specializing in the growth of coca, by far the most profitable crop. Since then the FARC has given up

Marxism-Leninism in favor of a vague populist doctrine called Bolivarism and the promise of better government than the Bogotá authorities. The FARC decided to demand a certain percentage of the income for protection money from the farmers ("reluctantly" according to sources close to them).[22] The farmers were quite willing to pay up; they might have had to pay more to groups of gangsters. ELN (National Liberation Army), a group consisting of pro-Castro elements as well as left-wing Christian militants, found another source of income in extorting money from the oil companies. Whenever the companies refused to pay up, the pipelines were bombed, sometimes as often as once a week.[23]

The other main source of income for the terrorists was kidnapping. More than half the kidnappings worldwide occur in Colombia each year — perhaps three to four thousand, and it has become a growth industry. Nine out of ten of those kidnapped regain their freedom, if the rules of the game are observed. Virtually none of the kidnappers is ever apprehended.

FARC, which has some ten to fifteen thousand fighters under arms, gained control of a considerable part of the country.[24] In view of the funds at its disposal — its income is estimated at almost $400 million a year, about half protection money, the rest revenue from kidnapping — FARC could obtain modern arms, which were often superior in firepower to those of the government forces, and they inflicted heavy defeats on the government. Hundreds of soldiers were taken prisoner between 1996 and 1999. Many of them were released when peace talks began in 1999, but the negotiations were not successful and fighting resumed at the end of two years of talks.[25]

The rise and the persistence of guerrilla warfare and terrorism in Colombia can be explained against a background of the weakness of the central government, its neglect of the farming community, and a tradition of violence (*violencia*) which is probably stronger than in any other Latin American country. In the two years of lawlessness after World War II, some two hundred thousand are believed to have been killed. In the fighting since 1986, some forty thousand people were killed, two to three thousand each year. While the Colombian government has tried with American help to carry out an ambitious reform project (the Colombia Plan), these attempts have been half-hearted and not very successful.[26] The FARC has tried to gain influence on national politics by mean of establishing a legal political party, the UP (Unión Patriótica), but its leaders and many militants were assassinated by terrorists of the extreme right. As a result this door remained closed to the FARC, which in turn brought about an intensification of their terrorist activities.[27]

There is a danger of a spillover of guerrilla warfare and terrorism to the neighboring countries, hence the interest taken by the United States in what is essentially a domestic problem. The question of most interest to the outside observer is how can a guerrilla and terrorist movement which has become the third largest drug syndicate (after Cali and Medellín) preserve its ideological purity? The consumption of drugs among the militants is banned, as it was in Afghanistan under the Taliban. But the issue of drug smuggling quite apart — and the FARC has become involved over the years in every stage from production to delivery abroad — there is the fact that FARC has become the wealthiest terrorist movement in history. Its ambitions in contrast to al Qa'ida are limited: they want to seize power in Colombia, not the whole of Latin America let alone the whole world. One of the central issues in FARC and ELP ideology is the struggle against government corruption, but the presence of so much money in the hands of the terrorists is bound to create similar problems. Whereas there is no doubt about its revolutionary origins, its operations over the years owe as much to banditry as to left-wing ideology: indiscriminate killing of civilians such as the bombing of a church in Bellavista (2002) in which more than a hundred people including forty children were killed, attacks against fellow revolutionaries of the ELN in a battle for domination, the kidnapping of peasants, and other such actions. From time to time the FARC would apologize for some massacre, which, it maintained, was the result of a misunderstanding. But the "misunderstandings" were so many that the apologies became less and less credible.[28] While the FARC has become stronger, the more left-wing ELN has declined and counts at the present time no more than about four thousand fighters. Lastly, there are the right-wing AUC groups, also said to be financed by drug money.[29] In Colombia, as in some other countries, terrorism has become a way of life, but eventually it will probably transform itself into a political movement.

The Coming Crises

The United States, Western Europe, Russia, and, of course, Israel remain the main targets in the years to come. Other foci of tension include above all countries of the Middle East as well as Central Asia and Africa, where Islam has made progress in recent decades and where as a result it has claimed a greater say in politics. There has been a cycle of violence in Nigeria, a country with hundreds of tribes and ethnic groups where disputes about land rights are frequent. More recently, however, clashes along religious lines have been more frequent. The Hausa-speaking Muslims in the north have insisted on introducing Sharia as the law of the land; in eleven regions this is now the case.

The immediate reasons for a major riot are often accidental. In Kano, the capital of the north, an otherwise peaceful anti-American demonstration in October 2001 turned in to a large-scale anti-Christian riot. Even earlier in Kaduna, which had been the capital under the British, two hundred were killed, and five hundred in Jos in September 2001; many more, according to some sources.[30] Poverty does play a role as does envy of the other community. But the essential cause triggering violence was the introduction of the Sharia, first in Zamfara (January 2000) and later on in other districts. Altogether some six thousand Nigerians are believed to have been killed in clashes between Muslims and their opponents during the last two years. Sharia courts meant amputation for crimes like theft and stoning to death of women for adultery. It manifested itself in things small and not so small — it meant vigilante groups roaming the streets looking for transgressors, open-air cinemas were closed down, single-sex taxis and schools were introduced. Alcohol was banned, men were advised to grow a beard. Mosques and churches were burned to the ground with religious preachers playing an inflammatory role.

The advance of Islam in Nigeria, not just as a religion but as a dominating political system, was bound to provoke a major confrontation. At the present time the Nigerian constitution is still secular but radical Islam wants to change this, and there have been calls for attacking not just the infidels — meaning Christians and pagans — but also the army. Governor Bukar Ibrahim of Yobe, a Sharia state, has made it known that he was prepared to fight a civil war to preserve the supremacy of the Muslim religious over the civil law.[31] Violence in these conditions more likely than not will assume the form of communal clashes rather than guerrilla warfare or terrorism, but terrorism could be part of it.

The same is true, broadly speaking, in Middle Eastern countries where the radical Islamic opposition wants to overthrow the establishment, such as in Egypt or Saudi Arabia or in a country like Iran where radical Islam has been in power for years and has generated a backlash. One of the more promising regions for the spread of jihadism is Southeast Asia, especially Indonesia in view of its deep economic and political tensions. The Indonesian Lashkar Jihad (the army of Jihad) was founded in April 2000. While bitterly hostile to the West and America, it is critical of Osama bin Laden, because his groups spread disunity, accusing other fundamentalist groups, rulers, and the clergy of heresy. Lashkar Jihad came into being to help the Muslims in Eastern Indonesia against the Christian residents in the Moluccans. In this conflict the Christians suffered badly, and many of them had to leave their homes. The Indonesian government brokered a peace agreement, but this was regarded as a government-Christian conspiracy by the Lashkar who want to get rid of the minority altogether; in any case their ambitions are wider than this regional dispute. No mention has been made of another guerrilla war raging since the early 1990s, that of the OPM (Organization Free Papua) and other local conflicts. With the weakening and disintegration of central state power in Indonesia, the spread of conflict and possibly the descent into chaos cannot be ruled out.[32] After the end of the war in Afghanistan, Indonesia reportedly became an important base of the activities of various radical Islamic groups. The aim of these radicals (known under the name of the "Ngruki network") was to establish an Islamic state consisting not only of Indonesia but also of Malaysia and the Philippines; the leaders of this movement had been in exile under Soeharto but returned after the downfall of his regime. They were few in number but, as an authoritative report noted in August 2002, even a relatively small number were capable of creating a great deal of havoc.[33] By and large certain trends have emerged: The bloodiest civil and tribal wars in Africa have ceased or declined in intensity. This refers, for instance to Rwanda/Burundi, Eritrea, Sierra Leone, Kongo-Kinshasa, and Angola. But the presence of hundreds of thousands of refugees in neighboring countries — for instance, in the camps of Guinea — constitute a potential for a recurrence of violence, and an increase of tension in South Africa cannot be ruled out.

The list of present and potential conflicts is endless. They will take various forms — civil war, guerrilla warfare, insurrection, and terrorism, as we have known will also play a role. Against the background of a wider armed conflict, terrorism usually recedes into the background. If tens or hundreds of thousands of people are killed, the fate of a single human being no longer seems of great importance. However, as past history has shown, terrorism could still be of importance in being the trigger which causes a wider conflict.

No mention has been made of terrorist campaigns of long standing such as the one conducted by the IRA in Northern Ireland or the ETA throughout Spain. Some of these campaigns are in abeyance, others continue, but they are regional in character and do not aim at the export of their revolution to foreign countries. They are not in the same category as the international terrorism that seems to be the prominent feature of the movement in the early twenty-first century.

War against the West

Predicting future trends in terrorism has always been next to impossible. The actors involved have been few, their actions often erratic, and the behavior of small groups in a society is no more predictable than that of very small particles in the physical world. In retrospect, one can point to objective factors which made it likely that the Irish patriots would engage in terrorism in the late nineteenth and early twentieth centuries or why periodic outbursts of terrorist violence occurred in Russia in the decades before the revolutions of 1917. But there were other countries inside Europe and abroad where terrorism could have been expected with equal justification but did not take place. Why did anarchism appear in some countries but not in others? Why did some terrorist groups show great activity during certain periods but were inactive during others? The efficiency of the state security forces undoubtedly played a role, but it is not sufficient to provide a satisfactory answer. Accident obviously also played an important role, in the appearance of certain ideologies and the presence of leaders preaching and practicing terrorist violence.

The same is true today, except that the stakes have grown immensely. Reviewing the history of terrorism over a period of 150 years there can be little doubt that its political effects in contrast to the publicity it received were small. Terrorists alerted public opinion to certain grievances, and to social and national injustice, but more often generated counterforces which in the end defeated them. The more successful terrorism was in destabilizing society, the more effective the mobilization of the antiterrorist forces which led to the downfall of the militants — Russia in 1905–6 and Latin America in the 1970s are obvious examples.

But what was true in the past is no longer necessarily true at present and may not apply in the future. The smaller the group, the more difficult it is to trace and to penetrate, the more far-fetched and strange its motivation and ideology is likely to be. Very small groups of people do not aim at conducting propaganda, building up political mass movements, and seizing power; they aim at destruction in the hope that out of the ruins of what they have destroyed a better world will emerge or at least one more in line with their ideology. Furthermore, society has become far more vulnerable than it has ever been in the past as the result of urbanization and technological progress. Not only have the arms become far more lethal, the targets have become so much softer.

Lastly, prospects have greatly increased for the use of terrorism as substitute warfare precisely because old-fashioned, conventional warfare has become much more risky and expensive; there is the temptation to inflict harm on an enemy through the use of substitutes. Such practices are based on the hope that state-sponsored terrorism will be difficult to prove conclusively. These assumptions are almost certainly mistaken, but the temptation will still be great and miscalculations may lead precisely to what the initiators wanted to avoid — regular warfare, possibly with the use of weapons of mass destruction.

The world is passing at present through a transitional period as far as the weapons of terrorism are concerned, the damage that is caused, and also its basic strategies. The form of terrorism prevalent at the present time is religious or nationalist in inspiration, or a mixture of the two, and the weapons used are improved versions of conventional weapons, more effective explosives, missiles, and so on. Suicide terrorism has made terrorism both more indiscriminate and more deadly. But at the same time, the search has been under way for non-conventional weapons which might kill not thousands but possibly hundreds of thousands. And while there is every reason to believe that jihad and similar doc-trines will persist for a long time to come, there are on the political horizon a great many other potential sources of terrorist motivation. At the same time the danger of escalation has greatly increased, terrorist provocation turning into a full-scale war.

We shall point in the following to some of the threats ahead. No one can say how long the transition period through which we live may last — it could be a matter of years or of decades. Some of the dangers invoked may never happen, while others may materialize sooner than anticipated.

The Future of Jihad

No end is in sight to the activities of Islamist groups which believe that the only way to achieve their mission on earth is armed struggle — that is to say, terrorism and in some circumstances guerrilla warfare. As far as they are concerned jihad is both an individual and collective duty of a true believer, not just the daily prayers or the pilgrimage to Mecca. It has been endlessly repeated that the majority of Muslims want to live in peace with their neighbors, a statement that is as correct as it is irrelevant. The believers in jihad are a minority, in most countries a small minority, but they can count on a substantial periphery of sympathizers, more than sufficient to sustain long campaigns of terrorism. No end is in sight to the conflict between Israel and the Palestinians.

For more than a decade, some Western observers have pointed to the decline of political Islamism, a correct observation in the long run but one of limited relevance with regard to the present activities of the terrorists. Despite all its confident assertions, Islamism does not have an answer to the political, social, and economic problems of the Muslim world — any more than socialism or nationalism or the other "Western" ideologies that have been tried, failed, and rejected. In the countries in which Islamism has been in power or has been politically very active, in Afghanistan and Iran, in Sudan and Algeria, it has been a disaster. But it has the advantage vis-à-vis other ideologies that it is historically deeply rooted, that it is part and parcel of the whole cultural tradition of the Islamic world and its way of life.

The attraction of radical Islamism in the Muslim diaspora, in Europe and other parts of the world continues to be substantial. It has been argued by French experts such as Olivier Roy and Gilles Kepel that radical Islam has been based on an alliance between the devout middle class, the urban poor, and sections of the young generation, and that this alliance has broken down.[1] But this applies more to countries such as Egypt and Algeria than to others, and given the dismal economic situation in the Arab world, a resurgence of radical forces cannot be ruled out. In any case, the integration of Muslims in Europe has been a failure as far as the majority of the new immigrants is concerned. Even if the governments and peoples of Western Europe had tried harder to engage in ecumenical dialogues and positive steps to help the immigrants find their place in society and become part of it, the result would probably not have been different. Many of the immigrants had no wish to be integrated into a society the basic values of which they did not share, with cultural traditions they did not appreciate, and to emulate a way of life many aspects of which they abhorred. In many European countries there has been (and continues to be) reluctance to face reality as far as the real obstacles to integration in these societies are concerned. Nor is there much awareness as far as the true mood prevailing in the immigrant minorities is concerned.[2]

For Islamist preachers, these unassimilated and in part perhaps unassimilable communities have been fertile ground to find converts, especially among the younger generation and this is unlikely to change in the near future. On the contrary, as the second generation of Muslim immigrants has pressed their demands with greater insistence and confidence, they have generated all over Europe anti-immigration countermovements, which in turn has aggravated existing tensions. Obviously, the Muslim communities, or in any case large parts of them, will become more acculturated in the future; there will be more intermarriage and other forms of social mixing; and the communities will become preoccupied with their own affairs rather than Islamic internationalism. But this process, more likely than not, will take decades if not generations, and it will have little political impact in the near future.

According to well-informed observers of the Russian scene, the chances that the Russian establishment will be able to integrate the Muslim minorities are virtually nonexistent; the number of extremist groups is steadily rising and there are many young proselytes.[3] International Muslim organizations have given them millions of dollars to establish camps and courses for both ideological indoctrination and the teaching of military arts. The young members of the congregations are said to be mostly fundamentalists.[4]

The prophets of the decline of political Islam might still be right, but not within the time frame they had in mind.[5] Most Muslim countries continue to face very serious problems of every kind, and improvement is not in sight. Economic growth has been far lower than in any other part of the world except Africa, and the standards of living have been stagnant or falling. Further deterioration seems likely in countries such as Algeria and Egypt, Pakistan and Indonesia; violent changes in Saudi Arabia, Jordan, Iraq, and elsewhere are possible, and even the more repressive dictatorships such as Syria are not as stable as they may appear. Whatever the consequences of the upheavals, it is quite likely that bad governments will be replaced by ones that are worse and more repressive.

The roots of Muslim rage are known, and they are unlikely to disappear in the foreseeable future. On the contrary, as frustration persists, an increase in political violence seems likely. Some of this may be turned inwards; there has been for a long time a dispute among Islamic radicals whether terrorism should be mainly directed against the enemy at home or abroad. Since terrorism directed against domestic targets has been less popular than acts of violence against foreigners, the former has been less prevalent in the past — with, of course, notable exceptions such as Algeria. In view of the time-honored tradition in the Muslim world to put most or all of the blame of its failures on foreigners rather than on their own shortcomings and not to engage in self-criticism, jihad against the infidels has been the preferred mode of action. But this could change at a time of acute crisis such as a civil war; for the extremists, all Muslims who do not share their convictions are no better, in principle, than the infidels, and the battle against them is still a religious duty.

Antiglobalism

The terrorism of the future will also find support from a variety of other quarters including small and very small groups, political and religious. In the past, terrorism was based almost always on easily identifiable political groups, national or social, but technological developments have made carrying out terrorist campaigns possible for tiny sects, for local groupuscules, and eventually for individuals on the pattern of the Unabomber or the individual who sent out the anthrax letters in the United States. The number of such groups is immense and constantly changing. All that can be done in the following section is to indicate some of the main directions from which the terrorist attacks of the future could come, always mindful of the fact that terrorism can, in principle, occur on the margins of every radical movement, and perhaps some that are not even radical. They can come from the left and from the right: Maxime Brunerie, who tried to shoot President Jacques Chirac, was a member of French neo-Nazi groups. The massacre at Nanterre municipality of mainly left-wing local politicians (2002) was carried out by Richard Durn, a sympathizer with the green movement; the murder soon after of Pym Fortuyn, the Dutch politician, by a confirmed animal liberationist.

The umbrella movement for many of the radical organizations is antiglobalism. The very name is misleading and has been accepted by the antiglobalists only with great reluctance. They are not, of course, opposed to making trade or communications between countries easier, nor do they wish to abolish the world postal union (so that it would become difficult or impossible to send letters or parcels from one country to another) or making travel between countries more difficult, be it only because it would hurt antiglobalists as much as anyone else, since in their strategy they rely on free movement between various parts of the world.

Antiglobalism means opposition to capitalism, neoliberalism, and corporate power. It regards globalization as a synonym for the Westernization or the Americanization of the world. It believes that globalization perpetuates social injustices or even aggravates them. And it is of course true, as a leading economist put it, that global capitalism is much more concerned with expanding the domain of market relations than with democracy, expanding education, and enhancing social opportunities.[6] As another leading economist has put it, globalization is not helping many poor countries — open capital markets, free trade, and privatization are making less developed countries not necessarily more stable.[7]

Opposition to globalization is by no means limited to the far left. There are active reactionary and neofascist antiglobalists who want the world to return to a golden age located somewhere in the distant past. Groups of the extreme right can justly argue that they have warned against globalism in the form of a secret world government well before the left did.[8] As the left sees it, globalism is "market fundamentalism," the belief that there is only one possible direction for human development, and "the map is held by an elite of economists and corporate flacks, to whom must be ceded all power once held by institutions with any shred of democratic accountability."[9]

The initiative to organize an antiglobalist movement of the far left seems to have come originally from a conference with the ambitious name "International Encounter for Humanity and against Neoliberalism" in a Mexican village called La Realidad (1996), which decided to go to war against neoliberalism and to establish for this purpose an intercontinental network of resisters ("by all the rebels in the world," in the words of subcomandante Marcos of the Zapatistas). Its first major appearance was in Seattle (1999) during the meeting of the World Trade Organization when a great deal of property was destroyed in downtown Seattle. Since then, massive, often violent, demonstrations have taken place on the occasion of gatherings of the IMF, the World Bank, or generally speaking meetings of prime ministers or finance ministers of the leading developed nations (Goeteborg, Genoa, Davos, New York, Quebec City, and elsewhere). While the movement did not attract all the rebels of the world, it attracted a great many of them who shared some basic tenets but did by no means agree on all fundamental ideological questions or on the strategy to be followed. In the demonstrations, representatives of groups called "Critical Mass" and "WOMBLES" could be seen. The former is a group of cyclists that wants an end to car culture, the other stands for White Overall Movement Building Liberation through Effective Struggle — a direct-action anarchist movement like the Italian Ya Basta. There is "No Sweat" protesting against sweat shops and the Campaign against Arms Trade, there are anti-vivisectionists, and the enemies of McDonald's restaurants.

In some respects antiglobalism was heir to the old socialist and communist tradition, which had suffered a fatal blow with the breakdown of the Soviet system and the watering-down of socialism in countries such as China. But the Marxism of the left was not very attractive for a new generation, nor did it seem promising to rely on the industrial proletariat as the carrier of the ideals of a new society. The New Left did not have many answers either. Hard as the Trotskyites tried (and their experience over the decades with "entryism," or infiltration, was unrivaled), they had to take second place to the anarchists who, for what they lacked in organizational know-how, they made up in radical enthusiasm. Among the most active in the ranks of the movement were the "Autonome," anarchist groups of the sort who had operated since the 1980s in Germany and Italy.[10] They were anticapitalist in their great majority but in contrast to the Trotskyites put equal or greater stress on values such as human rights and free speech.[11]

Some of the members of the antiglobalist movement were not opposed in principle to capitalism; some wanted corporations abolished and others just to make them comply with human and ecological rights.[12] It should be added at least in passing that critics of globalism in its present form and its leading institutions such as the World Bank and the IMF include leading economists and even leading businessmen such as George Soros.

These ideological divergences did not, however, lead to a split. The more doctrinaire Marxists thought the anarchist ideology primitive and inconsistent and were convinced that sooner or later they would come to adopt a Marxist outlook. More important, at least in the short run, was the debate about strategy, or to be precise, about the use of violence. The more militant members argued, not without justification, that the movement had attracted worldwide attention not as the result of orderly demonstrations, however large, but because of the use of violence — smashing windows, throwing Molotov cocktails, and battling with the police. The fact that one of the demonstrators in Genoa was killed by the police gave the movement a martyr and thus added to its prestige.

The antiglobalists provided a stage for a great many causes other than the struggle against IMF and the World Bank — for instance, the fight of the

Palestinians against Israel, the cause of migrants trying to enter Western Europe from North Africa and the Middle East but not being accepted, various green and environmentalist groups, several anarchist and quasi-anarchist factions such as the German Autonome and the Italian Tute Bianche (white overalls), as well as a variety of Trotskyite factions.[13]

Why include the cause of Palestinian suicide bombers and discriminate against those from Sri Lanka, not to mention the many other national or social liberation struggles from Colombia to Kashmir, from Algeria to Central Asia, the IRA and the Basque ETA and the Albanians? The reason, no doubt, was that the inclusion of these causes would have led to dissent inside the antiglobalist movement, whereas in the case of the Palestinians there was little reason to fear this. There was a mutual interest — the antiglobalists were gaining a sizeable reservoir of foot soldiers for their demonstrations, and the Palestinians were becoming part of a much wider movement for the liberation of all mankind.

However, the wider the antiglobalists were casting their nets, the more their message became watered down. Originally their movement had been launched to lead the struggle of all the rebels with the emphasis on the exploited and oppressed in the third world. But it was precisely in the countries of the third world that antiglobalism found least interest and support. In the Arab world, globalization (*aulama*) had been discussed for years by intellectuals, but they had been preoccupied mainly with its cultural aspects — the threat to the cultural tradition (including the very language) and thus the identity of the Arabs as the result of creeping Americanization.[14] It should have been clear, however, that rejection of globalization also meant rejection of modernity and secularism and the preservation of the status quo. The activist wing of the antiglobalization movement, such as ATTAC (founded in France in 1998), had its work cut out for itself, appearing on the scene at a time of an economic downturn. They demanded a "global economy based on solidarity" — but what did this mean in practical terms? And in what way did such slogans address the problems of the poorer countries? Left-wing and humanist in inspiration, antiglobalism was not an obvious ally for the Muslim world. Arab intellectuals did by not any means reject globalism *tout court* but only dissociated themselves from certain aspects, such as the threats to their cultural identity. At the same time, many were reluctant to support a fundamentalist antiglobalism preaching cultural isolation of the Muslim world and preservation of medieval traditions.[15]

Even those in the Muslim and Arab world dealing with the economic, social, and environmental consequences of globalism were preoccupied in the last resort with its impact on cultural rather than economic life. They were opposed to the conditions imposed by the IMF and the World Bank on third-world nations, and they had no enthusiasm for liberal capitalism.[16] At the same time they were only too aware that they needed Western economic help and that the terrorist attacks of September 2001 had not only done harm to the West, but even greater damage to the economies of North Africa and the Middle East.

If Arab intellectuals did not see the fight against corporate capitalism as their main assignment at the present time, this applied to an even greater extent to bin Laden and the other leaders of the jihadist movement. They opposed American and Western corporations if they established branches in Israel, but not because of any specific anticapitalist convictions. Radical Islamism was not in favor of capitalism, nor did it have sympathies for materialist socialism — another Western importation. As far as they were concerned, the teachings of Islam provided all the answers to economic and social problems. But in fact, Islam as a religion that had developed more than a millennium ago did nothing of the kind. There is no reason to consider a billionaire an enemy if he happened to be a pious Muslim observing the commandment of the religion, paying *zakat* and supporting the radicals in their struggle.

If there is an Islamic theory of imperialism, it resembles less Lenin's or Rosa Luxemburg's but more the ideas developed at the beginning of the twentieth century by some of Mussolini's predecessors such as Enrico Corradini and Prezzolini about the class struggle of "proletarian nations" against the rich and the exploiting nations of the West. (Bin Laden and al Zawahiri never developed a theory of imperialism, but there are many hints that they regarded Islam a proletarian religion and its believers exploited by the infidels.) Fascist Italy accepted the concepts of its ideological predecessors but these ideas led neither to socialism in one country nor to a socialist world order, but merely to a demand for the redistribution of colonies — in other words, to a counterimperialism.

Some Western sociologists had come to regard Islamic radicalism as a "new social movement" of the quasi-revolutionary kind they had envisaged in the 1970s and 1980s. But in fact, Islamism (like other religions and also political movements such as fascism) had no firm beliefs as far as the economic and social order is concerned. There was room for populists claiming to speak on behalf of the poor and oppressed. But there was also room for entrepreneurs of no mean ability such as bin Laden, whose business activities during his stay in Sudan would have done credit to a senior executive of an American corporation. For radical Islam, the West — and, above all, America — are the great threat, and their aim was and remains to weaken it politically, militarily, and economically. But economic issues are still not the central ones. As far as Islam is concerned, it is preoccupied with a religious vision of the future and hence its limited interest in antiglobalism.

Political Radicalism and Terrorism

The antiglobalist movement as such has not supported terrorism, just as the anarchism of Pyotr Kropotkin and Elisee Reclus never preached assassination. But on the margins of the anarchist movements there were militant cells or individuals who did engage in acts of violence, including terror. It cannot be excluded that the same will happen in the future, especially if the antiglobalists — as it seems likely — will fail to make much headway through its traditional strategy of mass demonstrations and propaganda.[17]

Various Trotskyite and New Left groups have not been able to agree on a correct strategy. Marxists have been in principle against individual terrorism, but just as Marx and Engels at times sympathized with the terrorism of the Irish and the Russian revolutionaries, Trotsky expressed himself (in a famous controversy against Karl Kautsky) in favor of collective in contrast to individual terrorism. His followers have taken great pain to point out that what the master had in mind had nothing to do with the terrorism of recent decades. Trotsky's opposition to terrorism was not based on moral scruples but on pragmatic considerations. What was the point of killing a bourgeois minister if several other ministerial hopefuls were already waiting in the wings, only too eager to replace the one who had been eliminated by revolutionaries? Trotskyites have emphasized time and again that they did not reject terrorism because of bourgeois morality, but simply because it did not help their cause and was merely grist for the capitalist mills. For this reason, some Trotskyite sects have also rejected terrorist attacks against civilians carried out by "national liberation movements." Trotskyites have not participated in terrorist campaigns, at least not to any significant extent. But ideologically and politically their attitude has been ambiguous despite the sad fate of Trotsky who, like his son Leon Sedov and other leading members of the Fourth International, was killed by Stalinist assassins.

Mention has been made of the Algerian Trotskyite Parti des Travailleurs, which has been accused by other Trotskyites of "serving as the handmaiden of the Islamic fundamentalists."[18] However, political support for terrorism has not been limited to countries such as Algeria, in which extreme nationalism and religious radicalism have been strong. Some of the leading Trotskyite groups in Western Europe such as the SWP (Socialist Workers Party) in Britain have also refused to condemn the al Qa'ida attacks in September 2001 because such condemnation would play into the hands of "Western imperialism and the further mass murder which Bush and Blair intend to unleash on the world."[19] The SWP attitude toward terrorism in the past in Spain, Ulster, Latin America, and the Middle East has not been different. While they have reiterated on many occasions that they oppose individual terrorism, they have not dissociated themselves from collective terrorism; in fact (to use Leninist language) they have objectively supported it, or in the words of other Trotskyites, acted as "uncritical cheer leaders" for the methods and policies of terrorist groups.[20] According to observers on the far left scene, they have taken unofficially an even more positive view of radical Islamist terrorism, but for political reasons ("entryism") thought it unwise to press the point in public. Whereas other groups on the far left have taken a dim view of the theories about the progressive and anti-imperialist character of al Qa'ida and similar organizations, the

SWP and some other groups have taken a more sanguine view.[21] As writers in the *Weekly Worker,* the organ of the CPGB (the British Communist Party) argued, anti-imperialists must desire the victory of the Taliban even though such views should be hidden in political mass work, for it would be a mistake to organize an antiwar movement around slogans such as "Victory to the Taliban."[22]

National Bolshevism has a history dating back many decades, but politically it never amounted to very much. In our time, however, there has been a confluence of elements of the extreme right and the far left with an admixture of religious groups with anti-Americanism as the common denominator. So far this meeting of minds has expressed itself mainly in the realm of ideology, but it would not come as a surprise if individuals or small groups at the margins of this movement one day will advocate and practice strategic violence.

Terrorism and the New Left

What of terrorism and the New Left? If the Trotskyites welcomed the Khomeini revolution in Iran, arguing that progressive movements in backward countries often appear in their initial phases in a religious guise, other New Left thinkers have been somewhat more skeptical concerning the anticapitalist and progressive character of radical Islamism.[23] But they too have been reluctant to distance themselves from fanatical religious and nationalist groups that weakened the imperialist enemy.

The recent decade has not been a successful era from their point of view, nor have there been new ideological impulses (except antiglobalism) to provide a fresh impetus for its followers. But the old ideals and ideas have had some resonance, and they found their expression, for instance, in the revival of the Che Guevara cult. Guevara was killed in Bolivia, isolated and defeated, and with him there disappeared the strategy of revolutionary guerrilla warfare. Like his comrades of the Cuban revolution, Che had believed in and practiced terrorism; in 1957 his group tried to kill the dictator Fulgencio Batista. But in later years he became a firm opponent of terrorism and thought that urban terrorism was the source of corruption of the revolutionary movement.

After his death, Guevara was forgotten for many years even in Cuba, his adopted home, but this was followed by a renaissance in the Americas as well as in some European quarters. He was the subject of several long biographies, movies, and even boutiques were named for him.[24]

How to explain this revival? Social tensions in many Latin American countries have not diminished in recent decades, and economic progress, to put it cautiously, has been uneven. The Cuban revolution attracted many at the time, but its subsequent history did not leave many admirers. Che on the other hand symbolized not only the revolutionary spirit but purity and martyrdom, Jesus Christ with a Kalashnikov. There was a revolutionary-idealist reservoir in Latin America, and to these young men and women the figure of Che appealed.

But it was difficult to envisage Guevara as a politician, and while there had been a certain resurgence of guerrilla warfare such as in Colombia, it was also difficult to envisage him as the head of an armed band engaging in narcoterrorism. This leaves open the terrorist alternative, which Che rejected in his lifetime but which might appeal to a new generation. Unemployment in the megacities of Latin America has reached high proportions (about 20 percent in São Paulo, 25 percent in Buenos Aires). Homicide, robberies, kidnapping, and other such crimes have reached unprecedented proportions. It seems only a question of time until a new form of "social terrorism" or organized terrorist banditry is going to emerge. Some radical groups will see in these trends a confirmation of their belief that these are the consequences of globalization and that bourgeois democracy (or any other form of democracy) will be incapable of solving these problems. In fact, these trends are rooted in technological innovations which make part of the labor force redundant — and the poverty of the local economies fails to create new places of work in the service sector.

Another revolutionary guru of political violence fared less well. Frantz Fanon had also died young and had been "pop" as far as a whole generation of young admirers was concerned. His books were widely read on American campuses and among French intellectuals. He too was forgotten but had a certain revival in the 1990s which was limited, however, to the groves of academe — or to be precise, to the postcolonial school.[25] The reasons were obvious — Fanon should have chosen another country for his activities and his theories. The last thing needed in Algeria in the 1990s, devastated by many years of terrorism, was another apostle of violence.

The "Third Position"

Well before the far left and the anarchists discovered the dangers of globalization, the extreme right was fighting this enemy to the best of their ability, except that in those early days the threat was known under another name: "The New World Order." As John F. McManus, president of the John Birch Society, put it, his group had opposed world government (and globalism, as he sees it, was precisely aiming at such government) for decades only to be derided by the liberal media as believers in primitive conspiracy theories.[26] Another leading opponent of globalism was William Pierce, the author of the *Turner Diaries*, who had claimed for many years that the internationalization of production and the deindustrialization of the United States were two sides of the same coin.[27] A world without national boundaries is bound to lead to racial integration, mongrelization, and leveling — in short into impoverishment and subordination to an interdependent New World

Order. Only a national cleaning day, a "day of the ropes," could stop this process, when tens of thousands of traitors will be hanged from lamp posts and trees.[28]

The extreme right put the stress on the national aspects — that is to say, the growing danger (as they saw it) of their countries losing sovereignty and their specific national character being swamped by foreign mass culture. They would hardly march with the Trotskyites and anarchists in favor of unrestricted mass immigration to their countries, for they loathed multiculturalism and stood for monocultural nation-states. But they shared with the left their hatred of neo-liberalism and also found common ground on such issues as support for the struggle of the anti-imperialist forces in the Middle East and elsewhere. They marched together with the left-wing activists in Seattle and on other occasions. There was a fascinating synergism between the far right and the extreme left in Europe as well as in the United States, which expressed itself, among other things, in the opposition to the war against terrorism.[29]

This gave birth to the so called "third position" (known in France and Italy as *Troisième Voie* or *Terza Posizione*, respectively) or, in the words of their critics, third-position fascism.[30]

The idea of a coalition between the extreme left and the extreme right, between nationalism and socialism (or, to be precise, anticapitalism) goes back to the Soviet Union in the 1920s, appearing in the early 1930s on the margins of the Nazi movement (Otto Strasser), and then taken up in the 1980s by the French right and on a more primitive ideological level by American neo-Nazis such as the Aryan Nations Congress and WAR, calling for support of the white working class against monopoly capitalism and the corporations. On the German terrorist scene, the attempts to bring about a synthesis between ideas of the far left and the extreme right date back to the days of Baader-Meinhof. This showed itself in playing the nationalist card. The U.S. forces in Germany were an occupation army; the unique character of Nazism and the Holocaust was played down by arguing that National Socialism had been nothing but a creature of monopoly capitalism. In brief, the motivation, while it expressed itself mainly in a revolutionary phraseology, had been to a considerable extent nationalist.[31] In other words the ultranationalist and neofascist views expressed by Horst Mahler and some other former terrorists of the left at the present time had been there, at least *in statu nascendi*, even thirty years earlier. What has been said about left-wing terrorism in Germany applies to a similar degree to left-wing terrorism in other European countries such as Italy and Greece.

Determined efforts were made by groups of the extreme right to bring about a left-right unity of action in the effort to smash capitalism.[32] For the extreme right in the United States and Europe, communism was no longer a serious enemy; in any case both capitalism and communism had been invented and sustained by the Jews. Anti-Semitic slogans — sometimes gross, sometimes more subtle — made their appearance in Britain, France, and Germany. In the words of a close observer of the terrorist scene, the extreme right considered the whole coun-terculture generation (antiglobalism, anti-WTO protests, ecowarriors, fighters for animal rights) as a potential constituency: "They push fascism as a revolutionary movement of the left."[33] Or, to quote the slogan of the most active sections of the contemporary Russian far right: "Fascism — Red and Unbounded." As a historian of these groups (the National Bolshevik party) noted, "third positionism" incor-porates Stalinist, Leninist, and partly even anarchist and New Left influences, especially in their countercultural forms.[34]

With this new initiative came a great deal of political interchange, of traveling of leading figures of the far right to visit comrades-in-arms in foreign countries. Whereas in the past national Bolsheviks or national revolutionaries had never seen their ambition in establishing an international network, this became the fashion in the late 1990s. Before his death in July 2002 William Pierce, author of the *Turner Diaries*, the bible of all terrorists of the far right (including Timothy McVeigh), went to Europe, where he met with Horst Mahler, once a pillar of Baader-Meinhof.[35] In his "Red Army" days, Mahler had welcomed the Black September killing of the Israeli athletes at the Munich Olympic Games as a courageous anti-imperialist commando raid.[36] Above all, there were frequent visits to Iran, Iraq, and other Arab countries. Something like an International Third Position (ITP) came into being with, inevitably, its own Web sites linking like-minded groups from many countries.

In years past there would have been little purpose in dwelling on the activities of small sects and eccentric individuals. They were of small importance, even from the point of view of collectors of abstruse political doctrines. However, this situation has changed for at least two reasons. Very small groups of people now have access to weapons of unprecedented destructiveness and, to repeat it once again, the smaller the group, the greater the likelihood that it will be motivated by wholly irrational motives. Second, there is the possibility that these small groups will look for powerful sponsors and that, on the other hand, governments eager to cause mischief may want to make use of such groups for their own purposes. Out of its weakness a new strategy has emerged and the groupuscules have become the prevailing form of the national revolutionary trend and left-wing fascism. Initially their emphasis was on cultural motives (or rather counterculture); in Russia, for instance, they have become the most prominent force among the counterculture of the young generation, and in Germany too they have been doing well. What began with the noise of many rock and metal bands and skinhead antics could end with the noise of the Kalashnikov and the bomb.[37] Arab governments and in particular Iran have cooperated with the grouplets of the European extreme right.

During the 1980s, Libya was the main sponsor of extremist groups in Europe, including terrorist groups. When Libya reduced its activities, its function was taken by Teheran and Baghdad. This collaboration expressed itself on the polit-ical and ideological level; among frequent visitors to Saddam Hussein were Jean

Marie Le Pen and Joerg Haider, as well as neo-Nazis from Germany and Russia.[38] According to the publications of the European extreme right, the anti-American attacks of the Muslim terrorists had been wholly justified, and the Arab countries were the natural allies of the patriotic forces in the West.[39]

Such close collaboration between European and American neo-Nazis with the radical Islamists created political problems of various sorts: One of the key planks of right-wing populism in Europe is, of course, opposition to the influx of immigrants, who mostly come from Muslim countries. The European neo-Nazis may admire the Muslim anti-American militants from the Middle East and North Africa, but only from a safe distance.

Key figures in these transactions were François Genoud and Ahmed Huber (who converted to Islam), who had been prominent in neo-Nazi circles for decades; representatives of the PLO in Europe; as well as businessmen and arms dealers, sometimes of Middle Eastern origin. It is most unlikely that elderly neo-Nazis or proponents of the Third Position will take an active part in the organization of terrorist groups in Europe or America. But they help as paymasters and in various other ways; above all, they have followers younger in age, more dynamic, and probably more fanatic. From these quarters, among others, terrorist violence could come in future years. People of this ilk have been talking and writing for a long time about the need for fighting. Some of them may have the courage of their convictions.

The factions of the extreme left and the extreme right both believe in revolution on a global scale, and they do not think that this aim can be achieved through democratic means such as parliamentary elections. What if — after years of intensive propaganda, of demonstrations and other political action — they realize that they are no nearer to their aim than before? There is, of course, always the hope that following some major political or economic upheaval — a war or a deep economic crisis — their influence will suddenly increase. But it is still most unlikely that, even if these sects were not split into dozens of fragments, they would experience anything near political power. In these conditions, violence, including terrorism, must appear the only alternative to resignation and ending the struggle for the liberation of mankind.

It stands to reason that the majority of the extremists, certainly in Europe, will not opt for the terrorist alternative, just as the majority of the followers of the New Left in 1968 did not turn to terrorism. Their ideological mentors, middle-aged professors of English literature or other such subjects or the opponents of automobile culture, are unsuited by temperament to terrorist action beyond vandalism, a few shop windows smashed and motor cars burned. They know only too well that this approach will not work. But there is usually a younger generation — more radical, less hampered by the negative burden of the past — which may opt for terrorism. Ideology in this context is important, but it is less important than a predisposition to aggression and violent action.

The ideological justification for terrorism can be manifold. The Unabomber was not a man of the left, but thought that the enemy was modern, large-scale technology which had to be destroyed; capitalism was not his target, but modern technological civilization.[40] (The choice of his victims had nothing to do with his ideology; it was indiscriminate, but this is quite typical for contemporary terrorism.) The aim of extreme ecoterrorists could be the reduction of the number of people alive to about one quarter or one fifth of the present number, which from an environmental point of view is far too large. It could be the oppression of Muslims or the religious duty of jihad, or the oppression of mankind by globalist, capitalist corporations, or the threat to the existence of the Aryan race.

All these causes are well known and have been mentioned more than once in these pages. But the issues at stake could even be far more obscure. This terrorism could be the work of very small groups whose very existence is not known to a broader public, individuals who feel a burning hatred against a society that has had grieved them in one way or another. It could be the work of mad individuals; the vision of the mad scientist known from science fiction becoming reality. There are in all probability many thousands of such people all over the globe, and among them there are bound to be some who have not only the motivation but the know-how to stage terrorist campaigns far more sophisticated and deadly than the parcel bombs sent out by the Unabomber or the person who sent out the letter that caused the anthrax infections in the United States. The Unabomber, it will be recalled, was apprehended only because his own family gave him away; the identity of the anthrax letter writer has never been established.

State-Sponsored Terrorism

The obvious tools of governments eager to engage in substitute terrorism are Islamic groups, and the link between Iran and the Lebanese Hizbullah has been the classic example. The U.S. Department of State report for 2001 mentioned Iran as the most active player in the field of international state terrorism, even before, in February 2002, George Tenet had come on record with a similar statement. This was much to the surprise and also often to the dismay of those who have stressed for years the gradual liberalization of the Iranian regime. While the rulers of Iran made certain concessions to the public after the death of Khomeini, it is also true that the revolutionary fervor of the young militants has largely disappeared. But with all this, the elected government is largely impotent as far as the foreign and military policy of the country is concerned. Real power is still in the hands of the diehards; the rearmament of Iran, including the build-up of unconventional arms, has continued undiminished. While open terrorist attacks sponsored by Iran have decreased, the support for terrorist groups abroad has continued.

The reasons are manifold. The Iranian leaders had hoped that the Khomeini revolution would have an impact well beyond Iran, but they were disappointed, underrating the depth of the schism between Sunnis and Shi'ites in the Muslim world. During the years that followed, they had some support (and extended support) of Shi'ite groups in Lebanon, in Afghanistan, and also among some minor Palestinian groups such as Islamic Jihad, but on the whole the Arab world, the Caucasian and Central Asian Muslim leaders with the exception of Syria, kept their distance.

The Iranian leadership has been apprehensive about the danger of being isolated, well aware of the long-term Iraqi designs in the Gulf and the possibility that the Iraqis, trying to obtain weapons of mass destruction, would resume hostilities at some future date. In these circumstances, the Iranian rulers decided to take an extreme position as far as the Palestinian-Israeli conflict was concerned, assuming that such a position would strengthen their position and constitute something like reinsurance in the Arab world. That the Iranians were fundamentally opposed to Israel goes without saying, but Israel was still not on the top of their political concerns. The decision to extend military and financial help to Hizbullah in Lebanon and some of the Palestinian groups had more complicated reasons. The case of *Karena II*, the ship loaded with fifty tons of Iranian arms destined for the Palestinians, only confirmed what had been known for years. The delivery of thousands of missiles to Hizbullah seemed a guarantee that the conflict would not come to an early end.

On a variety of occasions, such as an international "rejectionist" conference in Teheran in May 2002, the Iranian leadership again declared that it was in principle opposed to any peace process, and Rafsanjani, one of the most prominent among them, had even earlier discussed the advisability of using nuclear bombs as an instrument of foreign policy. It also took a leading part in promoting what outside observers called a "culture of suicide (martyr) terrorism" on the assumption that this was the most effective weapon the Palestinians could use.[41] The Teheran meeting signified a new stage in Iranian involvement in terrorism abroad. Up to that date Iran had preferred to make financial allocations to foreign groups through the Lebanese Hizbullah; but the Palestinian Islamic Jihad had complained of being shortchanged, whereupon the Teheran government, in consideration of the suicide attacks carried out by Islamic Jihad, decided to give it greatly enhanced support directly.[42]

Iran also kept contact with terrorist groups in Afghanistan before and after Taliban rule, and it has undertaken efforts to destabilize the Jordanian government. The Iranian Revolutionary Guard Corps and the Ministry of Intelligence and Security have been active in Syria, Lebanon, Turkey, and to a limited extent in Central Asia and Pakistan. It also reportedly made it possible for members of al Qa'ida to cross Iran on their way to the Caucasus after their defeat in Afghanistan.

If Israel had been a country adjacent to Iran, the Teheran government would probably have shown greater caution in its support for the anti-Israeli fighters. But in view of the safe distance, the Iranian rulers apparently believed that the risks they were taking were reasonable. These assumptions that could be mistaken for support of terrorist groups can seldom be kept secret for any length of time; furthermore, there is always the danger that the "substitutes" will not be under full control, that the conflict may escalate and in the end involve the sponsoring state. By and large, terrorism has become an instrument of Iranian foreign policy, something to be supported in certain circumstances abroad; but it is highly doubtful whether candidates for suicide terrorism could still be found inside Iran after twenty-five years of fundamentalist rule.

In view of its exposed position, Iraq has been more cautious than Iran in extending help to outside terrorist groups, but it has provided shelter to Iraqi radicals as well as the remnants of the Abu Nidal group and the PFLP. (Abu Nidal committed suicide or was killed in Baghdad in summer of 2002.) What matters in the final analysis is the willingness of these two countries as well as of some others to use outside terrorist groups for the purpose of their own foreign political interests, as Italy and some Balkan countries had done in the 1930s.

Battle Lines Blurred

Writers about terrorism have been criticized in recent years for not drawing a clear enough line between terrorism and other forms of violence, political and nonpolitical. This is perfectly true, but it merely reflects the emergence of new realities. It has been pointed out repeatedly that terrorism has become indiscriminate in the choice of its targets in recent decades, much in contrast to "classic terrorism." But this is by no means the only change that has taken place with regard to the dividing line between political terrorism and crime. There were, in the history of terrorism, cases in which terrorists also engaged in robberies and other forms of crime (the Bande Bonnot in Paris on the eve of World War I), but these were fairly rare exceptions. Since the 1970s, there has been a convergence of terrorism and the narcotics trade, which has made drug dealing one of the main sources of income of terrorist gangs. The case of Colombia has been mentioned; according to estimates the FARC had an annual income of some $500 million in the late 1990s.[43] However, the FARC is by no means the only such group. Others involved were the Real IRA, the Kurdish PKK, various Turkish groups, the Kosovo Liberation Army (KLA), various Central Asian groups such as the Islamic Movement of Uzbekistan, the Sri Lanka "Liberation Tigers," Abu Sayaf in the Philippines and, of course, Afghanistan on a massive scale under Taliban rule. The Ranvir Sena in the Indian state of Bihar was founded originally as a private army to protect the high-caste big landowners, but over time it became almost entirely engaged in criminal activities.[44]

The involvement with the drug trade has taken a variety of forms: income from smuggling drugs from the Far and Middle East to Europe and America, but also protection money collected from the peasants growing the crops from which the drugs are extracted. The massive income has enabled the terrorist groups to acquire sophisticated weapons and to engage in costly operations which otherwise would not have been possible. On the other hand, the massive involvement with crime has posed both ideological and practical problems to those engaged in narcoterrorism. Both the leaders of the Marxist and the Islamic narcoterrorist groups faced a dilemma inasmuch as they did not want their followers corrupted by practices they condemned in principle. They produced ingenious formulas according to which the handling and sale of drugs was permitted as it greatly helped their cause, but they were forbidden to consume these drugs. But this did not always work, and it was even more difficult to prevent the indirect effects of great sums of money streaming in. Corruption has many faces on every level. The funds accruing from narcobusiness made the terrorists a more dangerous enemy. They enabled the Tamil Tigers to buy speedboats to evade the control of the government, and the FARC to acquire weapons the government's troops did not have.

On the other hand there is, of course, a basic difference between the aims of political terrorism and narcobusiness. Criminals, on the whole, are conservative; terrorists are not. The latter want political power, changes in society and politics; the narco dealers, on the other hand, have a vested interest in the preservation of the status quo, which guarantees their income. There is a basic clash of interests which is bound to have consequences in the long run. So far there has been no known instance of a terrorist group voluntarily giving up this source of income.

Terrorist groups have engaged in criminal activities of other kinds, such as kidnapping wealthy individuals for ransom; this was often the practice in Latin America in the 1970s, and it is pursued at the present time in Colombia and in the Philippines. Among the recruits of the jihadists have been a substantial number of robbers and petty criminals — such as the Chalabi brothers in France (the "banlieue south" gang); Nizar Trabelsi, the professional soccer player in Brussels of whom mention has been made; the London shoe bomber and José Padilla (al Muhajir); not to mention the members of Chechen and Central Asian gangs. But these facts are mainly of sociological interest; the income from these sources is small in comparison with the narco business.

Terrorism and the Weapons of Mass Destruction

It is only a question of time until radiological, chemical, or biological weapons will be used more or less systematically by terrorist groups; the first steps in this direction have been made. This issue has been widely discussed, and there is a huge literature on its various aspects.[45] The fact that these weapons have been accessible in principle, if not always in practice, has led some to believe that this danger has been exaggerated. But the fact that great technical difficulties exist, that many of these operations may abort, should not blind one to the fact that with every year that passes, access becomes easier and the opportunities to use these weapons greater. There is much reason to believe that if such attacks should be carried out in the near future, many, perhaps the great majority, will fail, or will have a smaller effect than anticipated. But it should also be clear that if only one out of ten, one out of hundred such attempts succeeds, the damage caused, the number of victims will be infinitely higher than at any time in the past. According to a U.S. government estimate dating back ten years, the possible number of fatalities in the case of an efficient biological attack (ebola, smallpox, tularemia, anthrax) could be 1 million; of an atomic bomb detonated in a major city, one hundred thousand.[46] But it is equally possible that the number of victims, especially in the case of an attack with biological agents, could be much higher. Most of the terrorist groups of the past would not have used such weapons, and some of them will refuse to do so in the future. Some of the ideologists of megaterrorism in the nineteenth century such as Karl Heinzen and Johannes Most did mention at the time the likelihood (indeed the necessity) that hundreds of thousands, if not millions, of human beings would have to be killed. But these were fiery speeches and editorials, and as far as can be ascertained, Heinzen and Most were not involved in the murder of a single person. There were certain restraints in the nineteenth century which no political leader, however extreme, would overstep.[47] The only exception were fictional characters, supercriminals, and evil geniuses trying to blackmail cities, countries, or the whole world, or to engage in a campaign of vengeance. Jack London, in a forgotten short story entitled "The Enemy of All the World" (1907), was a pioneer of this genre, but there were others even before World War I.[48]

However, in the late twentieth century, with the growth of fanaticism, especially of the religious-nationalist kind, such restraints have become weaker or are no longer existent. In Pakistan, quasi-religious shrines have been erected to honor the Islamic bomb in major cities, and there is little doubt that if terrorist groups of this kind would gain possession of such weapons, they would not hesitate to use them even if the consequences would be suicidal. For here again a jihadi belief could offer comfort, for even if everyone will die, the soul of the true believer will be saved or because they are invulnerable by the grace of God: "A thousand shall fall at thy side, and ten thousand at thy right hand, but it shall not come nigh thee." Or as Muhammad Atta advised his comrades: God is with the believers and the angels are guarding his steps. "Carlos" was not a religious believer, probably not even a person with strong ideological convictions, but there is little doubt that he would have used weapons of mass destruction had they been at the disposal of his group.

At the present time, state arsenals and laboratories are the main source of such weapons, which leads to the issue of state-sponsored terrorism discussed earlier on. But there is also the possibility that as the result of a coup, or a civil war or some other breakdown of power and control, terrorist groups may gain access to such arsenals and laboratories. There is unfortunately an almost unlimited number of possibilities of things that may go wrong. Those arguing that since a disaster has not happened yet, it will not happen in the future, are on weak ground.

Nineteenth-century terrorism was to a large extent "propaganda by deed," and to a certain degree this was true also in the decades thereafter. But is it still correct? Terrorism continues to be a struggle for public opinion, but beyond this obvious statement generalizations have become difficult. On the Web sites of left-wing guerrilla and terrorist movements, such as the FARC or the Zapatistas, the emphasis is on peace and progress; if they have been forced to commit acts of violence, this was a regrettable necessity provoked by the repressive policy of the government. That narcoterrorism and kidnappings are not mentioned goes without saying; instead, there is considerable stress on human rights, social justice, and the misdeeds of the globalists.

The Web sites of terrorist groups (especially those in English) deal in great detail with the persecutions against them, the fate of their comrades-in-arms who were taken prisoner and are now tortured or, at best, kept in inhuman conditions. They are the victims; the state and their opponents are the real terrorists. Such propaganda is not in the main destined for domestic consumption but for liberal and left-wing circles in North America and Europe.[49] This appears quite clearly from the location of the Web sites; thus, for instance, the supporters of the Peruvian Shining Path operated out of Berkeley, California, as did the Zapatistas; the Kurdish militants out of Holland; the Tamil Tigers and the Palestinian Hamas were based in London; and some Irish groups in an American university.[50]

Right-wing terrorist groups, on the other hand, are more outspoken and less inclined to invite commiseration. They may invoke the threats facing their countries and societies in apocalyptic terms, but they have no interest in establishing popular fronts. Lastly, the radical Muslim groups do not hide or downplay the fact that they engage in violence but, on the contrary, intend to frighten and demoralize their enemies: Allah is with them and will protect them, their cause is invincible, those opposing them are doomed and will be destroyed.

The main audience of the radical Muslim terrorists is not the Western world but the Islamic countries and above all the Arab public; in this context, television for the time being is far more important than the Internet. The Lebanese Hizbullah has its own station, and the rest of the Arab world is reached by the terrorists through the official Arab TV stations and, of course, the Qatar-based Al Jezira. The scenes shown — Arab heroism on one hand and suffering on the other — are bound to generate support expressing itself in the pressure of public opinion on the Arab and Muslim governments to extend greater help to those fighting the holy war against the infidels.

Historically, some terrorist groups have been more successful than others attracting outside support; thus the activities of the Irish patriots of the nineteenth century and the Russian socialist revolutionaries generated far more sympathy than the assassinations carried out by the anarchists. In our age the Palestinians received far more publicity than other nationalist terrorist movements, even though the number of victims in other terrorist campaigns (Algeria, Colombia, Sri Lanka, Central Asia, India, etc.) was much higher. The world media concentrated on the Israeli-Arab conflict; many correspondents and television crews were stationed there, whereas other terrorist campaigns, usually in distant countries, were either out of bounds for coverage by the media because of the physical dangers involved or considered of little public interest.[51] This resulted in a curious imbalance: Most of the comment and the generalizations on terrorism were based on the Arab-Israeli conflict (and perhaps a few other campaigns well covered by the media) whereas terrorism elsewhere went often almost unnoticed. The number of victims of terrorism in the Indian state of Tripura — one theater of terrorist conflict out of several on the Indian subcontinent — was larger in the 1990s than that in the Israeli-Palestinian conflict, but Tripura was unknown territory. There were neither books nor articles about the subject, let alone television coverage.

Why the heavy emphasis on terrorism in one or two countries and the neglect of terrorist campaigns, often deliberate, in others? Some publicity was given in the world media to the civil war in Algeria in view of its traditional ties with France (and also because at one stage the Algerian Islamic radicals extended their activities to the European continent), but the killing of a hundred thousand Kurds was largely ignored. The same is true for bloodshed on a major scale that took place in Rwanda as late as 2002. On July 27, 2002, the *New York Times*, starting on the front page, devoted a report of thousands of words to the massacres which had taken place in the Indian state of Gujarat and in which close to a thousand lives had been lost. It had occurred five months earlier and at the time received little if any coverage in the world's media, nor had the UN Security Council been convened to deal with the explosive situation.

A variety of reasons caused this lopsided coverage. The fact that Palestine was a land holy to some of the world's religions did of course play a role. But it was also true that in many countries the media simply did not have access, because for the governments involved, terrorism was an embarrassment and they had no wish to invite reports that would reflect negatively about their countries. Was it perhaps because terrorism in Israel/Palestine was so dangerous because it could trigger off a wider war? But the same was true with regard to Kashmir, and yet foreign correspondents have not been seen on the Indian subcontinent in great numbers. The political outlook of the media and the correspondents, their predilections and aversions played an important role, and in this respect too they found much more interest (and often became emotionally more involved) in the Israeli-Arab conflict than in others in faraway countries about which they and their public knew little and cared less.

With all the dangers inherent in the Israeli-Arab dispute, a fixation on this issue is bound to lead to mistaken conclusions, not just because terrorism is a far wider phenomenon, but also because such fixation tends to lose sight of other threats. The main threat is the proliferation of weapons of mass destruction. Inasmuch as governments and states are concerned, this subject is outside the concerns of the present study. But there is the probability that some of these weapons will be at the disposal not just of government and traditional terrorist groups, but even of very small grouplets and perhaps even individuals. Science fiction has envisaged for more than a century the figure of the mad scientist threatening one or more countries or perhaps the whole world with destruction unless his demands are fulfilled. Many years before the first nuclear bomb was dropped, a story was published in which a scientist of this kind threatened to shift the earth's axis by means of atomic bombs unless his demands that war would cease were fulfilled.[52] This happened to be a noble aim, but there were other far more villainous threats; as another writer noted shortly after Hiroshima, "Just as there are unstable radioactive atoms, so there are unstable men."[53] The Unabomber and the person (or persons) who mailed the anthrax letters were in all probability the forerunners of a new species of terrorists of an infinitely more threatening potential, except for the fact that they used old-fashioned arms, not as yet weapons of mass destruction.[54]

One of the basic differences between terrorism today and a hundred years ago is the indiscriminate choice of targets. Another is the growing element of madness in contemporary terrorism. This proposition is bound to produce contradiction (if not outrage) on the part of some, but the evidence to this effect is overwhelming. Not every paranoiac is a terrorist, but in every terrorist there are paranoid fears at least to some degree. Terrorists engage in conspiracy, and it is only natural that they should suspect their enemies of acting in the same way. Typical symptoms of paranoia, individual and collective, are suspicion of others, concern with hidden motives, hostility and an unforgiving attitude, poor capacity to engage in self-criticism, and a poor sense of humor. The prognosis of individual cases of paranoia is poor because people with this disorder tend to resist treatment. The prognosis for groups suffering from paranoia seems to be no better.[55]

The terrorists of the far right are, virtually without exception, believers in conspiracies such as the imposition of a world government to subjugate their country and race and giant plots of every kind. The worldview of the extreme left is similar in character, but only the identity of the plotters is different: capitalism, imperialism, the giant corporations. Hamas invokes the *Protocols of the Elders of Zion* in its program; other radical Islamic groups firmly believe that the whole world is united in a conspiracy against Islam and those professing it.[56] In all Muslim countries but Turkey, a majority of the population believed that the terrorist attacks of September 11 were carried out by the Israeli Mossad (but they did not believe that Osama bin Laden was an agent of the Mossad).[57] The number of conspiracy theories is infinite, and many millions all over the world believe the most fantastic concoctions spread by impostors or deranged minds.[58]

Many of these theories are relatively harmless, such as the various UFO accounts, but others are anything but innocent. There is a great deal of free-floating rage and aggression which could find many outlets. A small group of dissident members of Egypt's Nasserist party stormed the headquarters of their party in Cairo in July 2002. One of them, a young man named Ahmed Kamal, standing on the first-floor balcony, threatened to cause an explosion. A journalist of the daily Al Ahram quoted an eyewitness, a young saleswoman in the shop opposite: "Kamal was screaming incomprehensible things. At one point he was saying, 'I want to blow up the whole world,' pacing about the balcony and frantically speaking to someone on his mobile."[59] In the end, the event ended more or less peacefully, but one day someone like Kamal will be able to inflict a great deal of damage though not perhaps blow up the whole world. If the nineteenth-century terrorism was the era of "propaganda by deed," the twenty-first century could be the age of catastrophic terrorism.

Even in the unlikely case that all global conflicts will be resolved — that all political, social, and economic tensions of this world will vanish — this will not necessarily be the end of terrorism. The combination of paranoia, fanaticism, and extremist political (or religious) doctrine will find new outlets. It is the reservoir from which the terrorism of today and tomorrow attracts its followers. Perhaps it is not part of the human condition, but it certainly is part of the condition of certain sections and individuals. There are bound to be ups and downs as far as the frequency and the political impact of terrorism is concerned. But there is a huge reservoir of aggression, and for this reason terrorism will be with us as far as one can look ahead.

Toward a Definition, or Humpty Dumpty and the Problem of Terrorism

After thirty years of hard labor there still is no generally agreed definition of terrorism. On the contrary, as far as the media are concerned, circumlocution has become the order of the day.[1] This is not surprising because there is no universally accepted definition as to what fascism or communism is or democracy and nationalism or virtually any other political phenomenon. Terrorism more perhaps than most concepts has generated widely divergent interpretations. An author writing in the 1980s listed more than a hundred definitions, and since then there have been numerous additions.

These difficulties could have been foreseen from the very beginning and not just because it was unlikely that terrorists and their well-wishers would ever agree with their victims about the nature of their actions, nor would Indians and Pakistanis, Israelis and Palestinians, Spanish and Basque, and all the other parties involved. The term "terrorism" has now everywhere a bad, negative connotation — in contrast, for instance, to "guerrilla," which enjoys a far more positive reputation. There are books about guerrilla productions of plays and movies and even guerrilla marketing. There are, to the best of my knowledge, no texts about terrorist marketing. For this reason terrorists, with a very few exceptions, have tried hard not to be labeled as such, and some writers too have shown great inventiveness choosing neutral terms such as militants, activists, commandos, raiders, resistants, insurgents, urban guerrillas, or in the worst case, gunmen. (But gunmen do not always use guns, quite apart from the fact that some of the gunmen are gunwomen; gunpersons would be a more accurate term.) A new entry in *Roget's Thesaurus* is needed to find further synonyms for terrorism.[2]

There are other obstacles to overcome in the search for a definition of terrorism. It is a very old phenomenon and it has changed its character and meaning over time and from country to country. It is most unlikely that any contemporary definition of terrorism would even come close to describing terrorism in 1850 or

1930, just as a definition of democracy in ancient Greece would be of little help with regard to democracy in the modern world.

According to title 22 of the United States Code, terrorism is premeditated, politically motivated violence perpetrated against noncombatant targets by sub- national groups or clandestine agents, usually intended to influence an audience. But the "politically motivated" has become debatable over time, or at least insuf- ficient, and the "noncombatants" is certainly no longer true. Most terrorist groups in the contemporary world have been attacking the military, the police, and the civilian population. For this reason, the definition suggested by an Israeli author proposing to name terrorists those who aim to attack randomly the civilian may not be very helpful in the real world.

In the past, it was frequently true that terrorists tried to influence an audience — the famous "propaganda by deed" concept of nineteenth-century anarchists. But if terrorists can kill thousands of people and cause immense mate- rial damage, as the possibility to defeat the enemy by arms alone becomes more feasible, the psychological weapon is no longer that important.

The attempts to find a definition go back to the days of the League of Nations in 1937 ("all criminal acts directed against a state . . . and intended to create a state of terror in the minds of particular persons or the general public"). But this definition was found wanting even at the time and was never generally accepted. A UN definition proposed in 1999 argued that terrorism consisted of criminal acts intended to provoke a state of terror, and these were in any circumstances unjus- tified whatever the considerations — that of a political, philosophical, ideological, racial, ethnic religious, or other nature. But this too was rejected by many gov- ernments who found the condemnation too sweeping. The United Nations has not agreed on a definition of terrorism and for obvious reasons never will. It is frequently argued that terrorists should be treated according to the Geneva con- ventions signed after World War II and the two protocols added in 1977; these conventions, however, do not mention terrorism, and even if they would it would still not be clear who will be the "bona fide terrorists" entitled to protection under these conventions. The tendency in international law has been toward establish- ing rules to enforce restraint in war, whereas the prevailing tendency among terrorist groups is, on the contrary, to shed restraints which are not in their inter- ests. Furthermore, international law concerning the rules of war is, by necessity, lagging behind technological developments in warfare; it was formulated before weapons of mass destruction became widely accessible.

When the Arab states gathered in 1989 and again in the 1990s to talk about terrorism, there was similar dissent. Syria and several other countries insisted that the armed fight against foreign occupation was not terrorism but justified struggle for national liberation. But such reservations, even if justified, made it clearly impossible ever to agree when terrorism was terrorism and when it was

national liberation: many Lebanese citizens would regard the Syrian military presence in Lebanon foreign occupation whereas the Damascus government clearly
would not.

An academic expert (A. P. Schmid) suggested in 1992 a simple expedient:
namely, to consider an act of terrorism the peacetime equivalent of a war crime.
But this would have meant that the perpetrators of an attempt to kill Adolf Hitler
in the 1930s (or Pol Pot or any other postwar dictator) would have to be judged as
war criminals, hardly a plausible proposition. The Central Intelligence Agency has
been mainly preoccupied with international terrorism, which it defined as conducted with the support of foreign governments or organizations and/or directed
against foreign nations, institutions, or governments. The CIA has also published
valuable annual surveys, but the self-imposed restriction on dealing with "international terrorism" led to many anomalies. If for instance an Egyptian terrorist
group ambushed and killed a group of foreign tourists, this would be listed in its
surveys, but if the victims were Egyptians it would not be included. (What if the
tourists had dual nationality?) Countries in which terrorism was endemic such as
Sri Lanka and Colombia would not qualify under the category of "international
terrorism," unless of course they also engaged in international activities such as
smuggling drugs.

The search for a definition received fresh impetus after the events of September 2001 when new legislation was introduced in many Western countries. The
European Union proposed a draft according to which terrorism was considered
an act aimed at seriously altering or destroying the political, economic, and social
structure by member countries, a rather clumsy attempt of definition because a
social revolution could be peaceful as well as violent. Terrorism was defined as
an organized act of violence or threat of violence that caused terror and fear
such as killing, assassination, the taking of hostages in airplanes and ships, and
the use of bombing aiming at advancing political aims. The same draft also went
into considerable detail as far as punishment for murder and other crimes was
concerned. This provoked the ire of the human rights advocates, for they feared
that "urban violence" might be interpreted in too sweeping a way. What if a
legitimate demonstration would turn a little violent? Would it be considered an
act of terrorism and punished accordingly?

Such concerns were often divorced from realities. Even though Britain under a
Labor government had introduced a Prevention of Terrorism Act in 1974, it had
remained in fact the country in which terrorists had almost unlimited freedom of
maneuver, not only with regard to freedom of speech and organization but also
as far as their personal safety was concerned. The same was true in Germany
where mosques (and, to a certain extent, even cultural centers) enjoyed something akin to extraterritoriality; the security forces could observe how young men
were indoctrinated and even enlisted for armed struggle but they could not intervene. Terrorists wanted for murder in their home countries such as Egypt or for

terrorist conspiracy in Italy and the United States were not extradited. Even Syria had been more forthcoming in regards to extraditing Egyptian terrorists without much fanfare.

Why should the issue of definition be of such importance? It is, of course, of no consequence in nondemocratic societies where terrorists (or persons suspected of terrorism) can be detained and sometimes executed for crimes of state, such as treason, without much regard for legal niceties. It is of importance in Western societies — in the arrest and the legal prosecution of terrorists. But even in this context, the definition of terrorism is of limited significance only because terrorists are normally sentenced for crimes committed, such as murder or kidnapping, and not for terrorist opinions voiced. It is only when membership in a terrorist organization becomes a crime that the definition of terrorism is of importance.

Several misconceptions have obfuscated the issue. A great deal of mischief has been caused by trying to define terrorism in the light of current events or events in one country only. Terrorism at the present time is mainly religious Islamic in character, but thirty years ago it was preponderantly left-wing and at other times it emanated from the extreme right. Terrorism has been in certain conditions justified. Even the Catholic Church recognized that tyrannicide was admissible in certain circumstances. Resistance against a brutal dictatorship in which no other means of redress existed cannot be condemned on moral or any other grounds. But this refers mainly to past periods in which terrorism was the *ultima ratio*, the last resort of those striving for freedom. Nineteenth-century terrorists went out of their way not to hit innocents; latter-day terrorists had no such scruples but on the contrary often targeted the innocent. More recently, terrorism has often become the *prima ratio* of small groups trying to impose their extreme views on a dissenting majority.

According to an old and widespread sophism, "one man's terrorist is another man's freedom fighter." This is true in the sense that criminals and victims will seldom agree on the nature of a crime; quite frequently people do not agree about a traffic accident. It is as true as saying that St. Francis and Mother Teresa had many admirers, but so had Hitler and Stalin and that therefore there is not really much to choose between them. But there is no room for moral relativism (or nihilism) in a civilized society, and there are yardsticks by which to measure human actions. Eichmann and Pol Pot, even if they had sympathizers, will not be proposed for sainthood.

Why the great coyness concerning the use of the word "terrorism" and "terrorists"? Why the use of ludicrous terms such as "armed struggle" or "Red Army" or "guerrilla" or "Red Brigade"? This was not always the case. The Russian revolutionaries of a century ago were far less sensitive and openly talked about their terrorist struggle. Boris Savinkov, the head of the terrorist organization of the Russian Social Revolutionaries, called his recollections, published before World War I, *Memoirs of a Terrorist*. It became a classic and was translated into many languages. Why should Western media eighty years later think such a choice of terms impermissible? It had, of course, to do with the change that has taken place in terrorist practice; it was one thing to plan the assassination of a dictator or a police chief, which would generate support at least on the part of some of the public. The indiscriminate murder of innocent people, of small children and elderly people, does not make for good public relations. In other words, the new terrorism is different from the old, and while today's terrorists want to practice it, they resent the label. The media were quite willing to respect their sensitivity.

There have been, as always, a few exceptions when ideologues of terrorism have made no bones about their views and strategies. Thus, for instance, Sheikh Azzam, bin Laden's teacher, who has been mentioned more than once in these pages:

> We are terrorists, and terrorism is our friend and companion. Let the West and East know that we are terrorists and that we are terrifying as well. We shall do our best in preparation to terrorize Allah's enemies and our own. Thus terrorism is an obligation in Allah's religion.[3]

There is the unfortunate and often ridiculous practice in some of the media to call a spade not a spade but an agricultural implement. It is understandable that, to give but one example, international news agencies such as Reuters feel uneasy about the use of the term "terrorist" because it might offend the terrorists and perhaps even endanger their correspondents in Gaza, on the West Bank, and other parts of the world. But it would have been more honest if Steven Jukes, head of the Reuters news department, had admitted that the use of terms such as "militants" or "activists" to identify terrorists is motivated by fear and perhaps also the wish not to lose customers, rather than the desire to be objective and tell the truth. The British Broadcasting Corporation (BBC) followed a more selective policy — not using the term "terrorist" in the Middle East but feeling free to use it in other parts of the world. The *Chicago Tribune* decided to forgo the use of the term "terrorism" because "it is tendentious and propagandistic, and because today's terrorist sometimes turns out tomorrow's statesman." By the same token, every political term could and should be dismissed as tendentious and even propagandistic, and while today's terrorist may indeed be tomorrow's statesman, this does not change the fact that at one stage he practiced terrorism. Reuters's decision provoked a great deal of cynical comment: Why not call Jack the Ripper an "amateur abdominal surgeon" and Timothy McVeigh (of Oklahoma City fame) "a person who left a volatile cargo in a nonparking zone"? Why not redefine Pol Pot a recruiter for farming work or Eichmann an activist demographer? Like Humpty Dumpty, some of the media decided that when they use a term "it means just what they choose it to mean."[4]

But the issue is, of course, a serious one. To call a terrorist an "activist" or a "militant" is to blot out the dividing line between a suicide bomber and the active member of a trade union or a political party or a club. It is bound to lead to constant misunderstanding: If an Indian journal publishes statistics about political activists killed in Jammu and Kashmir in the 1990s, the figures do not refer to people who have killed but were killed: candidates in elections.[5] If Reuters's head office in London or that of the *Chicago Tribune* were destroyed in a bomb attack, or if their staff, male and female, would have their throats cut by a group of invaders while sitting at their desks, it is unlikely that their colleagues would call the perpetrators "activists."

Another red herring frequently encountered is the argument that the whole preoccupation with terrorism by small groups of people is misplaced because terrorism exercised by governments has been far more bloody, causing far more victims. This too is perfectly true, for, to give but two obvious examples, the terror exercised by Nazi Germany and Stalinist Russia, not to mention the aggressive wars waged, has caused far more victims than all terrorist groups in history. This argument has been used by the terrorists themselves, arguing that there is no difference between their activities and those by governments and states. It has also been employed by some sympathizers, and it rests on the deliberate obfuscation between all kinds of violence, of which there has been a great deal in the history of mankind ever since Cain killed his brother Abel. This argument ignores the fact that the very existence of a state is based on its monopoly of power. If it were different, states would not have the right, nor be in a position, to maintain that minimum of order on which all civilized life rests. It would not be entitled to apprehend thieves or murderers; it would not even be entitled to collect taxes and enforce traffic regulations such as driving on the right (or the left) side of the road. It would, not, of course, be entitled to have a foreign policy, except of course the right of giving some of its revenue to other, less fortunate countries.

Lastly, there has been a tendency to refrain from the use of the term "terrorism" not so much for political reasons but because of ignorance. In the 1970s and 1980s, the term "urban guerrilla" was widely used in order to identify terrorists, partly perhaps because the term "guerrilla" seemed more value-free and objective, but largely no doubt because of genuine lack knowledge. The difference between "terrorist" and "guerrilla" is not a semantic one but one of essence. The strategy of guerrillas is to establish bases (sometimes called *foci*) usually far away from the populated centers of a country and the reach of the authorities, so-called liberated zones in which the guerrillas build their own institutions such as schools, openly conduct propaganda, and mobilize the population — in fact, a countergovernment. These liberated zones are gradually expanded; the military units are drilled and equipped, and they grow in size and engage in battle with the government troops until they prevail — or are defeated. This was the strategy of Mao and all the other major guerrilla movements in the period after World War II. Such open activities are, of course, impossible in big conurbations (even less in small towns) because the terrorists cannot operate in major units. They have nowhere to hide and to retreat and would invite defeat by the government forces. The true guerrilla leaders such as Che Guevara have been opposed in principle to military operations in cities; the towns were for them the "graveyard of the revolutionaries" — not only for tactical reasons but also because of the temptations of life in the big cities.

True, in some instances, such as the Algerian war of liberation, guerrillas also engaged in urban terrorism; in Ulster the IRA tried to establish (not very success-fully) liberated zones in cities such as Belfast, and al Qa'ida has tried its luck in all kinds of operations including terrorism and guerrilla tactics. The same is true for the Chechen in the Northern Caucasus. But these have been the exceptions rather than the rule. An "urban guerrilla" is a contradiction in terms; the use of the term is either based on ignoring what "terrorism" and "guerrilla" mean or it is deliberately misleading, an attempt to improve the image of the terrorist.

With all these misunderstandings, deliberate and involuntary, it is still true that, as Brian Jenkins has put it, people reasonably familiar with the terrorist phenomenon will agree 90 percent of the time about what terrorism is, just as they will agree on democracy or nationalism or other concepts. In fact, terrorism is an unmistakable phenomenon, even if the search for a scientific, all-comprehensive definition is a futile enterprise. Many years ago I wrote that any definition beyond "the systematic use of murder, injury, and destruction, or the threat of such acts, aimed at achieving political ends" will result in controversy, and arguments will go on for ever. The position of the student of terrorism is not unlike that of a physician dealing with a disease, the exact causes of which remain unknown to this day, or a drug of which it is not known how precisely it functions. But this will not prevent him from diagnosing the disease, or from prescribing the drugs that are applicable.

Notes

1. Roots of Terrorism?

1. Ted Honderich, a British philosopher, argued that the terrorism of 2001 was connected with the poverty of countries like Malawi, Mozambique, Zambia, and Sierra Leone. Ted Honderich, *After the Terror* (Edinburgh, 2002).

2. A study by Alan Krueger and Jitka Maleckova of Princeton and Prague University, respectively, made this point; the study was prepared for the World Bank but encountered opposition and could not be published. Robert Barro, *Business Week*, June 10, 2002. It was subsequently published in the *New Republic*, "Does Poverty Cause Terrorism?" (June 24, 2002). A study of Israeli Jewish terrorists in the 1970s and 1980s reached similar results — a pattern of higher education and better-paying occupation than the average. But the findings about the role of "education," which are also mentioned in the Krueger/Maleckova study, are not conclusive for they do not clarify the essence of education involved, whether it refers, for instance, to a liberal education based on humanist values or on a mainly technical training accompanied by political and religious indoctrination. The equation of various kinds of education is not helpful and might be quite misleading.

3. Hizb al Tahrir in Britain and other jihadist groups have argued all along that a clash between Islam and other civilizations is inescapable. See "The Inevitability of the Clash of Civilizations," *khilafah.com* (September 2002).

4. According to political correctness, human beings are born as tabula rasa; there are no innate traits; men and women are born good and corrupted by society. Neurobiological research into the foundations of human nature has been hamstrung because of the legacy of the racialist theories of Nazi Germany. Hence the reluctance to acknowledge that people may not be born entirely "characterless" and that they are not wholly formed by culture. Are there equal levels of talent, tolerance, and aggression at birth? If people are born with anything, this should be the subject of study. The issue is discussed in Steven Pinker's *The Blank Slate* (New York, 2002). The relevance for the study of terrorism is obvious; that terrorists are not genetically programmed goes without saying; further on in this study we shall deal with the crucial role of indoctrination in the making of suicide bombers. But the question whether biological factors are at all involved, and if so, to what extent, still remains to be investigated.

2. The Origins of Islamic Terrorism

1. The essential work on fundamentalism in the contemporary world is the Fundamentalism project edited by Martin E. Marty and R. Scott Appleby, including *Fundamentalism Observed, Fundamentalism and Society, Fundamentalism and the State*, and particularly *Accounting for Fundamentalisms* (Chicago, 1994).

239

2. About the early period of the history of the Brotherhood, see Richard Mitchell, *The Society of the Muslim Brothers* (London, 1969).

3. The literature about the "special apparatus" is in Arabic, especially the books by Abdulaziz Ramadan (1982), Ahmed Adil Kamel (1987), and Mahmud al Sabgh (1989). There are references in Gilles Kepel, *Muslim Extremism in Egypt* (London, 1985).

4. Hashem Kassem, "Muslem Brotherhood, part 2: Violence and Assassination," *www.eastwestrecord.com EWR* 77 (November 19, 2001).

5. Hassan al Banna, *Majmuat ar Rasa'il*, 72 (Alexandria, 1950), quoted in Abdelwahab Meddeb, *La Maladie de l'Islam* (Paris, 2002).

6. On Qutb as a leading Islamic thinker, Emmanuel Sivan, *Radical Islam* (New Haven, 1985), chaps. 3 and 4. Yvonne Haddad in John L. Esposito, ed., *Voices of Resurgent Islam* (New York, 1983); Gilles Kepel, *Muslim Extremism in Egypt*, which also includes a bibliography of Qutb, 68; the list of books by Qutb available in English translation is available on the Internet; Johannes J. G. Jansen, *The Dual Nature of Islamic Fundamentalism* (Ithaca, N.Y., 1997), 47–54; for a fairly full bibliography mainly of works in Arabic on Qutb's heirs, see Gehad Auda in Marty and Appleby, *Fundamentalism Observed*, 406–7; for a recent critical assessment of Qutb, Helmi el Namnam, *Sayyed Qutb va thawrat yuliu* (Cairo, 1999).

7. About the confrontation between the older and the younger generation among the Brotherhood, see Hisham Mubarak, *Al irhabiyun qadimoun* (Cairo, 1995). See also Abdel Aziz Ramadan, "Fundamentalist Influence in Egypt," in Marty and Appleby, *Fundamentalism and the State.*

8. There is a rich literature about Shukri. The essential facts appear in Kepel, *Muslim Extremism in Egypt*, 79–102, and in Jansen, *The Dual Nature of Islamic Fundamentalism*, 75–94.

9. Kepel, *Muslim Extremism in Egypt*, 78ff.

10. Gehad Auda, in *Fundamentalism Observed.*

11. The literature on these groups, almost exclusively in Arabic, is surveyed in François Burgat, *L'Islamisme en face* (Paris, 2001), 115–18. A valuable critical study is Eberhard Serauky, *Im Namen Allahs* (Berlin, 2001).

12. Patrick Gaffney, "Fundamentalist Preaching and Islamic Militancy in Upper Egypt," in H. Scott Appleby, *Spokesmen for the Despised* (Chicago, 1997), 257ff.

13. Abdel Rahman wrote a book about Jihad, quotations from which appear as government exhibits in *United States v. Abdel Rahman et al.* A short summary is provided by Andrew V. MacCarthy, "Prosecuting the New York Sheikh," March 1, 1997, *www.ict.org.il/articles/articledet.cfm/articleid-95.*

14. Johannes J. G. Jansen, *The Neglected Duty: The Creed of Sadat's Assassins and Islamic Resurgence in the Middle East* (New York, 1986), 123. This is a detailed analysis of the doctrine of Faraj and his followers. The quotation is from *Jihad: The Absent Obligation*, (London, 1999).

15. Kepel, *Muslim Extremism in Egypt*, chap. 7, "To Assassinate Pharaoh."

16. Estimates range between four and ten million.

17. For background about the Copts, see W. E. Wakin, *A Lonely Minority* (New York, 2000), and J. Watson, *Among the Copts* (New York, 1999); for current affairs, see *www.Copts.com.*

18. Ahmed Moussa, *Al Ahram*, August 12, 1998.

19. Aiman al Zawahiri's *Knights under the Prophet's Banner* was published in installments in *Al sharq el awsat* (London), during late November and early December 2001.

An abridged translation appeared in *FBIS* (Foreign Broadcast Information Service) on January 10, 2002. The text given here is from the fifth installment published in Arabic on December 2, 2001. In a book about Zawahiri by one-time comrade-in-arms Muntasser al Zayat, Zawahiri appears in a not very flattering light. *Ayman al Zawahiri kama araftuh* (Zawahiri as I knew him) (Cairo, 2002).

20. Al Zawahiri, *Knights under the Prophet's Banner*, installment 6.

21. Ibid., installment 1.1.

22. *Hawaraat Mamnua* (Forbidden discussions, 1995), in which he criticized both the government and the terrorists for perpetuating acts of violence by constantly provoking each other. See also Joyce M. Davis, *Between Jihad and Salaam* ((New York, 1997), 107ff. In 2000, Sheikh Umar seems to have had second thoughts and through the good offices of his American lawyer conveyed a message to his followers in Egypt to renew their struggle, *New York Times*, April 10, 2002.

23. Zawahiri, *Knights under the Prophet's Banner*, installment 9.

24. Ahmed Hussein Hassan, *Al Gama'at al syasia al Islamiyah* (Cairo, 2000).

25. Sivan, *Radical Islam*, 118.

26. Khaled al-Berry, *La terre est plus belle que le paradis* (Paris, 2002).

27. Charles Pellat, "Liwat" in *Encyclopedia of Islam* (Leyden, 1934). Arno Schmitt and Jehoeda Sofer, *Sexuality and Eroticism among Males in Moslem Societies* (New York, 1992). Felix Guttari, ed., *Trois milliards de pervers* (Paris, 1972).

28. Yasmina Khadra, *A quoi rêvent les loups?* (Paris, 2002), gives a fictional account of the conversion of a young Algerian, Walid Nafa. The author (his name is a pseudonym) was a former senior officer in the Algerian security forces.

29. Jansen, *The Neglected Duty*, 65.

30. Interview with Xavier Raufer, "GIA, radiographie d'une machine a tuer," *Humanité*, February 18, 1997.

31. "Murder on the Bosporus," *Middle East Quarterly* (June 2000).

32. Said Zahraoui, *Entre l'horreur et l'espoir* (Paris, 2000), 101.

33. Michael Prazan, *Les Fanatiques: Histoire de l'Armee Rouge Japonaise* (Paris, 2002), 43ff.

34. *New York Times*, February 25, 2002.

35. William Pierce [pseud. Andrew MacDonald], *The Turner Diaries* (Hillsboro, W.Va., 1980).

36. The documentation about the fate of the Algerian girls raped by members of the Islamic Armed Groups is abundant. See, for instance, Zazi Sadoui, "Femmes sous lois musulmans," *www.wlumi.org/english/publications.dossiers.dossiers16/algeria-martyrdom.htm*.

37. Homosexuality was acceptable in early Islam. According to tenth-century Islamic jurists it was permitted with one's own slaves, though not necessarily with strangers. In any case there was no legal punishment (*hadd*) for it. "Pervasive was this passion in circles high and low," according to the historian Adam Mex, *The Renaissance of Islam* (London, 1937), 358.

38. Hechmi Daoui, newsletter of the International Association for Analytical Psychology (on the Web site of IAAP). See also the same author's *L'amour en Islam* (Paris, 2001). The author believes that the long passage of the ordinary Muslim through the anal sadist phase during his upbringing causes the emergence of masochism, symbolized by the death wish of the religious man.

39. Hisham Mubarak, "A Tragedy of Errors: Afghan Militants the Real Danger," www.cairotimes.com, in which he argued in 1998 that the government was wasting its breath focusing on Western Europe at a time when the real danger was in Afghanistan.

40. A brief account of the confrontation appears in Hashem Kassem, "The Muslim Brotherhood in Syria," *East West Record*, December 10, 2001.

41. Another brief and reliable account of the Hama massacre is in a travel guide: Andrew Beattle and Timothy Pepper, *Syria, the Rough Guide* (London, 1998), 129.

42. Karam Zuhdi, Najeh Ibrahim, Usama Hafez, and Ali Sherif. Another leader, Hamdi Aberrahman, had been pardoned the year before. The series entitled *Tasheeh al Mafaheem* (Correction of Concepts) sold more than one hundred thousand copies in a few weeks (*Neue Zürcher Zeitung*, March 27, 2002). The Gama'a leaders who figured as authors were not released from prison but were given tolerable conditions; all of them married while in prison, and children were born to them.

43. *Al Mussawar*, June 19, 2002, interview with Makram Mohamed Ahmad, editor-in-chief. A similar apology was made by the IRA in July 2002, but it concerned only attacks in which noncombatants had been killed or injured.

44. Jallan Halawi, *Al Ahram Weekly*, June 27, 2002.

3. Jihad

1. Walter Laqueur, *The History of Terrorism*, new ed. (New Brunswick, N.J., 2001).

2. Karl Laske, *Ein Leben zwischen Hitler und Carlos: François Genoud* (Zurich, 1996).

3. Oliver Schroem, *Im Schatten des Jackals. Carlos und die Wegbereiter des internationalen Terrorismus* (Frankfurt, 2002).

4. "The Striving Sheikh: Abdullah Azzam," www.islam.org.au/articles14/azzam/htm. Also Sohheil Laher, "Abdullah Azzam on Jihad," www.calvin.use.edu. Some of Azzam's writing have appeared in English, such as *Defence of Muslim Lands* (London, 2000). His last will appears in another English-language compilation entitled *Declaration of War*, together with the fatwa of 1998. Maktabah al Ansaar brought out this volume in England, ca. 1999.

5. Yoni Fighel, "Sheikh Abdulla Azzam," ICT Research; G. Kepel, *Jihad* (Cambridge, Mass., 2002).

6. Laher, "Abdullah Azzam on Jihad."

7. Ibid.

8. There is a history of the Arabs congregating in Afghanistan by Mohamed Salah, *Waqai sanwat al jihad* (Years of Jihad) (Cairo, 2001).

9. Among the more reliable accounts are those by Peter L. Bergen, *Holy War Inc.* (New York, 2001), and Ahmed Rashid, *Taliban* (New Haven, 2000), which is also a good guide to the years of Taliban rule in Afghanistan.

10. Evidence of Jamal el Fadl, a defector from al Qa'ida, on the second day of the proceedings in the trial against the group that had tried to blow up the World Trade Center in 1993, cryptome.org/usa-v-ubl-dt.htm.

11. The various bin Laden biographies deal with his stay in Sudan. See, for instance, Bergen, *Holy War Inc.*, 79ff.

12. The sources on the activities of al Qa'ida during the early years are sparse. Bin Laden gave occasional interviews to Western reporters; the main source of information was the Arabic press published in London, *Al Quds al Arabi*, and above all *Al Hayat*, also published in the British capital. See also Esther Webman, "Political Islam at the Close of

the Twentieth Century," and the same author's "The Polarization and Radicalization of Political Islam," published by the Dayan Center and accessible on its Web page.

13. The first detailed portrait of Zawahiri in English appeared in the *New Yorker,* September 16, 2002 (Lawrence Wright, "The Man behind Bin Laden"). It is based mainly on interviews with family members and friends.

14. One of the most revealing documents of this genre is an illegal pamphlet, *Istratijia al muwadjaha ma al gharb* ("The strategy of confrontation with the West," place and date of publication unknown). This is quoted and interpreted in detail in Eberhard Serauky, *Im Namen Allahs* (Berlin, 2000), chap. 3.

15. *Al Quds al Arabi,* February 23, 1998.

16. Webman, "The Polarization and Radicalization of Political Islam."

17. The text and commentary in Bernard Lewis, "License to Kill," *Foreign Affairs* (November–December 1998).

18. MEMRI, special dispatch 381, June 12, 2002, based on the Center of Islamic Research and Studies *www.alneda.com* later changed to *http://66.34.191.223.* This series of three articles was entitled "In the Shadow of the Lances." Excerpts were published earlier in *Der Spiegel,* June 9, 2002. See also *Al Sharq al awsat,* June 7, 2002.

19. For various theories on the compilation and publication of the "Encyclopedia of Terror," see Reuel Gerecht, *Middle East Quarterly* (summer 2001).

20. Sections of this manual were made public by the U.S. Department of Justice as an exhibit in the trial against the accused in the 1993 bombing of the World Trade Center. The quotations are from pages 78–79. A recruiting tape of Osama bin Laden with comments by several experts has been published by Columbia International Affairs Online, August 2002, *www.ciaonet.org.*

21. "The Afghan Alumni Terrorism," ICT Research. On the fate of the Afghan Arabs who returned to Algeria after the end of the war against the Russians, see a series of eight articles by Muhammad Mukadam in the London-based daily *Al Hayat,* November 23–30 ("Rikhlat al Afghan al Jazairin min al Qa'ida ala l'Jama'a").

22. *arabicnews.com,* November 9, 1998.

23. Robert G. White, *Vanguard of Nazism* (Cambridge, Mass., 1952).

24. Craig Meyer, *Los Angeles Times,* October 7, 2001.

25. "The Afghan Alumni Terrorism."

26. *Frankfurter Rundschau,* October 24, 2001.

27. Michele Tribalat et al., *La republique et l'Islam entre crainte et aveuglement* (Paris, 2002).

28. *New York Times,* July 16, 2002.

29. "Farewell Message from Azzam Publications," November 20, 2001, on the Azzam Web site.

30. *London Times,* October 2, 2002.

31. This refers, for instance, to Richard Reed, the "shoe bomber" who became a convert in Feltham prison near London.

32. Alain Bauer and Xavier Raufer, *La guerre ne fait que commencer* (Paris, 2002), 224ff. Muslim writers have put some of the blame on the French media which, they claim, are responsible for the negative image of Muslims in France. Alain Boyer, *L'Islam en France* (Paris, 1998), 330.

33. *Strait Times,* Singapore, December 23, 2001.

34. David Pujadas and Ahmed Salam, *La tentation du Jihad* (Paris, 1995); G. Nonne-mann, ed., *Muslim Communities in the New Europe* (New York, 1998), chap. 11.

35. Bauer and Raufer, *La guerre ne fait que commencer,* 222.

36. Laurent Mucchielli, *Le Monde,* November 18, 2001; "Les interrogations de Ban-lieues," *Le Monde,* November 7, 2001.

37. *www.Racismeantiblanc.bizland.com.*

38. *Los Angeles Times,* October 21, 2001.

39. *New York Times,* November 24, 2001.

40. "A l'interieur d'Al Qaida," *Le Nouvel Observateur,* November 29, 2001.

41. *Le Monde,* September 9, 1998.

42. A collection of Bakri's declarations appears in MEMRI, Inquiry and Analysis 73, October 23, 2001.

43. *Al Hayat* (London), July 31, 2002, translated in MEMRI, August 9, 2002, Special Dispatch 410.

44. *Daily Mirror,* London, September 7, 1996.

45. *The Independent,* London, February 4, 2002.

46. *Guardian,* London, February 17, 2002.

47. Daily news and comments issued by the spokesmen of Hizb ul Tahrir can be found on the Web site *Khilafah.com.*

48. M. Anir Ali, "American Elections and Hizb al Tahrir," online at *www.iiie.net/Articles/HizbatTahrir.html.*

49. Many articles on these lines were published during August and September 2002 on the Hizb ul Tahrir Web site, *Khilafah.com.*

50. H. P. Raddatz, *Hamburger Abendblatt,* January 8, 2002; *Taz,* "Viel Kopfschuetteln," January 16, 2002; H. P. Raddatz, *Von Allah zum Terror?* (Munich, 2992).

51. *Taz,* February 9, 2002.

52. *Verfassungsschutzbericht 2000* (Bonn, 2001) passim; *Islamischer Extremismus und seine Auswirkungen auf die Bundesrepublik Deutschland,* BfV (Cologne, 1996).

53. On al Qa'ida in Southeast Asia, see Rohan Gunaratna, *Inside Al Qaeda* (London, 2002), chap. 4.

54. Oliver Stroem, "Der Prediger und die frommen Killer," *Die Zeit,* August 28, 2002.

4. Suicide

1. MEMRI, special dispatch N 226 (June 2001).

2. *The Encyclopedia of Islam,* vol. 4 (Leyden, 1934), 260.

3. Ibid.

4. Ibid.

5. MEMRI, "Debating the Religious, Political and Moral Legitimacy of Suicide Bombings," part 4, July 27, 2001.

See also Christoph Reuter, *Mein Leben ist eine Waffe* (Munich, 2002), 251ff.

6. See, for instance, Abdul Wahid Hamid, "Companions of the Prophet: Al Baraa Ibn Malik Al-Ansari," *www.islam101.com/people/companions/albara.html.*

7. Ibid., and also see Abul Rahman Al-Makki, "Fidayee Activities in Shariah," *www.markazdawa.org/English/magazines.*

8. Mario Liverani, *Akkad, the First World Empire* (Padova, 1993).

9. Michael Sommer, "Krieg im Altertum als soziales Handeln," in *Militärgeschichtliche Zeitschrift* 59 (2000): 297–322. Also Brian Ferguson, "Explaining War," in *The Anthropology of War*, ed. J. Haas (Cambridge, 1990), 26–50.

10. On Valhalla see *Bulfinch's Mythology* (New York, n.d.)

11. *Chanson de Roland*, ed. C. Segre (Milan, 1974).

12. Glinka's opera was first performed in 1836 and is the Russian national opera par excellence.

13. Theodor Koerner, "Bundeslied vor der Schlacht," quoted in G. Mosse, *Fallen Soldiers* (Oxford, 1990).

14. Mosse, *Fallen Soldiers*, Langemarck is usually referred to in English as Bixchote. On Langemarck, Ernst Juenger, *Der Kampf als inneres Erlebnis* (Berlin, 1922), but also Hitler, *Mein Kampf.*

15. Jay Baird, *To Die for Germany* (Bloomington, 1990). Ester Rossmeissel, *Maertyrerstilisierungen der Literatur des dritten Reiches* (Dresden, 2000); Sabine Behrenbeck, *Der Kult um die toten Helden* (Vierow, 1996).

16. Werner Jaekel, "Gegenwart der Toten," in *Rufe in das Reich*, ed. Herbert Boehme (Berlin, 1934).

17. Holzapfel in Boehme, ed., *Rufe in das Reich*, 284.

18. Boehme, ed., *Rufe in das Reich*, 17.

19. "An Interview — The Iron Guard," in *New Nation* the quarterly journal of the National Front, UK (summer 1985).

20. Kadmon, "Corneliu Codreanu, Struggle, and Seclusion," in *members.tripod.com/~ centenar/cce6.html.*

21. Julius Evola, *Men among the Ruins* (Rochester, Vt., 2002).

22. There is a considerable amount of kamikaze literature in English, for instance, Maurice Pinguet, *Voluntary Death in Japan* (Cambridge, 1993); Denis and Peggy Warner, *The Sacred Warriors* (New York, 1982); Rikihei Inoguchi et al., *The Sacred Wind* (Westport, Conn., 1959). For Japanese sources, see the bibliography in Mako Sasaki, "Who Became Kamikaze Pilots?" *Concord Review*, 1995, *www.tcr.org/kamikaze.html.*

23. Sasaki, "Who Became Kamikaze Pilots?".

24. Klaus Scherer, *Kamikaze* (Ludicium, 2001).

25. George Sweeney, "Irish Hunger Strikes and the Cult of Self Sacrifice," *Journal of Contemporary History* (1993): 421–37.

26. Stephen F. Dale, "Religious Suicide in Islamic Asia," *Journal of Conflict Resolution* (March 1988): 37–59.

27. On the Tamil Tigers, R. Hoole et al., *The Broken Palmyra* (Claremont, Calif., 1990); Manoj Joshi, "On the Razor's Edge," *Studies in Conflict and Terrorism* (January 1996); Jakob Rosel, *Der Bürgerkrieg in Sri Lanka* (Baden Baden, 1998); Sacho Sri Kantha, "The Prabhakaran Phenomenon" (thirty-six installments so far), *www.sangam.org.*

28. Ayman al Zawahiri, "Fursan taht ra'ayat al naby." This autobiography of the leading Egyptian terrorist was published in eleven installments in *Al Sharq al awsat* (London) between December 2 and 12. A detailed portrait of Osama bin Laden by Kamel al Tawil appeared in several installments in the London-based *Al Hayat*, between October 4 and October 9, 2001. See also Hisham Mubarak, *Il irhabiyun qadimoun* (Cairo, 1995), and Eberhard Serauky, *Im Namen Allahs* (Berlin, 2001).

29. Peter Schalk, "The Revival of Martyr Cults," *Temenos* 33 (1997), and P. Kharunakaran, "Great Heroes Week," *Weekend Express*, November 22, 1998.

30. Maitree, "The LTTE as a Tamil Civil Religion," chap. 2, *http://people.we.mediaone/ maitree.thesis*. For the central role of discipline see "The Prabhakaran Phenomenon," part 15, "Demand of Discipline."

31. Hoole et al., *The Broken Palmyra;* Rosel, *Der Bürgerkrieg in Sri Lanka;* Kantha, "The Prabhakaran Phenomenon."

32. *South Asia Intelligence Review* (SAPR) (July 2002), *satport@satp.org.*

33. Amos Harel, "The 100th Suicide Bomber," *Ha'aretz,* October 8, 2001; Ely Carmon, in *Countering Suicide Terrorism* (Herzliya, 2001). According to more recent statistics (*Ha'aretz,* September 29, 2002) there were 145 suicide bombers between 1993 and September 2002. This included terrorists who were caught before they were able to accomplish their mission. Fifty-two of them were sent by Hamas, forty by Fatah, and thirty-five by Jihad Islami. These figures refer only to bombers with explosives strapped to their body or driving booby-trapped vehicles.

34. *New York Times,* April 14, 2002.

35. Douglas E. Streusand, "What Does Jihad Mean?" *Middle East Quarterly* (September 1997); Emmanuel Sivan, *Radical Islam* (New Haven, 1990); Hanna F. Kassis, A *Concordance of the Quran* (Berkeley, 1983); Nimatullah Sjunainah, *Tanzim el Djihad* (Cairo, 1988); Fred Donner, "The Sources of Islamic Conception of War," in *Just War and Jihad,* ed. John Kelsay and James Turner Johnson (Westport, Conn., 1991).

36. On Ibn Taimiyah, Henri Laoust, *Essai sur les doctrines socials et politiques de Taki e Din Ahmad bin Taimiyyah* (Cairo, 1939). There has been an Ibn Taimiyah renaissance during the 1990s; the Library of Congress catalogue lists 198 new books about him and his teachings during the last decade, virtually all in Arabic. There are, however, many translations of selections from his main work *Al siyassah al shari'ya fi islah al ra'I va al-ra'iyah* ("Governance according to God's law in reforming both the ruler and his flock"), especially the sections concerning jihad.

37. *New York Times,* April 13, 2002.

38. "Virgins? What Virgins?" *Guardian,* January 12, 2002.

39. Christopher Luxenberg (pseud.), *Die Syro-Aramäische Lesart des Koran* (Berlin, 2000).

40. Zeev Shiff, *Ha'aretz,* August 9, 2002.

41. *Ha'aretz,* July 19, 2002.

42. Boaz Ganor, Yoram Schweitzer, and Reuven Paz in *Countering Suicide Terrorism* (Herzliya, 2001). To give but one example, Abu Danush, a very young Palestinian from a village near Jenin whose mission failed, had eight brothers and sisters. He had undergone hardly any religious training, but from the age of twelve he had wanted to die as a *shahid,* and though he did not come from a particularly observant family, religious instruction in school contributed to his decision to volunteer with the Islamic Jihad. Arnon Ragul in *Kol Ha'ir,* Jerusalem, March 22, 2002.

43. Suzanne Goldenberg, "A Mission to Murder," *Guardian,* June 11 and 12, 2002.

44. *Taz* (Berlin), June 15, 2002.

45. *Al Sharq al Awsat,* June 5, 2002.

46. Tarrad al Omari, *Al Watan,* December 22, 2002.

47. Reuven Paz, "Programmed Terrorists," *ICT,* December 13, 2001; Hassan Mneimneh and Kanan Makiya, "Manual for a Raid," *New York Review of Books,* January 17, 2002.

48. "What Drove a Boy from Bromley?" *Sunday Telegraph,* December 30, 2001.

49. Shaul Shay, "Suicide Terrorism in Lebanon," in *Countering Suicide Terrorism*; Yoram Schweitzer, "Suicide Terrorism," *ICT*, April 21, 2000.

50. Dogu Ergil, in *Countering Suicide Terrorism*.

51. Peter Schalk, "The Revival of Martyr Cults among Ilavar," *Temenos* 33 (1997): 151–90.

52. The term "overvalued idea" was coined by the German psychiatrist and neurologist Carl Wernicke around 1900. It has been used with regard to all kinds of compulsive disorders.

53. Goldenberg, "A Mission to Murder."

54. Latifa ben Mansour, *Frères musulmans, frères feroces* (Paris, 2002), 218–22.

55. Haruki Murakami, *Underground: The Tokyo Gas Attack* (London, 2000).

56. Three copies of this letter were found, and it is assumed that Muhammad Atta was the author. The Arabic text was published by the FBI: *www.fbi.gov/pressrel01letter.htm*. An English translation in Mneimneh and Makiyah, *New York Review of Books*, January 17, 2002. On Atta, see Elena Lappin, "Atta in Hamburg," *Prospect* (September 2002).

57. Ibid.

58. For documents in defense of the practices of these cults and sects see *www.cesnur.org*; for critical comments, *www.kelebekler.com/cesnur*.

59. The precise text is *plures efficimus quoties metimur a vobis, semen est sanguis Christianorum* — "the more ye mow us down, the more we grow, the seed is the blood of the Christians."

60. Gal Luft, "The Palestinian H bomb," *Foreign Affairs* (July 2002); Walter Laqueur, *Times Literary Supplement*, September 6, 2002.

61. "The Debate over Martyrdom Operations," part I, MEMRI, July 4, 2002.

5. Israel and the Palestinians

1. Quoted in Benny Morris, *Righteous Victims* (New York, 1999), 271.

2. Walter Laqueur, *The Road to War* (London, 1969, Pelican edition), 302–5.

3. Of Arafat biographies the following ought to be mentioned: Danny Rubinstein, *Arafat, dyokan* (Tel Aviv, 2001); Alan Hart, *Terrorist or Peacemaker* (London, 1984), an official biography; Andrew Gower and Rony Walker, *Behind the Myth* (London, 1999); Said Aburish, *From Defender to Dictator* (London, 1999), a hostile account.

4. On the early history of Fatah, Helena Cobban, *The Palestinian Liberation Organization* (Cambridge, 1984), and Ehud Yaari, *Strike Terror* (Tel Aviv, 1970). See also Olivier Carre, *L'Ideologie palestinienne de resistance* (Paris, 1972). Later works include the very detailed book by Y. Sayigh, *Armed Struggle and the Search for State* (New York, 1997), and A. Frangi, *The PLO and Palestine* (Totowa, N.J., 1983).

5. Ely Karmon, "Fatah and the Popular Front for the Liberation of Palestine 1968–1990," *ICT*, November 25, 2000. The literature about the PFLP and the PDFLP is extensive. The best bibliography known to me is in Gerrit Hoekmann, *Zwischen Ölzweig und Kalaschnikow: Geschichte und Politik der palästinensischen Linken* (Munster, 1996), 231–40.

6. On the PFLP, see Harold Cubert, *The PFLP's Changing Role in the Middle East* (London, 1997). On Islamic Jihad, Meir Hatina, *Islam and Salvation in Palestine: The Islamic Jihad Movement* (Tel Aviv, 2001).

7. R. Erlich, "The History of Israeli Policy in Lebanon," *ICT*, June 29, 2000.

8. Ariel Merari, "Israeli Preparedness for High Consequences Terrorism," Belfer Center, Harvard University, October 2000.

9. There is not yet a comprehensive history of the first Intifada. Zeev Schiff and Ehud Ya'ari, *Intifada* (New York, 1990), appeared well before its end.

10. On the early history of Hamas, Khaled Hroub, *Hamas* (Washington, D.C., 2000); Ziad Abu Amr, *Islamic Fundamentalism in the West Bank and Gaza* (Bloomington, Ind., 1994); Ahmed Rashid, *Hamas* (Annandale, Va., 1993); A. Nusse, *Muslim Palestine* (Amsterdam, 1998); Anat Kurz and Nahman Tal, *Hamas: Radical Islam in a National Struggle* (Tel Aviv, 1997).

11. Hroub, *Hamas*.

12. The text of the charter is in ibid., 267ff.

13. *www.palestine-info.com/hamas*.

14. Kurz and Tal, *Hamas*, 38; Roni Shaked and Aviva Shabi, *Hamas* (Jerusalem, 1994), 256–69; Menachem Klein, "Competing Brothers," in *Religious Radicalism in the Greater Middle East*, ed. Bruce Maddy-Weitzman and Efraim Inbar (London, 1997); Ali Jarbawi, *Hamas' Bid to Lead the Palestinian People* (Annandale, Va., 1994).

15. Ely Karmon, "Hamas Terrorism Strategy," *ICT*, November 19, 1999; *www.ict.org.il*.

16. Mahmud el Zahar, in *Al Majalla*, London, August 15, 1999, quoted in "Hamas," *ICT*.

17. Boaz Ganor, "Suicide Terrorism, an Overview," *ICT*, February 15, 2000. On the peace process and terrorism, Franck Debie and Sylvie Fouet, *La paix en miettes* (Paris, 2001).

18. N. T. Anders Strindberg, *Studies in Conflict and Terrorism* (July 2002): 271.

19. *palestineremembered.com/al-Ramla/Zarnuqa/Story455/html* (an interview with Fathi Shiqaqi). See Boaz Ganor, "The Islamic Jihad," *ICT special report*, and Hatina, *Islam and Salvation*.

20. "Fatah Tanzim," *www.ict.org.il*.

21. "Force 17," *www.ict.org.il*.

22. On Hizbullah, Martin Kramer, "The Oracle of Hizbullah," in R. Scott Appleby, *Spokesmen for the Despised* (Chicago, 1997) (with detailed bibliography); Nizar Hamzeh, "Lebanon's Hizbullah" in *Third World Quarterly* (1993): 321ff. Magnus Ranstorp, "Hizbullah's Command Leadership," *www.st-and.ac.uk/academic/intrel/research*, and Ranstorp, *Hizballah in Lebanon* (London, 1997); A. Husain, *Party of God* (London, 2002); Saad Ghorayeb, *Hizbullah, Politics and Religion* (London, 2002). On early Hizbullah terrorism in Lebanon, Edgar O'Balance, *Islamic Fundamentalist Terrorism, 1979–1995* (New York, 1997), chap. 4. There is a recent Arabic language history of Hizbullah, Tareq Azab, *Hizbullah beyn al Haqaiq wa Awham al gharb* (Hizbullah between facts and Western Illusions) (Cairo, 2000).

23. The dangers of such a policy were obvious even in 1967. See Laqueur, *The Road to War*.

24. Gal Luft, "The Palestinian H Bomb," *Foreign Affairs* (July 2002).

25. Ehud Sprinzak, *Brother against Brother* (New York, 1999), 239–43; Eliezer Don-Yehiya, "The Book and the Sword," in Martin E. Marty and R. Scott Appleby, eds., *Accounting for Fundamentalism* (Chicago, 1994).

26. Goldstein's admirers published a posthumous volume in his memory: Michael Ben Horin, ed., *Baruch hagever* (Jerusalem, 1995).

27. *Ha'aretz*, May 16, 2002.

28. Sprinzak, *Brother against Brother*, 274–75.

29. Ibid., 211. Meir Kahane wrote a number of books such as *Never Again* (Los Angeles, 1972), *The Story of the Jewish Defense League* (New York, 1975), and *Forty Years* (Miami, 1983).

30. Judith Tydor Baumel, "Kahane in America," *Studies in Conflict and Terrorism* 22 (1999).

31. Michael Lueders, "Arabische Intellektuelle," *Frankfurter Rundschau*, March 20, 2002.

6. Intelligence Failure?

1. The poem was written in 1828 as part of a cycle entitled *Konrad Wallenrod*. There are several English and German translations, but the Russian is the best.

2. The classic work on surprise attack is Roberta Wohlstetter, *Pearl Harbor* (Stanford, 1962). During the last years of the Cold War, academic work on this topic became very popular. See, for instance, Richard K. Betts, *Surprise Attack* (Washington, D.C., 1982). A massive recent addition to this genre (on the Yom Kippur War) is Uri Bar Yosef, *Hatzofe shenirdam* (The watchman fell asleep) (Tel Aviv, 2001).

3. The literature on surprise attack addresses itself without exception to surprise in war rather than in a terrorist campaign.

4. U.S. Department of Justice/Federal Bureau of Investigation, *Terrorism in the United States: Thirty Years of Terrorism. A Special Retrospective Edition* (Washington, D.C., 1999).

5. Van Atta, *New York Times*, June 2, 2002.

6. Statement made in the House Committee on national security, February 12, 1998.

7. Released in National Security Archives, College Park, Md. *www.gwu.edu/nsarchiv/* NSAEBB file: "Terrorism and Usama bin Laden," document 1.

8. *Joint Inquiry Staff Statement Part I*, Eleanor Hill, Staff Director Joint Inquiry Staff, September 18, 2002.

9. Ibid., 9.

10. Daniel Benjamin and Steven Simon, *New York Review of Books*, December 20, 2001.

11. Quoted in Richard Betts, "Fixing Intelligence," *Foreign Affairs* (January–February 2002).

12. Joint Inquiry Staff Statement, reported in the *New York Times*, September 23, 2002.

13. Department of Defense, *USS Cole Commission Report*, January 9, 2001, executive summary. *www.defenselink.mil/pubs/cole 20010109.html*.

14. "Advisory Panel to Assess Domestic Response Capabilities for Terrorism Involving Weapons of Mass Destruction," December 15, 1999, and subsequent reports.

15. *Countering the Changing Threat of International Terrorism*, Report of the National Commission on Terrorism (Washington, D.C., 2000).

16. Ibid.

17. Jake Tapper in *salon.com/politics/feature2001/09/12/bush*.

18. Letter, *Commentary* (February 2002).

19. John Miller and Michael Stone, *The Cell* (New York, 2002).

20. Seymour M. Hersh, "What Went Wrong?" *New Yorker*, October 8, 2001.

21. Peter Grose, *Gentleman Spy* (New York, 1994).

22. "Missed Signals," *New York Times*, December 30, 2001.

23. Dan Eggen and Bob Miller, "Bush Was Told of Hijacking Dangers," *Washington Post*, May 16, 2002; Bob Woodward and Dan Eggen "Aug. Memo Focused on Attacks in U.S.," *Washington Post*, May 18, 2001; as well as many other articles in the *Washington Post* and *New York Times*, between May 16 and May 20, 2002.

24. Stephen Hess, *International News and Foreign Correspondents* (Washington, D.C., 1995). See also Neil Hickey, "Over There," *Columbia Journalism Review* (November–December 1996). About the coverage of terrorism in the American media before and after September 11, see the special issue of the *Columbia Journalism Review* (January–February 2002), in particular Michael Parks, "Beyond Afghanistan: Foreign News: What's Next?"

25. To give but a few examples: Jessica Stern, *The Ultimate Terrorists* (Cambridge, Mass., 1999), was published by Harvard University Press; Bruce Hoffman, *Inside Terrorism* (New York, 1998), by Columbia University Press; Paul R. Pillar, *Terrorism and U.S. Foreign Policy* (Washington, D.C., 2001), by the Brookings Institution; Walter Laqueur, *The New Terrorism* (New York, 1999), by Oxford University Press. After September 11, virtually any book which had anything to do with Afghanistan, Pakistan, Islamism, and so on was guaranteed high sales for a few weeks or months.

26. For instance, Seymour M. Hersh, "What Went Wrong?" *The New Yorker*, October 8, 2001; Thomas Powers, "The Trouble with the CIA," *New York Review of Books*, January 17, 2002.

27. Craig Calhoun et al., *Understanding September 11* (New York, 2002); Eric Hershberg, *Critical Views of September 11* (New York, 2002). Most of the contributors to the volume edited by Hershberg came from universities in the third world trying to enlighten their obtuse American colleagues ("Of course, not all American intellectuals are myopic and insensitive," 325).

28. Most of what is said in the following refers only to the Arab world, and not all of it either. It was one of the unfortunate consequences of the Said controversy and its aftermath that "Orientalism" became more or less a synonym for Arab studies, whereas in fact it encompasses, of course, a far wider framework.

29. John L. Esposito, *The Islamic Threat: Myth or Reality?* 3d ed. (New York, 1999). Esposito pursued his arguments in a later book *Unholy War: Terror in the Name of Islam* (New York, 2002).

30. Esposito, *The Islamic Threat*, 280.

31. Ibid.

32. Esposito, *Unholy War*, 158.

33. Fawaz Gerges, "The Ultimate Terrorist: Myth or Reality?" *Daily Star*, Beirut, March 12, 2001.

34. Bernard Lewis, "The Roots of Muslim Rage," *Atlantic Monthly* (September 1990), republished on the Internet in 2001. It was originally a Jefferson lecture, given in Washington, D.C. Lewis had been one of the first, if not the first, Western scholars to note the revival of Islamic fundamentalism. See B. Lewis, "The Return of Islam," *Commentary* (January 1976).

Lewis was not forgiven that he had been right early on and acted as a warner. "Eminent historian of Islamic civilization, he turns propagandist when commenting on the contemporary Middle East." Juan Goytisolo, "Une vision orientaliste," *Le Monde Diplomatique* ("Islam contre Islam," Manière de voir 64), July–August 2002.

35. Edward W. Said, *Covering Islam* (New York, 1997) (originally published in 1981). This refers to the new introduction to the Vintage edition.

36. Said refers here to a book by French scholar Olivier Roy, *The Failure of Political Islam* (Cambridge, Mass., 1994).

37. Afterword to the 1994 edition of Edward Said, *Orientalism* (New York, 1979).

38. Martin Kramer, *Ivory Towers Built on Sand* (Washington, D.C., 2001), conclusion. Kramer is an American-born and American-trained historian at Tel Aviv University.

39. Ibid. The reference to the loss of confidence on the part of foundations seems slightly exaggerated for the Ford Foundation, the Pew Foundation, and others that continued their financial support for the post-Orientalist school.

40. Ibid., 122.

41. A considerable part of the post-Orientalists were Jewish but anti-Israeli in orientation. There were also several Arab experts critical of radical Islamism and its violent potential, but in contrast to the former they were outside the academic mainstream. There had been studies of the worldwide rise of religious fundamentalism including South Asia, Israel, and even the United States such as the famous "Chicago" study. Martin Marty and Scott Appleby published during the 1990s a series of massive volumes written by many hands. This included *Fundamentalism and the State, Fundamentalisms Observed, Accounting for Fundamentalisms,* and others. This work constituted a landmark in the study of the phenomenon. It had been initiated by students of theology rather than the Middle East. Edward Said and his followers did not like this project either, even though it could not possibly be construed as an attack on Islam. But as he saw it, it had failed to provide a clear definition of the phenomenon and it could therefore stir up alarm and consternation among the public (Said, *Covering Islam,* 17). In brief, the general tendency was to shy away from the subject, as the Victorians had shied away from sex.

42. Bernard Lewis, *Foreign Affairs* (September 1996).

43. F. Gregory Gause III, "Who Lost Middle Eastern Studies? The Orientalists Strike Back," *Foreign Affairs* (March–April 2002). The book in question is Mamoun Fandy, *Saudi Arabia and the Politics of Dissent* (New York, 1999).

44. Steve Heydemann, "Defending the Discipline," *Journal for Democracy* (July 2002).

45. Khaled Abou el Fadl, "Islam and the Theology of Power," *Middle East Report* 221 (winter 2001).

46. Kramer replied to some of his critics in "Arabic Panic," *Middle East Quarterly* (July 2002).

47. Bassam Tibi, *Challenge of Fundamentalism* (Berkeley, 1998); *Fundamentalismus im Islam, eine Gefahr für den Weltfrieden* (Darmstadt, 2000); and other works. Gilles Kepel's most recent book is *Jihad* (Cambridge, Mass., 2002).

48. Martina Sabra in *Neue Zürcher Zeitung,* September 20, 2002; Matthias Karmann, *Die Welt,* September 20, 2002.

49. The best guidebook to actors, authors, concepts, etc., is Alex P. Schmid and Albert J. Jongman, *Political Terrorism* (New Brunswick, N.J., 1988). This is the second, revised edition of this standard handbook; the first edition is now difficult to obtain but can be more highly recommended.

50. I am grateful to Professor David Fromkin, Mr. Brian Jenkins, and Professor Martha Crenshaw for having shared with me their recollections about their early steps in the discipline.

51. E. V. Walter, *Terror and Resistance* (Oxford, 1969); Th. P. Thornton, "Terror as a Weapon of Political Agitation," in *Internal War,* ed. H. Eckstein (New York, 1964).

52. Walter Laqueur, *Terrorism* (London, 1976), 4–6.

53. After 9/11 there was a veritable explosion of books and articles on terrorism; on the first anniversary, many academic journals published special issues devoted to this subject, including both analysis and policy recommendations by leading political science theorists.

While this new interest in a hitherto neglected field was welcome, the value of these contributions was not obvious. They reminded one all too often of a medical diagnosis by a leading physician of a patient with whom the doctor had had no direct contact.

54. Schmid and Jongman, *Political Terrorism*, 62ff.

55. Chomsky elaborated and repeated his views in many books and articles over the years, some written in collaboration with E. S. Herman, such as the *Political Economy of Human Rights*, 2 vols. (Nottingham, 1979). See also M. Stohl, *Myths and Realities of Political Terrorism* (New York, 1979). A recent detailed restatement by Chomsky of his position is "Terror and Just Response," *www.zmag.org*, July 2, 2002.

56. On psychological theories trying to explain terrorism, see Schmid and Jongman, *Political Terrorism*, 87–98.

57. Andrew Silke, "The Devil You Know: Continuing Problems with Research on Terrorism," *Terrorism and Political Violence* (winter 2001).

58. Laqueur, *Terrorism* (1977), 226.

59. Brian Jenkins, *Will Terrorists Go Nuclear?* (Santa Monica, Calif.: Rand, 1976), 6–7; Brian Jenkins, "International Terrorism," in *International Terrorism and World Security*, ed. David Carlton and Carlo Schaerf (London, 1975), 15; Brian Jenkins, "Will Terrorists Go Nuclear? A Reappraisal," in Harvey W. Kushner, *The Future of Terrorism* (Thousand Oaks, Calif., 1998), 249.

60. J. Bowyer Bell, *A Time of Terror* (New York, 1978), 121.

61. Laqueur, *Terrorism* (1977), 231. W. Laqueur, *The Age of Terrorism* (Boston, 1987), 319.

62. Bruce Hoffman's *Inside Terrorism* (New York, 1998) contained a long chapter on religious terrorism. Mark Juergensmeyer in *Terror in the Mind of God* (Berkeley, 2000) and in other works dealt with the phenomenon in considerable detail. There were also studies of Iranian-sponsored terrorism, Hizbullah, and Hamas, as well as the growth of religious terrorism on the Indian subcontinent.

63. Hoffman, *Inside Terrorism*, 94.

64. Walter Laqueur, *The New Terrorism* (New York, 1999), 282.

65. Walter Laqueur, "Reflections on Terrorism," *Foreign Affairs* (fall 1986).

66. Nina J. Easton, "Putting Theory into Practice," *Los Angeles Times*, November 18, 2001.

67. Benjamin Beit Halahmi, "Ten Comments on Watching Closely the Gaps Between Beliefs and Actions," *Terrorism and Political Violence* (spring 2002): 123.

68. Some seventy-one attacks had occurred up to that date in which chemical and biological weapons had been used, but only one U.S. fatality resulted.

69. Steven Simon and Daniel Benjamin, "America and the New Terrorism," *Survival* (spring 2000), and "America and the New Terrorism: An Exchange with Contributions by Olivier Roy, Bruce Hoffman, Reuven Paz, Steven Simon, and Daniel Benjamin," *Survival* (summer 2000).

70. Simon and Benjamin, *Survival* (spring 2000): 59.

71. *New York Times*, August 19, 2002.

7. The Far Right

1. *New York Times*, September 8, 2002.

2. Quoted here from *truthorfiction.com/rumors/falwell-robertson-wtc.htm*.

3. Ibid.

4. *www.splcenter.org/intelligenceproject/ip-4t3.html.*

5. Quoted in Nicholas Goodrick-Clarke, *Black Sun* (New York, 2001), 302.

6. *www.splcenter.org/intelligenceproject/ip-4t3.html.*

7. Ibid.

8. *www.adl.org/terrorism_/default.asp,* posted October 29, 2001.

9. *www.adl.org/terrorism_/default.asp,* "What They Are Saying," November 28, 2001.

10. *www.splcenter.org.*

11. *www.adl.org/terrorism.* David Irving, November 8, 2001; Robert Faurisson, November 9, 2001.

12. *Al Watan,* March 7, 2002.

13. *www.adl.org.*

14. *www.splcenter.org.*

15. *www.adl.org.*

16. "Ein Schluck von der eigenen Medizin," Pressemitteilung *Aktionsbüro Norddeutschland,* September 12, 2001, quoted in *Verfassungsschutzbericht 2001* (Berlin, 2002).

17. Horst Mahler, "Der Untergang des judaeo-amerikanischen Imperiums," online at *www.deutsches-kolleg.org/deutscheskolleg/untergang.html.*

18. Dugin is the author of countless articles and books. Some can be found online at *www.patriotica.narod.ru.*

19. Fyodor Girenok, Alexander Panarin, Alexander Dugin — speeches made at a round table economic-philosophical meeting, Moscow, October 6, 2001. For the views of Zatulin, Delyagin, and Andranik Migranyan, see *Svobodnaya Mysl* (December 2001).

20. This was the argument used, for instance, by Mathias Broeckers, *Verschwörungen, Verschwörungstheorien und die Geheimnisse des 11.9* (Frankfurt, 2002).

21. "Der kabbalistische und andere Aspekte des WTC Attentates," *www.ostara.org/zeitge/wtc17.htm.* Ostara was a quasi-religious political sect just before and after World War I which played a certain role in the prehistory of Nazism. See also Anthony Judge, "Conspiracy and Terrorism," November 18, 2001, *www.uia.org/musings/uncommo6.htm.*

22. Thierry Meyssan, *L'effroyable imposture* (Paris, 2001). In April 2002 this book placed at the top of the French bestseller list (*Le Point,* April 5, 2002). The conspiracy literature sold more copies than even the bestellers of the extreme right and far left.

23. Sayed Qutb, *Fi zilal al Quran* vol. 1, 108.

24. MEMRI, January 8, 2002, lists some fifty-five different conspiracy versions published by leading Arab newspapers and TV and radio stations, including not only *Al Ahram, Al Akhbar,* and others published in the Arab world, but also the Arab press in London and Iranian papers such as the Tehran *Keyhan.*

25. *Al Akhbar,* Cairo, October 26, 2001.

26. *Al Ra'i,* Jordan, September 13, 2001 (quoted in MEMRI).

27. *Al Dustour,* Jordan, September 13, 2001 (quoted in MEMRI).

28. Warren Richey, "Muslim Opinion Sees Conspiracy," *Christian Science Monitor,* November 6, 2001; a fairly representative example of Arab academic reaction is the winter 2002 issue of the quarterly *Al Dimuqratiyah,* Cairo, with contributions by Gamal Zahran, Abdel Alim Mohamed, and others.

29. *Al Quds al Arabi,* London, February 9, 2002.

30. *Al Watan,* September 18 and 25, 2001 (Saudi Arabia).

31. In an interview with Yusri Foda broadcast by *Al Jazira*, September 11, 2002. See also *MEMRI*, September 13, 2002, "The Events of September 11 and the Arab Media," and Abdeljabber Adwan in *Daily Star* (Beirut), September 19, 2002.
32. *Al Ahram*, September 20, 2002.
33. Mick Hume, "The Anti-Imperialism of Fools," *New Statesman*, June 21, 2002.
34. Todd Gitlin, "The Rough Beast Returns," *Mother Jones*, June 17, 2002.
35. Naomi Klein quoted in Hume, "The Anti-Imperialism of Fools."

8. Anti-Americanism

1. Tom Friedman, *New York Times*, February 13, 2002.
2. See, for instance, "The U.S. Image Abroad," *Research Report 1998*, USIA Washington, Office of Research and Media Reaction.
3. Tom Friedman, *New York Times*, October 2, 2002.
4. An extensive survey of public opinion polls was provided by Karlyn Bowman, *American Public Opinion on the Terrorist Attacks* (Washington, D.C.: American Enterprise Institute, August 2002).
5. Bobby Fischer, *Die Welt*, January 29, 2002.
6. On October 11, 2001, at a meeting at MIT.
7. Susan Sontag's *obiter dicta* appeared first in *Frankfurter Allgemeine Zeitung* and *Le Monde* and subsequently in the *New Yorker*; Eric Foner in the *London Review of Books*, October 4, 2001. Sontag's modified version in *Frankfurter Allgemeine Zeitung*, November 11, 2001; Oliver Stone quoted by Jeffrey Wells, *Reel.Com*, October 10, 2001.
8. Quoted in Paul Hollander, *The Weekly Standard*, October 22, 2001.
9. Christopher Hitchens, "Against Rationalization," *Nation*, October 8, 2001. The debate between Hitchens and Chomsky went on for weeks. Hitchens was bitterly attacked by British left-wingers, for instance Scott Lucas, "The Dishonorable Policeman of the Left," *New Statesman*, May 27, 2002.
10. Michael Walzer, "Excusing Terror," *The American Prospect*, October 22, 2001. A manifesto of American political scientists and philosophers critical of European, especially German, pacifists who had denounced American reactions to the terrorists attacks hardly received any attention in the United States but a great deal in Germany, and the controversies continued for many months. Peter Schneider, *Der Spiegel*, August 26, 2002.
11. Stanley Kurtz, *Chronicle of Higher Education*, October 26, 2001.
12. Emily Eakin, *New York Times*, November 24, 2001.
13. On these meetings, see *Chronicle of Higher Education* during September and October 2001.
14. Ibid.
15. "Scholars of Islam Speak Out against Terrorism," *http://groups.colgate.edu/aarislam/response.htm*.
16. Ibid.
17. A daily collection of anti war articles can be found on the Web site *www.antiwar.com/viewpoints.html*.
18. Frances Trollope, *Domestic Manners of the Americans* (New York, 1949, originally published London, 1832). The fact that Mrs. Trollope went to America to improve the shaky finances of her family but failed may have had a certain impact on her writing. But the book made her a celebrity and generated a small fortune.

19. *Der Amerikamuede* (Frankfurt, 1855). Later the book was forgotten but rediscovered after World War II, and republished in 1982 and 1986.

20. *Profil*, Vienna, September 24, 2002.

21. Anti-American attitudes were frequent in the *Süddeutsche Zeitung* and *Der Stern* right from the beginning. *Der Spiegel* and *Frankfurter Allgemeine Zeitung* published both anti- and pro-American comments. A collection of interesting quotations from German academics, artists, and entertainers appeared in *Die Welt* October 19, 2001. On the Adrienne Goehler statement and similar pronouncements, see Henryk M. Broder, *Kein Krieg, nirgends* (Berlin, 2002), 27–42.

22. *Neues Deutschland*, September 13, 2001; *Interim*, November 1, 2001; *Interim* November 15, 2001; Flugblatt, "Bündnis gegen den Krieg"; Aufruf der Gruppe "organisierte Autonome"—all quoted in *Verfassungsschutzbericht 2001* (Berlin, 2002), 182–84.

23. Johannes J. G. Jansen, *The Dual Nature of Islamic Fundamentalism* (Ithaca, N.Y., 1997).

24. The text of the manifesto was published by *www.uni-muenster.de/ArabistikIslam*.

25. *London Review of Books*, October 4, 2001.

26. Quoted in the *London Times*, September 21, 2001.

27. Bryan Appleyard, "Why Do They Hate America?" *London Sunday Times*, September 22, 2001.

28. Ibid.

29. Anatole Kaletsky, "Our Pathological Need to Talk Up the Enemy," *London Times*, September 20, 2001.

30. Appleyard, "Why Do They Hate America?"

31. François Duday, *Le Point*, October 5, 2001.

32. *London Times*, December 21, 2001.

33. Her first article was published originally in the *Frankfurter Allgemeine Zeitung* on September 28, in the *Guardian*, September 29, 2001, also in *Le Monde*.

34. The second article ("Brutality Smeared in Peanut Butter") also appeared in the *Guardian* on October 23, 2001. In addition there were long interviews in the German weekly *Der Spiegel* and elsewhere. For an Indian assessment of Ms. Roy, see Amrit Dhillon, "Dam Hypocrite," *The Spectator*, April 20, 2002. For a critical assessment by a fellow ecologist see Ramachandra Guha, *The Hindu*, November 26, 2000. Another broadside against Ms. Roy appeared in *Outlook India* ("Roy Is Lying," Balbir K. Punj, May 27, 2002). Ms. Roy was again in trouble when it appeared that some of her comments on the troubles in Guajarat had been factually untrue (*Outlook India*, July 1, 2002).

35. While Ms. Roy was widely criticized in India, she was warmly welcomed by her supporters in New York. About a meeting in Cooper Union, Jordan Mejias, *Frankfurter Allgemeine Zeitung*, September 16, 2002.

36. *New York Times*, February 4, 2002. Rushdie's article was reprinted in several countries.

37. *London Times*, August 7, 2002.

38. *Le Monde*, November 1, 2001; on Baudrillard in New York, *Frankfurter Rundschau*, February 5, 2002.

39. Jacques Juillard, "Misère de l'anti-americanisme," *Liberation*, November 13, 2001. Jean François Revel, "Le terrorisme fauteur de pauvreté," *Le Point*, October 12, 2001, had appeared even earlier. Other notable answers to Baudrillard were those by Alain Minc also in *Le Monde*, and by Bernard Henri Levy in *Le Monde*, December 27, 2001, which

said that the real confrontation was between Islamists and the secular in the East and pacifists and humanists in the West. He thought the outcome of the war in Afghanistan was not only a defeat for fundamentalism but also of anti-Americanism; time had come to reflect upon the multiple impotence of Europe and the systematic blindness of some of its intellectuals. Quoted here from *Frankfurter Rundschau*, December 28, 2001. B. H. Levy on German anti-Americanism, *Der Spiegel* 49 (2001).

40. Quoted here from *Taz*, October 10, 2001.

41. Translation by Chris and Paola Newman, *fallaci.blodgspot.com*.

42. Umberto Eco, "La Guerra senza passione e ragione," *La Repubblica*, October 5, 2001.

43. *La Repubblica*, October 5, 2001; for another attack, see Laurent Joffrin ("un livre idiot"), in *Le Nouvel Observateur*, June 27, 2002. Joffrin argued that Fallaci's assertion that a "thought police" was at work in the West as far as radical Islam was concerned was quite untrue. But it is also true that suit was brought to prevent the publication of Fallaci's book in France and that so far (summer 2002) it has not found an English-language publisher.

44. Michael Naumann, *Die Zeit*, April 10, 2002.

45. Y. Trofimov and C. Fleming, *Wall Street Journal*, April 8, 2002. *The New Statesman* in London and *The Nation* published cartoons that were interpreted as being anti-Semitic.

46. These and other illustrations are quoted from "International Far Right Reactions to the Terrorist Attacks in the US," *Searchlight, www.searchlightmagazine.com*. See also Peter Beaumont, *Observer*, February 17, 2002, and *Le Monde*, February 18, 2002, about anti-Semitism in France.

47. Fatemah Farg, "Do We Hate Them?" *Al Ahram Weekly*, October 18, 2001.

48. What Amartya Sen wrote about antiglobalism ("Anti-Globalization Protests Are Not about Globalization") in *New Perspectives* 18, no. 4, is also correct to a large extent with regard to anti-Americanism.

49. Andre Glucksman, *Dostoievski a Manhattan* (Paris, 2002). Interview with Glucksman in *Der Spiegel* 21 (2002).

9. Battlefields of the Future 1

1. Vijai Nair, "The Nuclear Dimension of the War on Terrorism," in *AAKROSH (Asian Journal on Terrorism and Internal Conflicts)* (January 2002): 19ff.

2. *Jane's Intelligence Review* (January 1998): 34. See also "Pakistan, Sectarian Violence," published by an official Canadian source. *www.irb.ac.ca/research/publications/pak17_e.htm*, as well as *Modern Asian Studies* (July 1998): passim.

3. Pakistan: Madrassas, "Extremism and the Military," published by International Crisis Group *ICG Asia Report* no. 36 (July 29, 2002).

4. Abbas Rashid and Farida Shaheed, "Pakistan: Ethno-Politics and Contending Elites, Chronology of Riots," United Nations Report, Research Institute for Social Development, n.d. See also *Human Rights Watch World Report 1999*, "Pakistan," *www.hrw.org/worldreport/Asia-09.htm*; Ian Talbot, *Pakistan: A Modern History* (London, 1998).

5. *The Herald*, January 1998. *The Herald* is the leading monthly organ of the Dawn group of newspapers in Karachi.

6. B. Raman, *SAPRA INDIA*, "Musharraf, Bin Laden, and the Lashkar" and "Lashkar e Taiba: A Backgrounder," July 2, 2001.

7. *South Asia Intelligence Review* (SAIR), August 12, 2002.

8. Chetan Bhatt, *Hindu Nationalism* (Oxford, 2001), 50; Sobhag Mathur, *Hindu Revivalism and the Indian National Movement* (Jodhpur, 1996).

9. Stanley J. Tambiah, *Levelling Crowds* (Berkeley, 1996), 251.

10. Sudhir Kakar, "The Time of Kali," *Social Research* (fall 2001); also Sudhir Kakar, *The Color of Violence* (Chicago, 1996). On various explanations for intercommunal tensions, see Charles Tilly, "Contentious Conversation," *Social Research* (fall 1998).

11. Kakar, "The Time of Kali."

12. Ibid.

13. For the early days of the conflict, see Karan Singh, *Heir Apparent* (Oxford, 1982).

14. Sumantra Bose, *The Challenge in Kashmir* (New Delhi, 1997); S. Bose, "Kashmir," *Survival* (autumn 1999); Victoria Schofield, *Kashmir in Conflict* (London, 2000). Sumit Ganguly, *The Crisis in Kashmir* (Cambridge, 1997); Congressional Research Service, *Kashmir: Recent Developments and U.S. Concerns*, June 21, 2002, updated September 5, 2002.

15. Yogindar Sikand, "The Changing Course of the Kashmiri Struggle," *Muslim World* (April 2001).

16. *www.dawacenter.com/ijtiman/salafi-e.html.*

17. *Times of India*, December 14 and 15, 2001.

18. For regular reviews and analyses of terrorism on the subcontinent from an Indian point of view see *SAPRA INDIA* homepage and the weekly *SAIR* (*South Asia Intelligence Review*) — for instance, on terrorism in Assam and West Bengal, September 8, 2002.

19. The two Chechen wars have produced a great amount of literature. The most balanced Russian account as far as the general background is concerned is V. A Tyshkov, *Obshestvo v vooruzhonnom Konflikte* (Moscow, 2001). See also D. E. Furman, ed., *Chechnya I Rossiya*, Vypusk 3 (Moscow, 1999). A recent survey of the historical background is Vladimir Degoyev, *Bolshaya Igra na Kavkaze* (Moscow, 2001). Western accounts of the war are too numerous to be cited here, but Yo'av Karni, *Highlanders* (New York, 2000), deserves to be singled out, a journalist's account of visits to regions which few others ever visited. On the military aspects of the two Chechen wars see Olga Oliker, *Russia's Chechen Wars, 1994–2000* (RAND, 2000). Also of importance is *Central Asia and the Caucasus* published in Sweden and accessible on the Internet. The insurgents have their own Web sites; chechnyanews.com, however, hardly deals with Chechnyan affairs, and kavkaz.org is mainly Islamist propaganda.

20. Emil Pain, "The Second Chechen War," *Central Asia and the Caucasus* 4 (2000).

21. Tyshkov, *Obshestvo v vooruzhonnom Konflikte*, 479.

22. Ibid., 414.

23. *Neue Zürcher Zeitung*, English ed., January 15, 2002.

24. Igor Dobaev, "Islamic Radicalism in the North Caucasus," *Central Asia and the Caucasus* 6 (2000); Svante E. Cornell, "Conflicts in Northern Caucasus," *Central Asian Survey* 17, no. 3 (1998).

25. "Wahhabism," in *Severny Kavkaz* (February 2001).

26. Nadeshda Emelyanova, "Islam in the Northern Caucasus," *Central Asia and the Caucasus* (December 2001).

27. E. Fakhri and N. Ibrahimov, in *Baku Zerkalo*, February 27, 2002. On the origins of the Hizb ul Tahrir, see Suha Taji-Farouki, *A Fundamental Quest: Hizb al Tahrir and the Search for the Islamic Caliphate* (London, 1996).

28. "Central Asia's Islamic Threat," *Institute of War and Peace Reporting*, November 15, 2001; Ghonchei Tazmini, "The Islamic Revival in Central Asia," *Central Asian Survey* 20, no. 1 (2001). Uwe Halbach, *Zentralasien in Bedrängnis* (Berlin, 2001).

29. "Bukhara Shuns Radical Islam," *Institute for War and Peace Reporting* (IWPR), November 17, 2000. For general background see Barnett Rubin et al., eds., *Calming the Ferghana Valley* (Washington, D.C., 1999). For general background see also Roy Allison, ed., *Central Asian Security* (London, 2001).

30. Mohadin Mesbahi, "Tajikistan, Iran, and the International Politics of the Islamic Factor," *Central Asian Survey* 16, no. 2 (1997).

31. Iskandaer Mehman and Turat Akimov, "Incursions Part of Larger Picture," *IWPR* (August 18, 2000) *www.iwpr.net/index/pl?archive/*.

32. Ahmed Rashid, *Jihad* (New Haven, 2002), chap. 6.

33. Muzaffar Olimov, "Ob ethnopoliticheskoi i konfessionalnoi situatsii," *Tsentralnaya Aziya i Kavkas*, originally published in *Vostok* 2 (1994).

34. Quotations from "Sistema Islama," Bahodyr Musaev, "Religious Extremism Threatens Uzbeksitan," *Central Asia and the Caucasus* 5 (2000).

35. Ibid.

36. Rashid, *Jihad*, chap. 7.

37. Mehman and Akimov, "Incursions Part of Larger Picture."

38. Galina Bukkharbaeva, *IWPR*, May 19, 2000.

39. Edward Poletaev, *IWPR*, May 11, 2001.

10. Battlefields of the Future 2

1. *The Turner Diaries* was written by a physicist who used the pseudonym Andrew MacDonald (Hillsboro, W.Va., 1980).

2. Tore Bjorgo, ed., *Terror from the Extreme Right* (London, 1995); Jeffrey Kaplan and Leonard Weinberg, *The Emergence of a Euro-American Radical Right* (New Brunswick, N.J., 1998); Robert Antonio, "After Postmodernism: Reactionary Tribalism," *American Journal of Sociology* 106 (2000): 1.

3. *Verfassungsschutzbericht* for 1999, 2000, and 2001 (Berlin, 2000, 2001, 2002). Regional reports are published by the various Läender of the German republic.

4. David Michaels, "Neo-Nazi Terrorism," *Jewish Community Security Group* (London: April 21, 2000).

5. But see, for instance, Johannes and Germana von Dohnanyi, *Schmutzige Geschäfte und heiliger Krieg* (Zurich, 2002).

6. George Kasimeris, *Europe's Last Red Terrorists: The Revolutionary Organization 17 November* (London, 2001).

7. Edmondo Berselli, "Perche uccidonono le colombe," *L'Espresso*, March 22, 2002.

8. "Caserta 24/Il testo di rivendicazione delle Brigate Rosse," *Dagospia.com*, March 21, 2002.

9. The Algerian Trotskyite party (Parti des Travailleurs) opposes terrorism but does not support the government in its struggle against the armed gangs. It opposed the military operations against bin Laden and was accused by other groups of the extreme left of collaboration with "fascist Islamism."

10. Louisa Hanoune and Ghania Mouffok, *Une autre voix pour l'Algerie* (Paris, 1996), quoted here from the German translation *Terroristen fallen nicht vom Himmel* (Zurich, 1997), 18. On life under the threat of Islamist terrorism, see the novels of Latifa ben Mansour and by the same author, *Frères Musulmans, frères feroces: Voyage dans l'enfer du discours islamiste* (Paris, 2002).

11. Said Zahraoui, *Entre l'horreur et l'espoir* (Paris, 2000), 162.

12. Frantz Fanon, *The Wretched of the Earth* (Harmondsworth, U.K., 1967), 73; David Macey, *Frantz Fanon* (New York, 2001).

13. The return of the Afghans is described in a series of articles in the London newspaper *Al Hayat,* the first of which appeared on November 23, 1999.

14. An extensive bibliography of books and articles on the subject has been published at Cornell University, and can be found under *www.library.cornell.edu.*

15. Severine Labat, *Les Islamistes algeriens* (Paris, 1995). *Courrier International,* January 11, 1996; *Nouvel Observateur,* August 31, 1995; *Liberation,* January 13, 1996.

16. "The Civil Concord: A Peace Initiative Wasted," July 9, 2001. Brussels, 2001.

17. Hamida Layachi, "Banditisme et islamisme arme vont aujourd'hui de pair in Algerie," *Le Monde,* June 16, 2000; Quintan Viktorowicz, "Centrifugal Tendencies," *Arab Studies Quarterly* (July 2001); Michael Humphrey, "Violence, Voice and Identity in Algeria," *Arab Studies Quarterly* (winter 2000).

18. An estimate by Interpol. Jiri Dienstbier in *Die Welt,* April 3, 2002.

19. Thomas M. McKenna, *Muslim Rulers and Rebels: Everyday Politics and Armed Resistance in the Southern Philippines* (Berkeley, 1998); T. J. S. George, *Revolt in Mindanao* (Kuala Lumpur, 1980); Cesar A. Majul, *The Contemporary Muslim Movement in the Philippines* (Berkeley, 1985).

20. Sean L. Yom, "Abu Sayaf," CSIS, "Briefing Notes" (Washington, D.C., n.d.). "Abu Sayaf's Link," *Asiaweek,* January 25, 1999.

21. Roman D. Ortiz, "Insurgent Strategies in the Post-Cold War: The Case of the Revolutionary Armed Forces of Colombia," *Studies in Conflict and Terrorism* 25 (2002).

22. Maurice Lemoine, "La Bataille de sud Bolivar," *Le Monde Diplomatique* (October 2001).

23. Rafael Pardo, "Colombia's Two-Front War," *Foreign Affairs* (July 2000).

24. Steve Macko, "Colombia the World Leader in Kidnapping," ERRI Daily Intelligence Report, December 8, 1997; Steve Macko, "Kidnapping a Latin American Growth Industry," *ENN Daily Intelligence,* April 30, 1997.

25. *Armed Conflicts Report 2001: Project Ploughshares,* Institute of Peace and Conflict Studies (Waterloo, Ontario, Canada). "Profiles of Colombian Rebel Groups," ERRI Special Report, January 9, 2002.

26. Albert Garrido, ed., *Guerrilla y el Plan Colombia* (Caracas, 2001).

27. FARC, "The Illegality of Legal Opposition in Colombia." This and many other FARC communiques were published on the FARC Web site *www.farc-ep.org/pagina_ingles.*

28. About the Bellavista massacre, *Washington Post,* May 9, 2002. About the killing of ELN militants, *Frankfurter Allgemeine Zeitung,* May 6, 2002. See also "La guerre secrete," *Le Point,* May 3, 2002.

29. Julia E. Sweig, "What Kind of War for Colombia?" *Foreign Affairs* (August 2002).

30. Gamal Nkrumah, "Crossing Swords with the Shariah," *Al Ahram Weekly,* August 29, 2002.

31. Paul Marshall, *The Talibanization of Nigeria: Sharia Law and Religious Freedom* (New York, 2002).

32. Richard W. Baker, ed., *Indonesia* (Singapore, 1991); Geoff Forester, ed., *Post-Soeharto Indonesia* (Singapore, 1999).

33. "Al Qaeda in South East Asia: The Case of the 'Ngruki Network' in Indonesia," *International Crisis Group,* Brussels, August 8, 2002, *www.crisisweb.org.*

Conclusion: War against the West

1. For a discussion of the Kepel thesis, see Malcolm Yapp, *Times Literary Supplement*, June 28, 2002; Malise Ruthven, *Prospect* (July 2002); Walter Laqueur, *Atlantic Monthly* (March 2002).

2. For some illustrations concerning Northern Europe, see Bruce Bawer, "Tolerating Intolerance," *Partisan Review* (July 2002).

3. Both Mawdoodi and Qutb were published in Russian in the early 1990s. Al Maududi, *Osnovy Islama* (Moscow, 1993), and S. Qutb, *Budushshe prinadlezhit islamu* (Moscow, 1993), as well as other books by these two authors.

4. Alexei Malashenko and Magomedov quoted by Nabi Abdullaev, *St. Petersburg Times*, June 7, 2002; Igor Rotar, "Under the Green Banner: Islamic Radicals in Russia and the Former Soviet Union," *Religion, State and Society* (June 2002).

5. Olivier Roy, *The Failure of Political Islam* (Cambridge, Mass., 1994); Olivier Roy, *L'Islam mondialisé* (Paris, 2002); Gilles Kepel, *Jihad* (Cambridge, Mass., 2002).

6. Amartya Sen in *American Prospect* (January 2002).

7. Joseph E. Stiglitz, *Globalization and Its Discontents* (New York, 2002).

8. According to the annual (2002) report of the German Office for the Protection of the Constitution (*Verfassungsschutzbericht*) and many other sources.

9. David Graeber, "The New Anarchists," *New Left Review* (January 2002).

10. Georges Katsiaficas, *European Autonomous Movements* (Boston, 1997).

11. Barbara Epstein, "Anarchism and the Anti-Globalist Movement," *Monthly Review* (September 2001).

12. Ibid.

13. On the Tute Bianche, see *www.tutebianche.org*, and Danio Azzelini, Telepolis, n.d.; on the German Autonomen "Geronimo," *Feuer und Flamme* and *Schutt und Asche* (n.p., 2001).

14. Amin al Houli, ed., *Al arab va al aulama* (Beirut, 1997). Mustafa al Nahar, *Did al aulama* (Cairo, 1999). For a short summary of the discussion, see Amr Hamazawi, "Die Angst vor den kulturellen Folgen," in *Weltlage*, ed. Felicitas von Aretin and Bernd Wannemacher (Opladen, 2002).

15. Ali Harb, *Hadith an nihayat* (Casablanca, 2000); "Globalization and the Arab World," *Arab Studies Quarterly* (summer 1999).

16. Jamal Amin, *Al Aulama* (Beirut, 1999).

17. For lists of links on the activities of the movement, see, among many others, *www.leftbankbooks.com/~matthew*, the Web site of the Centre for Research on Globalization (*www.globalresearch.ca*) as well as *www.destroyimf.org* and others.

18. *The Internationalist* (summer 2001): 28. The Algerian P.T. belongs to the Trotskyite group known in France as the Lambertists.

19. Quoted in Peter Taafe, *The Socialist* (September 29, 2001), organ of CWI (Committee for a Workers International).

20. Ibid.

21. For an SWP analysis of radical Islamic fundamentalism and terrorism, see Chris Harman, *The Prophet and the Proletariat*, 5th ed. (London, 2002).

22. *www.cpgb.org.uk*, quoted in Joseph Green, "The Socialist Debate on the Taliban," *www.Communist.voice.org*.

23. For instance, Frederic Jameson, "Globalization and Political Strategy," *New Left Review* (July–August 2000).

24. Among the biographies John Lee Anderson, *Che Guevara: A Revolutionary Life* (London, 1997), should be singled out.

25. Homi K. Bhabha, "Remembering Fanon," in *Colonial Discourse and Postcolonial Theory*, ed. P. Williams and L. Christman (New York, 1994).

26. Gary Benoit, "Globalism's Growing Grasp," in *New American* (February 2000).

27. The hero decides to kill mixed couples in order to trigger a racial war. On Pierce and the National Alliance, see Martin Durham, "From Imperium to Internet," *Patterns of Prejudice* (July 2002): 50–61. The number of hate groups on the extreme right is legion. A *Hate Directory* of such groups (and games) compiled by Raymond A. Franklin is available in PDF on the Internet and in hard copy: *www.bcpl.net/~frankli/hatedir.htm*.

28. "A Virtual Guided Tour of Far Right Anti-Globalist Ideology," Part II, Tyranny. *www.maxwell.syr.edu*.

29. Some illustrations are given by Franklin Foer, "Home Bound," *New Republic*, July 22, 2002.

30. "Third Position Fascism" and "Right Woos Left," published by The Public Eye, *www.publiceye.edu*.

31. Oliver Tolmein, *Vom deutschen Herbst zum 11. September* (Hamburg, 2002), 35–46.

32. Chip Berlet, *Right Wing Populism in America: Too Close for Comfort* (New York, 2000), chap. 16.

33. Kevin Coogan quoted in Michael Reynolds, "Virtual Reich," *www.vanguardnetwork* *.com/index181.htm*. Coogan is the author of an important study of a forerunner of the third position, Francis Parker Yockey (2000). I am particularly grateful for the help extended by him and by Dr. Jeffrey M. Beale, who have done pioneering work in the field of Western European national revolutionary groupuscules.

34. Markus Mathyl, "The National Bolshevik Party and Arctogaia," *Patterns of Prejudice* (July 2002): 75.

35. *The Turner Diaries* sold more than 350,000 copies up to 1999, even though it was not advertised or reviewed in the media. Pierce's other book (*The Hunter*) sold more than 500,000. If correct, this is considerably more than the circulation of the best-selling authors of the far left such as Noam Chomsky.

36. Quoted in Anton Maegerle and Heribert Schiedel, "Krude Allianz," *www.doew.at/ thema/rechts/allianz.html*.

37. Roger Griffin, "The Primacy of Culture," *Journal of Contemporary History* 1 (2002); Jeffrey M. Bale, "National Revolutionary Groupuscules and the Resurgence of Left-Wing Fascism," *Patterns of Prejudice* 3 (2002).

38. The French organization S.O.S. Enfants d'Iraq was headed by Le Pen's wife.

39. A great many declarations of this kind can be found in Maegerle, quoted above.

40. Paragraph 200–208 of the manifesto of the Unabomber (accessible on the Internet).

41. *Neue Zürcher Zeitung*, June 2, 2002; for a review of Iranian terrorist operations in other countries, see Shaul Shay, *Terror beshlikhut haimam* (Herzliya, 2001).

42. *Al Sharq al Awsat*, London, June 8 and 9, 2002; *Al Hayat*, London, June 7, 2002, quoted in MEMRI, Special Dispatch 387, June 11, 2002.

43. In Frank Cilluffo, evidence before the U.S. House of Representatives Justice Committee, Subcommittee on Crime, December 13, 2000.

44. *South Asia Intelligence Review* 7 (2002).

45. Among the many studies in this field only a few can be mentioned. Jessica Stern, *The Ultimate Terrorists* (Cambridge, Mass., 1999); Ron Purver, *Chemical and Biological Terrorism*,

Canadian Security Intelligence Service, June 1995; Joshua Lederberg, *Biological Weapons* (Cambridge, Mass., 1999); Jonathan B. Tucker, ed., *Assessing Terrorist Use of Chemical and Biological Weapons* (Cambridge, Mass., 2000); Office of Technology Assessment, *Proliferation of the Weapons of Mass Destruction: Assessing the Risks*, U.S. Government (Washington, D.C., 1993).

46. These figures are based on estimates published by the Agency of Homeland Defense (2002).

47. For a discussion of the writings of Heinzen and Most, see Walter Laqueur, *Terrorism* (New York, 1977), 28–32, 56–62.

48. Brian Stableford, "Man-Made Catastrophes," in *End of World*, ed. Eric Rabkin et al. (Carbondale, Ill., 1983).

49. Based on a three-year study by Gabriel Weimann and Yariv Tsfati of the University of Haifa, Communications Department. Links to many Web sites sponsored by terrorist organizations can be found on *www.bombsecurity.com/extremist.html.*

50. Yariv Tsfati and Gabriel Weimann, *Terror on the Internet*, 2002: 9. This paper was subsequently published in *Terrorism and Political Violence* (September 2002). Many, probably most, neo-Nazi Web sites were also located in the United States and could therefore not be taken to court by European governments.

51. To give but one example, as these lines are written, on July 5, 2002, a terrorist group killed thirty civilians and wounded more in a market town near Algiers. On July 13 an Islamist terrorist group killed twenty-seven Hindu ragpickers, including women and children, in a Jammu slum. The incidents were not shown on television outside Algeria and India, and leading world newspapers reported the news in a few sentences.

52. "The Man Who Rocked the Earth," quoted in David Dowling, *Fictions of Nuclear Disaster* (Iowa City, 1987), chap. 2: "The Mad Scientist and Armageddon."

53. John Campbell Jr., *The Atomic Story* (New York, 1991), 24.

54. David Albright et al., "bin Laden and the Bomb," *Bulletin of the Atomic Scientists* (January 2002).

55. See, for instance, Alistair Munro, *Delusional Disorder: Paranoia and Related Diseases* (Cambridge, 1999).

56. "Esa al Kanadi," *The Secret World* (Maktabah al Ansaar, n.d.), is a typical product of the Islamic school of conspiratology.

57. Harold Evans, *London Times*, June 28, 2002.

58. For a representative selection, see Robert Anton Wilson, *Everything Is under Control: Conspiracies, Cults and Cover-Ups* (San Francisco, 1998), or the Web site of Conspiracy Nation. See also Jeffrey M. Bale, "The Cult Wars," part 1 and 2, *Hit List*, vols. 2, 4, and 5.

59. *Al Ahram Weekly*, July 11, 2002.

Appendix: Toward a Definition, or Humpty Dumpty and the Problem of Terrorism

1. Omar Malik, *Enough of the Definition of Terrorism* (Washington, D.C., 2001).

2. An analysis of the terms used by American and British journalists operating in the Middle East shows that "militant" and "activist" are the most popular expressions used to evade the term "terrorist," but "fighter," "extremist," "resistant," "commando," "raider," "combatant," "urban guerrilla," and "martyr" are also frequently used, whereas "partisan" is now antiquated. "Gunman" is frequently used. According to many journalists and editors, a militant or an activist may commit a terrorist act, but this does not make him a terrorist;

the use of the adjective is sometimes permitted. So is the term "suicide bomber." Quite often, a hostage taken by terrorists is not killed or murdered (which would be a loaded term) but executed. (To "remove" him or her would be even more neutral.)

These terminological rules do not apply to other parts of the world — for instance, Kashmir, the Philippines, or even Europe. British newspapers will not usually refer to Irish groups engaging in terrorism as activists, and American media have not called the attackers of September 11, 2001, "militants." Sometimes they are, however, called "alleged terrorists." In Britain, some liberal newspapers use the terms "terrorism" and "terrorists" but often in quotation marks; however, if governments are accused of terrorism, the quotation marks are dropped. Circumlocution is more frequently used by news agencies and daily newspapers than by periodicals. Left-wing media have no hesitation to use the term "terrorism" if the perpetrators are neofascists or neo-Nazis. Moreover, the linguistic confusion is not limited to the media; the difference between what the authorities call a "hate crime" and what others call "terrorism" is not always readily obvious.

3. This is quoted here from the recruiting tape of Osama bin Laden. Fawaz A. Gerges, "Eavesdropping on Osama bin Laden," *Columbia International Affairs* online (August 2002), *www.ciaonet.org.*

4. Lewis Carroll, *Through the Looking Glass.*

5. *South Asia Intelligence Review,* August 19, 2002. The number of politicians killed between 1990 and 2002 was 411.

Bibliography

Much of the current literature on terrorism is available on the Internet. Some of the best links can be found through the following organizations and on the following Web sites:

Terrorismlibrary.com. See also *Mipt.org* (Oklahoma City National Memorial Institute for Prevention of Terror).

University of Michigan Document Center: America's war against terrorism. This is probably the most extensive list of links available concerning 9/11 and the background.

The University of Pennsylvania Library (Penn Reads about Conflict and Terrorism).

Useful links about Islamism can be found on a French-language Web site, *www.agora.qc.ca.* In English: Yahoo Directory Islam Jihad.

An excellent collection of antiwar and anti-antiterrorist articles is *www.antiwar.com/viewpoints.html;* on Islamism and Islamic terrorism *khilafah.com;* and other links offered in *kavkaz.com.*

ICT, Institute of Counter Terrorism, Herzliya, Israel, presents documents and analytical articles about terrorism in the Middle East and elsewhere.

Terrorism Research Center Links: *www.islam-online.*

On cults of every kind: *www.cultinformation.org.uk/articlel_printable.html.*

Works of Reference

Ahmed, Moussali. *Historical Dictionary of Islamic Fundamentalism.* Lanham, Md., 1999.

Anderson, Sam, and Stephan Sloan. *Historical Dictionary of Terrorism.* Metuchen, N.J., 1995.

Annual Patterns of Global Terrorism. U.S. Department of State.

Atkins, Stephen E. *Terrorism: A Reference Handbook.* Denver, 1992.

Beckett, Ian. *Encyclopedia of Guerrilla Warfare.* Santa Barbara, Calif., 1997.

Crenshaw, Martha, and John Pimlott, ed. *Encyclopedia of World Terrorism.* 3 vols. Armonk, N.Y., 1998.

Lakos, Amos. *Terrorism 1980–90: A Bibliography.* Boulder, Colo., 1991.

Bibliographies

All the following are available on the Internet:

Annotated Bibliography of Government Documents Related to the Threat of Terrorism and the Attack of September 11, 2001. Oklahoma Department of Libraries.

Bibliography of Terrorism and Conflict in South Asia.

Chemical, Biological and Nuclear Terrorism. Dudley Kent Library.

Homeland Defense and Domestic Terrorism. Naval War College.

Insurgencies, Terrorist Groups and Indigenous Movements: An Annotated Bibliography. Foreign
    Military Studies Office.
Islam Jihad — Yahoo Directory .
The September 11 Sourcebooks. National Security Archive.
Terrorism: A Bibliography of Selected Rand Publications 1980–2001.
Terrorism and Insurgent Organizations. Air University Library.
Terrorism and Political Violence: An International Bibliography.
Terrorism Bibliography (FEMA).

Journals

Terrorism and Political Violence.
Studies in Conflict and Terrorism.

Books

The literature about various aspects of terrorism has developed exponentially during the
last two years. The following list includes some of the more important works.

Abanes, Richard. American Militias. Downers Grove, Ill., 1996.
Abd-allah, Umar. The Islamic Struggle in Syria. Berkeley, 1983.
Abdo, Geneive. No God but God. New York, 2000.
Adams, James. The Financing of Terror. New York, 1986.
Adamson, Kay. Algeria: A Study in Competing Ideologies. London, 1998.
Adinolfi, Gabriele, et al. Noi, terza posizione. Rome, 2000.
Agnivesh, Swami, et al. Harvest of Hate; Guajarat under Siege. New Delhi, 2002.
Agronomov, A. I. Jihad, svyashennaya voina mukhammedan. Moscow, 2002.
Anderson, Walter, et al. The Brotherhood in Saffron. Boulder, Colo., 1987.
Anti-Defamation League. Extremism on the Right: A Handbook. New York, 1988.
Appleby, Scott. Spokesmen for the Despised. Chicago, 1997.
Arjomand, Said. The Turban for the Crown. New York, 1988.
Arquilla, John. Networks and Netwars. Santa Monica, Calif., 2001.
Ashmaoui, Mohamed Said al. Al islam al siyasi. Cairo, 1987.
Asprey, Robert B. War in the Shadows. New York, 1975.
AUNAR. Subversion: La historia olvidada. Buenos Aires, 1999.
Aust, Stefan. The Baader-Meinhof Group. London, 1987.
Axell, Albert, and Hideaki Kase. Kamikaze. Harlow, U.K., 2002.
Backes, Uwe. Bleierne Jahre. Erlangen, 1991.
Bale, Jeffrey. The Secret Cold War and European Right-Wing Terrorism. forthcoming.
Barkun, Michael. Millennialism and Violence. London, 2002.
———. Religion and the Racist Right. Chapel Hill, N.C., 1997.
Bauer, Alain, and Xavier Raufer. La guerre ne fait que commencer. Paris, 2002.
Beam, Louis. Leaderless Resistance. n.p., n.d.
Begin, Menahem. The Revolt. Jerusalem, 1977.
Bell, J. Bowyer. The IRA, 1968–2000. London, 2002.
———. Terror Out of Zion. New York, 1977.
Benjamin, David, and Steven Simon. The Age of Sacred Terror. New York, 2002.
Bennett, John M., et al. Sendero Luminoso in Context. New York, 1998.
Bergen, Peter. Holy War Inc. New York, 2001.

Bergqvist, Charles, et al. *Violence in Colombia 1990–2000*. Wilmington, Del., 2001.
Bjorgo, Tore. *Terror from the Extreme Right*. London, 1995.
Bonavena, Pablo, et al. *Origines e desarrollo de la guerra civil en Argentina*. Buenos Aires, 1998.
Bose, Sumantra. *The Challenge in Kashmir*. New Delhi, 1997.
Boyer, Paul. *When Time Shall Be No More*. Cambridge, Mass., 1992.
Brackett, D. W. *Holy Terror: Armageddon in Tokyo*. New York, 1996.
Burgat, François. *L'Islamisme en face*. Paris, 2001.
Chubin, Sharam. *Whither Iran?* London, 2002.
Ciment, James. *Algeria: The Fundamentalist Challenge*. New York, 1997.
Cirincione, Josef, et al. *Deadly Arsenals*. Washington, D.C., 2002.
Clark, Robert. *The Basque Insurgents ETA*. Madison, Wisc., 1984.
Clarke, Thurston. *By Blood and Fire*. New York, 1981.
Cobban, Helena. *Palestinian Liberation Organization*. New York, 2002.
Coogan, Kevin. *Dreamer of the Day*. New York, 1999.
Corcoran, James. *Bitter Harvest*. New York, 1995.
Cordesman, Anthony. *Terrorism, Asymmetric Warfare and Weapons of Mass Destruction*. New York, 2001.
Crenshaw, Martha., ed. *Terrorism in Context*. New York, 1995.
Cubert, Harold. *The PFLP's Changing Role in the Middle East*. London, 1997.
Curcio, Renato. *Mit offenem Blick*. Berlin, 1997.
Dartnell, Michael Y. *Action Directe*. London, 1995.
Dees, Morris, with James Corcoran. *Gathering Storm: America's Militia Threat*. New York, 1996.
Dobson, Christopher. *Black September*. London, 1975.
Drake, Richard. *The Aldo Moro Murder Case*. Cambridge, Mass., 1995.
Ehrenfeld, Rachel. *Narco-Terrorism*. New York, 1990.
Eickelman, D. F., and James Piscatori. *Muslim Politics*. Princeton, 1996.
Emerson, Steven. *American Jihad*. New York, 2002.
Enroth, Ronald. *Youth Brainwashing*. Grand Rapids, 1977.
Esposito, John. *Iran at the Crossroads*. New York, 2001.
———. *The Islamic Threat: Myth or Reality?* New York, 1999.
———. *Political Islam*. Boulder, Colo., 1997.
———. *Unholy War: Terror in the Name of Islam*. New York, 2002.
Evola, Julius. *Revolt against the Modern World*. Rochester, Vt., 1995.
Falkenrath, Richard, et al. *America's Achilles' Heel*. Cambridge, Mass., 1998.
Firestone, Reuven. *Jihad: The Origins of Holy War in Islam*. New York, 1999.
Fischer, Thomas. *Politische Gewalt in Latein Amerika*. Frankfurt, 2000.
Flynn, Kevin, and Gary Gerhard. *The Silent Brotherhood*. New York, 1995.
Frank, Hans, and Kai Hirschmann, ed. *Die weltweite Gefahr*. Berlin, 2002.
Fregosi, Paul. *Jihad in the West*. New York, 1998.
Fuller, Graham. *Algeria*. Santa Monica, Calif., 1996.
Fuller, Graham, et al. *A Sense of Siege*. Boulder, Colo., 1995.
Galvis, Constanza. *The Heart of the War*. London, 2000.
Ganguly, Sumit. *The Crisis in Kashmir*. Cambridge, 1997.
Geraghty, Tony. *The Irish War*. Baltimore, 2000.
Gerges, F. A. *America and Political Islam*. New York, 1999.

Ghosh, Parta. *BJP and the Evolution of Hindu Nationalism.* New Delhi, 1999.

Ginat, Joseph. *The Palestinian Refugees.* Norman, Okla., 2001.

Goren, Roberta. *The Soviet Union and Terrorism.* London, 1984.

Gorenberg, Gershom. *The End of Days.* New York, 1999.

Hammuda, Adel. *Qanabil vamasahif.* Cairo, 1989.

Hanoune, Louisa. *Une autre voix pour l'Algerie.* Paris, 1996.

Hart, Alan. *Arafat: A Political Biography.* London, 1994.

Hasan, Mushirul. *Legacy of a Divided Nation: India's Muslims since Independence.* London, 1997.

Hatina, Meir. *Islam and Salvation in Palestine: The Islamic Jihad Movement.* Tel Aviv, 2001.

Heehs, Peter. *Nationalism, Terrorism, Communalism: Essays in Modern Indian History.* New Delhi, 1998.

Heller, Joseph. *The Stern Gang.* London, 1995.

Henze, Paul. *The Plot to Kill the Pope.* New York, 1983.

Hettige, Siripala T., et al. *Sri Lanka at Crossroads.* New Delhi, 2000.

Heyman, Philip. *Terrorism and America.* Cambridge, Mass., 1998.

Hoekmann, Gerrit. *Zwischen Ölzweig und Kalaschnikow: Geschichte und Politik der paläestinensischen Linken.* Munster, 1996.

Hoffman, Bruce. *Inside Terrorism.* New York, 1998.

Hoge, James, ed. *How Did This Happen.* New York, 2001.

Hole, Guenther. *Fanatismus.* Freiburg, 1995.

Hoole, Rajan, et al. *The Broken Palmyra.* Claremont, Calif., 1990.

Horenberg, Gershom. *The End of Days.* New York, 2000.

Horgan, John, and Max Taylor. *The Psychology of Terrorism.* London, 2002.

Hroub, Kemal. *Hamas.* New York, 2000.

Huntington, Samuel P. *The Clash of Civilizations.* New York, 1996.

Jaber, Hala. *Hezbollah: Born with a Vengeance.* New York, 1997.

Jansen, Johannes J. G. *The Dual Nature of Islamic Fundamentalism.* Ithaca, N.Y., 1997.

———. *Militant Islam.* New York, 1980.

———. *The Neglected Duty.* New York, 1986.

Jenkins, Brian. *The Likelihood of Nuclear Terrorism.* Santa Monica, 1985.

Johnson, James Turner. *The Holy War Idea in Islam.* University Park, Pa., 1997.

Juergensmeyer, Mark. *The New Cold War?* Berkeley, Calif., 1994.

———. *Terror in the Mind of God.* Berkeley, Calif., 2000.

Kaltenbach, Jeanna-Helene, et al. *La republique et l'Islam.* Paris, 2002.

Kaplan, David, and Andrew Marshall. *The Cult at the End of the World.* London, 1995.

Kaplan, Jeffrey. *Millennial Violence.* London, 2002.

———, and Leonard Weinberg. *The Emergence of a Euro-American Radical Right.* New Brunswick, N.J., 1998.

Kaplan, Robert D. *Eastward to Tartary.* New York, 2000.

Karan, Vijaya. *War by Stealth; Terrorism in India.* New Delhi, 1997.

Karni, Yo'av. *The Highlanders.* New York, 1999.

Kelsay, John. *Islam and War.* Louisville, Ky., 1993.

Kepel, Gilles. *Jihad.* Cambridge, Mass., 2002.

———. *Le prophete et pharaon.* Paris, 1984.

———. *The Revenge of God.* New York, 1995.

Kohlhammer, Siegfried. *Die Feinde und die Freunde des Islam.* Göttingen, 1996.

Kramer, Martin. *Arab Awakening and Islamic Revival.* New Brunswick, N.J., 1996.
———. *Hezbollah's Vision of the West.* Washington, D.C., 1989.
———. *Ivory Towers Built on Sand.* Washington, D.C., 2001.
Kumar, Amrita, et al. *Lest We Forget.* New Delhi, 2002.
Kupperman, Robert, and Darrel Trent. *Terrorism, Threat, Reality, Response.* Stanford, Calif., 1979.
Laqueur, Walter. *The History of Terrorism.* New ed. New Brunswick, N.J., 2001.
———. *The New Terrorism: Fanaticism and the Arms of Mass Destruction.* New York, 1999.
Lederberg, Joshua. *Biological Weapons.* Cambridge, Mass., 1999.
Lesser, Ian. *Countering the New Terrorism.* Santa Monica, Calif., 1999.
Lewis, Bernard. *Islam and the West.* New York, 1993.
———. *What Went Wrong.* New York, 2002.
Lewis, Philip. *Islamic Britain.* London, 1994.
Lia, Brynjar, et al. *Globalization and the Future of Terrorism.* London, 2002.
Lifton, Robert J. *Destroying the World to Save It: Aum Shinrikyo.* New York, 2000.
Linz, Juan. *Conflicto en Euzkadi.* Madrid, 1986.
L'Islam en France et en Allemagne. *Identités et citoyennetés.* La Documentation Française. Paris, 2001.
Litvinov, N. D. *Terroristicheskie Organizatsii.* Moscow, 1999.
MacDonald, Andrew. *Hunter.* Hillsboro, W.Va., 1989.
———. *The Turner Diaries.* Arlington, 1985.
Malik, Omar. *Enough of the Definition of Terrorism.* Washington, D.C., 2001.
Manikkalingam, Ram. *Tigerism and Other Essays.* Colombo, 1995.
Mansour, Latifa ben. *Frères Musulmans, frères feroces: Voyage dans l'enfer du discours islamiste.* Paris, 2002.
Martinez, Luis. *The Algerian Civil War.* New York, 2000.
Marty, Martin, and Scott Appleby. *Fundamentalism and the State.* Chicago, 1993.
Marwa, Ved. *Uncivil Wars: Pathology of Terrorism in India.* New Delhi, 1999.
Menashri, David. *Post-Revolutionary Politics in Iran.* London, 2001.
Michel, Lou, et al. *American Terrorist: Timothy McVeigh.* New York, 2001.
Mikolus, Edward, et al. *International Terrorism in the 1980s.* Ames, Iowa, 1989.
Mishal, Shaul, et al. *The Palestinian Hamas.* New York, 2000.
Mitchell, Richard P. *The Society of the Muslim Brothers.* London, 1969.
Moretti, Mario. *Brigate Rosse.* Berlin, 2000.
Morris, Benny. *Righteous Victims.* New York, 1999.
Moyano, Maria. *Argentina's Lost Patrol.* New Haven, 1995.
Mubarak, Hisham. *Il irhabiyun qadimoun.* Cairo, 1995.
Munro, Alastair. *Delusional Disorder: Paranoia and Related Diseases.* Cambridge, 1999.
Murakami, Haruki. *Underground: The Tokyo Gas Attack.* London, 2000.
Mylroie, Laurie. *Study of Revenge.* Washington, D.C., 2000.
Niehoff, Debra. *The Biology of Violence.* New York, 1999.
Norval, Morgan. *Triumph of Disorder: Islamic Fundamentalism.* Indian Wells, Calif., 2001.
O'Balance, Edgar. *Islamic Fundamentalist Terrorism, 1979–1995.* New York, 1997.
———. *Kurdish Struggle.* London, 1995.
Palmer, David Scott, ed. *Shining Path of Peru.* New York, 1994.
Pena, Manuelo Vicente. *La paz de las FARC.* Bogotá, 1997.
Peters, Rudolf. *Islam and Colonialism.* The Hague, 1979.

Petrichev, Viktor. *Zametki o terrorizme.* Moscow, 2001.

Politkovskaya, Anna. *A Dirty War.* London, 2001.

Popov, Pavel. *Politicheski terrorizm v Rossii.* Moscow, 2000.

Post, Jerrold, ed. *Studies in the Jihad against the Tyrants.* London, 2002.

Pillar, Paul R. *Terrorism and U.S. Foreign Policy.* Washington, D.C., 2001.

Pipes, Daniel. *Conspiracy.* New York, 1997.

Praza, Michel. *Fanatiques: Histoire de l'armee rouge japonaise.* Paris, 2001.

Pujadas, David, and Ahmed Salam. *La tentation du Jihad.* Paris, 1995.

Puri, Harish. *Terrorism in Punjab.* New Delhi, 1999.

Quandt, William. *Between Ballots and Bullets: Algeria's Transition.* London, 1998.

Qutb, Sayed. *Ma'alim fi al tariq.* Legal edition. Cairo, 1989.

———. *In the Shade of the Quran.* Nairobi, Kenya, n.d.

Rabasa, Angel, et al. *Colombian Labyrinth.* Santa Monica, Calif., 2001.

Rabert, Bernhard. *Links und Rechts.* Bonn, 1995.

Ramadan, Abdulaziz. *Jama'at al taqfir fi misr.* Cairo, 1995.

Ramazani, Rouhollah K. *Revolutionary Iran.* Baltimore, 1996.

Ranstorp, Magnus. *Hizballah in Lebanon.* London, 1997.

Rashid, Ahmed. *Jihad: The Rise of Militant Islam in Central Asia.* New Haven, 2002.

———. *Taliban.* New Haven, 2000.

Reeve, Simon. *The New Jackals.* New York, 2000.

Reich, Walter, ed. *Origins of Terrorism.* Cambridge, Mass., 1990.

Reinders, Ralf, et al. *Die Bewegung 2. Juni.* Berlin, 1997.

Reuter, Christoph. *Mein Leben ist eine Waffe.* Munich, 2002.

Rich, Paul, and Thomas Mockaitis. *Terrorism and Grand Strategy.* London, 2002.

Ritter, Scott. *Endgame: Solving the Iraqi Problem.* New York, 1999.

Roberts, Brad. *Terrorism with Chemical and Biological Weapons.* Alexandria, Va., 1997.

Roy, Olivier. *The Failure of Political Islam.* Cambridge, Mass., 1994.

———. *L'Islam mondialisé.* Paris, 2002.

Rubin, Barry. *The Tragedy of the Middle East.* New York, 2002.

Saad, Ghorayeb. *Hizbullah: Politics and Religion.* London, 2001.

Said, Edward. *Orientalism.* New York, 1979.

Saussure, Thierry de, et al. *Les miroirs de fanatisme.* Geneva, 1996.

Sayigh, Y. *Armed Struggle and the Search for State.* New York, 1997.

Schmid, Alex P., and Albert J. Jongman. *Political Terrorism.* New Brunswick, N.J., 1984.

Schofield, Victoria. *Kashmir in the Crossfire.* London, 1996.

Schubarth, Wilfred, et al., ed. *Rechtsextremismus in der Bundesrepublik Deutschland.* Opladen, 2000.

Schwagerl, Joachim. *Rechtsextremes Denken.* Frankfurt, 1993.

Seale, Patrick. *Abu Nidal.* New York, 1992.

Senaratne, Jagath. *Political Violence in Sri Lanka.* Amsterdam, 1997.

Serauky, Eberhard. *Im Namen Allahs.* Berlin, 2001.

Sfeir, Antoine. *Dictionnaire mondial de l'Islamisme.* Paris, 2002.

Shaked, Ronni, and Aviva Shabi. *Hamas.* Tel Aviv, 1974.

Simon, Jeffrey. *The Terrorist Trap.* Bloomington, Ind., 2001.

Singh, Sarab Jit. *Operation Black Thunder: An Eyewitness Account of Terrorism in Punjab.* New Delhi, 2002.

Sivan, Emmanuel. *Radical Islam.* New Haven, 1990.

————, and Menahem Friedman, eds. *Religious Radicalism and Politics in the Middle East.* New York, 1990.

Snow, Robert. *The Militia Threat.* New York, 1999.

Smith, Sebastian. *Allah's Mountains: The Battle for Chechnya.* London, 2001.

Sprinzak, Ehud. *Brother against Brother.* New York, 1999.

Stern, Jessica. *The Ultimate Terrorists.* Cambridge, Mass., 1999.

Stone, Martin. *Agony of Algeria.* New York, 1996.

Stora, Benjamin. *La guerre invisible: Algerie années 90.* Paris, 2001.

Sullivan, John. *ETA and Basque Nationalism.* London, 1988.

Swami, Narayan. *Tigers of Lanka.* New Delhi, 1997.

Taheri, Amir. *Holy Terror.* New York, 1987.

Talbott, Strobe, ed. *The Age of Terror.* New York, 2001.

Tarasov, Alexander. *Levoradikaly.* Moscow, 1997.

Taylor, Max, and John Horgan. *The Future of Terrorism.* London, 2000.

Taylor, Peter. *Provos: The IRA and Sinn Fein.* London, 1997.

Teitelbaum, Joshua. *Holier Than Thou.* Washington, D.C., 2000.

Tibi, Bassam. *The Challenge of Fundamentalism.* Berkeley, 1998.

————. *Krieg der Zivilisationen.* Hamburg, 1995.

Tolmein, Oliver. *RAF Das war für uns die Befreiung.* Hamburg, 1999.

————. *Vom deutschen Herbst zum 11. September.* Hamburg, 2002.

Tranfaglia, Nicola, and Diego Novelli. *Vite sospese.* Milan, 1988.

Tribalat, Michele, et al. *La republique et l'Islam entre crainte et aveuglement.* Paris, 2002.

Tucker, Jonathan. *Toxic Terror.* Cambridge, Mass., 2000.

Ustinov, Vladimir. *Obvinyaetsya terrorizm.* Moscow, 2002.

Veer, Peter van den. *Religious Nationalism: Hindus and Muslims in India.* Berkeley, 1994.

Velásquez, Alejo Vargas. *Guerra, violencia y terrorismo.* Bogotá, 1999.

Waldmann, Peter. *Terrorismus: Provokation der Macht.* Munich, 1998.

Wallis, Rodney. *Lockerbie.* Westport, Conn., 2001.

Whittaker, David. *The Terrorism Reader.* London, 2001.

Wilkinson, Paul. *Terrorism versus Democracy.* London, 2000.

Willis, Michael. *Islamist Challenge in Algeria.* New York, 1996.

Wolfgang, Marvin E., and F. Ferracuti. *The Subculture of Violence.* London, 1969.

Wunschik, Tobias. *Baader Meinhof's Kinder.* Opladen, 1997.

Yagil, Limor. *Terrorists et Internet.* Montreal, 2002.

Ziad, Abu Amr. *Islamic Fundamentalism, Muslim Brotherhood and Islamic Jihad.* Bloomington, Ind., 1994.

Index